# *hands-on*
# science
# and Technology
### *An Inquiry Approach*

## Grade 3

*Series Editor*
Jennifer Lawson

PORTAGE & MAIN PRESS

Winnipeg • Manitoba • Canada

Portage & Main Press gratefully acknowledges the financial support of the Province of Manitoba through the Department of Sports, Culture, and Heritage and the Manitoba Book Publishing Tax Credit, and the Government of Canada through the Canada Book Fund (CBF), for our publishing activities.

**Hands-On Science and Technology, Grade 3
An Inquiry Approach**

ISBN: 978-1-55379-709-8
Printed and bound in Canada by Prolific Group

0 1 2 3 4 5 6 7 8 9 10

Download the image banks that accompany this book by going to the Portage & Main Press website at <www.portageandmainpress.com/product/HOSTBANKGR3/>. Use the password **MATERIALS** to access this free download.

**Assistant Editors:**
Leigh Hambly
Laura McKay
Desirae Warkentin

**Science and Technology Consultant:**
Brad Parolin

**Indigenous Consultant:**
Kevin Reed

**Makerspace Contributors:**
Joan Badger
Todd Johnson

**Resource Consultant:**
Astrid DeCairos

**Book and Cover Design:**
Relish New Brand Experience Inc.

**Cover Photos:**
Kirsten Phillips

**Illustrations:**
ArtPlus Ltd.
26 Projects
Jess Dixon

## PORTAGE & MAIN PRESS

www.portageandmainpress.com
books@portageandmainpress.com
1-800-667-9673
Winnipeg, Manitoba
Treaty 1 Territory and homeland of the Métis Nation.

MIX
Paper from
responsible sources
FSC
www.fsc.org
FSC® C006215

# Contents

## Introduction to *Hands-On Science and Technology, Grade 3*    1

Introduction to Hands-On Science and Technology    2

Program Introduction    2

The Inquiry Approach to Science and Technology    2

21st Century Teaching and Learning    3

The Goals of the Science and Technology Program    3

Hands-On Science and Technology Strands and Expectations    4

Hands-On Science and Technology Fundamental Concepts and Big Ideas    4

Hands-On Science and Technology Program Principles    5

Infusing Indigenous Perspectives    5

Cultural Connections    7

Land-Based Learning    7

Technology    7

Sustainability    7

Program Implementation    8

Program Resources    8

Classroom Environment    11

(Planning Units) Timelines    12

Classroom Management    12

Classroom Safety    12

Scientific Inquiry Skills: Guidelines for Teachers    12

Observing    12

Questioning    13

Exploring    13

Classifying    13

Measuring    14

Communicating, Analyzing, and Interpreting    14

Predicting    15

Inferring    16

Inquiry Through Investigating and Experimenting    16

Inquiry Through Research    16

Online Considerations    17

Addressing Students' Early Literacy Needs    17

Technological Problem Solving    17

Makerspace    18

## The Hands-On Science and Technology Assessment Plan    20

Assessment *for* Learning    21

Assessment *as* Learning    21

Assessment *of* Learning    22

Performance Assessment    23

Portfolios    23

Evidence of Student Achievement Levels for Evaluation    24

Important Note to Teachers    24

References    25

Assessment Reproducibles    26

## Unit 1: Growth and Changes in Plants    43

Introduction    44

Unit Overview    48

Curriculum Correlation    49

Resources for Students    51

Websites    53

1 What Do We Know About Plants and Their Needs?    56

2 What Are the Parts of a Plant?    61

3 What Are Some Special Features of Plants?    66

4 How Do Plants Adapt in Order to Survive?    77

5  What Is the Life Cycle of a Plant? 83

6  What Parts of Plants Do We Eat? 93

7  What Are the Different Ways in Which Plants Are Grown for Food? 99

8  How Can We Investigate the Needs of Plants? 104

9  How Can We Design a Terrarium to Sustain Living Things? 116

10  In What Other Ways Are Plants Important to Humans? 125

11  How Can Dye Be Made From Plants? 130

12  How Do Plants and Animals Depend on Each Other? 136

13  How Do Plants Help Reduce Erosion? 141

14  How Can We Protect Plants? 145

15  Inquiry Project: What More Can I Learn About Plant Products? 150

**Unit 2: Strong and Stable Structures** 155

Introduction 156

Unit Overview 159

Curriculum Correlation 160

Resources for Students 161

Websites and Online Videos 162

1  What Is a Structure? 164

2  Where Are Structures Found? 169

3  Which Materials Are Stronger Than Others? 174

4  What Are Joints? 186

5  How Can We Build Structures to Be Stronger and More Stable? 195

6  How Can We Build a Frame That Is Strong and Stable? 201

7  What Structures Has Nature Engineered? 208

8  How Are Structures Around the World Similar and Different? 215

9  What Are Some Careers in Design and Building? 221

10  What Other Structures Can We Build? 225

11  Inquiry Project: What More Can I Learn About Important Buildings and Structures? 238

**Unit 3: Forces Causing Movement** 243

Introduction 244

Unit Overview 247

Curriculum Correlation 248

Resources for Students 249

Websites and Online Videos 251

1  What Is a Force? 254

2  How Is a Force a Push or a Pull? 260

3  What Is Friction? 265

4  Which Objects Do Magnets Attract? 268

5  How Is a Magnet Made? 276

6  How Can a Magnetic Force Be Altered? 283

7  How Is Earth Like a Giant Magnet? 292

8  What Are Helpful Uses and Harmful Effects of Magnets? 299

9  What Is Static Electricity and How Is It Created? 305

10  How Does Humidity Affect Static Electricity? 309

11  How Can the Force of Static Electricity Be Demonstrated Safely? 314

12  How Does an Electroscope Work? 319

13  What Effect Does Gravity Have on Different Objects? 325

14  What Are Some Forces of Nature? 335

15  How Are Forces Used to Move Toys? 339

16  How Can Safety Devices Be Used to Reduce the Effects of Forces? 343

17  Inquiry Project: How Can I Design a Toy or Game That Uses Forces? 346

## Unit 4: Soils in the Environment 351

Introduction 352

Unit Overview 355

Curriculum Correlation 356

Resources for Students 357

Websites and Online Videos 359

1 What Do We Know About Soil? 361

2 What Are the Different Types of Soil? 368

3 How Can Soil Components Be Separated? 375

4 How Much Water Can Different Soil Types Absorb? 381

5 How Do Different Soils Affect the Growth of Plants? 387

6 What Lives in Soil? 396

7 How Does Rainfall Affect Soil? 401

8 How Can Organic Materials Be Recycled? 405

9 How Do Humans Use Earth Materials? 412

10 Inquiry Project: What More Can We Learn About Products Made From Earth Materials? 415

## References 424

## Appendix: Image Bank 425

## About the Contributors 443

# Introduction to
# *Hands-On Science and Technology, Grade 3*

# Introduction to Hands-On Science and Technology

## Program Introduction

**Hands-On Science and Technology** helps develop students' scientific and technological literacy through active inquiry, problem solving, and decision making. With each activity in the program, students are encouraged to explore, investigate, and ask questions as a means of heightening their own curiosity about the world around them. Students solve problems through firsthand experiences, and by observing and examining objects within their environment. In order for young students to develop scientific and technological literacy, concrete experience is of utmost importance—in fact, it is essential.

## The Inquiry Approach to Science and Technology

As students explore science and technology concepts, they should be encouraged to ask questions to guide their own learning. The inquiry model is based on five components:

1. formulating questions
2. gathering and organizing information, evidence, or data
3. interpreting and analyzing information, evidence, or data
4. evaluating information, evidence, or data, and drawing conclusions
5. communicating findings

Using this model, the teacher becomes the facilitator of the learning process, and students initiate questions; gather, organize, interpret, and analyze information; evaluate findings and draw conclusions; and communicate their learning. As such, the process focuses on students' self-reflections as they ask questions, discover answers, and communicate their understanding.

Using an inquiry approach involves beginning with more structured inquiry, and moving to guided inquiry and, finally, open inquiry.

- In structured inquiry, the teacher may provide the initial question and structure the procedures to answer that question. Students follow the given procedures and draw conclusions to answer the given question.

- In guided inquiry, the teacher provides the research question, but students are involved in designing ways to answer the question and communicate their findings.

- In open inquiry, students formulate their own question(s), design and follow through with a developed procedure, and communicate their findings and results. According to Banchi and Bell (2008), "Open inquiry activities are only successful if students are motivated by intrinsic interests and if they are equipped with the skills to conduct their own research study."

In implementing an inquiry approach to science and technology, questions and ideas form the foundation of the teaching and learning process. The following excerpt from the Ontario Literacy and Numeracy Secretariat speaks clearly to this approach:

> While all students ask questions and express interests in world phenomena, it takes creative and responsive teaching to transform wonder into knowledge. To begin, inquiry works best in a classroom in which ideas are placed at the centre. Establishing a culture in which students are encouraged to express ideas but also to respectfully challenge and test one another's ideas is an important first step in the inquiry process. This spirit of inquiry is achieved by welcoming ideas and trusting that even the simplest questions can lead to something greater and not yet evident. Like any good growing system, these questions need time to germinate. Students' ideas can be expressed in many forms (questions, comments, diagrams, pictures, dance, etc.) and serve the important purpose of advancing student understanding of a topic. When the classroom culture is one that views ideas as improvable,

Portage & Main Press, 2017 · *Hands-On Science and Technology · Grade 3* · ISBN: 978-1-55379-709-8

students work hard to continuously improve the quality, coherence and utility of ideas—both individually and collectively (Scardamalia 2002).

## 21st Century Teaching and Learning

In this rapidly changing and globalized world, it is more important than ever to prepare students to lead fulfilling lives, be productive contributors, and thrive in our society. Educators are responding to this challenge through evolving practice that challenges students in engaging and meaningful ways. The **Hands-On Science and Technology** program responds to this challenge by ensuring it reflects best practices that focus on 21st Century Competencies. According to Michael Fullan (2013), these competencies are:

- **Critical thinking:** Critical thinking is the ability to explore problems, weigh alternate solutions, and arrive at solutions. It also involves problem solving and making effective decisions, and applying them to real-world contexts.
- **Communication:** Communication refers to the ability to communicate effectively through reading, writing, speaking, listening, viewing, and representing. It also involves the ability to use a variety of information sources and digital tools.
- **Collaboration:** Collaboration requires the ability to work in teams, learning from and contributing to the learning of others.
- **Creativity:** Creativity involves exploring new ideas, being innovative, and thinking outside the box. Being creative also means looking at novel ideas and finding ways to put ideas into action.
- **Citizenship:** Citizenship involves thinking like a local and a global citizen, considering the values and worldviews of others, and having a genuine interest in solving complex real-world problems that affect human and environmental sustainability.
- **Character:** Character involves specific traits such as perseverance, resilience, and being a life-long learner.

These competencies are the foundation of the inquiry-based approach used in **Hands-On Science and Technology**. As such, teachers take on a facilitation role as students use these skills to explore, investigate, research, design, create, and solve problems in the world around them. To provide a connection between science and technology activities and 21st Century Competencies, each lesson in **_Hands-On Science and Technology, Grade 3_** identifies one or more competencies that teachers may focus on during the activity. This provides teachers with the opportunity to make ongoing links between the science and technology curriculum and 21st century classroom teaching and learning.

## The Goals of the Science and Technology Program

Science and technology play fundamental roles in the lives of Canadians. In the introduction to _The Ontario Curriculum, Grades 1–8: Science and Technology_ (2007, 3), the Ministry of Education states:

> During the twentieth century, science and technology played an increasingly important role in the lives of all Canadians. Science and technology underpin much of what we take for granted, including clean water, the places in which we live and work, and the ways in which we communicate with others. The impact of science and technology on our lives will continue to grow. Consequently, scientific and technological literacy for all has become the overarching objective of science and technology education throughout the world.

Portage & Main Press, 2017 · Hands-On Science and Technology · Grade 3 · ISBN: 978-1-55379-709-8

*The Ontario Curriculum* identifies three goals that form the foundation of the science and technology program. In keeping with this focus on scientific and technological literacy, these goals are the bases for the lessons in the **Hands-On Science and Technology** program:

**Goal 1**

to relate science and technology to society and the environment

**Goal 2**

to develop the skills, strategies, and habits of mind required for scientific inquiry and technological problem solving

**Goal 3**

to understand the basic concepts of science and technology

## Hands-On Science and Technology Strands and Expectations

The Ontario science and technology curriculum for all grade levels is organized into four strands, as follows:

1. Understanding Life Systems
2. Understanding Structures and Mechanisms
3. Understanding Matter and Energy
4. Understanding Earth and Space Systems

Two sets of expectations are listed for each grade in each strand: (1) overall expectations, and (2) specific expectations.

The overall expectations describe, in general terms, the knowledge and skills that students are expected to demonstrate by the end of each grade. There are three overall expectations for each strand in each grade in science and technology.

The specific expectations describe the expected knowledge and skills in greater detail.

**NOTE:** The overall and specific expectations must all be accounted for in instruction and assessment, but evaluation focuses on the three overall expectations (Ontario Ministry of Education 2010, 38).

The overall and specific expectations for each strand are presented in chart format in the introduction to each unit. Alongside each specific expectation, corresponding lessons are identified.

## Hands-On Science and Technology Fundamental Concepts and Big Ideas

Fundamental concepts are key ideas that provide a framework for the acquisition of all scientific and technological knowledge. These concepts also help students to integrate scientific and technological knowledge with knowledge in other subject areas, such as mathematics and social studies. The fundamental concepts addressed in the curriculum for science and technology are:

- matter
- energy
- systems and interactions
- structure and function
- sustainability and stewardship
- change and continuity

Big ideas are the enduring understandings that students carry with them into the future. Big ideas are often transferable to other subjects and to real-life experiences.

The fundamental concepts and big ideas for each grade and strand can be found in a chart in the introduction to each unit of the **Hands-On Science and Technology** program.

Portage & Main Press, 2017 · Hands-On Science and Technology · Grade 3 · ISBN: 978-1-55379-709-8

## Hands-On Science and Technology Program Principles

- Effective science and technology programs involve hands-on inquiry, problem solving, and decision making.
- The development of students' skills, attitudes, knowledge, and understanding of Science, Technology, Society, and the Environment (STSE) issues form the foundation of the science and technology program.
- Children have a natural curiosity about science and the world around them. This curiosity must be maintained, fostered, and enhanced through active learning.
- Science and technology activities must be meaningful, worthwhile, and relate to real-life experiences.
- The teacher's role in science and technology education is to facilitate activities and encourage critical thinking and reflection. Children learn best by doing, rather than by just listening. Instead of simply telling, the teacher, therefore, should focus on formulating and asking questions, setting the conditions so that students ask their own questions, and helping students to make sense of the events and phenomena they have experienced.
- Science and technology should be taught in conjunction with other school subjects. Themes and topics of study should integrate ideas and skills from several core areas whenever possible.
- The science and technology program should encompass, and draw on, a wide range of educational resources, including literature, nonfiction research material, audio-visual resources, and technology, as well as people and places in the local community.

- The science and technology program should be infused with knowledge and worldviews of Indigenous peoples, as well as with other diverse multicultural perspectives.
- Assessment of student learning in science and technology should be designed to focus on performance and understanding, and should be conducted through meaningful assessment techniques carried out throughout each unit of study.

## Infusing Indigenous Perspectives

Indigenous peoples are central to the Canadian context, and it is important to infuse their knowledge into the learning experiences of all students. The intentional integration of Indigenous knowledge in the **Hands-On Science and Technology** series helps to address the Calls to Action of the Truth and Reconciliation Commission of Canada (2015), particularly the call to "integrate Indigenous knowledge and teaching methods into classrooms" (Action 62) and the call for "building student capacity for intercultural understanding, empathy, and mutual respect" (Action 63).

Indigenous peoples of the past depended on the natural environment to survive. The environment shaped their way of life: geography, vegetation, climate, and natural resources of the land determined the ways they survived. By observing the land and its animal inhabitants, the environment also taught them to survive. The traditional territories of the First Nations and Métis peoples cover Ontario, and many Inuit have moved to urban centres in the province. The worldviews of these peoples and their approaches and contributions to science and technology are now being acknowledged and incorporated into educational programs. It is also important to recognize the diversity of Ontario's Indigenous peoples and to focus on both the traditions and contemporary lives

Portage & Main Press, 2017 · *Hands-On Science and Technology · Grade 3* · ISBN: 978-1-55379-709-8

of the Indigenous communities in your area. Contact personnel in your school district—Indigenous consultants and/or those responsible for Indigenous education—to find out what resources (e.g., people, books, videos) are available to you and your students.

In incorporating Indigenous perspectives, it is important to value Traditional Ecological Knowledge (TEK). TEK has been defined as:

> ...the knowledge base acquired by indigenous and local people over many hundreds of years through direct contact with the environment. It includes an intimate and detailed knowledge of plants, animals, and natural phenomena, the development and use of appropriate technologies for hunting, fishing, trapping, agriculture, and forestry and a holistic knowledge, or "worldview" which parallels the scientific disciplines of ecology (Inglis 1993).

Indigenous peoples developed technologies and survived on this land for millennia because, in part, they were good scientists. They used observation and experimentation to refine their technologies such as building canoes and tipis and discovering food-preservation techniques. As such, TEK serves as an invaluable resource for students and teachers of science and technology.

Throughout the **Hands-On Science and Technology** program, there are many opportunities to incorporate culturally appropriate teaching methodologies from Indigenous worldviews. First Peoples Pedagogy indicates that making connections to the local community is central to learning (First Nations Education Steering Committee 2016). As one example, both Elders and Métis Senators offer a wealth of knowledge that can be shared with students. Consider inviting an Elder or a Métis Senator as a guest into the classroom in connection with specific topics being studied (as identified within the given lessons throughout the unit). An Elder or a Métis Senator can guide a nature walk, share stories and experiences, share traditional technologies, and help students understand Indigenous peoples' perspectives of the natural world. Elders and Métis Senators will provide guidance for learners and opportunities to build bridges between the school and the community. Here are a few suggestions about working with Elders and Métis Senators:

- Some Indigenous keepers of knowledge are more comfortable being called "Knowledge Keepers" than "Elders" or "Métis Senators." Be sensitive to their preferences.

- It is important to properly acknowledge any visiting Elders and Métis Senators and their knowledge, as they have traditionally been and are recognized within Indigenous communities as highly esteemed individuals. There are certain protocols that should be followed when inviting an Elder or a Métis Senator into your classroom. The Lakehead District School Board has protocols available at: <https://www.lakeheadschools.ca/aboriginal-education/>.

- It is especially important to connect with Indigenous peoples and Elders and Métis Senators in your local area, and to study local issues related to Indigenous peoples in Ontario. Consider contacting Indigenous education consultants within your local school district or with the Ontario Ministry of Education to access referrals. Also, consider contacting local Indigenous organizations for referrals to Elders and Métis Senators, and other knowledge keepers. Such organizations may also be able to offer resources and opportunities for field trips and land-based learning.

Portage & Main Press, 2017 · *Hands-On Science and Technology · Grade 3* · ISBN: 978-1-55379-709-8

## Cultural Connections

To acknowledge and celebrate the cultural diversity represented in Canadian classrooms, it is important to infuse cultural connections into classroom learning experiences. It is essential for teachers to be aware of the cultural makeup of their class, and to celebrate these diverse cultures by making connections to curricular outcomes. In the same way, it is important to explore other cultures represented in the community and beyond, to encourage intercultural understanding and harmony.

Throughout the **Hands-On Science and Technology** program, suggestions are made for connecting science and technology topics to cultural explorations and activities.

## Land-Based Learning

Land-based learning replaces the classroom walls with the natural land. For all students, land-based learning offers firsthand opportunities to observe, explore, and investigate the land, waters, and atmosphere of the natural world. Land-based learning promotes a healthy interplay between society and nature and helps students envision a world where there is meaningful appreciation and respect for our natural environment—an environment that sustains all life forms. Many lessons in *Hands-On Science and Technology, Grade 3* incorporate land-based learning activities, whether it be a casual walk around the neighbourhood to examine trees or a more involved exploration of local waterways. When land-based learning connections are made in *Hands-On Science and Technology, Grade 3* lessons, the following icon is used:

## Technology

Digital learning, or learning with information and communication technology (LwICT), is an important component of any classroom. As such, technological supports available in schools—including digital cameras, computers/tablets, interactive whiteboards (IWB), projectors, document cameras, audio-recording devices, and even calculators—can be used with and by students to enhance their learning experiences. When technology connections are made in *Hands-On Science and Technology, Grade 3* lessons, the following icon is used:

## Sustainability

The **Hands-On Science and Technology** program provides numerous opportunities for students to investigate issues related to sustainable development. Asking students the following question can often help to clarify for them what is meant by sustainability: "Is there enough for everyone, forever?" Exploring sustainability also connects to Indigenous worldviews about respecting and caring for the Earth. The three pillars of sustainability are the environment, society, and the economy. When sustainability links are made in *Hands-On Science and Technology, Grade 3* lessons, any or all of the sustainability pillars may be the focus of this connection, and are identified by the following icon:

Portage & Main Press, 2017 · Hands-On Science and Technology · Grade 3 · ISBN: 978-1-55379-709-8

## Program Implementation

### Program Resources

*Hands-On Science and Technology, Grade 3* is organized in a format that makes it easy for teachers to plan and implement. The book opens with an introduction (which includes assessment reproducibles) and is divided into four units that cover the selected topics of study for the grade level. The units relate directly to the strands, expectations, fundamental concepts, and big ideas outlined in the *The Ontario Curriculum, Grades 1–8: Science and Technology* (2007) document. Each unit also has its own introduction, which summarizes the general goals for the unit. This introduction provides background information for teachers, planning tips, and lists of vocabulary related to the unit, as well as other pertinent information such as how to embed Indigenous perspectives into units of study.

Additionally, the introduction to each unit includes both a list of related resources (books and online videos) and a list of annotated websites suitable for students.

Each unit is organized into numbered lessons comprised of topics and activities based on the overall and specific expectations. Lessons are arranged in the following format:

**Lesson title:** The title of each lesson is posed as a guided inquiry question, which is related to the expectations being addressed.

**Information for Teachers:** Some lessons provide teachers with the basic scientific and technological knowledge they will need to present the activities. This information is offered in a clear, concise format, and focuses specifically on the topic of study.

**21st Century Competencies:** At the start of each lesson, the key competencies focused on during the various activities (critical thinking, communication, collaboration, creativity, citizenship, character) are identified.

**Materials:** A complete list of materials required to conduct the main activities is provided. The quantity of materials required will depend on how you conduct activities. If students are working individually, you will need enough materials for each student. If students are working in groups, the materials required will be significantly reduced. Many of the identified items are for the teacher to use for display purposes, or for making charts for recording students' ideas. In some cases, visual materials (e.g., large pictures, sample charts, diagrams) have been included with the lesson to assist the teacher in presenting ideas and questions, and to encourage discussion. Some lessons include Image Banks. Black-and-white thumbnails of Image Bank visuals can be found in the Appendix, on page 425. Colour images of these thumbnails can be downloaded from the Portage & Main website (go to: <www.portageandmainpress.com/product/ HOSTBANKGR3>. Use the password **MATERIALS** to access this free download.) These images may be displayed or printed, depending on the availability of projectors, their use in specific activities, and the needs of students.

**Activate:** This activity is intended to activate prior knowledge, review previous lessons, and engage students in the lesson. The guided inquiry question for the lesson is also introduced in this section. Teachers may choose to record the question for display throughout related investigations. For example, the guided inquiry question might be recorded on a sentence strip and displayed for students to refer to during activities and discussion.

**Action:** This section details a step-by-step procedure, including higher-level questioning techniques, and suggestions for encouraging the acquisition of new knowledge and skills. In some cases, one lesson may involve several Action activities, which are identified as Action: Part One, Action: Part Two, and so on.

**Learning Centre:** Included with most lessons are independent student learning opportunities that focus on the expectations. These learning centres promote differentiated instruction, and are based upon multiple-intelligences research. Within a unit, each centre focuses on a different intelligence (some centres focus on more than one), to provide opportunities for students to use areas of strength and also to expose them to new ways of learning. The following intelligences, identified by the accompanying icons, are focused on in *Hands-On Science and Technology, Grade 3*:

- **Verbal-Linguistic:** These learners think in words and enjoy reading, writing, word puzzles, and oral storytelling. When a learning centre focuses on Verbal-Linguistic intelligence, the following icon is used:

- **Logical-Mathematical:** These learners think by reasoning and enjoy problem solving, puzzles, and working with data. When a learning centre focuses on Logical-Mathematical intelligence, the following icon is used:

- **Visual-Spatial:** These learners think in visual pictures and enjoy drawing and creating visual designs. When a learning centre focuses on Visual-Spatial intelligence, the following icon is used:

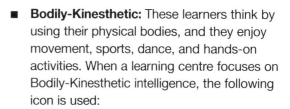

- **Bodily-Kinesthetic:** These learners think by using their physical bodies, and they enjoy movement, sports, dance, and hands-on activities. When a learning centre focuses on Bodily-Kinesthetic intelligence, the following icon is used:

- **Musical-Rhythmic:** These learners think in melodies and rhythms and enjoy singing, listening to music, and creating music. When a learning centre focuses on Musical-Rhythmic intelligence, the following icon is used:

- **Interpersonal:** These learners think by talking to others about their ideas and enjoy group work, planning social events, and taking a leadership role with friends or classmates. When a learning centre focuses on Interpersonal intelligence, the following icon is used:

- **Intrapersonal:** These learners think within themselves and enjoy quietly thinking, reflecting, and working individually. When a learning centre focuses on Intrapersonal intelligence, the following icon is used:

- **Naturalistic:** These learners learn by classifying objects and events and enjoy anything to do with nature and scientific exploration of natural phenomena. When a learning centre focuses on Naturalistic intelligence, the following icon is used:

▶

Portage & Main Press, 2017 · *Hands-On Science and Technology · Grade 3* · ISBN: 978-1-55379-709-8

■ **Existential:** These learners learn by probing deep philosophical questions and enjoy examining the bigger picture as to why ideas are important. When a learning centre focuses on Existential intelligence, the following icon is used:

Teachers are encouraged to explore the topic of multiple intelligences with their students and to have students identify ways they learn best, and ways that are challenging for them. Guidelines for this process are included in the book *Teaching to Diversity* by Jennifer Katz (see References, page 25).

**NOTE:** Many learning-centre activities offer excellent assessment opportunities—both formative and summative—that teachers can take advantage of through student conferences/interviews. Teachers can then use the **Individual Student Observations** sheet, on page 27, to record assessment data. See the next section of *Hands-On Science and Technology, Grade 3* for more information on assessment.

The activity at each learning centre is described on a task card that remains at the centre, along with any required supplies and materials. When implementing the learning centre, it is important to review the task card prior to having students work at the centre, to ensure they are familiar with the content and the expectations.

**Consolidate and Debrief:** Students are provided with ways to demonstrate what they have learned through consolidation and reflection. This process allows for synthesis and application of inquiry and new ideas. The activities in this section are intended as a review of the main ideas of the lesson, focusing on fundamental concepts, big ideas, and overall and specific expectations. The guided inquiry question for the lesson is also reviewed in this section, and students are

encouraged to share their knowledge, provide examples, and ask further inquiry questions.

With each lesson, teachers are also encouraged to embed learning by adding to graphic organizers; communicating investigations and ideas in a science and technology journal; having students record, describe, and illustrate new vocabulary; and adding new vocabulary to the classroom word wall (a bulletin board or poster paper for displaying new science and technology terminology). Both teachers and students can add to the word wall throughout the unit, or even all year. New vocabulary may also include terminology in Indigenous languages and other languages that reflect the cultural diversity of the classroom and the community.

Also in this section, teachers are encouraged to explore the 21st Century Competencies with students, in order to determine how these skills have been used by students throughout the lesson.

**Enhance:** This section includes optional activities to extend, enrich, and reinforce the expectations. Many lessons can be enhanced with interactive activities, available through Portage & Main Press's website. For directions on how to access an activity, check the Enhance section of each lesson. These activities can be used on interactive whiteboards and on computers.

**Activity Sheets:** Lessons include reproducible activity sheets, which are designed to correlate with the expectations being focused on. Activity sheets are sometimes used during the main activity in a lesson, often to record results of investigations. At other times, the activity sheets are used as follow-up to the main activities.

Students can work independently on the sheets, in small groups, or you may read over the sheets

Portage & Main Press, 2017 · *Hands-On Science and Technology · Grade 3* · ISBN: 978-1-55379-709-8

together and complete them in a large group setting. Activity sheets can also be projected using document cameras or interactive whiteboards. Since it is important for students to learn to construct their own charts and recording formats, teachers may decide to use the activity sheets as examples of ways to record and communicate ideas about an activity. Students can then create their own sheets rather than use the ones provided.

NOTE: Activity sheets are meant to be used only in conjunction with, or as a follow-up to, the hands-on activities. The activity sheets are not intended to be the science and technology lesson in itself or the sole assessment for the lesson.

### Assessment *for, as,* and *of* Learning:

Based on current research about the value of quality classroom assessment (e.g., Davies 2011), suggestions are provided for authentic assessment, which includes assessment *for* learning, assessment *as* learning, and assessment *of* learning. These assessment strategies focus specifically on the expectations that relate to a particular lesson.

Keep in mind that these suggestions are merely ideas to consider; teachers are also encouraged to use their own assessment techniques and to refer to the other assessment strategies outlined in detail in the Assessment section of **Hands-On Science and Technology, Grade 3**, on pages 20 to 24.

## Classroom Environment

The classroom environment is inclusive of the diverse backgrounds and learning needs of all students. The strengths students bring to school are identified and nurtured. At the same time, every student is supported in order to meet with success. The classroom environment must also foster the conditions that are required for inquiry and discussion. To promote inquiry in the classroom, consider doing the following:

- Encourage students to ask questions and to appreciate different perspectives.
- Foster a nonthreatening atmosphere in which all students are comfortable sharing.
- Provide lots of opportunities for students to reflect on questions, share ideas, and generate further questions for inquiry.
- Promote discussion with and between students, as they need to talk about ideas with each other and with the teacher to help make meaning.
- Model for students how to gather the information they need so they have an adequate foundation for discussion.
- Ensure questions are clear and vocabulary is appropriate to learners.
- Avoid dominating discussion.
- Provide equal opportunities for all learners to participate.
- Model good questions and questioning strategies.
- Guide students in discovering answers to questions.

The classroom setting is an important component of the learning process. An active environment—one that gently hums with the purposeful conversations and activities of students—indicates that meaningful learning is taking place. When studying a specific topic, the room should display related objects and materials: student work; pictures and posters, maps, graphs, and charts made during activities; and anchor charts of important concepts, procedures, skills, or strategies that are co-constructed with students. Visuals serve as a source of information and reinforce concepts and skills that have been stressed during lesson activities, and also serve to support those students who are visual learners. Charts outlining success criteria are also displayed in the classroom.

▶

Portage & Main Press, 2017 · *Hands-On Science and Technology · Grade 3* · ISBN: 978-1-55379-709-8

## (Planning Units) Timelines

No two groups of students will explore topics and material at the same rate, and so planning the duration of units is an important responsibility of the teacher. In some cases, students will not complete the lesson's activities during one block of time. Also, students may be especially interested in one topic and want to expand upon it. The individual needs of the class should be considered; there are no strict timelines involved in **Hands-On Science and Technology**. It is important, however, to spend time on every unit in the program so that students focus on all the curriculum expectations established for the grade level.

## Classroom Management

Although hands-on activities are emphasized throughout this program, how these experiences are handled is up to the teacher. In some cases, teachers may have all students manipulating materials individually; in others, teachers may choose to organize the class into small groups. This encourages the development of social skills, enables all students to be active in the learning process, and means less cost in terms of materials and equipment. Again, classroom management is up to the teacher, since it is the teacher who ultimately determines how students in their care function best in the learning environment.

## Classroom Safety

Occasionally, especially when safety concerns are an issue, teachers may decide to demonstrate an activity, while still encouraging as much student interaction as possible. The nature of scientific and technological experimentation means that safety concerns do arise from time to time. Throughout **Hands-On Science and Technology, Grade 3**, whenever there is a potential safety issue that teachers

need to be aware of, the concern is flagged with the following safety icon:

## Scientific Inquiry Skills: Guidelines for Teachers

The **Hands-On Science and Technology** program is based upon a scientific inquiry approach. While involved in the activities of **Hands-On Science and Technology, Grade 3**, students use a variety of scientific inquiry skills as they answer questions, solve problems, and make decisions. These skills are not unique to science and technology, but they are integral to students' acquisition of scientific and technological literacy. The skills include initiating and planning, performing and recording, analyzing and interpreting, as well as communicating and the ability to work in teams. In the primary grades, basic skills should focus on scientific inquiry and problem solving.

The following guidelines provide a framework that can be used to encourage students' skill development in specific areas.

### Observing

Students learn to perceive characteristics and changes through the use of all five senses. Students are encouraged to safely use sight, smell, touch, hearing, and taste, in order to gain information about objects and events. Observations may be qualitative (by describing properties such as texture or colour), quantitative (by describing properties such as size or number), or both.

Observing includes:

- gaining information through the senses
- identifying similarities and differences, and making comparisons

Portage & Main Press, 2017 · Hands-On Science and Technology · Grade 3 · ISBN: 978-1-55379-709-8

It is important to encourage students to communicate their observations in a variety of ways, including orally, in writing, by sketching labelled diagrams, and by capturing evidence digitally, such as with a camera or tablet.

## Questioning

Generating thoughtful inquiry questions is an essential skill for students when participating in inquiry-based learning. Teachers should encourage students to be curious, and to extend their questions beyond those posed to them. Students should ask questions that can be answered through tests/experimentation, and formulate a specific question to investigate. Then, students can create, from a variety of possible methods, a plan to find answers to the questions they pose (Ontario Ministry of Education 2007).

## Exploring

Students need ample opportunities to manipulate materials and equipment in order to discover and learn new ideas and concepts. During exploration, students need to be encouraged to use all of their senses and observation skills. Oral discussion is also an integral component of exploration; it allows students to communicate their discoveries. At a deeper level, oral discussion also allows students to make meaning by discussing inconsistences/misconceptions, and by comparing/contrasting their observations with others. This is the constructivist model of learning, which is essential in inquiry-based learning.

## Classifying

Classification is used to group or sort objects and events and is based on observable properties. For example, trees can be classified as those with leaves (deciduous) and those with needles (coniferous). Two strategies for sorting involve the use of sorting mats and Venn diagrams. Sorting mats show distinct groups,

while Venn diagrams intersect to show similar characteristics among sets.

For example:

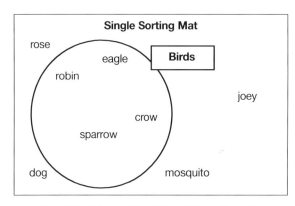

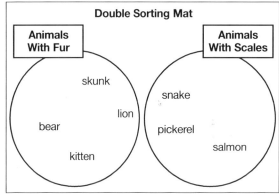

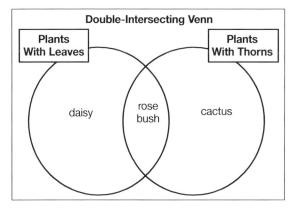

Portage & Main Press, 2017 · Hands-On Science and Technology · Grade 3 · ISBN: 978-1-55379-709-8

## Measuring

Measuring is a process of discovering the dimensions or the quantity of objects or events. In the primary grades, measuring activities first involve the use of nonstandard units of measure, such as interlocking cubes or paper clips to determine length. This allows students to build understanding of how to observe, compare, and communicate dimensions and quantity. This is a critical preface to measuring with standard units. By the time students are in grade three, they are using standard measuring tools. For example, they will measure mass/weight, length, volume, and temperature using standard units. They will also measure the passage of time using seconds, minutes, and hours.

An essential skill of measurement is estimating. Students should be encouraged regularly to estimate before they measure, whether in nonstandard or standard units. Estimation allows students opportunities to take risks, use background knowledge, and enhance their skills in measuring by comparing estimates and actual results.

## Communicating, Analyzing, and Interpreting

In science and technology, one communicates by means of diagrams, graphs, charts, maps, models, and symbols, as well as with written and spoken languages. Communicating includes:

- reading and interpreting data from tables and charts
- making tables and charts
- reading and interpreting data from pictographs
- making pictographs
- making labelled diagrams
- making models
- using oral and written languages

- sequencing and grouping events, objects, and data according to attributes

When presenting students with charts and graphs, or when students make their own as part of a specific activity, there are guidelines that should be followed:

- A pictograph has a title and information on one axis that denotes the items being compared (note that the first letter on both the title and the axis text is capitalized). There is generally no graduated scale or heading for the axis representing numerical values.

| Favourite Dessert | | | | |
|---|---|---|---|---|
| | | 🍦 | | |
| | | 🍦 | | |
| | 🥧 | 🍦 | | |
| 🎂 | 🥧 | 🍦 | | |
| Cake | Pie | Ice Cream | | |

- A bar graph is another common form of scientific communication that students use in grade three. Bar graphs should always be titled so the information communicated is easily understand. These titles should be capitalized in the same manner as one would title a story. Both axes of the graph should also be labelled and capitalized the same way. In most cases, graduated markings are noted on one axis and the objects or events being compared are noted on the other. On a bar graph, the bars must be separate, as each bar represents a distinct piece of data.

Portage & Main Press, 2017 · Hands-On Science and Technology · Grade 3 · ISBN: 978-1-55379-709-8

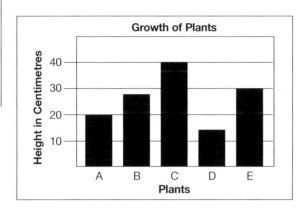

**Growth of Plants**

**Data Chart**

| Local Snowfall | | |
|---|---|---|
| **Month** | **2016/2017 Snowfall (cm)** | **Average Snowfall (cm)** |
| October | 7 | 5 |
| November | 9 | 8 |
| December | 23 | 20 |
| January | 29 | 25 |
| February | 16 | 18 |
| March | 11 | 10 |

■ A tally chart is a means of recording data as an organized count. The count is grouped in 5s for ease of determining the total by counting by 5s.

| Favourite Sport | | |
|---|---|---|
| **Sport** | **Tally** | **Total** |
| baseball | ⦀⦀ | 6 |
| hockey | ⦀⦀ ⦀⦀ | 10 |
| soccer | ⦀⦀ ⦀⦀ ⦀ | 12 |

■ A chart (table) requires an appropriate title, and both columns and rows need specific headings. Again, all titles and headings require capitalization of the first letter as in the title of a story. In some cases, pictures can be used to make the chart easier for young students to understand. Charts can be made in the form of checklists or can include room for additional written information and data.

**Checklist Chart**

| What Substances Dissolve in Water? | | |
|---|---|---|
| **Substance** | **Dissolves in Water** | **Does Not Dissolve in Water** |
| Beads | | √ |
| Sugar | √ | |
| Drink Mix | √ | |
| Rice | | √ |
| Pepper | | √ |

Communicating also involves using the language and terminology of science and technology. Teachers should encourage students to use the appropriate vocabulary related to their investigations (e.g., *object, metal, pliable, absorbent, characteristic*). The language of science and technology also includes terms such as *predict, infer, estimate, measure, experiment,* and *hypothesize*. Teachers should use this vocabulary regularly throughout all activities and encourage their students to do the same. As students become proficient at reading and writing, they can also be encouraged to use the vocabulary in written form. In each unit, students develop word walls, and their own Science and Technology Glossary in which they can record the terms they have learned, and define them in their own words.

## Predicting

Predicting refers to the question, "What do you think will happen?" For example, ask students to predict what they think will happen to a blown-up balloon that is placed in a basin of water. It is important to provide opportunities for students to make predictions and for them to feel safe doing so.

## Inferring

In a scientific context, inferring generally refers to asking why something occurs. For example, ask students to infer why a blown-up balloon

Portage & Main Press, 2017 · *Hands-On Science and Technology* · Grade 3 · ISBN: 978-1-55379-709-8

▶

floats when placed into a basin of water. Again, it is important to encourage students to take risks when making inferences. Instead of explaining scientific phenomena to them, students should be given opportunities to infer for themselves, using a variety of perspectives, and then building their knowledge base through inquiry and investigation.

## Inquiry Through Investigating and Experimenting

When investigations and experiments are conducted in the classroom, planning and recording both the process and the results are essential. The traditional scientific method uses the following format:

- purpose: what we want to find out, or a testable question we want to answer
- hypothesis: a prediction; what we think will happen, and why
- materials: what we used to conduct the experiment or investigation
- method: what we did
- results: what we observed and measured
- conclusion: what we found out
- application: how we can use what we learned

This method of recording investigations may be used in later school years. However, in primary grades, it is more useful to focus on a narrative style of lab report such as:

- what we want to know
- what we think might happen
- what we used
- what we did
- what we observed
- what we found out

A simpler four-question narrative may also be used with any age group. The structure includes the following questions:

1. What was I looking for?

- Describe the question you were trying to answer, or the hypothesis/prediction you were testing.
2. How did I look for it?
   - Tell what you did. Include materials and method.
3. What did I find?
   - Describe observations and data.
4. What does this mean?
   - Draw conclusions, and consider applications to real life.

This narrative may be done in a variety of ways: orally as a class, recording findings as a class, having students use drawings and writings, or a combination of these.

Throughout **Hands-On Science and Technology**, a variety of methods are used to encourage students to communicate the inquiry process, including those above. In addition, other formats such as concept maps and other graphic organizers are used.

## Inquiry Through Research

In addition to hands-on inquiry, research is another aspect of inquiry that involves finding, organizing, and presenting information related to a specific topic or question. Scientific inquiry involves making observations, exploring, asking questions, and looking for answers to those questions. Even at a young age, students can begin to research topics studied in class if they are provided with support and guidelines. Accordingly, guided research is a teaching and learning strategy that is encouraged throughout the **Hands-On Science and Technology** program. Guided research provides an opportunity for students to seek further information about subjects of inquiry, personal interests, or topics of their choice. As such, students are empowered and engaged in the process. Guided research encourages students to do the following:

Portage & Main Press, 2017 · Hands-On Science and Technology · Grade 3 · ISBN: 978-1-55379-709-8

- Ask questions of interest related to a topic being studied by the class.
- Choose resources.
- Collect information.
- Make a plan to present findings.
- Present research in a variety of ways.

Guided research encourages teachers to do the following:

- Provide opportunities for students to ask questions of personal interest.
- Provide accessibility to appropriate resources.
- Model and support the research process.
- Offer opportunities for students to present their findings in a variety of ways and to a variety of audiences.

In the **Hands-On Science and Technology** program, the approach for scientific inquiry is one of gradual release. The teacher provides substantial support in initial inquiry experiences, and gradually presents students with more and more opportunities for directing their own research. Suggestions for guiding research are presented regularly throughout **Hands-On Science and Technology, Grade 3**.

## Online Considerations

As our technological world continues to expand at an accelerating rate, and increasing information is available online, students will turn to the Internet more and more to expand their learning. Accordingly, **Hands-On Science and Technology, Grade 3** is replete with opportunities for students to use online resources for researching and investigating. Teachers are encouraged to talk often with students about safety protocols when online. At all times, teachers need to be vigilant in supervising student use of the Internet. Similarly, teachers should review websites and bookmark those appropriate for student use.

Teachers are also encouraged to discuss plagiarism with students: Copying information word for word—whether from a book, the Internet, or other resource—is wrong. Such information should always be paraphrased in the student's own words, and the source of the information cited. Photos, drawings, figures, and other images found online should also only be used with permission and citation of the source. Alternatively, students can source images for which permission has already been granted for use, such as through Creative Commons Canada. (Creative Commons is a nonprofit organization that "promotes and enables the sharing of knowledge and creativity…[and which] produces and maintains a free suite of licensing tools to allow anyone to easily share, reuse, and remix materials with a fair 'some rights reserved' approach to copyright." See <http://ca.creativecommons.org>.)

## Addressing Students' Early Literacy Needs

The inquiry process involves having students ask questions and conduct investigations and research to answer these questions. At the grade-three level, some students may benefit from support for research, reading, and writing. Consider having volunteers, student mentors, or educational assistants support students during these processes to help young students with reading, research, and writing.

## Technological Problem Solving

Throughout **Hands-On Science and Technology, Grade 3**, students have opportunities to use technological problem-solving skills to design and construct objects. For example, in unit 1, lesson 9, students design and construct a terrarium to sustain living things.

Portage & Main Press, 2017 · Hands-On Science and Technology · Grade 3 · ISBN: 978-1-55379-709-8

The technological problem-solving process involves having students seek solutions to practical problems. There are specific steps to the process:

1. **Identify a need.** Recognize practical problems and the need to solve them.
2. **Create a plan.** Seek alternate solutions to a given problem, create a plan based on a chosen solution, and record the plan in writing and using labelled diagrams.
3. **Develop a product or prototype.** Construct an object that solves the given problem, and use predetermined criteria to test the product.
4. **Communicate the results.** Identify and make improvements to the product, and explain the changes.

The technological problem-solving process also involves research and experimentation.

When the technological problem-solving process is featured in a lesson of *Hands-On Science and Technology, Grade 3*, the following icon is used:

## Makerspace

To foster open inquiry, each unit of *Hands-On Science and Technology, Grade 3* suggests a Makerspace. In a general sense, a Makerspace is a collaborative do-it-yourself environment, where participants share ideas and explore hands-on projects. In the school setting, a Makerspace is usually cross-curricular and should allow for inquiry, discovery, and innovation. Sometimes, the Makerspace is housed in a common area such as the library, which means it is space used by the whole school community. A classroom Makerspace is usually designed as a centre where students create do-it-yourself projects, learning together and collaborating on cross-curricular ideas or classroom themes. It is important to remember

learning is not directed here. Rather, teachers simply create conditions for learning to happen.

There is no list of required equipment that defines a Makerspace; however, the centre may evolve to foster inquiry within a specific topic. Students are given the opportunity to work with a variety of age-appropriate tools, as well as with everyday and recycled materials. Additionally, arts-and-crafts are often integrated into Makerspace offerings. Materials to consider at Makerspace centres include:

- general supplies (e.g., graph or grid paper for planning and designing, pencils, markers, paper, cardstock, cardboard, scissors, masking tape, duct tape, glue, rulers, metre sticks, tape measures, elastics, string, Plasticine, modelling clay, fabric/cloth, straws, pipe cleaners, tin foil)
- arts-and-craft supplies (e.g., construction paper, paint, brushes, glitter, foam, fabric)
- building materials (e.g., sticks, wooden blocks, wooden dowels, toothpicks, Popsicle sticks, balsa wood, and age-appropriate tools such as hammers, nails, screwdrivers, screws)
- commercial products (e.g., LEGO, LEGO Story Starter, WeDo, MakeDo, Mechano, Plus-Plus, Kinex, Keva Planks, Dominoes, Wedgits)
- technology (e.g., Green Screen, tablets, Coding/Programming [Beebots, Code-a Pillar], apps such as Hopscotch, Tynker, Scratch Jr., Tickle)
- reference materials (e.g., books, videos, websites, visuals)

Work with students to develop a collaborative culture in which they tinker, invent, and improve on their creations throughout each unit. Ask students for ideas on how to stock the Makerspace, based on their project ideas, and then work collaboratively to acquire these supplies. The Internet may also provide lots of good ideas.

Also, set up a recycling bin in your Makerspace for paper, cardboard, clean plastics, and other materials students can use in their creations. This is a good opportunity to stress the idea that Makerspaces can help reuse many items destined for a landfill. Discuss which items can/ should be placed in this bin.

Some things to consider when planning and developing a Makerspace centre are:

- Always address safety concerns, ensuring that materials, equipment, and tools are safe for student use. Include safety gloves and goggles, as appropriate.

- Consider space and storage needs. Mobile carts and/or bins are handy for storing materials and tools.

- Work with students to write a form letter to parents/guardians, explaining the purpose of the Makerspace, and asking for donations of materials.

In *Hands-On Science and Technology, Grade 3*, each unit includes a variety of suggestions for Makerspace materials, equipment, and challenges related to the specific science and technology topics of study, while correlating with other subject areas. Suggested materials and challenges are intended to support inquiry, discovery, creation, and innovation related to the unit expectations.

Since the Makerspace process is intent upon solving design problems, it is helpful to have visuals at the Makerspace centre to encourage innovation, creativity, and technological problem solving. Critical aspects of technological problem solving are:

- careful planning, including the consideration of alternate solutions
- purposeful selection of tools and materials
- testing, retesting, and modifying a product or process

- communicating the solution
- recommending changes or improvements

In addition, the Makerspace process is collaborative in nature, and, therefore, it is important to focus on skills related to working with others. Collaboration skills include:

- contributing ideas and questions
- respecting and accepting the contributions of others
- negotiating roles and responsibilities
- remaining focused, and encouraging others to stay on task
- completing individual commitments

Before students begin working at a Makerspace centre, it is suggested that teachers review technological problem-solving skills and collaborative skills with students. With students, co-construct criteria for each skill, record on chart paper, and display at the Makerspace centre. As an alternative, challenge students to create posters for the Makerspace centre that convey what technological problem solving and collaboration look like. These visual prompts can be referred to before, during, and after students work at the centre, as a means of guiding and assessing the process.

As students create, photograph their creations to share with the class, and discuss the unique properties of their designs. Model appropriate digital citizenship with students by asking their permission to photograph and share their creations. It is also suggested that teachers facilitate regular debriefing sessions as a class, after students have spent time at the Makerspace centre. Consider focusing this discussion on the 21st Century Competencies (critical thinking, communication, collaboration, creativity, citizenship, and character) as an anchor for reflective practice with this learning.

Portage & Main Press, 2017 · *Hands-On Science and Technology · Grade 3* · ISBN: 978-1-55379-709-8

# The Hands-On Science and Technology Assessment Plan

Portage & Main Press, 2017 · Hands-On Science and Technology · Grade 3 · ISBN: 978-1-55379-709-8

The **Hands-On Science and Technology** program provides a variety of assessment tools that enable teachers to build a comprehensive and authentic daily assessment plan for students. Based on current research about the value of quality classroom assessment (Davies 2011), suggestions are provided for authentic assessment, which includes assessment *for* learning, assessment *as* learning, and assessment *of* learning.

Ontario's policy on assessment is outlined in the document *Growing Success: Assessment, Evaluation, and Reporting in Ontario Schools* (see: <www.edu.gov.on.ca/eng/policyfunding/success.html>). The document (2010) outlines a fundamental shift in the roles of teachers and students in the learning process:

> In a traditional assessment paradigm, the teacher is perceived as the active agent in the process, determining goals and criteria for successful achievement, delivering instruction, and evaluating student achievement at the end of a period of learning. The use of assessment for the purpose of improving learning and helping students become independent learners requires a culture in which student and teacher learn together in a collaborative relationship, each playing an active role in setting learning goals, developing success criteria, giving and receiving feedback, monitoring progress, and adjusting learning strategies. The teacher acts as a "lead learner," providing support while gradually releasing more and more responsibility to the student, as the student develops the knowledge and skills needed to become an independent learner.

The primary purpose of assessment is to improve student learning. Assessment *for* learning provides students with descriptive feedback and coaching for improvement. Assessment *as* learning helps students self-assess by developing their capacity to set their own goals, monitor their own progress, determine their next steps in learning, and reflect on their learning. Assessment *of* learning is summative in nature and is intended to identify student progress in relation to learning expectations. The challenge for educators is to integrate assessment seamlessly with other learning goals. The Ontario assessment model uses the following process:

- **Establish learning goals from curriculum expectations.** Lessons include learning goals in student-friendly language that have been developed from curriculum expectations. These learning goals are shared with students and used to guide instruction.

- **Develop success criteria.** These descriptors are written in student-friendly language to help students understand what successful learning looks like. Criteria can be established by the teacher, using assessment task exemplars of student work, or by using the Achievement Chart from *The Ontario Curriculum, Grades 1–8: Science and Technology* (2007, 26–27). Success criteria can also be determined in collaboration with students.

- **Provide descriptive feedback.** In conversations with students, identify what criteria they have and have not met, and provide any needed instruction. At this stage, teachers work with students to identify next steps to determine how students may improve. This may include differentiating instruction.

- **Use information for peer and self-assessment.** Students assess their own work and the work of others to determine what still needs to be done.

- **Establish individual goals.** Students determine what they need to learn next and how to get there.

The **Hands-On Science and Technology** program provides assessment suggestions, rubrics, and templates for use during the teaching/learning process. These suggestions include tasks related to assessment *for* learning, assessment *as* learning, and assessment *of* learning.

## Assessment *for* Learning

It is important for teachers to assess students' understanding before, during, and after a lesson. The information gathered helps teachers determine students' needs and then plan the next steps in instruction. Students may come into class with misconceptions about science and technology concepts. By identifying what they already know, teachers can help students make connections and address any challenging issues.

To assess students as they work, use the assessment *for* learning suggestions provided with many of the activities.

While observing and conversing with students, teachers may use the **Anecdotal Record** template and/or the **Individual Student Observations** template to record assessment *for* learning data.

- **Anecdotal Record:** To gain an authentic view of a student's progress, it is critical to record observations *during* lessons. The **Anecdotal Record** template, on page 26, provides the teacher with a format for recording individual or group observations.

- **Individual Student Observations:** When teachers wish to focus more on individual students for a longer period of time, consider using the **Individual Student Observations** template, on page 27. This template provides more space for comments and is especially useful during conferences, interviews, or individual student performance tasks.

## Assessment *as* Learning

It is important for students to reflect on their own learning in relation to science and technology. For this purpose, teachers will find a **Student Self-Assessment** template, on page 31, as well as a **Student Reflections** template on page 32.

In addition, the **Science and Technology Journal**, on page 28, will encourage students to reflect on their own learning. Teachers can copy several sheets for each student, cut the sheets in half, add a cover, and bind the sheets together. Students can then create their own title pages for their journals. For variety, you may also have students use the blank reverse side of each page for other reflections, such as drawing or writing about:

- new science and technology challenges
- favourite science and technology activities
- real-life experiences with science and technology
- new terminology
- new places explored during investigations

Students may also journal in other ways, such as by adding notes to their portfolios, or by keeping online science and technology blogs or journals to record successes, challenges, and next steps relating to the learning goals.

---

**NOTE:** This Science and Technology Journal template is provided as a suggestion, but journals can also be made from simple notebooks or recycled paper.

---

Another component of assessment *as* learning involves opportunities for students to reflect on their use of 21st Century Competencies. During each lesson, teachers should spend time discussing and reflecting on the competencies being focused on. The intent here is to enhance students' understanding of how and when

Portage & Main Press, 2017 · *Hands-On Science and Technology · Grade 3* · ISBN: 978-1-55379-709-8

they use the competencies during the inquiry process. For this purpose, teachers may project a copy of the **21ˢᵗ Century Competencies Reflection** template, on page 29, and complete it as a class, using words and pictures to communicate students' reflections. A completed **Sample 21ˢᵗ Century Competencies Reflection** is included on page 30.

---

**NOTE:** Since no lesson addresses all six competencies, teachers can focus specifically on those covered in a lesson. Students can then explore the meaning of those skills at a deeper level.

---

Another component of assessment *as* learning utilizes the **21ˢᵗ Century Competencies Student/Teacher Reflection** template, which is found on page 33. This is completed by students at the end of the unit, in order to encourage them to reflect on how they have used the competencies. Students record their reflections in the rectangles on the template, and teachers provide descriptive feedback in the outer ovals.

---

**NOTE:** Depending on their literacy level, students may complete the assessment in various ways. For example, the sheets may be used as guides for oral conferences between teacher and student, or an adult may act as a scribe for the student, recording their responses. Alternatively, students may complete the sheets independently or with guidance and support as needed.

---

**NOTE:** This descriptive feedback from teachers may also be considered assessment *for* learning. Even though this feedback is provided at the end of the unit, students will consider the anecdotal comments as they continue to develop their 21ˢᵗ Century Competencies.

---

Students should also be encouraged to reflect on their cooperative group work skills, as these are directly related to 21ˢᵗ Century Competencies, as well as to the skills scientists use as they collaborate in team settings. For

this purpose, a **Cooperative Skills Self-Assessment** template is on page 34.

Student reflections can also be done in many ways other than by using these templates. For example, students can do the following:

- Interview one another to share their reflections on science and technology.
- Write an outline or brief script and make a video reflection.
- Create an electronic slide show with an audio recording of their reflections.

## Assessment *of* Learning

Assessment *of* learning provides a summary of student progress related to the accomplishments of the learning goals at a particular point in time. It is important to gather a variety of assessment data to draw conclusions about what a student knows and can do. As such, consider collecting student products, observing processes, and having conversations with students. Teachers should also consider which student work is formative and which is summative. Only the most recent and consistent evidence should be used.

Assessment *of* learning suggestions are provided with the culminating lesson of each unit of the **Hands-On Science and Technology** program. Teachers may use the **Anecdotal Record** template, on page 26, the **Individual Student Observations** template, on page 27, and the **Rubric**, on page 36, to record student results.

Always assess a student's individual accomplishments, not group work. However, you may assess how an individual student works within a group. Such skill development includes the ability to listen to others respectfully, share ideas, and participate actively in the inquiry process. For this purpose, use

Portage & Main Press, 2017 · *Hands-On Science and Technology · Grade 3* · ISBN: 978-1-55379-709-8

the **Cooperative Skills Teacher Assessment** template on page 37.

## Performance Assessment

Both assessment *for* learning and assessment *of* learning include performance assessment. Performance assessment is planned, systematic observation and assessment based on students actually doing a specific science and technology activity. Teacher- or teacher/ student-created rubrics can be used to assess student performance.

A **Sample Rubric** and a **Rubric** template for teacher use are on pages 35 and 36. For any specific activity, before the work begins, the teacher and students should together discuss success criteria for completing the task. This will ensure that the success criteria relate to the lesson's learning goals. The teacher can then record these criteria on the rubric.

When conducting assessment *for* learning, the rubric can be reviewed with students to determine strengths, challenges, and next steps related to learning goals.

When conducting assessment *of* learning, the rubric can be used to determine summative data. For example, teachers can use the rubric criteria to assess student performance, and students can receive a check mark for each criterion accomplished to determine a rubric score from a total of four marks. These rubric scores can then be transferred to the **Rubric Class Record** template, on page 38.

When using the rubric for assessment *of* learning, consider using four levels of achievement to correlate with the Ontario Science and Technology Achievement Chart (see pages 26 and 27 of *The Ontario Curriculum*).

For example:

1. achievement that falls much below the provincial standard
2. achievement that approaches the provincial standard
3. achievement that meets the provincial standard
4. achievement that surpasses the provincial standard

The **Hands-On Science and Technology** program provides numerous opportunities for students to apply their skills. By considering the same levels of achievement throughout the year, teachers should be able to track student learning and determine when students have a thorough understanding and demonstrate in-depth application of concepts and skills.

## Portfolios

A portfolio is a collection of work that shows evidence of a student's learning. There are many types of portfolios—the showcase portfolio and the progress portfolio are two popular formats. Showcase portfolios highlight the best of students' work, with students involved in the selection of pieces and justification for choices. Progress portfolios reflect students' progress as their work improves and aim to demonstrate in-depth understanding of the materials over time.

Select, with student input, work to include in a science and technology portfolio or in a science and technology section of a multi-subject portfolio. Selections should include representative samples of student work in all types of science and technology activities. Templates are included to organize the portfolio (**Portfolio Table of Contents** is on page 39, and **Portfolio Entry Record** is on page 40).

Portage & Main Press, 2017 · *Hands-On Science and Technology · Grade 3* · ISBN: 978-1-55379-709-8

**NOTE:** In an Indigenous context, portfolio creation may differ in that the student and teacher may select completed work from a coming-to-know perspective that reflects participatory learning. Students reflect on their own understanding of the world around them or have a sense of negotiating another point of view.

**NOTE:** From an Indigenous perspective, assessment is community-based, qualitative, and holistic, and includes input from all the people who influence an individual student's learning—parents, caregivers, Elders, Métis Senators, community members, and educators. An assessment that includes all these perspectives provides a balanced understanding of what represents success for Indigenous students and their families/community. A strong partnership between parents/guardians/communities and school improves student achievement. Teachers should be aware that some Indigenous students may feel apprehensive about a formal process of assessment; others may find that Western achievement goals do not fit their worldviews.

## Evidence of Student Achievement Levels for Evaluation

At the end of each unit, the teacher can determine achievement levels for each student. Assessment *of* learning information gathered throughout the unit can be used to identify these levels, according to the Ontario Science and Technology Achievement Chart.

The most recent and consistent assessment information should be used to determine levels of achievement. A reproducible, **Achievement Chart for Science & Technology**, on page 41 and 42, is included for teacher reference.

## Important Note to Teachers

Throughout the **Hands-On Science and Technology** program, suggestions are provided for assessment *for* learning, assessment *as* learning, and assessment *of* learning. Keep in mind that these are merely suggestions. Teachers are encouraged to use the assessment strategies presented in a wide variety of ways, and to ensure that they build an effective assessment plan using these assessment ideas, as well as their own valuable experiences as educators.

Portage & Main Press, 2017 · *Hands-On Science and Technology · Grade 3* · ISBN: 978-1-55379-709-8

# References

Banchi, Heather, and Randi Bell. "The Many Levels of Inquiry," *Science and Children* 46.2 (2008): 26–29.

Cameron, Caren, and Kathleen Gregory. *Rethinking Letter Grades: A Five-Step Approach for Aligning Letter Grades to Learning Standards.* Winnipeg: Portage & Main Press, 2014.

Creative Commons Canada. (See: <http://ca.creativecommons.org>.)

Davies, Anne. *Making Classroom Assessment Work* (3rd ed.). Courtenay, BC: Connections Publishing, 2011.

First Nations Education Steering Committee. *Science First Peoples Teachers Resource Guide,* 2016.

Fullan, Michael. *Great to Excellent: Launching the Next Stage of Ontario's Education Agenda,* 2013.

Inglis, Julian T. *Traditional Ecological Knowledge: Concepts and Cases.* Ottawa: International Development Research Centre, 1993.

Katz, Jennifer. *Teaching to Diversity: The Three-Block Model of Universal Design for Learning.* Winnipeg: Portage & Main Press, 2012.

Manitoba Education and Training. *Kindergarten to Grade 4 Science: Manitoba Curriculum Framework of Outcomes*, 1999. (See: <www.edu.gov.mb.ca/>)

Ontario Ministry of Education. *Growing Success: Assessment, Evaluation, and Reporting in Ontario Schools,* 2010. (See: <www.edu.gov.on.ca/>.)

_____. *The Ontario Curriculum, Grades 1–8: Science and Technology,* 2007. (See: <www.edu.gov.on.ca/>.)

Scardamalia, M. "Collective Cognitive Responsibility for the Advancement of Knowledge." In *Liberal Education in a Knowledge Society.* Edited by Barry Smith. Chicago: Open Court, 2002, quoted in Ontario Literacy and Numeracy Secretariat. "Inquiry-based Learning," Capacity Building series 32, p. 4 (May 2013).

Toulouse, Pamela. *Achieving Aboriginal Student Success.* Winnipeg: Portage & Main Press, 2011.

Truth and Reconciliation Commission of Canada: Calls to Action, 2015. (See: <www.trc.ca>.)

Portage & Main Press, 2017 · *Hands-On Science and Technology · Grade 3* · ISBN: 978-1-55379-709-8

**Date:** _____

# Anecdotal Record

## Purpose of Observation: _____

| Student/Group | Student/Group |
|---|---|
| Comments | Comments |
| Student/Group | Student/Group |
| Comments | Comments |
| Student/Group | Student/Group |
| Comments | Comments |

Portage & Main Press, 2017 · *Hands-On Science and Technology · Grade 3* · ISBN: 978-1-55379-709-8

**Date:** _____

# Individual Student Observations

## Purpose of Observation: _____

| |
|---|
| Student: _____ |
| Observations |
| |
| Student: _____ |
| Observations |
| |
| Student: _____ |
| Observations |
| |

Portage & Main Press, 2017 · Hands-On Science and Technology · Grade 3 · ISBN: 978-1-55379-709-8

# Science and Technology Journal

Date: _____    Name: _____

Today, I _____

I learned _____

I would like to learn more about _____

# Science and Technology Journal

Date: _____    Name: _____

Today, I _____

I learned _____

I would like to learn more about _____

Date: _____    Name: _____

# 21ˢᵗ Century Competencies Reflection

Inquiry Question: _____

| 21ˢᵗ Century Skill | What did it look like when we used this skill? | What did it sound like when we used this skill? | What did it feel like when we used this skill? |
|---|---|---|---|
| Critical Thinking | | | |
| Communication | | | |
| Collaboration | | | |
| Creativity | | | |
| Citizenship | | | |
| Character | | | |

Portage & Main Press, 2017 · Hands-On Science and Technology · Grade 3 · ISBN: 978-1-55379-709-8

# Sample 21ˢᵗ Century Competencies Reflection

**Inquiry Question:** _____

| 21ˢᵗ Century Skill | What did it look like when we used this skill? | What did it sound like when we used this skill? | What did it feel like when we used this skill? |
| --- | --- | --- | --- |
| Critical Thinking | We were solving problems. | What do you think we should do? Do you think that would work? Why don't we try another way? | It was interesting. |
| Communication | We were talking together and drawing pictures. | What do you think? I like your idea! Let's draw a plan. | We were happy. |
| Collaboration | We worked as a team. | Let's do it together. Now it's your turn. | It was exciting! |
| Creativity | | | |
| Citizenship | | | |
| Character | | | |

SAMPLE

Portage & Main Press, 2017 · Hands-On Science and Technology · Grade 3 · ISBN: 978-1-55379-709-8

**Date:** _____  **Name:** _____

# Student Self-Assessment

## Looking at My Science and Technology Learning

1. What I did in science and technology: _____

_____

_____

2. In science and technology I learned: _____

_____

_____

3. I did very well at: _____

_____

_____

4. One science and technology skill that I am working on is: _____

_____

_____

5. I would like to learn more about: _____

_____

_____

6. One thing I like about science and technology is: _____

_____

_____

**Note:** The student may complete this self-assessment or the teacher can scribe for the student.

Portage & Main Press, 2017 · Hands-On Science and Technology · Grade 3 · ISBN: 978-1-55379-709-8

**Date:** _____     **Name:** _____

# Student Reflections

| What I Did | What I Learned |
|---|---|

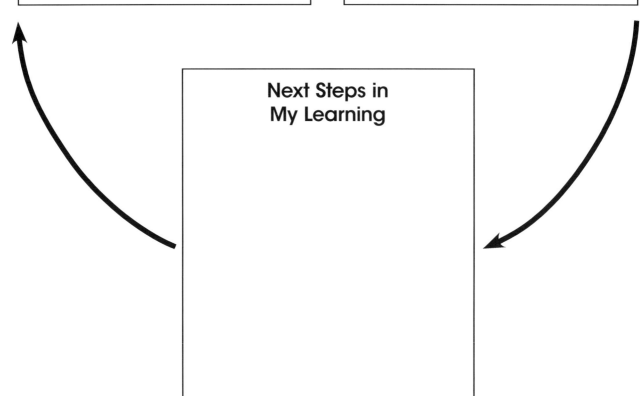

Next Steps in
My Learning

Portage & Main Press, 2017 · Hands-On Science and Technology · Grade 3 · ISBN: 978-1-55379-709-8

# 21st Century Competencies Student/Teacher Reflection

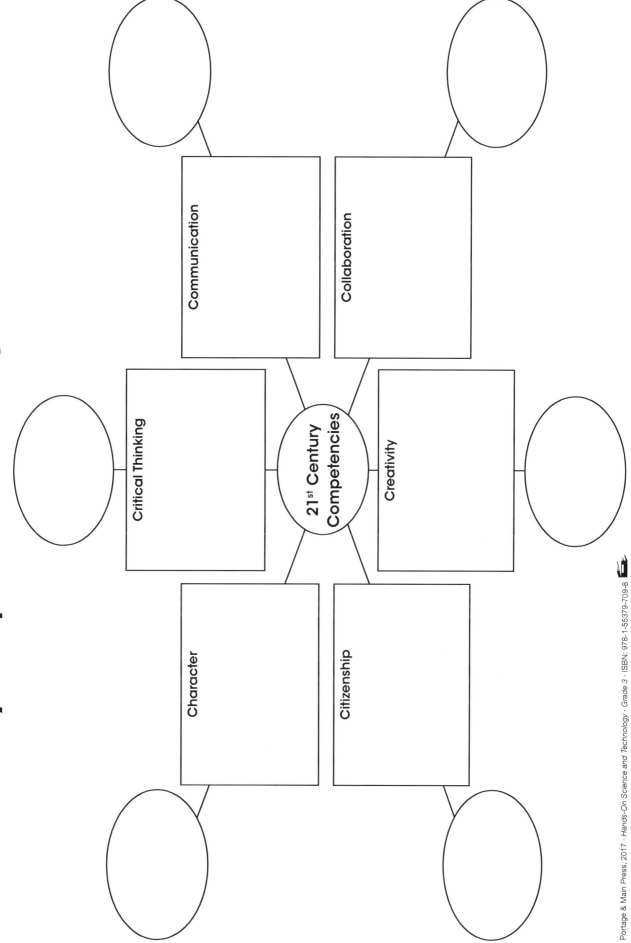

Portage & Main Press, 2017 · *Hands-On Science and Technology · Grade 3* · ISBN: 978-1-55379-709-8

# Cooperative Skills Self-Assessment

## Students in my group:

_____          _____

_____          _____

## Group Work – How Did I Do Today?

| Group Work | How I Did (✔) | | |
|---|---|---|---|
| | ☺ | 😐 | ☹ |
| I shared ideas. | | | |
| I listened to others. | | | |
| I asked questions. | | | |
| I encouraged others. | | | |
| I helped with the work. | | | |
| I stayed on task. | | | |

I did very well in _____

_____

Next time I would like to do better in _____

_____

Portage & Main Press, 2017 · Hands-On Science and Technology · Grade 3 · ISBN: 978-1-55379-709-8

# Sample Rubric

**Science and Technology Activity:** Looking at Seeds

**Science and Technology Unit:** _____

**Date:** _____

4 Thorough understanding and in-depth application of concepts and skills

3 Very good understanding and application of concepts and skills

2 Basic understanding and some application of concepts and skills

1 Limited understanding and minimal application of concepts and skills

| Student | Criteria | | | | Rubric Score /4 |
| --- | --- | --- | --- | --- | --- |
| | Follows Directions | Makes Detailed Observations | Sorts and Classifies Seeds | Uses Appropriate Vocabulary to Communicate Ideas | |
| Jarod | ✓ | ✓ | ✓ | | 3 |
| Aisha | ✓ | ✓ | ✓ | ✓ | 4 |
| | | | | | |
| | | | | | |
| | | | | | |
| | | | | | |
| | | | | | |
| | | | | | |
| | | | | | |
| | | | | | |
| | | | | | |

SAMPLE

Portage & Main Press, 2017 · Hands-On Science and Technology · Grade 3 · ISBN: 978-1-55379-709-8

# Rubric

**4** Thorough understanding and in-depth application of concepts and skills

**3** Very good understanding and application of concepts and skills

**2** Basic understanding and some application of concepts and skills

**1** Limited understanding and minimal application of concepts and skills

Science and Technology Activity: _____

Science and Technology Unit: _____

Date: _____

| Student | Criteria | | | | Rubric Score /4 |
|---------|----------|---|---|---|-----------------|
|  |  |  |  |  |  |
|  |  |  |  |  |  |
|  |  |  |  |  |  |
|  |  |  |  |  |  |
|  |  |  |  |  |  |
|  |  |  |  |  |  |
|  |  |  |  |  |  |
|  |  |  |  |  |  |
|  |  |  |  |  |  |
|  |  |  |  |  |  |

# Cooperative Skills Teacher Assessment

Date: _____

Task: _____

_____

| Group Member | Cooperative Skills | | | | |
|---|---|---|---|---|---|
| | Contributes ideas and questions | Respects and accepts contributions of others | Negotiates roles and responsibilities of each group member | Remains focused and encourages others to stay on task | Completes individual commitment to the group |
| | | | | | |
| | | | | | |
| | | | | | |
| | | | | | |
| | | | | | |
| | | | | | |

Comments: _____

_____

_____

_____

Portage & Main Press, 2017 · Hands-On Science and Technology · Grade 3 · ISBN: 978-1-55379-709-8

# Rubric Class Record

| Student | Unit/Activity/Date | | | | | | | | |
|---|---|---|---|---|---|---|---|---|---|
| | Rubric Scores /4 | | | | | | | | |
| | | | | | | | | | |
| | | | | | | | | | |
| | | | | | | | | | |
| | | | | | | | | | |
| | | | | | | | | | |
| | | | | | | | | | |
| | | | | | | | | | |
| | | | | | | | | | |
| | | | | | | | | | |
| | | | | | | | | | |
| | | | | | | | | | |
| | | | | | | | | | |

| Scores on Specific Tasks | Assessment |
|---|---|
| 4 | Thorough understanding and in-depth application of concepts and skills |
| 3 | Very good understanding and application of concepts and skills |
| 2 | Basic understanding and some application of concepts and skills |
| 1 | Limited understanding and minimal application of concepts and skills |

Portage & Main Press, 2017 · Hands-On Science and Technology · Grade 3 · ISBN: 978-1-55379-709-8

**Name:** _____

# Portfolio Table of Contents

| Entry | Date | Selection |
|-------|------|-----------|
| 1. | _____ | _____ |
| 2. | _____ | _____ |
| 3. | _____ | _____ |
| 4. | _____ | _____ |
| 5. | _____ | _____ |
| 6. | _____ | _____ |
| 7. | _____ | _____ |
| 8. | _____ | _____ |
| 9. | _____ | _____ |
| 10. | _____ | _____ |
| 11. | _____ | _____ |
| 12. | _____ | _____ |
| 13. | _____ | _____ |
| 14. | _____ | _____ |
| 15. | _____ | _____ |
| 16. | _____ | _____ |
| 17. | _____ | _____ |
| 18. | _____ | _____ |
| 19. | _____ | _____ |
| 20. | _____ | _____ |

Portage & Main Press, 2017 · Hands-On Science and Technology · Grade 3 · ISBN: 978-1-55379-709-8

**Date:** _____     **Name:** _____

# Portfolio Entry Record

This work was chosen by_____

This work is _____

_____

I chose this work because _____

_____

_____

_____

_____

**Note:** The student may complete this form or the teacher can scribe for the student.

✂ - - - - - - - - - - - - - - - - - - - - - - - - - - - - - - - - - - - - - - - - - - - - - -

**Date:** _____     **Name:** _____

# Portfolio Entry Record

This work was chosen by_____

This work is _____

_____

I chose this work because _____

_____

_____

_____

_____

**Note:** The student may complete this form or the teacher can scribe for the student.

Portage & Main Press, 2017 · Hands-On Science and Technology · Grade 3 · ISBN: 978-1-55379-709-8

# Achievement Chart for Science & Technology

| Categories | Level 1 | Level 2 | Level 3 | Level 4 |
|---|---|---|---|---|

**Knowledge and Understanding** – Subject-specific content acquired in each grade (knowledge), and the comprehension of its meaning and significance (understanding)

| | The student: | | | |
|---|---|---|---|---|
| **Knowledge of content** *(e.g., facts; terminology; definitions; safe use of tools, equipment, and materials)* | demonstrates limited knowledge of content | demonstrates some knowledge of content | demonstrates considerable knowledge of content | demonstrates thorough knowledge of content |
| **Understanding of content** *(e.g., concepts, ideas, theories, principles, procedures, processes)* | demonstrates limited understanding of content | demonstrates some understanding of content | demonstrates considerable understanding of content | demonstrates thorough understanding of content |

**Thinking and Investigation** – The use of critical and creative thinking skills and inquiry and problem-solving skills and/or processes

| | The student: | | | |
|---|---|---|---|---|
| **Use of initiating and planning skills and strategies** *(e.g., formulating questions, identifying the problem, developing hypotheses, scheduling, selecting strategies and resources, developing plans)* | uses initiating and planning skills and strategies with limited effectiveness | uses initiating and planning skills and strategies with some effectiveness | uses initiating and planning skills and strategies with considerable effectiveness | uses initiating and planning skills and strategies with a high degree of effectiveness |
| **Use of processing skills and strategies** *(e.g., performing and recording, gathering evidence and data, observing, manipulating materials and using equipment safely, solving equations, proving)* | uses processing skills and strategies with limited effectiveness | uses processing skills and strategies with some effectiveness | uses processing skills and strategies with considerable effectiveness | uses processing skills and strategies with a high degree of effectiveness |
| **Use of critical/creative thinking processes, skills, and strategies** *(e.g., analysing, interpreting, problem solving, evaluating, forming and justifying conclusions on the basis of evidence)* | uses critical/ creative thinking processes, skills, and strategies with limited effectiveness | uses critical/ creative thinking processes, skills, and strategies with some effectiveness | uses critical/creative thinking processes, skills, and strategies with considerable effectiveness | uses critical/creative thinking processes, skills, and strategies with a high degree of effectiveness |

**Communication** – The conveying of meaning through various forms

| | The student: | | | |
|---|---|---|---|---|
| **Expression and organization of ideas and information** *(e.g., clear expression, logical organization)* **in oral, visual, and/or written forms** *(e.g., diagrams, models)* | expresses and organizes ideas and information with limited effectiveness | expresses and organizes ideas and information with some effectiveness | expresses and organizes ideas and information with considerable effectiveness | expresses and organizes ideas and information with a high degree of effectiveness |

Portage & Main Press, 2017 · Hands-On Science and Technology · Grade 3 · ISBN: 978-1-55379-709-8

# Achievement Chart for Science & Technology (Continued)

| Categories | Level 1 | Level 2 | Level 3 | Level 4 |
|---|---|---|---|---|
| **Communication** – (continued) | | | | |
| | **The student:** | | | |
| **Communication for different audiences** *(e.g., peers, adults)* **and purposes** *(e.g., to inform, to persuade)* **in oral, visual, and/or written forms** | communicates for different audiences and purposes with limited effectiveness | communicates for different audiences and purposes with some effectiveness | communicates for different audiences and purposes with considerable effectiveness | communicates for different audiences and purposes with a high degree of effectiveness |
| **Use of conventions, vocabulary, and terminology of the discipline in oral, visual, and/or written forms** *(e.g., symbols, formulae, scientific notation, SI units)* | uses conventions, vocabulary, and terminology of the discipline with limited effectiveness | uses conventions, vocabulary, and terminology of the discipline with some effectiveness | uses conventions, vocabulary, and terminology of the discipline with considerable effectiveness | uses conventions, vocabulary, and terminology of the discipline with a high degree of effectiveness |
| **Application** – The use of knowledge and skills to make connections within and between various contexts | | | | |
| | **The student:** | | | |
| **Application of knowledge and skills** *(e.g., concepts and processes, safe use of equipment and technology, investigation skills)* **in familiar contexts** | applies knowledge and skills in familiar contexts with limited effectiveness | applies knowledge and skills in familiar contexts with some effectiveness | applies knowledge and skills in familiar contexts with considerable effectiveness | applies knowledge and skills in familiar contexts with a high degree of effectiveness |
| **Transfer of knowledge and skills** *(e.g., concepts and processes, safe use of equipment and technology, investigation skills)* **to unfamiliar contexts** | transfers knowledge and skills to unfamiliar contexts with limited effectiveness | transfers knowledge and skills to unfamiliar contexts with some effectiveness | transfers knowledge and skills to unfamiliar contexts with considerable effectiveness | transfers knowledge and skills to unfamiliar contexts with a high degree of effectiveness |
| **Making connections between science, technology, society, and the environment** *(e.g., assessing the impact of science and technology on people, other living things, and the environment)* | makes connections between science, technology, society, and the environment with limited effectiveness | makes connections between science, technology, society, and the environment with some effectiveness | makes connections between science, technology, society, and the environment with considerable effectiveness | makes connections between science, technology, society, and the environment with a high degree of effectiveness |
| **Proposing courses of practical action to deal with problems relating to science, technology, society, and the environment** | proposes courses of practical action of limited effectiveness | proposes courses of practical action of some effectiveness | proposes courses of practical action of considerable effectiveness | proposes highly effective courses of practical action |

Source from: The Ontario Curriculum, Grades 1-8: Science and Technology, 2007.

Portage & Main Press, 2017 · Hands-On Science and Technology · Grade 3 · ISBN: 978-1-55379-709-8

# Unit 1

# Growth and Changes in Plants

# Introduction

This unit of **Hands-On Science and Technology, Grade 3**, focuses on the study of plants: their physical characteristics, along with each characteristic's specific function, the requirements plants need to survive, and their patterns of growth. Students will investigate, grow, and observe plants in their local environment. They will learn about similarities and differences in the physical characteristics of different plant species, as well as the changes that take place in different plants as they grow. Students will also learn about the importance of plants for the survival of humans and other animals, and the effects of both human activities and changes in environmental conditions on plants.

## Planning Tips for Teachers

- Collect a variety of live plants and an assortment of seeds and bulbs for examination and use in the classroom. Bean plants grow well and quickly, so students can observe them develop from seed to adult plant in a reasonably short period of time.

- Collect a variety of containers in which to put soil, as well as to grow the plants.

- Consider setting up a plant centre in a sunny area of the classroom, or at another location in the school, where students can observe, record, and discuss changes in plants on a regular basis.

- Collect numerous photos and pictures of plants for use in lesson activities and at learning centres. Resources for collecting pictures include:
  - wall calendars (current or outdated)
  - departments of forestry and natural resources
  - seed catalogues
  - forestry and environmental associations
  - gardening and plant magazines
  - horticultural societies
  - brochures and flyers
  - simplified plant guides/books
  - gardening books
  - nature-walk brochures from local, provincial, and national parks
  - photographs from home (Some images should be digital for use with a whiteboard/projection system.)

- Contact government departments and associations well in advance of studying the unit. Teachers may be able to obtain other related materials and services such as booklets, posters, videos, and presentations for classroom use.

- It is not necessary to teach this unit (or any other unit) in one block. Some teachers might consider splitting up the unit's activities to focus on plants during fall and spring when outdoor plant life is abundant; others might choose to study plants on an ongoing basis throughout the year. Nor is there a need to teach each unit of the curriculum as a discrete unit. Many meaningful links can be made by teaching this unit in conjunction with Soils in the Environment (unit 4).

- Develop a Makerspace centre. Classroom Makerspaces are usually designed as centres where students learn together and collaborate on do-it-yourself projects. Students are given the opportunity to work with a variety of age-appropriate tools, as well as everyday and recycled materials. Additionally, arts-and-crafts are often integrated into Makerspace offerings.

  For this unit, set up a Makerspace centre in your classroom that encourages informal learning about plants. Include general materials, such as those listed in the Introduction to **Hands-On Science and Technology, Grade 3**, as well as unit-specific materials. For example, provide a large collection of live plants, as well as

Portage & Main Press, 2017 · Hands-On Science and Technology · Grade 3 · ISBN: 978-1-55379-709-8

plant parts (e.g., slices of tree trunks, seeds, leaves, bark, fruit, and vegetables). Also, provide magnifiers, tweezers, soil samples, spray bottles, containers, and water.

Do-it-yourself projects may include anything related to the concepts within this unit. Projects that students might initiate include (but are not limited to):

- creating a field guide for local plants, edible plants, weeds, trees, or flowers
- creating a mosaic out of plant parts such as seeds, leaves, grasses, and bark
- designing and constructing a diorama featuring models of a variety of local plants
- creating models of trees in the different seasons
- creating a model of a neighbourhood that has a unique layout re: trees, plants, grasses, etc.
- creating a device or structure that helps to protect plants when they are young
- using what they know about the basic needs of plants, creating a device or structure that will help speed the growth of plants
- creating a model of a plant that displays their knowledge of plant parts (*stem, leaf, root, pistil, stamen, flower, adaptation*)
- creating a model greenhouse
- creating a device that automatically waters a plant
- examining slices of tree trunks and researching to discover what the rings tell you
- creating terrariums, or use glass jars in order to see roots growing (bulbs)
- using wet paper towels to sprout seeds
- using food colouring to see if they can change the colour of flowers (white carnations work well)

Literacy connections that might inspire projects include:

- *The Giving Tree* by Shel Silverstein
- *The Tiny Seed* by Eric Carle
- *A Fruit Is a Suitcase for Seeds* by Jean Richards
- *Pick, Pull, Snap!: Where Once a Flower Bloomed* by Lola M. Schaefer
- *Sunflower House* by Eve Bunting
- *Plants Can't Sit Still* by Rebecca E. Hirsch
- *Lola Plants a Garden* by Anna McQuinn
- *Finding Wild* by Megan Wagner Lloyd
- *The Reason for a Flower* by Ruth Heller

As inquiry questions are posed with each lesson, you will find these questions inspire other do-it-yourself projects related to the unit. Students may determine solutions to these questions through the creating they do at the Makerspace centre. Remember to not direct the learning here; simply create conditions for learning to happen.

## Indigenous Worldviews

Indigenous perspectives on the natural environment are based on the idea of sustainability. Many plants traditionally used by Indigenous peoples in Ontario are either no longer in existence or in danger of being lost forever. Indigenous perspectives, which are common to many other cultures as well, are embedded throughout this unit of **Hands-On Science and Technology, Grade 3** with the following understandings in mind:

- People from all cultures respect and appreciate nature's gifts.
- All life forms, no matter how small, are considered important and significant.
- By respecting plants, we are protecting the Earth.
- Plants have homes and communities just like animals and people do.

Portage & Main Press, 2017 · Hands-On Science and Technology · Grade 3 · ISBN: 978-1-55379-709-8

- Plants have powers to heal. Plants help animals and people survive.
- Indigenous science helps us understand how plants grow and develop.
- Western science helps us understand how plants grow and develop.
- We can learn about plants from each other.

## Indigenous Peoples' Uses for Plants

**Food:** The Indigenous peoples of North America farmed and gathered wild plants for food. Eastern Woodlands people cultivated maize (corn), beans, and squash (known as the Three Sisters). Sagamite, a soup made of cornmeal, with added fish, meat, or squash, was a staple. There is also evidence of similar crops grown among the Prairies people farther west, in the area where the Red and Assiniboine rivers meet. Tobacco and sunflowers were also grown in the Prairies.

Hundreds of species of wild plants were gathered for food. These included seeds, nuts, and grains (e.g., whitebark pine seeds, hazelnuts, acorns, and wild rice). Berries and fleshy fruits (e.g., saskatoons, blueberries, huckleberries, crabapples, rosehips, wild cherries) were important sources of vitamins along with wild greens, the shoots and leaves of various plants, and leaf vegetables (e.g., mustard greens, lamb's quarters, watercress). Roots (e.g., wild onion, balsam root, wild turnip) were harvested later in summer. Fungi, such as wild mushrooms, and certain tree barks were also eaten. In northern areas, people ate lichens; in coastal areas, they ate certain species of algae and seaweed.

**Medicinal plants:** Many plants can be used to treat illnesses and ailments. Some can be administered as teas (e.g., Labrador tea is used for kidney ailments and yarrow is used to treat colds and fever). Some plants are used as inhalants or as poultices applied to a certain part of the body (a poultice from the purple coneflower root, for example, treats sores and swelling). Others are mixed with fats to make ointments. Some plants are used as smudges in healing ceremonies (see sacred plants, below).

**Sacred plants:** Tobacco, sweetgrass, cedar, and sage are known as the four sacred medicines by the Anishinaabe people, though they are also used by other First Nations peoples in North America. These medicines are used mainly in smudging, where the smoke they produce is part of prayer and cleansing ceremonies. Some people believe the smoke from the sacred plants summons spirits that people can communicate with. Tobacco is the first medicine offered in a ceremony to communicate with the spirit world. Sweetgrass is used for healing and purification. Sage is known for its physical healing properties, and cedar is used for both purification and as a guardian spirit.

**Utility plants:** Plants were essential for day-to-day life. Wood from various trees was used to build structures (e.g., shelters, frames for wigwams); for transportation (e.g., canoes, snowshoe frames, toboggans); for tools and implements (e.g., arrow and spear shafts, digging sticks, chisel and adze handles); and toys and games. Bark was used to create containers, canoes, and as wrapping and lining. Plant fibres were used to make rope, fabric, mats, and baskets. Moss was used to line diapers. Many plants were used as dyes.

## Science and Technology Vocabulary

Throughout this unit teachers should use, and encourage students to use, vocabulary such as:

- *adaptation, air, basic needs, carbon dioxide, coniferous, deciduous, fibrous, flowers, leaves, life cycle, light, nutrients, ovule, oxygen, photosynthesis, pistil, pollen, root, seeds, soil, space, stamen, stem, taproot, water*

Portage & Main Press, 2017 · Hands-On Science and Technology · Grade 3 · ISBN: 978-1-55379-709-8

In lesson 1, students start a Science and Technology Glossary in which they record new vocabulary introduced throughout the unit. Also in lesson 1, teachers create a class word wall for the unit. The word wall can be created on a bulletin board, or simply on a sheet of poster paper, so as not to take up too much space. On the bulletin board or poster paper, record new vocabulary as it is introduced throughout the unit. Ensure the word wall is placed in a location where all students can see it and refer to the words during activities and discussion.

Teachers should also consider including vocabulary related to scientific inquiry skills, which includes terms such as:

- *access, ask, brainstorm, collect, compare, connect, consider, construct, cooperate, create, describe, develop, diagram, display, draw, estimate, examine, explain, explore, find, follow, graph, identify, improve, investigate, label, measure, observe, order, plan, predict, recognize, record, repeat, research, respond, select, sequence, test*

These terms might be displayed in the classroom as they relate to inquiry skills used throughout the year. Students can then brainstorm which skills they are using as they work through particular lessons. They could also discuss what the skill looks and sounds like as they explore and investigate.

Portage & Main Press, 2017 · *Hands-On Science and Technology · Grade 3* · ISBN: 978-1-55379-709-8

# Unit Overview

| Fundamental Concepts | Big Ideas |
|---|---|
| Systems and Interactions | ■ Plants have distinct characteristics.<br>■ There are similarities and differences among various types of plants. |
| Sustainability and Stewardship | ■ Plants are the primary source of food for humans.<br>■ Humans need to protect plants and their habitats.<br>■ Plants are important to the planet. |

## Overall Expectations

By the end of Grade 3, students will:

1. Assess ways in which plants have an impact on society and the environment, and ways in which human activity has an impact on plants and plant habitats.
2. Investigate similarities and differences in the characteristics of various plants, and ways in which the characteristics of plants relate to the environment in which they grow.
3. Demonstrate an understanding that plants grow and change and have distinct characteristics.

Portage & Main Press, 2017 · Hands-On Science and Technology · Grade 3 · ISBN: 978-1-55379-709-8

# Curriculum Correlation

| Specific Expectation | Lesson | | | | | | | | | | | | | | |
|---|---|---|---|---|---|---|---|---|---|---|---|---|---|---|---|
| | 1 | 2 | 3 | 4 | 5 | 6 | 7 | 8 | 9 | 10 | 11 | 12 | 13 | 14 | 15 |
| **1. Relating Science and Technology to Society and the Environment** | | | | | | | | | | | | | | | |
| **1.1** Assess ways in which plants are important to humans and other living things, taking different points of view into consideration, and suggest ways in which humans can protect plants. | | | | | | √ | √ | | √ | √ | | | | √ | √ |
| **1.2** Assess the impact of different human activities on plants, and list personal actions they can engage in to minimize harmful effects and enhance good effects. | | | | | | | | | | √ | | | | √ | |
| **2. Developing Investigation and Communication Skills** | | | | | | | | | | | | | | | |
| **2.1** Follow established safety procedures during science and technology investigations. | √ | √ | √ | √ | √ | √ | √ | √ | √ | √ | √ | √ | √ | √ | √ |
| **2.2** Observe and compare the parts of a variety of plants. | | √ | √ | | | | | | | | | | | | |
| **2.3** Germinate seeds and record similarities and differences as seedlings develop. | | | √ | | √ | | | | | | | | | | |
| **2.4** Investigate ways in which a variety of plants adapt and/or react to their environment, including changes in their environment, using a variety of methods. | | | √ | √ | | | | √ | | | | | | | |
| **2.5** Use scientific inquiry/ experimentation skills, and knowledge acquired from previous investigations, to investigate a variety of ways in which plants meet their basic needs. | | | √ | | √ | | | √ | | | √ | | | | |
| **2.6** Use appropriate science and technology vocabulary, including *stem, leaf, root, pistil, stamen, flower, adaptation,* and *germination,* in oral and written communication. | √ | √ | √ | √ | √ | √ | √ | √ | √ | √ | √ | √ | √ | √ | √ |
| **2.7** Use a variety of forms to communicate with different audiences and for a variety of purposes. | √ | √ | √ | √ | √ | √ | √ | √ | √ | √ | √ | √ | √ | √ | √ |

▶

Portage & Main Press, 2017 · Hands-On Science and Technology · Grade 3 · ISBN: 978-1-55379-709-8

| 3. Understanding Basic Concepts | | | | | | | | | | | | | | | |
|---|---|---|---|---|---|---|---|---|---|---|---|---|---|---|---|
| **3.1** Describe the basic needs of plants, including air, water, light, warmth, and space. | √ | | | | | | √ | | | | | | | | |
| **3.2** Identify the major parts of plants, including root, stem, flower, stamen, pistil, leaf, seed, and fruit, and describe how each contributes to the plant's survival within the plant's environment. | √ | √ | √ | √ | | √ | | | | | | | | | |
| **3.3** Describe the changes that different plants undergo in their life cycles. | | | | √ | | | | | | | | | | | |
| **3.4** Describe how most plants get energy to live directly from the sun and how plants help other living things to get energy from the sun. | √ | | √ | | | | | | | | | | | | |
| **3.5** Describe ways in which humans from various cultures, including Indigenous peoples, use plants for food, shelter, medicine, and clothing. | | | | | | √ | √ | | | √ | √ | | | | √ |
| **3.6** Describe ways in which plants and animals depend on each other. | | | | | | | √ | | √ | | | √ | | | |
| **3.7** Describe the different ways in which plants are grown for food, and explain the advantages and disadvantages of locally grown and organically produced food, including environmental benefits. | | | | | | √ | √ | | | | | | √ | | |
| **3.8** Identify examples of environmental conditions that may threaten plant and animal survival. | | | | | | | | | | | | | √ | √ | √ |

**1**

## Action: Part Two

Provide each student with one of the plant pictures from Image Bank: Local and Exotic Plants and one large sticky note. Tell students to keep their pictures to themselves at this point. Have them examine their picture and record on the sticky note what they see and what they think the name of the plant is, or what they think an appropriate name might be, based on the plant's appearance. Have students attach the sticky note to their picture.

Explain there are two copies of each picture, so for every picture held by a student, another student in the class has the same one. Challenge students to find their partner—the classmate who has the duplicate picture. Make sure students do not show their picture to anyone; each must first share an oral description of their plant, as well as guess the partner's plant by name (e.g., prickly stem, red flower at the top, medium-sized leaves—a rose) to determine if the plants are *likely* the same. If a match does not seem likely, those two students can move on in search of the classmate with their duplicate plant picture. Once all students are in pairs (with likely matches), have them share their recordings on sticky notes with each other.

After all pairs have shared, ask:

- What do all of the pictures have in common? (They are all plants. The plants all have green parts. They all need water, sunlight, and air to grow.)
- How are they different? (different types of plants, grow in different locations, different uses)
- What do you think you will be learning about in this lesson?

Have students share their ideas and background knowledge.

## Action: Part Three

Display a variety of plants for students to observe and examine. On chart paper, construct a KWHL chart for recording ideas. Title and label the chart, as in the following example:

| What Do We Know About Plants and Their Needs? | | | |
|---|---|---|---|
| **What We Know** | **What We Want to Know** | **How We Can Find Out** | **What We Learned** |
| | | | |
| | | | |

Discuss the first part of the chart's title with students. Ask:

- What is a plant?

Have students share ideas, and record this information in the first column of the chart. Let students know there are many good ideas, and they will use the information on the chart to agree on a definition for *plant*.

Create a class definition for the term *plant*, and record this on a separate strip of chart paper.

Discuss the second part of the title with students by asking:

- What do plants need in order to survive?

Have students share ideas, and use a different colour of marker to record this information in the first column of the chart. Remind students that there are many good ideas, and they will use the information on the chart to agree on some basic things that plants need to survive.

Create a class list of things plants need to survive and grow, and record on a separate sheet of chart paper with the same coloured marker as above.

Now, have students focus on the second column of the chart.

Portage & Main Press, 2017 · *Hands-On Science and Technology · Grade 3* · ISBN: 978-1-55379-709-8

Portage & Main Press, 2017 · *Hands-On Science and Technology* · *Grade 3* · ISBN: 978-1-55379-709-8

**1**

Ask:

- As we begin to study plants, what questions do you have about them?
- What would you like to learn about plants?

Have students share their ideas, and record these in the second column of the chart. This provides an opportunity for students to share special interests, and for you to consider these interests when planning future activities.

Introduce the concept of sustainability with regards to how we use and need plants (e.g., growing crops, building materials, exploring natural areas). Introduce the three pillars of sustainability—social (human health and well-being), environmental, and economic. Challenge students to notice when sustainability of plants is challenged or protected.

**NOTE:** For detailed information on sustainability education, refer to Ontario's Acting Today, Shaping Tomorrow website: <www.edu.gov.on.ca/curriculumcouncil/ShapeTomorrow.pdf>.

As students share questions, discuss ways they might find answers to these questions. Encourage them to think of a wide variety of ways to learn new ideas or to find answers to scientific questions. For example:

- researching classroom resources (e.g., books, magazines, posters)
- inviting guest speakers to the classroom
- going on field trips
- watching videos
- reading websites, blogs
- researching library resources
- researching resources from home (e.g., books, artifacts, family experts)
- writing letters to experts
- conducting experiments
- making observations
- going on nature walks in the community
- taking photograps

**NOTE:** Introduce resources students may not think of (e.g., simplified plant guides; nature-walk brochures from local, provincial, and national parks; gardening books).

Record all of these ideas in the third column of the KWHL chart.

Explain to students that as they explore plants and learn new things about them, they will record these ideas in the fourth column of the chart.

In a visible area of the classroom, display the KWHL chart, along with the class definition of the term *plant* and the list of what plants need in order to grow and survive. Students can refer to the information on the KWHL chart for the remainder of the unit.

Finally, discuss with students how this topic—plants and their needs—might apply to their own lives. Ask:

- How could you use what you learn about plants during your life?

Discuss examples (e.g., gardening, cooking, potential future careers).

Distribute several copies of Activity Sheet: Science and Technology Glossary (1.1.1) to each student. Have students begin their own glossaries for the unit. By the end of the unit, students will have completed several sheets, at which point they can cut apart the rows, alphabetize their words, and create booklets of vocabulary related to growth and changes in plants.

**NOTE:** The Science and Technology Glossary presents an excellent opportunity to celebrate cultural diversity by having students include words in other languages. Students may include terms in Indigenous languages or other languages spoken at home.

A variety of online dictionaries may be used as a source for translations. For example:
- ojibwe.lib.umn.edu/
- www.freelang.net/online/mohawk.php

Online dictionaries are also available for other languages that may be reflective of the class population.

**Activity Sheet**

Directions to students:

Begin your Science and Technology Glossary for the unit. Record the term *plant*, and include a definition and an illustration (1.1.1).

## Consolidate and Debrief

- Revisit the guided inquiry question: **What do we know about plants and their needs?** Have students share their knowledge, provide examples, and ask further inquiry questions.
- Add to the KWHL chart as students learn new concepts, answer some of their own inquiry questions, and ask new inquiry questions.
- Begin a class word wall to display new terms introduced throughout the unit. Include the words in other languages, as appropriate.

## Enhance 🖥️1

- Throughout the unit, ensure students have opportunities to learn about local plants and plants from around the world.

  There are many apps that allow students to identify plants. Leafsnap, for example, enables you to take a photo of a leaf and the app will identify the tree species. Other apps can be found at: <www.telegraph.co.uk/gardening/tools-and-accessories/the-best-apps-to-identify-unknown-plants-and-flowers/>.

- Have students create digital glossaries using Google apps such as Educreations, which allows for voice recording. Another option is to use Microsoft Word. For each term introduced, have students draw a text box, record the term and a definition for it, and then add an illustration or picture. For the latter, students may want to use a computer program such

as Kid Pix to draw digital pictures, insert clip-art pictures in Word, copy and paste pictures from websites, or draw their pictures by hand and have them scanned.

**NOTE:** If students are copying and pasting pictures from websites, take the opportunity to educate them about copyright with regards to photos and drawings. Explain that it is okay to copy, paste, and print online photos for personal use. However, they may not do this for mass distribution, or for selling a product in which the photo or picture is being used. The Creative Commons Canada website may also be a useful resource: <https://ca.creativecommons.org/>.

- Have students create slide shows throughout the unit, using a computer program such as Google Slides, PowerPoint, or Kid Pix, or a web-based application (e.g., Prezi). At this point, students can begin their slide shows by creating two slides, the first one as the title page "Plants" and the second slide defining what a plant is. Each slide created throughout the unit should include information, as well as illustrations students have either drawn or copied and pasted from the Internet. This activity may also be done as a class project, with each student creating a slide or two for each lesson. Establish criteria as a class as to what should be included on each slide.

- Access the interactive activity, Classifying Plants, in the Grade 3, Unit 1 folder of the ***Hands-On Interactive for Science and Technology, Grade 3*** download. Find this download at: <www.portageandmainpress.com/product/hands-on-interactive-for-science-and-technology-grade-3/>.

- Have students begin their do-it-yourself projects at the Makerspace centre. (See page 18 in the Introduction to ***Hands-On Science and Technology, Grade 3*** and page 44 in the Introduction to this unit for details on setting up the Makerspace centre.)

Portage & Main Press, 2017 · *Hands-On Science and Technology · Grade 3* · ISBN: 978-1-55379-709-8

# Science and Technology Glossary

| Illustration | Term | Definition |
| --- | --- | --- |
| Illustration | Term | Definition |
| Illustration | Term | Definition |

Portage & Main Press, 2017 · *Hands-On Science and Technology · Grade 3* · ISBN: 978-1-55379-709-8

# 2 | What Are the Parts of a Plant?

## Information for Teachers

The basic parts of plants include: root, stem, leaf, flower, pistil, stamen, sepal, petals, and seeds.

In this lesson, students will be removing potted plants from their pots, and examining all the parts of a plant. A day or two before conducting this activity, water the plants to be used (see Materials, below), as it is easier to remove a plant from moist soil than from dry soil.

## 21st Century Competencies

**Communication** and **Critical Thinking**: Students will observe and compare plants, identifying the main parts. They will then complete a labelled diagram of a plant.

## Materials

- newspaper
- variety of small plants in bloom, one for each student or pair of students (Plants suitable for classroom use can often be found at local gardens, grocery stores or markets, or florists. Ask for plants that are a bit "tired" and not suitable for sale, explaining these can still be used for teaching purposes. If live plants are unavailable, print pictures from the Internet, or cut out pictures from magazines.)
- soft paintbrushes
- plastic knife
- chart paper
- markers
- transparent containers (optional)
- computer/tablet with Internet access (optional)
- digital camera (optional)
- printer (optional)
- repotting soil (optional)
- pots for repotting (optional)
- pictures of flowering plants
- Activity Sheet: What Are the Parts of a Plant? (1.2.1)
- Learning-Centre Task Card: Building a Model of a Plant (1.2.2)
- toothpicks
- paper
- various art supplies
- variety of recycled materials
- KWHL chart (from lesson 1)
- Science and Technology Glossary (1.1.1)

⚠️ **SAFETY NOTE:** Be aware of any student allergies in class. An easy entry point to a discussion about allergies is to talk about plants not allowed in hospital rooms (usually lilies).

## Activate

Review the previous lesson. Ask students:

- What is a plant?

Have students explain the characteristics of plants with which they are familiar.

On chart paper, construct a chart for recording students' ideas. For example:

| Names of Plants | Similarities | Differences |
|---|---|---|
|  |  |  |
|  |  |  |
|  |  |  |

Ask:

- What were some of the plants we looked at?

Record the names of two plants in the first column. Ask:

- What were some of the plants' similarities (things in common) we discussed in the last lesson?

Record these in the second column. Ask:

- What were some of the plants' differences we discussed in the last lesson?

Portage & Main Press, 2017 · *Hands-On Science and Technology · Grade 3* · ISBN: 978-1-55379-709-8

**2**

Record these in the third column. Repeat this process, comparing other pairs of plants.

Introduce the guided inquiry question: **What are the parts of a plant?**

## Action

Have students work individually or in pairs, and give each student or pair of students some newspaper, a dry paintbrush, and a flowering plant (or a picture of a flowering plant).

If actual plants are being used (rather than pictures), ask students to cover their desks with the newspaper. Then, slowly go through the following steps with students for gently removing the plant from its pot:

1. Put your hand over the top of the pot, and hold the plant stem gently between your fingers.
2. Turn the pot upside down while holding the stem in this way, supporting the plant and the soil.
3. Tap the edge of the pot against something hard, such as a table.
4. Gently use your other hand to pull the pot upwards to remove the plant.
5. If the plant does not come out easily, repeat steps 3 and 4.

**NOTE:** Remind students it is quite easy to break or damage a plant when removing it from a pot. It may be easier for pairs of students to work together to remove the plants from the pots, one student holding the plant and turning over the pot (steps 1 and 2) and the other student pulling on the pot. For stubborn plants, it sometimes helps to slide the blade of a plastic knife around the inside edge of the pot, to cut any roots that are protruding through the drainage holes. If all else fails, breaking or cracking the pot (if plastic) can help to remove the plant.

Tell students to lay their potless plants on top of the newspaper. Have them use a paintbrush to carefully brush away as much of the soil

clinging to the roots as they can. Then, have them identify any parts of the plant they know by writing the names beside the parts, directly on the newspaper. If a digital camera is available, have students take pictures of their labelled plant parts. Then, have students circulate the classroom, observing the other students' plants and parts labelled. Ask:

■ What do all of these plants have in common?

As students identify the plant parts—including roots, stem, leaves, flowers, and seeds—record the name of each part under "Similarities" on the chart (if not already noted). Once all of the plant parts have been identified, distribute a copy of Activity Sheet: What Are the Parts of a Plant? (1.2.1) to each student. Have students sketch their plant and label their diagram.

**NOTE:** Some of the similarities (and/or differences) students may notice in the plants are: shape of the leaves, type of roots, number of petals on flowers. Encourage students to be specific in their observations (as well as later on, in their drawings).

Keep the plant specimens for future observation and examination. They can be placed in transparent containers or allowed to dry, to observe what happens as they die. Alternatively, if plants have not been damaged, they may be replanted and used in subsequent lessons.

**Activity Sheet**
Directions to students:

Draw a diagram of your plant. Label these parts: root, stem, leaf, flower, seeds. Predict the function of each part. Identify your plant, and name five other plants you know about (1.2.1).

**NOTE:** Seeds and flowers may not be visible on all plants, so consider having students research their plants to draw more accurate diagrams.

Portage & Main Press, 2017 · *Hands-On Science and Technology · Grade 3* · ISBN: 978-1-55379-709-8

## Learning Centre

At the learning centre, provide toothpicks, paper, art supplies, a variety of recycled materials, pictures of flowering plants, and a copy of the Learning-Centre Task Card: Building a Model of a Plant (1.2.2).

Have students use the materials to create 3D models of one of the plants. Students can use toothpicks and paper to label all the plant parts. Have students take photos of their models with a digital camera (if available). Print the photos, and display these at the centre.

## Consolidate and Debrief

- Revisit the guided inquiry question: **What are the parts of a plant?** Have students share their knowledge, provide examples, and ask further inquiry questions.

- Add to the KWHL chart as students learn new concepts, answer some of their own inquiry questions, and ask new inquiry questions.

- Add new terms and illustrations to the class word wall. Include the words in other languages, as appropriate.

- Have students add new terms, definitions, and illustrations to their Science and Technology Glossary (1.1.1). When possible, encourage them to add words (and examples) in other languages, including Indigenous languages, reflective of the classroom population.

## Enhance

- Conduct a language-arts novel study, using the book *The Secret Garden*, by Frances Hodgson Burnett, or read the novel aloud to the class.

- Along with English words, students may learn science-related words in Indigenous languages such as Anishinaabe, Cree, and

others. In the same way, students may share science-related terminology in other languages that they speak at home. Also, consider opportunities to integrate basic French into a lesson by learning the terms in Canada's other official language. Words in other languages can be added to the Science and Technology Glossary (1.1.1) along with the English words, or students may keep a log of Indigenous words that they learn. Elders, Métis Senators, or other community members may also be able to help students to build science and technology vocabulary.

- Have students interview their parents/ guardians or grandparents about plants that are native to your region. Have them write a journal entry with a drawing of the plant and a story that their parents/guardians or grandparents shared.

- Access the interactive activity, Parts of a Plant, in the Grade 3, Unit 1 folder of the **Hands-On Interactive for Science and Technology, Grade 3** download. Find this download at: <www.portageandmainpress.com/product/hands-on-interactive-for-science-and-technology-grade-3/>.

- Have students continue their do-it-yourself projects at the Makerspace centre.

Portage & Main Press, 2017 · *Hands-On Science and Technology · Grade 3* · ISBN: 978-1-55379-709-8

# What Are the Parts of a Plant?

Draw a picture of your flowering plant in the large box below. Label these parts on your diagram:

| root(s) | stem | flower | leaf | seed(s) |
| --- | --- | --- | --- | --- |

Beside each labelled part, predict that part's function or job.

The plant I drew is a _____ .

Five other plants I know are:

1. _____

2. _____

3. _____

4. _____

5. _____

Portage & Main Press, 2017 · *Hands-On Science and Technology · Grade 3* · ISBN: 978-1-55379-709-8

# Building a Model of a Plant

1. Look at the plant pictures, then use any of the materials at this centre to create a three-dimensional model of a flowering plant.

2. Try to use different materials to represent the different parts of the plant.

3. Be sure to label the following parts using the toothpicks and paper:

   - root(s)

   - stem

   - leaves

   - flower(s)

   - seed(s)

4. Take a photograph of your model to display at the centre.

Portage & Main Press, 2017 · Hands-On Science and Technology · Grade 3 · ISBN: 978-1-55379-709-8

# 3 | What Are Some Special Features of Plants?

## Information for Teachers

**Roots:** Roots anchor a plant in place. Roots also seek out and store moisture and nutrients for the plant. There are two types of root systems: taproot and fibrous-root. A taproot is a long, thick root that grows down deep and straight (e.g., dandelion root, carrot, turnip, radish). A fibrous root has many root tips that spread out in all directions (e.g., grass, tomatoes, onions, most potted plants).

**Stem:** The stem has xylem cells, which transport water and other nutrients from the roots to the leaves. The stem also carries the food made in the leaves to all parts of the plant.

**Leaves:** Leaves make food for the plant to live and grow. They are filled with a pigment called "chlorophyll," which gives the leaves their green colour. Chorophyll captures energy from sunlight and combines it with water, minerals, and oxygen to produce food for the plant through a process called "photosynthesis."

Before beginning this lesson, teachers are encouraged to have students collect, as homework, a variety of leaves to bring to school. These will be used during the lesson.

## 21st Century Competencies

**Critical Thinking**, **Creativity**, and **Communication**: Students will do several activities to examine the features and functions of different plant parts. Then, at the learning centre, students will create and record songs to communicate their understanding of the features and jobs of different parts of plants.

## Materials

- *The Apple Tree* by Sandy Tharp-Thee
- chart paper
- markers
- drawing paper
- writing paper

- access to water
- audio-recording devices
- pencil crayons
- paper lunch bags
- trowels
- newspaper
- samples of fibrous roots and taproots
- potted plants (optional)
- containers or glasses of water (two for each working group)
- food colouring
- fresh celery with leafy tops (one for each working group)
- white carnations (one for each working group)
- sharp knife (adult use only)
- cactus
- variety of leaves collected by students (see Information for Teachers)
- *Living Sunlight: How Plants Bring the Earth to Life* by Molly Bang and Penny Chisholm, *Busy, Busy Leaves* by Nadia Higgins, or *Experiment with Photosynthesis* by Nadia Higgins
- measuring tools
- Activity Sheet A: What Is the Function of a Plant Root? (1.3.1)
- Activity Sheet B: What Is the Function of a Plant Stem? (1.3.2)
- Activity Sheet C: What Is the Function of Leaves on a Plant? (1.3.3)
- Learning-Centre Task Card: Plant Part Pop (1.3.4)
- KWHL chart (from lesson 1)
- Science and Technology Glossary (1.1.1)

## Activate

Read *The Apple Tree* by Sandy Tharp-Thee. This is the story of a Cherokee boy who plants an apple seed and learns about the tree's cycle through the seasons.

Portage & Main Press, 2017 · Hands-On Science and Technology · Grade 3 · ISBN: 978-1-55379-709-8

After reading, discuss the various parts of the tree. Have students identify:

- leaves
- seeds
- fruit
- branches

Discuss the growth and changes in the tree throughout the seasons, focusing on how the various parts grow and change. Ask:

- What part of the tree can we not see? (roots)
- Where are the roots of the tree?

Once all parts have been reviewed, explain to students that they are going to conduct a number of experiments to investigate the special features of plants. Through these tasks, they will learn how each part of a plant has a special role in its survival.

Divide the class into working groups (about four students per group). Have students stay in the same groups as they work through all the activities. First, discuss and record students' ideas of how to work successfully in a group. For example:

- Let everyone have a chance to speak.
- Listen while others speak.
- Respect the ideas of others.
- Ask questions of group members.
- Give positive feedback.
- Take part in getting the job done.

Introduce the guided inquiry question: **What are some special features of plants?**

### Assessment as Learning

As students conduct the following experiments and work together with their peers, have them reflect on their own cooperative skills. Distribute the Cooperative Skills Self-Assessment sheet, on page 34, to each student, and have students record their thoughts on how they worked cooperatively.

## Action: Part One

Have students collect their own root samples from weeds and other plants in the school yard. If this is not possible, use a variety of potted plants to investigate root systems.

> ⚠️ **SAFETY NOTE:** Before beginning this activity, be sure to discuss with students which plants are safe/appropriate to pick (e.g., dandelions, clover, small amounts of grass), and which plants are not (e.g., poison ivy, flower/garden plants, protected plants).

Discuss what students already know about plant roots. Ask:

- Have you seen the roots on a plant before?
- Have you pulled up grass or a carrot?
- Have you helped your family weed the garden?

Distribute a copy of Activity Sheet A: What Is the Function of a Plant Root? (1.3.1) to each student. Ask students to predict the role of the roots of a plant, and have them write their prediction in the space provided at the top of the sheet.

Encourage students to use their background knowledge and past experience to help them make this and subsequent predictions.

If the season permits, take students for a walk in the school yard. Have them work in their groups, and give each group a paper lunch bag. Ask students to find a weed in the ground. Before they dig up the weed, give each student drawing paper and pencil crayons or markers, and have students draw what they think their group's weed root system looks like in the "Predicted Root System" box on the activity sheet. Once all students have drawn their predictions, distribute trowels, and ask students to dig up their weeds and place them in their paper lunch bags.

▶

Portage & Main Press, 2017 · *Hands-On Science and Technology · Grade 3* · ISBN: 978-1-55379-709-8

Portage & Main Press, 2017 · Hands-On Science and Technology · Grade 3 · ISBN: 978-1-55379-709-8

**3**

Back in the classroom, have students soak their weeds in water to remove any soil around the roots. Ask them to compare their predictions of what they thought the roots would look like with the actual root system. Have students draw the actual root system next to their prediction in the "Actual Root System" box.

Display the weeds on a table covered with newspaper. Once all students have had an opportunity to view the root systems of different weeds, ask:

- Are all root systems the same?
- How are they different?
- Was it easy or difficult to dig up your root from the ground?
- What special role do you think roots play in the survival of a plant?

**NOTE:** If students did not collect examples of both fibrous roots and taproots, use samples that you have provided to observe, compare, contrast, and discuss.

Introduce the terms *taproot* and *fibrous root*. Have students sort the weeds collected according to the type of root system it has. Explain that the role of the roots is to anchor a plant in place, as well as to seek out and store moisture and nutrients for the plant. Ask:

- Why do you think some plants have a taproot system while others have a fibrous-root system?

To help students remember the difference between taproots and fibrous roots, have them stand straight up, legs together and arms at their sides. This is the taproot pose. For fibrous roots, have students stand shoulder-width apart with their arms stretched out, moving slightly up and down. This is the fibrous-root pose.

**Activity Sheet A**

Directions to students:

Record your prediction about the role of roots in a plant. Draw your prediction about what the root system of the weed your group found looks like. Draw the actual root system of the weed your group found. In your own words, describe the special function of roots, and name the two types of root systems (1.3.1).

## Action: Part Two

Have students discuss the stems of plants on display in the classroom. Ask:

- What is a stem?
- In the classroom plants, which parts are the stems? (Have students identify these.)
- What does the stem of a tree look like?

Distribute a copy of Activity Sheet B: What Is the Function of a Plant Stem? (1.3.2) to each student. Ask students to predict the role of stems in plants, then have them write their prediction at the top of the sheet.

Provide each group with two glasses or containers to hold water, food colouring, a celery stalk, a white carnation, some drawing paper, and pencil crayons or markers. Give students the following instructions:

1. Fill your two glasses or containers with water.
2. Put a few drops of food colouring into each glass.
3. Put the celery stalk into one glass and the carnation into the other.
4. Draw your plants in the "First Observations" box on the activity sheet.
5. Set the glasses or containers in the sunlight, and leave them overnight.
6. Record the results in the "Final Observations" box on your activity sheet.

**3**

Ask students:

■ Can you explain the role of the stem in the survival of a plant?

■ Why is this an important role?

Using a sharp knife (teacher or other adult only), cut off a section of the stems of the celery stalk and carnations so that students can examine the inside of the stem. Ask:

■ What does the inside of the stem look like?

■ Can you locate the tubes that carry the water up the stem in the celery and in the carnation?

■ How did you locate these tubes?

■ What else do you think stems may carry? (nutrients to different parts of the plant)

Display the cactus, and have students identify it and locate the stem. Explain to students that cacti have special stems called *fleshy stems*. Ask:

■ Do you think the role of the stem in a cactus is any different from the stems of any other plants?

■ Why is the stem so important for a cactus?

■ Where do cacti grow? What is their habitat? Why do you think cacti have fleshy stems?

Connect this exploration back to the previous one on root systems. Have students examine one of the unearthed plants to observe how the roots connect to the stems. Ask:

■ How do the roots and stems work together on plants?

**Activity Sheet B**
Directions to students:

At the top of the page, record your prediction about the role of the stem in a plant. Draw a diagram of the celery and the carnation just after you place them in the coloured water in the "First Observations" box. Draw your

observations of the celery and carnation stems at the end of the experiment in the "Final Observations" box. Explain, in your own words, the special function of the stem (1.3.2).

## Action: Part Three

**NOTE:** The concept of photosynthesis can be quite abstract for students at this age, as it is impossible for students to directly observe production of food by the plant. The activities that follow should assist students in gaining a basic understanding of the importance of leaves and the process of photosynthesis.

Provide each group with several leaves from those collected by students (from both coniferous and deciduous trees) to observe, examine, and discuss. Encourage students to identify similarities and differences.

Distribute a copy of Activity Sheet C: What Is the Function of Leaves on a Plant? (1.3.3) to each student. Ask students to predict the role of leaves in plants, then have them write their prediction at the top of the sheet.

Read aloud the book, *Experiment with Photosynthesis* by Nadia Higgins, *Busy, Busy Leaves* by Nadia Higgins, or *Living Sunlight: How Plants Bring the Earth to Life* by Molly Bang and Penny Chisholm.

**NOTE:** You may wish to read only those parts of the book that are appropriate for this investigation.

Ask students:

■ Why are leaves green?

■ Why do plants need chlorophyll?

■ What else does a green leaf need in order to make food for the plant? (sunlight)

Again, make connections between the functions of the various parts of the plant. Display unearthed plants, and have students describe the structure of the plants from roots, to stem, to leaves. Discuss the processes of each.

Portage & Main Press, 2017 · *Hands-On Science and Technology · Grade 3* · ISBN: 978-1-55379-709-8

# 3

### Activity Sheet C

Directions to students:

At the top of the page, record your prediction about the role of leaves in a plant. In the box, draw everything a green leaf needs in order to make food for the plant (recipe for plant food). In your own words, explain the special function of leaves (1.3.3).

## Learning Centre

At the learning centre, provide writing paper, pencils, audio-recording devices, and a copy of the Learning-Centre Task Card: Plant Part Pop (1.3.4).

Using a tune that is familiar to them or one that they make up, have students create and record songs that describe the special functions of one (or more) part(s) of a plant. Below is a list of melodies students can use as a structure for writing their own songs. It might be helpful to review these songs with students first, to remind them how each one is sung.

- *Farmer in the Dell*
- *Pop Goes the Weasel*
- *London Bridge Is Falling Down*
- *Row, Row, Row Your Boat*
- *Are You Sleeping?*
- *I'm a Little Teapot*
- *(Here We Go 'Round) the Mulberry Bush*
- *If You're Happy and You Know It*
- *Twinkle, Twinkle Little Star*
- *Mary Had a Little Lamb*
- *Jingle Bells*
- *The Muffin Man*
- *She'll Be Coming 'Round the Mountain*

## Consolidate and Debrief

- Revisit the guided inquiry question: **What are some special features of plants?** Have students share their knowledge, provide examples, and ask further inquiry questions.
- Add to the KWHL chart as students learn new concepts, answer some of their own inquiry questions, and ask new inquiry questions.
- Add new terms and illustrations to the class word wall. Include the words in other languages, as appropriate.
- Have students add new terms, definitions, and illustrations to their Science and Technology Glossary (1.1.1). When possible, encourage them to add words (and examples) in other languages, including Indigenous languages, reflective of the classroom population.

## Enhance

- During a class discussion, have students compare their predictions about the definitions and functions of plant parts from lesson 2 (see Activity Sheet: What Are the Parts of a Plant? [1.2.1]) with their predictions from this lesson (see Activity Sheet A: What Is the Function of Plant Roots? [1.3.1]; Activity Sheet B: What Is the Function of a Plant Stem? [1.3.2]; and Activity Sheet C: What Is the Function of Leaves on a Plant? [1.3.3]).
- In their working groups, have students compare and contrast their individual explanations of each plant part's function. First, have students take turns reading their explanations to each other. Then, have a spokesperson from each group report to the class about one explanation all group members had in common, and one explanation that was different among them.

▶

Portage & Main Press, 2017 · *Hands-On Science and Technology · Grade 3* · ISBN: 978-1-55379-709-8

**3**

- Play the "Root Pose" game. Call out "tap!" and have students pose like that type of root. Then, call out "fibrous!" and have students change their poses accordingly. Continue in this way—each time you call out a root type, students must change their pose (even if the change is from "fibrous" to a different "fibrous" pose). Begin to decrease the amount of time between callouts. Add in other plant parts and callouts, such as "wilted stem," "straight stem," "leaf facing the Sun," and "drooping leaf."

- Provide three potted, newly sprouted plants of the same size. Label them "plant 1," "plant 2," and "plant 3." Pinch all the leaves off plant 1. Pinch half the leaves off plant 2. Do not pinch any leaves off plant 3. Treat all plants the same otherwise, making sure they receive the same amount of sunlight and water. Have students observe the plants and measure differences in their growth. Discuss the importance of leaves in the growth of a plant.

**NOTE:** This investigation will take time to yield results, so take photographs along the way, if possible.

- Leaf rubbings: Place a leaf under a sheet of drawing paper, and lightly colour over it with a crayon. The stem and leaf pattern will be clearly displayed.

- Wax paper leaves: Turn leaves into beautiful art pictures, or save them for further study and classroom display, by placing them between sheets of wax paper, covering the wax paper with a cloth, and pressing with a warm iron. Leaf patterns will be apparent, and the leaves will be permanently maintained.

- Leaf skeletons: Collect various leaves, and place them between sheets of newspaper. Place books on top of the newspaper to add weight. After a few days, when the leaves have become dry and brittle, place one leaf between two sheets of paper, and use a hammer to gently pound the entire leaf surface. Remove the top sheet of paper, and observe the leaf skeleton. This is an excellent way to closely examine veins, stems, and the framework of leaves.

- Conduct an experiment to extract the chlorophyll from a leaf. This is an effective way to link the concept to what happens naturally to leaves in autumn. See the following link for directions: <https://www.quora.com/How-can-you-remove-chlorophyll-from-leaves>.

- Breathing leaves: Using one plant with several leaves, coat half of the leaves with petroleum jelly on both sides. Tie a piece of string or a twist tie loosely around the stem of each coated leaf so that you will remember which leaves have been treated. Leave the plant for several days, observing the changes in the leaves. The leaves covered with petroleum jelly will begin to die because they cannot take in air. (Leaves breathe through stomates on their underside, so it is important to thoroughly coat both sides with petroleum jelly for this experiment to work.)

- Patterned leaves: Using plants that have several large leaves, attach, with paper clips, small cutout circles or rectangles of black construction paper over sections of some of the leaves. Place the plants in a sunny area for several days, then remove the construction paper and observe the leaves. The areas covered with paper will be much paler, because these areas did not receive enough sunlight to make the production of chlorophyll profitable for the plant. Chlorophyll, which gives plants their green colour, is hard for plants to make so they only make it in areas that will be of maximum benefit to the plant. (Sunlight is

Portage & Main Press, 2017 · *Hands-On Science and Technology · Grade 3* · ISBN: 978-1-55379-709-8

Portage & Main Press, 2017 · *Hands-On Science and Technology · Grade 3* · ISBN: 978-1-55379-709-8

**3**

also necessary for photosynthesis, a process by which the plant creates its own sugar for food. Teachers can explain to students that without sunlight, plants die.)

- Moisture in leaves: Using a plant with several leaves, place a small, transparent plastic bag over a few of the leaves, then tie the bag securely with string. After a few days you will notice water droplets in the bag, because plants that use water also disperse water into the air.

- Use leaves for printmaking by dipping them into paint and pressing them onto art paper.

- Gather a group of leaves, and have students sort them according to size, veins, edges, texture, colour, and shape.

- Have students use collected plants to dry and press leaves or flowers. Press leaves, flowers, or small, full plants inside a folded sheet of wax paper, then place inside a book to help flatten them out. Leave like this for a number of days. Students can also press the plants directly into their student journals (by placing a book or two on top). Once pressed and dried, plants can be placed on a paper decorated with a border and then covered with plastic wrap or plastic protector sheets.

- Access the interactive activity, Special Features of Plants, in the Grade 3, Unit 1 folder of the *Hands-On Interactive for Science and Technology, Grade 3* download. Find this download at: <www.portageandmainpress.com/product/hands-on-interactive-for-science-and-technology-grade-3/>.

- Have students continue their do-it-yourself projects at the Makerspace centre.

# What Is the Function of a Plant Root?

## My Prediction

I think the function of the root is _____

_____

_____

_____

| Predicted Root System | Actual Root System |
|---|---|
|  |  |

## Function of Roots

The function of the root is _____

_____

The two kinds of root systems are _____

and _____ .

Portage & Main Press, 2017 · Hands-On Science and Technology · Grade 3 · ISBN: 978-1-55379-709-8

# What Is the Function of a Plant Stem?

## My Prediction

I think the function of the stem is _____

_____

_____

_____

| First Observations | Final Observations |
|---|---|
|  |  |

## Function of the Stem

The function of the stem is _____

_____

_____

Portage & Main Press, 2017 · Hands-On Science and Technology · Grade 3 · ISBN: 978-1-55379-709-8

# What Is the Function of Leaves on a Plant?

## My Prediction

I think the function of the leaves is _____

_____

_____

_____

## Recipe for Plant Food

_____

## Function of Leaves

The function of the leaves is _____

_____

_____

_____

Portage & Main Press, 2017 · Hands-On Science and Technology · Grade 3 · ISBN: 978-1-55379-709-8

# Plant Part Pop

Create a song, rap, or poem about the special function(s) of one or more plant parts:

- Work with a partner, in a group, or on your own.

- Choose one or more parts of a plant.

- Use a familiar tune (e.g., "Row, Row, Row Your Boat"), or make up a tune.

- Use the audio-recording device to record your song.

Portage & Main Press, 2017 · Hands-On Science and Technology · Grade 3 · ISBN: 978-1-55379-709-8

# 4 | How Do Plants Adapt in Order to Survive?

## Information for Teachers

An adaptation is a structure, function, or life process of a living thing that helps it to survive in its habitat. Some examples of plant adaptations are:

- Cacti have thick stems to store water.
- Cacti leaves are needles, which have a reduced surface area and, therefore, minimize water loss.
- Roots of grasses grow very deep to reach moisture.
- Cacti roots are shallow and spread out.
- Some plants have waxy leaves to minimize water loss.
- The seeds of maple trees have thin wings to spin and float in the wind.
- Dark colours help Arctic plants absorb the Sun's heat.
- In colder climates, the parts of the plant that grow above ground die in winter, but the roots are protected by the snow.
- Some flowers are brightly coloured to attract pollinators.

There are also many plants with protective adaptations that make them harmful to humans and other living things (e.g., spines on cacti or thorns on rosebushes, bitter taste in berries, poison ivy leaves that can cause rashes).

## 21st Century Competencies

**Critical Thinking** and **Communication**: Students will gather plant samples while on a nature walk, sort and classify the specimens, and examine various plant adaptations that aid in survival.

## Materials

- Image Bank: Plant Adaptations (see Appendix, page 429)
- pictures of harmful plants

- lunch-size paper bags or large zipper-lock plastic bags (one for each student)
- rope or pylon markers (to identify areas where students may collect natural materials)
- chart paper
- markers (in various colours)
- drawing supplies (e.g., pencils, pencil crayons, markers)
- Scotch tape or glue
- projection device
- samples of plant roots, stems, leaves, flowers, and seeds (other than those collected on the nature walk)
- Activity Sheet: How Do Plants Adapt in Order to Survive? (1.4.1)
- Learning-Centre Task Card: Working With Plant Words (1.4.2)
- KWHL chart (from lesson 1)
- Science and Technology Glossary (1.1.1)

## Activate

Discuss with students the parts of a plant and the functions of each. Also, discuss the types of roots. Talk about how the structure and function of plant parts help the plants survive.

Explain that animals have specific structures or functions that help them survive, as well. For example, ask:

- Why do you think a polar bear has a coat of white fur?
- Why do you think a duck has webbed feet?

Explain that these types of characteristics are called *adaptations*, and they enable a living thing to survive in its habitat.

Explain to students that some plants also have adaptations that help them survive in their environment. These adaptations are often related to the parts of the plant. Display Image Bank: Plant Adaptations. Have students examine and describe each picture. Ask:

Portage & Main Press, 2017 · Hands-On Science and Technology · Grade 3 · ISBN: 978-1-55379-709-8

**4**

■ What are some examples of how these plant parts help a plant to survive in its environment?

Record students' ideas on chart paper. Tell students they will be gathering and examining local plants in order to learn more about adaptations.

Introduce the guided inquiry question: **How do plants adapt in order to survive?**

## Action: Part One

Explain to students that they will be going on a nature walk to collect plants and plant parts. Discuss the importance of collecting plants in a safe way. Ask:

■ Why should you not pull the bark off the trunk of a tree or the leaves from its branches?

■ Are you aware of any types of plants that are harmful to humans? (e.g., poison ivy, poison oak, stinging nettle, poinsettia)

■ Why are they harmful? (some produce rashes, others are harmful if eaten)

■ How can you be safe from harmful plants?

Display pictures of harmful plants for students to examine and describe. Encourage them to learn to identify these plants so that they will know to stay away from them.

## Action: Part Two

Identify an area where students can collect examples of plant life (e.g., leaves, bark, twigs, pine cones, dandelions). Ensure the area is safe and acceptable for collecting these items. (If you will be going into a municipal or provincial park, be sure to get prior approval and follow any recommended guidelines.)

When you reach the site of your nature walk, tell students they are to collect different parts of plants. Use pylons or rope to mark off the

designated area, and explain to students that they are allowed to collect plants from that area only. Also, remind them to be respectful of living things (e.g., pick up leaves and bark from the ground rather than pull off a tree).

Explain to students that when they return to the classroom they will be comparing and sorting what they find. Give a paper or plastic bag to each student, and encourage students to look for various samples of different parts of plants. Tell them that whatever they collect must fit into the bag.

Back in the classroom, ask students to examine and sort what they found during the nature walk. Have them select a rule for how they will sort their own materials (e.g., by part, colour, shape). Once they have done this, have them circulate the classroom to observe how other students sorted their items.

Have students return to their seats, and ask questions such as:

■ Why did you choose your sorting rule?

■ Could you sort your collection another way? How?

■ Are the leaves pointed or rounded?

■ Is the bark smooth or rough?

■ Are any of the seeds the same size, colour, or weight?

■ What colour are the flower petals?

During these discussions, encourage students to closely observe their plant parts and describe them in detail, using all of their senses except taste. Also, compare students' collected plant parts with the classroom ones provided for the activity (teachers may want to sort their samples, as well). Encourage students to classify the plant parts in several different ways, and then challenge other students to identify the sorting rules.

Portage & Main Press, 2017 · *Hands-On Science and Technology · Grade 3* · ISBN: 978-1-55379-709-8

**4**

Finally, have a class discussion about the various plants and their parts, focusing on adaptations. Using one example, such as bark from a tree, ask:

■ How does this bark help a tree to survive in its environment?

Discuss the protective function of bark. Continue with other examples of plant adaptations, focusing on plant parts and their functions.

## Action: Part Three

Distribute to each student a selection of plant parts—from the collected samples, the classroom samples, or both. Make sure each student has at least two samples of roots, stems, leaves, flowers, and seeds. Also, distribute a copy of Activity Sheet: How Do Plants Adapt in Order to Survive? (1.4.1), glue or tape, and drawing materials to each student. Have students complete the activity sheet by selecting two samples of each type of plant part to compare.

### Activity Sheet
Directions to students:

Select two samples of each type of plant part from your collection to compare. For any samples that are small enough, tape or glue them onto the chart. If they are too big, draw a diagram of the sample plant part(s). Write about how each pair of plant parts is the same. From your collection, describe one example of a plant adaptation that helps it to survive in its environment (1.4.1).

## Learning Centre

At the learning centre, provide chart paper, coloured markers, and a copy of the Learning-Centre Task Card: Working With Plant Words (1.4.2).

Have students brainstorm a list of words associated with plants and record their

suggestions randomly on chart paper. Then, have students sort their words (e.g., by part, type) by circling them with different colours of marker.

---

**NOTE:** This learning centre can also be done electronically by having students brainstorm their words and then use them to create wordles. Go to: <www.wordle.net>. Note that this site includes options for colour-coding words.

---

## Consolidate and Debrief

■ Revisit the guided inquiry question: **How do plants adapt in order to survive?** Have students share their knowledge, provide examples, and ask further inquiry questions.

■ Add to the KWHL chart as students learn new concepts, answer some of their own inquiry questions, and ask new inquiry questions.

■ Add new terms and illustrations to the class word wall. Include the words in other languages, as appropriate.

■ Have students add new terms, definitions, and illustrations to their Science and Technology Glossary (1.1.1). When possible, encourage them to add words (and examples) in other languages, including Indigenous languages, reflective of the classroom population.

## Enhance

■ Plant part posters: Divide the class into five groups, and assign to each group a plant part. Distribute sheets of chart paper or large poster paper to the groups, and have students use art materials to title their page with their assigned plant part. Display any leftover samples collected during the lesson's nature walk, and allow students to gather as many examples of their assigned plant part as they want. Then, have students glue or tape the samples onto the chart or poster

Portage & Main Press, 2017 · *Hands-On Science and Technology · Grade 3* · ISBN: 978-1-55379-709-8

**4**

paper—they may be as creative as they want to be in decorating their plant part posters. Encourage students to avoid including two samples that are the same on one poster. Ask students to label any known samples on their posters (e.g., elm seed), and have them use books and/or websites to identify any unknown samples.

■ Have students play a matching game with the plant parts they have found. Have one student ask a question (e.g., Who has a smooth piece of bark that is white?). Students who have a match may hold up their matching plant part.

■ Have students identify the names of plants based on the characteristics of its parts (e.g., smooth white bark found on the ground often comes from a birch tree).

■ Have students continue their do-it-yourself projects at the Makerspace centre.

Portage & Main Press, 2017 · *Hands-On Science and Technology* · *Grade 3* · ISBN: 978-1-55379-709-8

# How Do Plants Adapt in Order to Survive?

| Plant #1 Part | Plant #2 Part | How They Are the Same |
|---|---|---|
| root | root | |
| stem | stem | |
| leaf | leaf | |
| flower | flower | |
| seed | seed | |

From your collection, describe one example of a plant's adaptation that helps it to survive in its environment.

_____

_____

_____

Portage & Main Press, 2017 · Hands-On Science and Technology · Grade 3 · ISBN: 978-1-55379-709-8

# Working With Plant Words

1. With the other members of your group, think of as many words about plants as you can, and record them in black on chart paper. Be sure to include words about adaptations of plants.

2. Discuss ways to sort the words.

3. Use one colour of marker to circle all words that belong together in one group, a different colour for words belonging in a second group, and so on. Some words may have more than one coloured circle around them (because they belong in more than one group), while others may not have any circles around them.

4. Include a key at the bottom of the chart paper that tells what each colour means.

Portage & Main Press, 2017 · Hands-On Science and Technology · Grade 3 · ISBN: 978-1-55379-709-8

# 5 | What Is the Life Cycle of a Plant?

## Information for Teachers

The stages of the life cycle of a flowering plant are:

1. seed
2. seedling (embryo)
3. adult plant (roots appear first, then stem, then leaves)
4. adult plant with flowers (pollination occurs)
5. adult plant with fruit (back to step 1)

**NOTE:** Many flowering plants do not appear to bear fruit, at least by the "typical" definition of fruit (e.g., apple, orange, plum). The seed of the plant, however, is encased in a fruit that develops from the flower. An example of this is wheat: wheat grains are considered to be the fruit of the plant. In the case of a bean plant, the bean is considered to be the fruit.

## 21st Century Competencies

**Communication**: Students will examine the life cycle of plants by growing their own specimens and tracking the growth and changes.

## Materials

- *The Apple Tree* by Sandy Tharp-Thee
- dry kidney beans or other dry bean seeds
- Activity Sheet A: Observations of My Plant (1.5.1)
- Information Cards: Life Cycle of a Plant (Photocopy and cut apart for classroom display.) (1.5.2)
- paper towels (one piece for each student)
- access to water
- centimetre rulers
- small plastic bags (one for each student)
- metre sticks
- large sheets of graph paper
- writing paper
- masking tape
- potting soil
- clear plastic cups or other containers
- markers

- digital camera
- mister/spray bottle filled with water
- variety of plants of different species and sizes
- Activity Sheet B: What Is the Life Cycle of a Flowering Plant? (1.5.3)
- Learning-Centre Task Card: Graphing Plant Height (1.5.4)
- KWHL chart (from lesson 1)
- Science and Technology Glossary (1.1.1)

**⚠ SAFETY NOTE:** If you are using a recycled spray bottle, it should be thoroughly cleaned first (preferably in a dishwasher, or by hand, with hot water and soap) to remove any residue of potential toxins (to humans and/or plants).

## Activate

Review the book, *The Apple Tree,* by Sandy Tharp-Thee, read in lesson 3. Discuss how the tree changed throughout the seasons. Ask:

- How did the tree's life begin?
- What did the seed turn into?
- How did the seedling change as it grew?
- How did the tree change throughout the seasons?
- How did the boy take care of the tree?

Discuss students' background knowledge of the needs of plants. Ask:

- What does a plant need in order to survive? (water, sunlight, soil/another growing medium, air/oxygen, warmth)

Explain to students that they will be planting seeds to grow their own plants. It is important for students to know that even with the proper care, some seeds will not grow into adult plants. Explain that they will track the growth of the ones that do survive, as the plants progress through their life cycle. Ask:

- Do you have any questions about what could happen when we plant the seeds?

Portage & Main Press, 2017 · *Hands-On Science and Technology · Grade 3* · ISBN: 978-1-55379-709-8

- What questions do you have about the life cycle of plants?

Encourage students' questions about the investigation. Add these questions to the KWHL chart created for the unit, or begin a new chart for this lesson.

Provide each student with four to six dry bean seeds. Have students observe and examine their seeds. Then, distribute a copy of Activity Sheet A: Observations of My Plant (1.5.1) to each student, and have students record the date, write a description of their seeds, and draw a diagram.

**NOTE:** At this point, students should leave the last column, "Height of Stem (cm)," blank.

Next, give each student a wet paper towel folded in half, a small plastic bag, and tape. Have each student follow these steps:

1. Place the dry bean seeds onto the wet paper towel.
2. Carefully fold the paper towel again, to cover the bean seeds.
3. Place the bean seeds and wet towel into a small plastic bag.
4. Seal the bag with tape.
5. Use a marker to label the bag with student's name.
6. Place labelled bag of the seeds in a warm area of the classroom.
7. Wait three to four days.

**NOTE:** The moisture on the paper towel is necessary for softening the seed coat surrounding the dry bean seed. Waiting a couple of days allows time for the seedling (embryo) to appear.

Introduce the guided inquiry question: **What is the life cycle of a plant?**

## Action: Part One

After a few days, return to each student their labelled bag containing the beans in a folded paper towel. Before students open their bags, ask:

- What do you think you will see? (possible answers: nothing, my seed, a root)
- Could some seeds look different from other seeds? Why or why not?

Now, tell students to carefully open their plastic bags. Teachers are encouraged to observe students' reactions, as well as make note of any interesting discoveries and use of vocabulary during this time. Encourage students to observe one another's seeds. Tell students to record the date, write a description of their seedlings, and draw a diagram on their activity sheet.

**NOTE:** Students will continue to use Activity Sheet A: Observations of My Plant (1.5.1) throughout the remainder of the unit as they observe their growing plants. Teachers should encourage students to observe their plants regularly and record observations on the activity sheet chart.

Give each student a clear plastic cup half filled with soil. Have students carefully lay the seeds in the soil with the embryo pointing down. Next, tell students to cover the seedlings with more soil and then water the seedlings, being sure not to add too much water. If available, have students use misters to avoid overwatering plants. Tell students to label their cups by using a marker to write their name on pieces of tape and affix to the cup. Put the cups in a warm, sunny area of the classroom. Have students take care of their plants by watering them as needed.

As the plants begin to grow, have students continue using Activity Sheet A (1.5.1) to note changes in their plants on a regular basis. Distribute centimetre rulers to students; each time they record observations of their plant, have them measure and include the height of the stem in centimetres.

Portage & Main Press, 2017 · *Hands-On Science and Technology · Grade 3* · ISBN: 978-1-55379-709-8

**5**

### Activity Sheet A

Directions to students:

Record the date, your observations, a diagram of your plant, and the height of the stem (1.5.1).

## Action: Part Two

Use a digital camera to take photographs of the plants at the various stages of growth (seed, seedling, adult plant, adult plant with flowers, adult plant with fruit). Have regular class discussions about the changes in the plants. Ask:

- When did the leaves start to appear?
- What colour are the leaves?
- What shape are the leaves?
- Do the leaves appear in pairs or one by one?
- What is the stem like?
- What parts of the plant are changing as it grows?
- What parts of the plant are staying the same as it grows?

Display the Information Cards: Life Cycle of a Plant (1.5.2). Mix them up, and have students sequence them in the correct order.

Have students examine their plants and these pictures and identify the current stage of the plants.

**NOTE:** As plants continue to grow, they may eventually need to be transplanted into larger pots.

Distribute a copy of Activity Sheet B: What Is the Life Cycle of a Flowering Plant? (1.5.3) to each student to complete.

### Activity Sheet B

Directions to students:

Label the stages of the plant's life cycle in order. Be sure to draw a diagram of your plant at each stage (1.5.3).

### Assessment of Learning

Have students refer to the Information Cards: Life Cycle of a Plant (1.5.2), along with Activity Sheet A (1.5.1) and Activity Sheet B (1.5.3), as they describe the life cycle of their bean plants. Use the Individual Student Observation sheet, on page 27, to record results.

## Learning Centre

At the learning centre, provide a variety of plants of different species and sizes, along with metre sticks, large sheets of graph paper, pencils, markers, writing paper, and a copy of the Learning-Centre Task Card: Graphing Plant Height (1.5.4).

Have students use a metre stick to measure the height of the various plants. Have them record all measurements taken, then use graph paper to create a bar graph showing the heights of the plants.

## Consolidate and Debrief

- Revisit the guided inquiry question: **What is the life cycle of a plant?** Have students share their knowledge, provide examples, and ask further inquiry questions.
- Add to the KWHL chart as students learn new concepts, answer some of their own inquiry questions, and ask new inquiry questions.
- Add new terms and illustrations to the class word wall. Include words in other languages, as appropriate.
- Have students add new terms, definitions, and illustrations to their Science and Technology Glossary (1.1.1). When possible, encourage them to add words (and examples) in other languages, including Indigenous languages, reflective of the classroom population.

Portage & Main Press, 2017 · *Hands-On Science and Technology · Grade 3* · ISBN: 978-1-55379-709-8

# 5

## Enhance

- Plant bulbs so students can observe another way plants grow. Compare the life cycle of plants grown from bulbs to the life cycle of plants grown from seeds.

- Read different versions of the story "Jack and the Beanstalk." Compare the story to students' knowledge of how bean plants grow.

- Have students continue creating their slide show presentations begun in lesson 1 (see Enhance, page 59). Ask students to either draw pictures or use photographs of their plants to show the life cycle of the bean plant. Tell students to include a different picture of a plant part on each slide, along with its name and its function. Then, have students use an audio-recording device to record themselves reading their descriptions of the life cycle of the bean plant. Students can continue working on these presentations throughout the remainder of the unit.

- Using what they have learned about the plant life cycle and plant growth, have students brainstorm useful tips for growing garden vegetables. Have them present their ideas in a brochure about caring for plants.

- As a class, plant a garden. Include several different plants (e.g., tomatoes, carrots, flowers). This will help demonstrate that each plant goes through a similar life cycle, but they are harvested at different stages in their life cycles. Explain how growing and harvesting crops year after year is a sustainable enterprise. If enough plants are grown, students could share a meal using the produce.

- For Indigenous content, consult two stories and associated learning activities in Michael J. Caduto and Joseph Bruchac, *Keepers of Life: Discovering Plants Through Native Stories and Earth Activities for Children*. The two relevant sections are:
  - "The Sky Tree," pages 31–41, which includes riddles about different types of plants and suggestions for learning about biomes using Indigenous symbols and ideas.
  - "The Thanks to the Trees," pages 45–54, which includes teachings about the significance of trees and other plants to Indigenous peoples.

- Invite a local community gardener or organizer to the classroom to discuss how they grow plants.

- Take a field trip to a community garden and/ or arrange for students to participate in planting or harvesting.

- Access the interactive activity, Life Cycle of a Plant, in the Grade 3, Unit 1 folder of the **Hands-On Interactive for Science and Technology, Grade 3** download. Find this download at: <www.portageandmainpress.com/product/ hands-on-interactive-for-science-and- technology-grade-3/>.

- Have students continue their do-it-yourself projects at the Makerspace centre.

Portage & Main Press, 2017 · *Hands-On Science and Technology · Grade 3* · ISBN: 978-1-55379-709-8

# Observations of My Plant

| Date | Observations | Diagram | Height of Stem (cm) |
|------|-------------|---------|---------------------|
|      |             |         |                     |
|      |             |         |                     |
|      |             |         |                     |
|      |             |         |                     |
|      |             |         |                     |
|      |             |         |                     |

Portage & Main Press, 2017 · *Hands-On Science and Technology* · Grade 3 · ISBN: 978-1-55379-709-8

# Life Cycle of a Plant

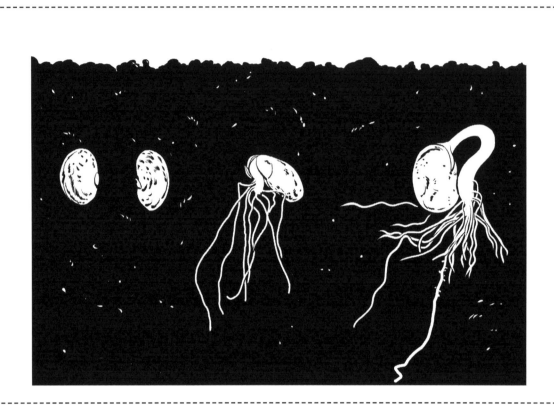

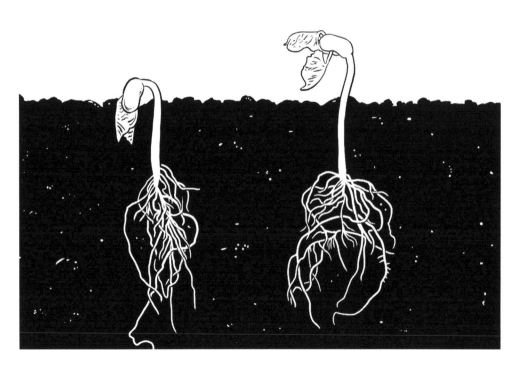

Portage & Main Press, 2017 · Hands-On Science and Technology · Grade 3 · ISBN: 978-1-55379-709-8

# Life Cycle of a Plant (continued)

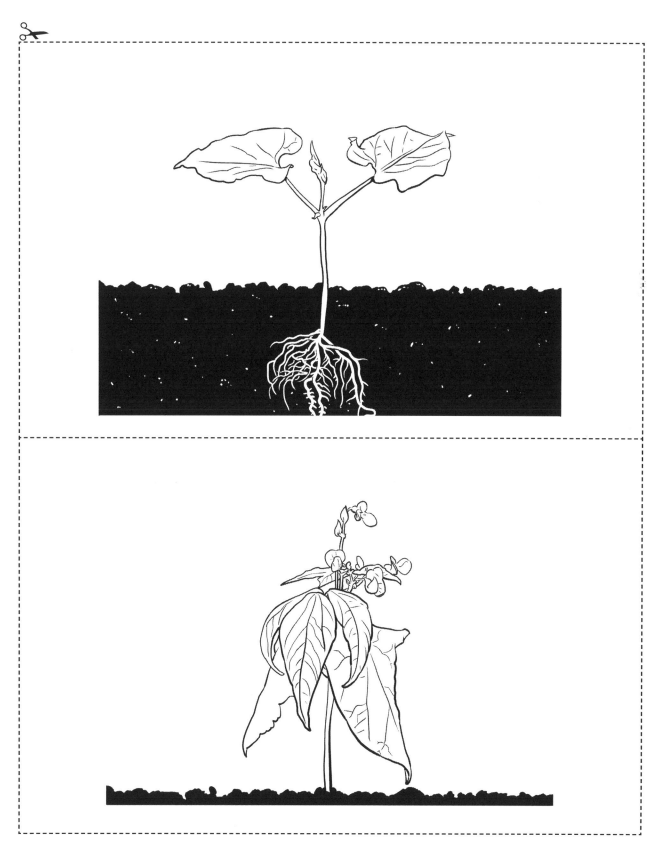

Portage & Main Press, 2017 · *Hands-On Science and Technology · Grade 3* · ISBN: 978-1-55379-709-8

# Life Cycle of a Plant (continued)

Portage & Main Press, 2017 · Hands-On Science and Technology · Grade 3 · ISBN: 978-1-55379-709-8

# What Is the Life Cycle of a Flowering Plant?

1._____

5._____

**The Life Cycle of
a Flowering Plant**

2._____

4._____

3._____

# Graphing Plant Height

1. Use a metre stick to measure the heights of the different plants at the centre.

2. Measure from the soil to the highest point of the plant.

3. Record this measurement for each plant.

4. Create a bar graph to display your data.

5. Be careful not to harm the plants!

Portage & Main Press, 2017 · Hands-On Science and Technology · Grade 3 · ISBN: 978-1-55379-709-8

# 6 | What Parts of Plants Do We Eat?

⚠️ **SAFETY NOTE:** Before beginning this lesson, teachers should familiarize themselves with any allergies students may have, and ensure students have no known allergies to any of the foods being brought into the classroom.

## 21st Century Competencies

**Critical Thinking**, **Communication**, and **Creativity**: Students will sort and classify various foods according to what part of a plant the food comes from. Students then design and cost out a meal using foods that come from various parts of plants.

## Materials

- basket or large container (large enough to hold all food samples below)
- roots humans eat (e.g., carrots, parsnips, beets)
- stems humans eat (e.g., celery, rhubarb, asparagus)
- leaves humans eat (e.g., lettuce, cabbage, spinach)
- seeds humans eat (e.g., peas, corn, pumpkin)
- flowers humans eat (e.g., cauliflower, broccoli, artichoke)
- fruit humans eat (e.g., tomato, apple, cucumber)
- herbs and spices humans eat (e.g., dill, mint, black pepper)
- unique foods from plants humans eat (e.g., chili peppers, leeks, kale)
- six Hula-Hoops
- six unlined index cards (Print the following plant parts onto the cards [one per card]: "Roots," "Stems," "Leaves," "Seeds," "Flowers," "Fruit.")
- paper towels or napkins (optional)
- plates (optional)
- knife (optional)
- newspaper flyers and magazines
- grocery-store flyers
- large sheets of white construction or art paper
- Plasticine or play dough
- scissors
- rulers (centimetre and metre)
- glue
- spoons or forks (for serving food) (optional)
- chart paper
- markers
- Activity Sheet: Plants on Your Plate Predictions (1.6.1)
- books about foods traditionally eaten by Indigenous peoples (e.g., *Byron Through the Seasons* by students and staff at Ducharme Elementary School, La Loche; *Lessons From Mother Earth* by Elaine McLeod; *Wild Berries* by Julie Flett; *Ziis-baak-daa-keng Maple Syrup Harvesting* by Lucy Pitawanakwat and Honourine Trudeau-Wright; *Manoomini-Mikaans-The Wild Rice Road* by Michael Fisher, Perry Bebamash, and Isabelle Osawamick; *The Story of Manoomin* by Fond du Lac Head Start; *A Native American Thought of It* by Rocky Landon and David MacDonald)
- Learning-Centre Task Card: Sorting Plant Food (1.6.2)
- KWHL chart (from lesson 1)
- Science and Technology Glossary (1.1.1)

**NOTE:** Teachers may consider bringing in enough of each kind of food listed above so all students have the opportunity to sample them. If food samples are not available, pictures of the foods mentioned may be used as an alternative to actual foods.

## Activate

Have students share recent experiences with plant foods. Ask:

- What kinds of fruits and vegetables did you eat yesterday or today?

Portage & Main Press, 2017 · *Hands-On Science and Technology · Grade 3* · ISBN: 978-1-55379-709-8

In addition to fresh fruits and vegetables, give students cues for other foods that come from plants (e.g., *corn*flakes, *Rice* Krispies, *rice* pudding, puffed *wheat* cereal, cream of *tomato* soup). This will help them see connections between the plant foods they eat and where the foods come from.

Record all students' responses on chart paper. Make sure to include your own plant food choices. Ask:

- What do you notice about your answers?
- Is there a way to group them together?

Have students discuss various ways to sort the plant foods.

Divide the class into working groups, and provide each group with a copy of Activity Sheet: Plants on Your Plate Predictions (1.6.1). Have the groups brainstorm foods they think come from each part of a plant and write or draw their ideas on the activity sheet.

When they have completed the activity sheet, have students in each group share their predictions with the rest of the class.

Introduce the guided inquiry question: **What parts of plants do we eat?**

## Action: Part One

Have students sit in a circle. Place the basket filled with all plant food samples in the centre of the circle. Place the Hula-Hoops around the basket.

Explain to students that the basket is filled with different types of fruits, vegetables, herbs, and spices that humans eat. Hold up each item, and have students identify it.

As a class, read the plant-part labels aloud, and place one label in the centre of each Hula-Hoop. Hold up each food item once again, and ask students:

- Which part of the plant does this food come from? (For example, black pepper is actually the dried fruit of a plant. Dill and mint are leaves from plants.)

Sort each food item into the appropriate group.

**NOTE:** Teachers may wish to cut up or divide the different food items so that all students can sample each one.

In their working groups, have students review the activity sheet again, circle correct predictions of foods in each plant-part group, and cross out any incorrect examples. If needed, ask students to add one example that humans eat for each plant part.

**Activity Sheet**
Directions to students:

Write or draw examples of the types of foods you think come from each part of a plant. After completing the Hula-Hoop class activity, circle the correct predictions (food examples) you recorded or drew for each plant part group, and cross out any incorrect examples. Add one more example to each group (1.6.1).

## Action: Part Two

Invite an Elder or a Métis Senator to share knowledge of plants that were/are traditionally eaten by Indigenous peoples (e.g., blueberries, raspberries, strawberries, blackberries, cranberries, beans, corn, squash, potatoes, sunflower seeds, hickory nuts). They can discuss and compare cultural practices of the past and present in terms of plants that are eaten, as well as how they were gathered and preserved.

The food preservation practices of Indigenous peoples in Canada enable them to preserve and store food long after gathering. They have many techniques for drying foods, using air, Sun, heat, and smoke. Pemmican (dried meat and fat, with nuts and berries often added) is an example of

Portage & Main Press, 2017 · *Hands-On Science and Technology · Grade 3* · ISBN: 978-1-55379-709-8

**6**

a food Indigenous peoples make. Traditionally, pemmican was stored in rawhide bags, and could last for months.

Read a variety of books about foods that were/ are traditionally eaten by Indigenous peoples, such as:

■ *Byron Through the Seasons,* created by students and staff at Ducharme Elementary School in La Loche, ON. This book describes activities such as fishing and hunting, moccasin sewing, food preservation, and cooking bannock over an open fire.

■ *Lessons From Mother Earth* by Elaine McLeod. In this story, a granddaughter learns the value of plants and gardens.

■ *Wild Berries* by Julie Flett portrays the process of blueberry picking.

■ *Ziis-baak-daa-keng Maple Syrup Harvesting* by Lucy Pitawanakwat and Honourine Trudeau-Wright is a bilingual Ojibwe-English resource that tells a personal story about maple syrup harvesting.

■ *Manoomini-Miikaans-The Wild Rice Road* by Michael Fisher, Perry Bebamash, and Isabelle Osawamick. This story focuses on two children who are on their way to an annual traditional rice camp. Activities and games are interspersed throughout the story. Go to: <http://www.sagchip.org/environment/ pdf/Minoomini-miikaans%20-%20The%20 Wild%20Rice%20Road.pdf>.

■ *The Story of Manoomin* by Fond du Lac Head Start. Learn the story of Manoomin, along with Ojibwe words and phrases, as you accompany a group of young people through the wild rice harvest.

■ *A Native American Thought of It* by Rocky Landon and David MacDonald. There is a section about wild rice under the chapter on food.

## Action: Part Three

Have students design a meal that uses various types of food from different parts of plants. Challenge students to calculate the cost of the meal, using prices from grocery-store flyers.

**NOTE:** If possible, as a class, prepare some of the meals that students have designed.

## Learning Centre

At the learning centre, provide large sheets of white construction or art paper, Plasticine or play dough, grocery-store flyers, scissors, rulers, and glue, along with a copy of the Learning-Centre Task Card: Sorting Plant Food (1.6.2).

Have students divide a sheet of paper into six sections and label them with the six plant parts: "Roots," "Stems," "Leaves," "Flowers," "Fruit," and "Seeds." Tell students to cut out from grocery-store flyers (or draw) examples of foods that come from plants. Have students sort their pictures into the six groups and then glue the pictures onto the appropriate sections of the paper. Suggest that they include at least two examples of food for each group. Then, have students use Plasticine or play dough to make a three-dimensional model of a plant food for each category.

## Consolidate and Debrief

■ Revisit the guided inquiry question: **What parts of plants do we eat?** Have students share their knowledge, provide examples, and ask further inquiry questions.

■ Add to the KWHL chart as students learn new concepts, answer some of their own inquiry questions, and ask new inquiry questions.

■ Add new terms and illustrations to the class word wall. Include the words in other languages, as appropriate.

Portage & Main Press, 2017 · *Hands-On Science and Technology · Grade 3* · ISBN: 978-1-55379-709-8

**6**

- Have students add new terms, definitions, and illustrations to their Science and Technology Glossary (1.1.1). When possible, encourage them to add words (and examples) in other languages, including Indigenous languages, reflective of the classroom population.

**Enhance**

- Introduce students to a variety of foods from plants that are common in other countries (e.g., plantain, mango, coconut, sugar cane). Extend the activity by having students sort these foods according to which part of the plant each comes from.

- Display, on individual index cards, pictures of different types of food from various parts of the plant. Have students play a game of concentration: Place all cards onto a table, facedown. If a student turns over two food cards that come from the same part of the plant, it is considered a match.

- Indian Breadroot (Prairie Turnip) was the single most important wild plant eaten by Indigenous peoples on the Prairies. The Cree name for this plant is mix-tas-coos-se-nena. The plant's stem breaks off and blows away once the seeds form. The root is a turnip-like vegetable that can be eaten raw. Strips of the root were dried in the Sun and stored in leather bags for the winter months. Roots were also boiled or crushed for use in soups or puddings. Wild breadroot is now hard to find because of agricultural practice; although it once grew wild on the Prairies, much of that land is now farmland. Have students use the Internet to access photographs of the plant and to research other plants used by Indigenous peoples, such as wild onion. Discuss the importance of sustaining plants for future generations, and for ensuring we use sustainable agricultural practices.

- Have students design and construct a composter to dispose of unused plant parts and to enrich soil for future planting.

- Have students research what parts of plants various herbs and spices come from.

- This lesson presents an excellent opportunity to educate students about social justice. Use various types of media (e.g., DVDs, online/TV documentaries, local newspaper articles) to raise awareness about food-supply shortages in local communities, as well as worldwide. Ask students for ideas about what they can do to help. Consider inviting a representative from a local food centre/organization/bank to speak to students about food shortages and how plant foods can help both in local communities and around the world.

- Have students play the World Food Program's "Free Rice Game," an educational game that helps to feed hungry people in developing countries around the world. For details, visit Hunger Response International at: <freerice.com>.

- Access the interactive activity, Plants That We Eat, in the Grade 3, Unit 1 folder of the *Hands-On Interactive for Science and Technology, Grade 3* download. Find this download at: <www.portageandmainpress. com/product/hands-on-interactive-for-science-and-technology-grade-3/>.

- Have students continue their do-it-yourself projects at the Makerspace centre.

Portage & Main Press, 2017 · Hands-On Science and Technology · Grade 3 · ISBN: 978-1-55379-709-8

# Plants on Your Plate Predictions

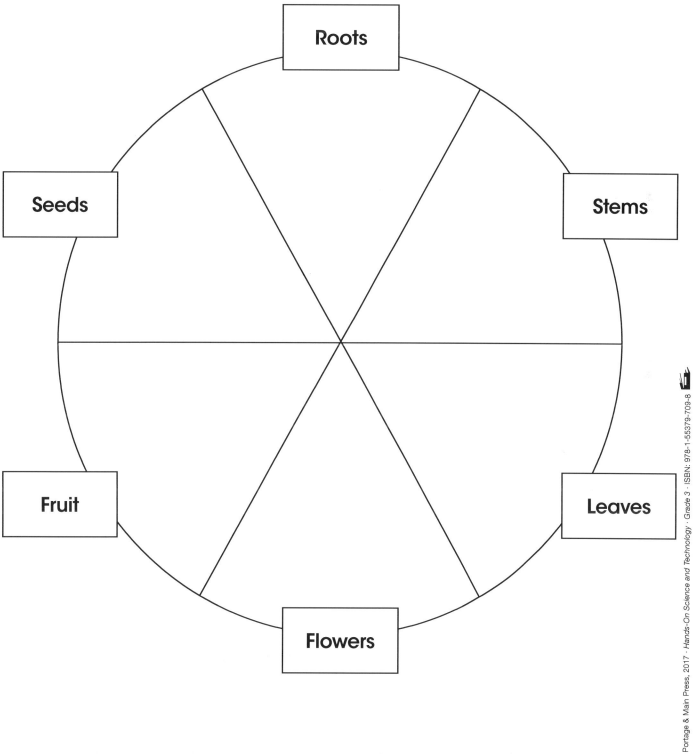

Portage & Main Press, 2017 · Hands-On Science and Technology · Grade 3 · ISBN: 978-1-55379-709-8

# Sorting Plant Food

1. Divide your sheet of paper into six sections.

2. Label the sections "Roots," "Stems," "Leaves," "Flowers," "Fruit," and "Seeds."

3. Cut out (from grocery-store flyers or magazines) or draw examples of foods that come from plants.

4. Sort your pictures into each of the six groups.

5. Glue the pictures onto the sections of the sheet where they belong. Make sure you have at least two examples in each group.

6. Use Plasticine or play dough to create a model of a plant food for each section of your sheet.

Portage & Main Press, 2017 · Hands-On Science and Technology · Grade 3 · ISBN: 978-1-55379-709-8

# 7 What Are the Different Ways in Which Plants Are Grown for Food?

## Information for Teachers

Plants are grown for food in a variety of ways and locations across Canada. The following are places where plants can be grown for food products:

- home gardens
- in the ground
- raised beds
- vertical gardens
- large-scale/industrial farming—These farms may grow one or two substantially large crops to sell to large companies who make certain food products. These farms may or may not produce organically grown food.
- greenhouses
- orchards
- small-scale farming/community supported agriculture (CSA)—These farmers offer weekly freshly picked food boxes to community members who pay a one-time fee prior to the growing season. CSA's typically produce organically grown food.

## 21st Century Competencies

**Communication**, **Critical Thinking**, and **Collaboration**: Students will investigate the pros and cons of a variety of locations for growing plants. They will also explore traditional Indigenous plants grown for food.

## Materials

- examples (or pictures) of food products grown from different places (e.g., home gardens, greenhouses, orchards, CSA)
- pictures of different places that food products are grown (e.g., home gardens—in the ground, raised beds, vertical gardens; large-scale/industrial farming; greenhouses; orchards; CSA)
- chart paper
- Activity Sheet: Plant Location (1.7.1)
- *The Three Sisters* by Michelle Corneau
- resources about the Three Sisters (e.g., https://blogs.cornell.edu/gblblog/files/2016/07/newlogoThree-Sisters-Exploring-an-Iroquois-Garden1-199h8hj-xupent.pdf)
- computer/tablet with Internet access (optional)
- Image Bank: Three Sisters (see Appendix, page 430)
- Image Bank: Wild Rice (see Appendix, page 430)
- markers
- pencil crayons
- poster paper
- KWHL chart (from lesson 1)
- Science and Technology Glossary (1.1.1)

## Activate

Show students different examples of food products. For each food product, ask:

- Where do you think this was grown?

As students brainstorm different locations, record their answers on a chart:

| Food Product | Location Type(s) |
|---|---|
|  |  |
|  |  |

Ask:

- Have you ever planted a garden? What kind? What did you plant?
- Have you ever visited a farm, greenhouse, orchard, or other place that grows plants? Describe what you saw.

Introduce the guided inquiry question: **What are the different ways in which plants are grown for food?**

Portage & Main Press, 2017 · *Hands-On Science and Technology · Grade 3* · ISBN: 978-1-55379-709-8

Portage & Main Press, 2017 · *Hands-On Science and Technology · Grade 3* · ISBN: 978-1-55379-709-8

**7**

## Action: Part One

Show students pictures of different places that food products are grown (e.g., home gardens—in the ground, raised beds, vertical gardens; large-scale/industrial farming; greenhouses; orchards; CSA). For each location, ask:

- What is the name of this?
- What do you think grows here?
- What are the advantages of food products grown here?
- What are the disadvantages of food products grown here?
- What are some environmental benefits of this location?

Add to the chart below, and record students' ideas:

| Food Product | | |
|---|---|---|
| Location Type(s) | | |
| Advantages | | |
| Disadvantages | | |
| Environmental Benefits | | |

Explain the location briefly, if necessary.

After each picture location is discussed, display the picture in the classroom.

## Action: Part Two

Tell students they will now research the different locations. Organize the class into small, working groups based on the following: have each student choose (or be given) a location (e.g., greenhouse, orchard, CSA, large-scale farming, home garden) and stand by the picture displaying that location. Next, provide each student with a copy of Activity Sheet: Plant Location (1.7.1). In their groups (based on location), students will first work individually on the activity sheet by brainstorming the advantages, disadvantages, and environmental benefits of their chosen location.

When they have completed the activity sheet, have students in each group share their individual brainstorms with the rest of their group. Each group will then create one poster describing the location, advantages, disadvantages, and environmental benefits of their location, as well as draw a picture representative of the location. Then, groups will share their poster with the rest of the class.

### Activity Sheet

Directions to students:

On your own, create a diagram of your chosen location and jot down the advantages, disadvantages, and environmental benefits of the location.

After you have completed the activity sheet and shared your ideas with their group, each group will create a poster. The poster will include a drawing of the location, a description of the location, as well as the advantages, disadvantages, and environmental benefits of the location (1.7.1).

## Action: Part Three

Explore how the Three Sisters are central to traditional Haudenosaunee life and culture. The Three Sisters refer to corn/maize, beans, and squash. These three plants are grown synergistically. The corn provides a vertical support for the beans, the beans fix nitrogen in the soil and act as support for the corn stalks, and the squash leaves reduce weeds and protect the base of the other two plants. Many of the ceremonial events of the Haudenosaunee are associated with the planting and harvesting of the Three Sisters.

Display Image Bank: Three Sisters, and have students describe the characteristics of the

**Hands-On Science and Technology · Grade 3**

**7**

plants, identify them, and discuss how they are growing.

Read the book, *The Three Sisters,* by Michelle Corneau. This Kanyen'kehà:ka (Gan-yeh-ga-ha-ga) story is about how the Three Sisters saved the people then, and are still feeding people today! The Kanyen'kehà:ka is one of Six Nations that together are the Haudenosaunee.

NOTE: For more background on the Three Sisters consult The Three Sisters: Exploring an Iroquois Garden at: <https://blogs.cornell.edu/gblblog/files/2016/07/newlogoThree-Sisters-Exploring-an-Iroquois-Garden1-199h8hj-xupent.pdf>.

Among the Anishinaabe, wild rice is a very important food and cultural symbol. The Anishinaabe originally lived along the East Coast but received a prophecy to migrate inland until they came to the land where "food grows on the water." That food was wild rice, which the Anishinaabe call "Manoomin," meaning "the good berry."

Display Image Bank: Wild Rice, and have students describe the characteristics of the plant, and discuss how/where it is growing and how it is harvested.

Encourage students to explore the harvesting and processing of wild rice further at the following website, which provides valuable information and images: <www.native-art-in-canada.com/wildrice.html>. Students can also view a video on wild rice harvesting at: <http://theways.org/story/manoomin>.

NOTE: For more information, including a traditional story and learning activities, consult, "Waynabozho and the Wild Rice," in *Keepers of Life: Discovering Plants Through Native Stories and Earth Activities for Children* by Michael J. Caduto and Joseph Bruchac, pages 219–234.

## Consolidate and Debrief

- Revisit the guided inquiry question: **What are the different ways in which plants are grown for food?** Have students share their knowledge, provide examples, and ask further inquiry questions.

- Add to the KWHL chart as students learn new concepts, answer some of their own inquiry questions, and ask new inquiry questions.

- Add new terms and illustrations to the class word wall. Include the words in other languages, as appropriate.

- Have students add new terms, definitions, and illustrations to their Science and Technology Glossary (1.1.1). When possible, encourage them to add words (and examples) in other languages, including Indigenous languages, reflective of the classroom population.

## Enhance

- Instead of creating posters, groups of students can create a presentation using programs such as PowerPoint or Prezi.

- Many foods in our contemporary diet originated in North America and South America (e.g., potatoes, corn, tomatoes, chilis, avocadoes, vanilla, chocolate, turkey, peanuts, maple syrup). To read about food origins, go to: <https://en.wikipedia.org/wiki/List_of_food_origins>.

- Invite members of the community who grow food products in different locations (e.g., orchard, greenhouse, large-scale/industrial farms, CSA) to discuss the location, what they grow, advantages, disadvantages, and environmental benefits of their location.

- Take a field trip to a local greenhouse, orchard, large-scale/industrial farm, or CSA in your area.

Portage & Main Press, 2017 · *Hands-On Science and Technology · Grade 3* · ISBN: 978-1-55379-709-8

**7**

- Create raised bed and vertical gardens. Plant the same plants in each, and assign groups different duties for the maintenance and care of the gardens. To make a math connection, track of the growth of the plants by measuring the gardens and creating graphs. To make a technology connection, take videos to monitor the growth, and use a program such as PowerPoint or Prezi to put together a final presentation.

- As a class, visit a heritage garden that features the Three Sisters and other plants important to Indigenous peoples.

- Have students participate in a debate-style discussion, highlighting the advantages, disadvantages, and environmental benefits of each type of garden.

- Access the interactive activity, Where Does Your Garden Grow?, in the Grade 3, Unit 1 folder of the ***Hands-On Interactive for Science and Technology, Grade 3*** download. Find this download at: <www.portageandmainpress.com/product/hands-on-interactive-for-science-and-technology-grade-3/>.

- Have students continue their do-it-yourself projects at the Makerspace centre.

Portage & Main Press, 2017 · Hands-On Science and Technology · Grade 3 · ISBN: 978-1-55379-709-8

# Plant Location

The location of growing plants that I chose is _____ .

Food products grown here: _____

| Diagram |
| --- |
|  |

| Advantages |
| --- |
|  |

| Disadvantages |
| --- |
|  |

| Environmental benefits |
| --- |
|  |

Portage & Main Press, 2017 · Hands-On Science and Technology · Grade 3 · ISBN: 978-1-55379-709-8

# 8 | How Can We Investigate the Needs of Plants?

## Information for Teachers

A *control* is a standard against which other conditions can be compared in a scientific experiment. Variables are those conditions that can influence the results. An *independent variable* is what the scientist changes in the experiment. The *dependent variable* is what is measured to see if it changes as the independent variable changes. For example, an experiment could measure the growth of two groups of plants, one under full sunlight for eight hours a day and the other under four hours of full sunlight per day. In this experiment, the amount of sunlight per day is the independent variable—the variable has been controlled. The growth rate of the plants is, in this case, the dependent variable.

**NOTE:** Although *independent variable* and *dependent variable* are the correct, formal terms, teachers may also choose to use the terms *changed variable* and *measured variable,* which may be more accessible language for students.

## 21st Century Competencies

**Critical Thinking** and **Communication**: Students will design experiments to test growing conditions and needs of plants, and graph the results.

## Materials

- four potted plants of similar type and size
- 30-centimetre rulers
- containers of water
- masking tape
- markers
- chart paper
- Activity Sheet A: How Sunlight Affects Plant Growth (1.8.1)
- Centimetre Graph Paper (1.8.2) (two copies per student)
- Activity Sheet B: How Does Water Affect Plant Growth? (1.8.3)
- Learning-Centre Task Card: Leaf Study (1.8.4).
- Learning-Centre Activity Sheet: Examining Leaves (1.8.5)
- Diagram: Leaf Margins (1.8.6)
- magnifying glasses
- leaves of several different sizes and shapes
- drawing paper
- pencil crayons
- bar graphs constructed by students (from lesson 5)
- KWHL chart (from lesson 1)
- Science and Technology Glossary (1.1.1)

## Activate

Display the four plants for students to examine. Ask:

- What does a plant need to live?
- How can we properly care for plants?
- What do you think would happen to a plant if it did not have water?
- What do you think would happen to a plant if it did not have light?

Discuss students' responses, and record their predictions on chart paper.

Introduce the guided inquiry question: **How can we investigate the needs of plants?**

## Action: Part One

Explain to students that they will be conducting an experiment to see how plants grow without something plants need. Tell them that when doing an experiment, scientists first come up with a question to answer. This is usually called the "purpose" or the "problem" of the experiment. Ask:

Portage & Main Press, 2017 · Hands-On Science and Technology · Grade 3 · ISBN: 978-1-55379-709-8

- What are some scientific questions you might ask about how plants would grow without something they need?
- How could you find answers to those questions?

Record students' questions, as well as their ideas for answering given questions.

Now, focus the discussion on scientific experimentation, and discuss the importance of testing only one plant need at a time (answering only one question, purpose, or problem at a time).

Discuss the terms *control, independent variable,* and *dependent variable* with students as each relates to this experiment. Explain how it is important to change only one variable at a time (the independent variable), and to measure one variable at a time (the dependent variable). If too many variables are introduced as one large experiment, it will be difficult to determine cause and effect. Further explain that in their plant experiments, taking away the sunlight is an example of the independent variable. What happens to the plant when the sunlight is removed is the dependent variable.

Now, affix a piece of masking tape to each of two of the pots, and label the plants:

- Control Plant With Water and Sunlight
- Plant With Water but No Sunlight

Next, have students observe and describe the present state of the two labelled plants, including their heights. Distribute a copy of Activity Sheet A: How Sunlight Affects Plant Growth (1.8.1) and a 30-centimetre ruler to each student. Have students use the rulers to measure the height of each plant and record the measurement on one of the two charts (one plant/measurement per chart).

Place each plant in an appropriate location according to its label (one in sunlight, the

other in an area with no sunlight). Observe the plants on a regular basis for the next few weeks, watering both plants as needed. Discuss changes as they occur, always comparing the control plant to the plant with no sunlight. Be sure to measure the plants' heights often, and record this information and any other changes on the activity sheet charts.

### Activity Sheet A

Directions to students:

Use the two charts to record the results of your experiment to find out what happens to plants without sunlight (1.8.1).

**NOTE:** This is a two-page activity sheet.

### Assessment for Learning

Assess students' background knowledge of bar graphs. Display bar graphs constructed by students in lesson 5 (see the Learning Centre activity, on page 85). Have students read and interpret the graphs based on questions posed. Also, have students identify criteria for a bar graph, by locating the required parts:

- appropriate title
- labelled *x* and *y* axes (horizontal and vertical)
- axes calibrations
- space between bars

Use the Anecdotal Record sheet, on page 26, to record results.

## Action: Part Two

Discuss with students their ideas about when to end the experiment. Students may agree to wait until the plant with no sunlight dies or students may decide to end the experiment before the plant dies, once a pattern has been established.

When the end of the experiment is decided, discuss the results. Review the activity sheet charts, and focus on patterns in the data, as well as variations. Have students generate questions about the data gathered.

Portage & Main Press, 2017 · *Hands-On Science and Technology · Grade 3* · ISBN: 978-1-55379-709-8

**8**

Distribute a copy of Centimetre Graph Paper (1.8.2) to each student, and have students use the data from the activity sheet charts to create a bar graph of the results.

**NOTE:** Depending on students' background experience constructing graphs, teachers may choose to guide this activity to ensure students include all required information on the graph. This can also be done as a whole-class activity on large graph paper.

Once bar graphs are complete, discuss students' graphs, and record statements on chart paper about their observations and results. As a class, use these statements to draw conclusions about the data, and record these conclusions on chart paper.

## Action: Part Three

Tell students they will be conducting another plant experiment, this time eliminating water for one of the plants.

Display two similar plants. Again, have students observe and describe the plants' present states, including height. Distribute a copy of Activity Sheet B: How Does Water Affect Plant Growth? (1.8.3) to each student, along with a 30-centimetre ruler. Have students measure the exact height of each plant and record each measurement onto one of the two charts.

Affix a piece of masking tape onto each pot, and label the plants:

- Control Plant With Water and Sunlight
- Plant With Sunlight but No Water

Discuss the terms *control, independent variable,* and *dependent variable* as they relate to this experiment. Explain that, for this experiment, removing the water is the independent variable and what happens to the plant will be the dependent variable.

Place both plants in the same location. Observe the plants on a regular basis for the next few

weeks, watering only the control plant. Discuss changes as they occur, comparing the control plant to the plant with no water. Have students measure plant height often and record this information on the activity sheet charts.

Review students' activity sheet charts, and focus on patterns in the data, as well as variations. Have students generate questions about the data gathered.

**Activity Sheet B**

Directions to students:

Use the two charts to record the results of your experiment to find out what happens to plants without water (1.8.3).

**NOTE:** This is a two-page activity sheet.

## Action: Part Four

Discuss with students when they think the experiment should end. Again, students might agree to wait until the plant receiving no water is dead; or, students might decide to stop the experiment before the plant dies, once a pattern has been established.

Once students determine the end of the experiment, distribute another copy of Centimetre Graph Paper (1.8.2) to each student. Have students use the data from the charts to create another bar graph of the results.

**NOTE:** Depending on students' background experience constructing graphs, teachers may choose to guide this activity to ensure that they include all required information on the graph. Again, this can also be done as a whole-class activity on large graph paper.

Once students have completed their bar graphs, discuss their graphs, and record statements about their observations and results on chart paper. As a class, use these statements to draw conclusions about the data, and record these conclusions on chart paper.

Portage & Main Press, 2017 · Hands-On Science and Technology · Grade 3 · ISBN: 978-1-55379-709-8

**8**

### Learning Centre

At the learning centre, provide magnifying glasses, leaves of several different sizes and shapes, drawing paper, and pencil crayons. Also, provide a copy of the Learning-Centre Task Card: Leaf Study (1.8.4), copies of the Learning-Centre Activity Sheet: Examining Leaves (1.8.5), and copies of the Diagram: Leaf Margins (1.8.6).

Have students choose two leaves from the selection and use a magnifying glass to examine the front and back of each leaf. Tell students to record their observations on the activity sheet (1.8.5). Have students refer to the diagram (1.8.6) when drawing their leaves. If they have time, tell them to use pencil crayons to make leaf rubbings of their two leaves.

**NOTE:** If available, an app (e.g., Leafsnap) on a tablet could be used to identify what types of leaves students are making rubbings from.

### Assessment as Learning

Have students reflect on what they learned about plants, and how accurately they conducted their experiments, recorded results, and constructed graphs. Have them use the Student Self-Assessment sheet, on page 31, to reflect on their learning.

### Consolidate and Debrief

- Revisit the guided inquiry question: **How can we investigate the needs of plants?** Have students share their knowledge, provide examples, and ask further inquiry questions.
- Add to the KWHL chart as students learn new concepts, answer some of their own inquiry questions, and ask new inquiry questions.
- Add new terms and illustrations to the class word wall. Include the words in other languages, as appropriate.
- Have students add new terms, definitions, and illustrations to their Science and Technology Glossary (1.1.1). When possible, encourage

them to add words (and examples) in other languages, including Indigenous languages, reflective of the classroom population.

### Enhance

- Have students make math connections by using the data from their bar graphs to write story problems for other students to answer.
- Have students conduct other experiments with plants, using questions they generate themselves. For example:
  - How does tap water and/or rainwater affect plants?
  - Does liquid fertilizer help plants grow?
  - What kind of soil is best for plant growth?

  Be sure to stress that any experiment should involve changing only one variable relative to the control, or they will have difficulty drawing conclusions afterward. If students focused on different questions like these, they could share results, and then, based on the results, try and develop the optimal growing conditions for plants in their class.

 **SAFETY NOTE:** If using liquid fertilizer for this activity, be sure to follow the instructions on the packaging for safe use.

- Discuss ways that humans work to keep plants alive. For example, in a greenhouse we can provide artificial light and water. In farmers' fields, irrigation may be used when there is a drought or dry conditions. These are sustainable practices.
- Access the interactive activity, Plants Need Water and Light, in the Grade 3, Unit 1 folder of the **Hands-On Interactive for Science and Technology, Grade 3** download. Find this download at: <www.portageandmainpress.com/product/hands-on-interactive-for-science-and-technology-grade-3/>.
- Have students continue their do-it-yourself projects at the Makerspace centre.

Portage & Main Press, 2017 · *Hands-On Science and Technology · Grade 3* · ISBN: 978-1-55379-709-8

**Date:** _____  **Name:** _____

# How Sunlight Affects Plant Growth

| Control Plant With Water and Sunlight | | |
|---|---|---|
| Date | Height | Observations |
| | | |

Portage & Main Press, 2017 · *Hands-On Science and Technology · Grade 3* · ISBN: 978-1-55379-709-8

**Date:** _____    **Name:** _____

## How Sunlight Affects Plant Growth (continued)

| Plant With Water but No Sunlight | | |
|---|---|---|
| Date | Height | Observations |
| | | |

Portage & Main Press, 2017 · *Hands-On Science and Technology · Grade 3* · ISBN: 978-1-55379-709-8

**Date:** _____      **Name:** _____

# Centimetre Graph Paper

Portage & Main Press, 2017 · Hands-On Science and Technology · Grade 3 · ISBN: 978-1-55379-709-8

Date: _____     Name: _____

# How Does Water Affect Plant Growth?

| Control Plant With Water and Sunlight | | |
|---|---|---|
| Date | Height | Observations |
| | | |
| | | |
| | | |
| | | |
| | | |
| | | |
| | | |

Portage & Main Press, 2017 · Hands-On Science and Technology · Grade 3 · ISBN: 978-1-55379-709-8

# How Does Water Affect Plant Growth? (continued)

| Plant With Sunlight but No Water | | |
|---|---|---|
| Date | Height | Observations |
|  |  |  |

Portage & Main Press, 2017 · Hands-On Science and Technology · Grade 3 · ISBN: 978-1-55379-709-8

# Leaf Study

A botanist is a scientist who studies plants. Today, you are going to be a botanist and study the leaves of plants.

1. Select two different-looking leaves.

2. Use a magnifying glass to examine the front and back of each leaf.

   ▪ Look closely at the size and shape of each leaf. This is the "leaf margin."

   ▪ Look closely at the vein system of the leaf.

3. With a pencil, draw the front and back of each leaf. Be as exact as you can—remember that you are a botanist!

4. Label your leaves based on the Leaf Margins card.

5. If you have time, use pencil crayons to make a leaf rubbing of each leaf on separate pieces of paper.

Portage & Main Press, 2017 · Hands-On Science and Technology · Grade 3 · ISBN: 978-1-55379-709-8

Date: _____     Name: _____

# Examining Leaves

| Front of Leaf A | Back of Leaf A |
|---|---|
|  |  |

Describe the leaf margin (size and shape) of Leaf A:

_____

_____

| Front of Leaf B | Back of Leaf B |
|---|---|
|  |  |

Describe the leaf margin (size and shape) of Leaf B:

_____

_____

Portage & Main Press, 2017 · Hands-On Science and Technology · Grade 3 · ISBN: 978-1-55379-709-8

# Leaf Margins

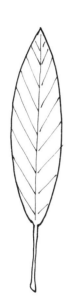 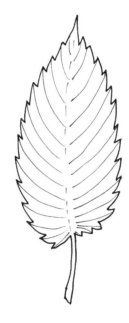 

entire       serrate       crenate

lobed       parted

Portage & Main Press, 2017 · Hands-On Science and Technology · Grade 3 · ISBN: 978-1-55379-709-8

# 9 | How Can We Design a Terrarium to Sustain Living Things?

## Information for Teachers

A terrarium is a container with a miniature landscape containing living plants and, sometimes, small live animals and other natural or decorative features. The container creates a greenhouse effect, holding in moisture and warmth to help the miniature environment thrive. A lidded container is used when the plants inside require more moisture (e.g., ferns, ivies). An open container is used when a drier environment is required for the plants inside (e.g., cacti, portulaca). Consequently, when designing a terrarium, it is important to research and use plants with similar needs for soil, warmth, moisture, and light.

A well-functioning terrarium is a visible example of sustainability. With proper care, a terrarium should be able to be sustained indefinitely.

## 21st Century Competencies

**Collaboration**, **Creativity**, and **Critical Thinking**: Students will work collaboratively to research and design a terrarium. They will include decorative features, and will compare their final product to another group's design.

## Materials

- variety of clear containers (e.g., glass jars of various sizes, fishbowls, two-litre plastic bottles, plastic milk jugs) (Many types of glass containers suitable for terrariums are available at dollar stores.)
- water
- stones or gravel
- activated charcoal (a very absorbent powdered charcoal, used in medicines)
- different types of soil (e.g., potting, peat, clay, sand)
- small plants (to fit into clear containers) (three for each pair of students)
- twigs
- other materials identified by students to create terrariums (e.g., stones, shells, decorative ornaments or figurines)
- poster board
- index cards
- chart paper
- markers
- dice
- game pieces
- computers/tablets with Internet access
- Activity Sheet A: Designing a Terrarium (1.9.1)
- Activity Sheet B: Building a Terrarium (1.9.2)
- Learning-Centre Task Card: Taking Care of Your Terrarium (1.9.3)
- Information Sheet: Terrarium Troubleshooting: Mistakes to Avoid (1.9.4)
- KWHL chart (from lesson 1)
- Science and Technology Glossary (1.1.1)

## Activate

Review with students what plants need to survive and thrive.

Have students imagine an ideal plant-growing environment. As a class, brainstorm, and record responses on chart paper.

Show students all available materials for creating a terrarium, including the containers. Ask:

- Have you ever seen a clear, closed container in which plants are growing?
- How could we design and construct an environment in one of the containers that will be sustainable for all living things inside it?
- How could we support plant growth in these kinds of containers?

Introduce the term *terrarium,* and record it on chart paper. Discuss students' understanding of or their experiences with terrariums. They may be more familiar with the term *aquarium,* which

Portage & Main Press, 2017 · *Hands-On Science and Technology* · *Grade 3* · ISBN: 978-1-55379-709-8

**9**

is also a container used to sustain living things but in an aquatic environment.

Ask:

- What kinds of things do you find in an aquarium that help the organisms in it survive?
- What might be needed in a terrarium to help organisms survive?

Record students' ideas on chart paper.

Introduce the guided inquiry question: **How can we design a terrarium to sustain living things?**

## Action: Part One

Tell students they will design, with a partner, their own terrariums. Provide each student with a copy of Activity Sheet A: Designing a Terrarium (1.9.1). Review the diagram of a terrarium on the activity sheet, and discuss the various layers of the environment. Have students infer the function of each layer. Record their ideas on chart paper.

With students, discuss the selection of plants for their terrariums. Explain that they must find at least three plants that prefer the same kind of soil, moisture, light, and warmth.

As a class, identify criteria for a terrarium design project. For example:

- must contain soil and air
- must contain at least three different plant species
- must allow for water to be added as needed
- must allow plants and other living things to survive long-term

Have student pairs discuss their ideas, conduct their plant research, and agree on materials and a design for their terrarium. This may include ideas for decorative features (e.g., twigs, special rocks, figurines, ornaments). Have students

discuss their designs with the teacher before building their terrariums. Finally, have student pairs draw and label their designs for their terrariums on Activity Sheet A: Designing a Terrarium (1.9.1).

### Activity Sheet A

Directions to students:

With your partner, draw and label your design for your terrarium (1.9.1).

NOTE: This is a two-page activity sheet.

## Action: Part Two

Using the materials available and their designs, have student pairs construct their terrarium. During the building phase, students may find it necessary to make changes to their original designs.

When students have completed their terrariums, distribute a copy of Activity Sheet B: Building a Terrarium (1.9.2) to each student. Have students draw the final design of their terrarium on the activity sheet, recording any changes made during construction.

Have students observe their terrariums over time and record their observations on the activity sheet.

### Activity Sheet B

Directions to students:

Draw and label the terrarium you and your partner constructed. Be sure to mention any changes you made from your original design, and why you made them. Observe your terrarium over time, and record your observations (1.9.2).

NOTE: This is a two-page activity sheet.

### Assessment of Learning

Observe students as they work together to design and construct their terrariums. Use the Cooperative-Skills Teacher Assessment sheet, on page 37, to record results.

▶

Portage & Main Press, 2017 · *Hands-On Science and Technology* · Grade 3 · ISBN: 978-1-55379-709-8

## Action: Part Three

Provide an opportunity for students to present their finished terrariums to the class. Challenge students to explain how their terrariums meet the identified criteria, and what they might change if they were to design another one.

### Assessment of Learning

On the Rubric, on page 36, record identified criteria for the terrarium design project. During students' presentations (Action: Part Three), assess their design projects. Record results.

## Learning Centre

At the learning centre, provide poster board, index cards, markers, a copy of the Learning-Centre Task Card: Taking Care of Your Terrarium (1.9.3), and the Information Sheet: Terrarium Troubleshooting: Mistakes to Avoid (1.9.4).

Have pairs or groups of students design a board game about proper terrarium care, using the Learning-Centre Task Card and the Information Sheet as a guide.

**NOTE:** Once students have completed their board games, keep the games at the learning centre for other students to play.

## Consolidate and Debrief

- Revisit the guided inquiry question: **How can we design a terrarium to sustain living things?** Have students share their knowledge, provide examples, and ask further inquiry questions.
- Add to the KWHL chart as students learn new concepts, answer some of their own inquiry questions, and ask new inquiry questions.
- Add new terms and illustrations to the class word wall. Include the words in other languages, as appropriate.

- Have students add new terms, definitions, and illustrations to their Science and Technology Glossary (1.1.1). When possible, encourage them to add words (and examples) in other languages, including Indigenous languages, reflective of the classroom population.

## Enhance

- Have two pairs of students work together to create a Venn diagram that compares their terrariums.
- Use an old aquarium to create a large terrarium. Place it near the entrance or in another common area inside the school.
- Discuss and research larger institutions that function like terrariums, such as the Montreal Biodôme (<espacepourlavie. ca/en/biodome>), which includes a First Nations Garden (<espacepourlavie.ca/en/ first-nations-garden>) a Chinese Garden (<espacepourlavie.ca/en/chinese-garden>) and a Japanese Garden (<espacepourlavie. ca/en/japanese-garden>). The Arizona Biosphere 2 Project (<www.b2science.org>) provides a similar exploration.
- Access the interactive activity, Effects of Soil and Nutrients on Plants, in the Grade 3, Unit 1 folder of the ***Hands-On Interactive for Science and Technology, Grade 3*** download. Find this download at: <www.portageandmainpress.com/ product/hands-on-interactive-for-science-and-technology-grade-3/>.
- Have students continue their do-it-yourself projects at the Makerspace centre.

Portage & Main Press, 2017 · *Hands-On Science and Technology · Grade 3* · ISBN: 978-1-55379-709-8

# Designing a Terrarium

- A terrarium is a container with a miniature landscape inside. It contains living plants and sometimes small, live animals and other natural and/or decorative features.

- When designing a terrarium, it is important to research and use plants with similar needs for soil, warmth, moisture, and light.

- Terrariums sometimes have lids when the plants inside need lots of moisture. When plants need less moisture, lids are not used.

- With proper design and care, plants in a terrarium should be able to grow for a long time.

Here is an example of the layers in a terrarium:

plants

potting soil

charcoal
rocks

Now, work with your partner to design your own terrarium!

Portage & Main Press, 2017 · Hands-On Science and Technology · Grade 3 · ISBN: 978-1-55379-709-8

# Designing a Terrarium (continued)

1. Record the criteria for this project:

_____

_____

_____

_____

2. What kinds of plants will you put in your terrarium? Explain why you chose these plants.

_____

_____

3. Draw and label your design for a terrarium.

```
┌─────────────────────────────────────────────┐
│                                               │
│                                               │
│                                               │
│                                               │
│                                               │
│                                               │
│                                               │
│                                               │
└─────────────────────────────────────────────┘
```

4. What materials will you need?

_____

5. How will you design your terrarium so that it can sustain life for anything living that you put inside?

_____

_____

Portage & Main Press, 2017 · Hands-On Science and Technology · Grade 3 · ISBN: 978-1-55379-709-8

# Building a Terrarium

1. Draw and label a diagram of your final product.

<br>
<br>
<br>
<br>
<br>
<br>
<br>
<br>
<br>
<br>

2. Describe how you changed your terrarium from your original design.

_____

_____

_____

3. How well do you think your terrarium will work to sustain life for the living things you put in it? Explain your answer.

_____

_____

_____

_____

Portage & Main Press, 2017 · Hands-On Science and Technology · Grade 3 · ISBN: 978-1-55379-709-8

# Building a Terrarium (continued)

4. Observe your terrarium over time. Make a chart to record dates and your observations.

5. How well does your terrarium sustain life for the living things you put in it?

_____

_____

_____

_____

6. How might you change its design if you were to build another terrarium?

_____

_____

_____

_____

_____

Portage & Main Press, 2017 · Hands-On Science and Technology · Grade 3 · ISBN: 978-1-55379-709-8

# Taking Care of Your Terrarium

It is important to take care of your terrarium so that the plants inside can live for a very long time.

1. With a partner or in a group, create a board game that can be played by two to four players.

   You will need:

   - poster board
   - index cards
   - markers
   - one die

   - place markers
   - information about common terrarium mistakes (included at the centre)

2. On poster board, draw a start and a finish line, and about 15 spaces.

3. Choose 10 spaces, and label them "Pick a Card."

4. From the index cards, make 10 cards a player picks up when they land on a space that says "Pick a Card":

   - At least one card should say the player must move back for not taking care of the terrarium. For example:

     □ The terrarium received no light because you forgot to open the curtains for a week. Move back three spaces.

   - At least one card should reward the player for properly caring for the terrarium. For example:

     □ The terrarium sits on the table in the sunroom, out of direct sunlight. Move forward two spaces.

   - Details for the other cards are up to you.

5. Once you have made all the cards and the game board, and have written how-to-play instructions, play your game. Share it with classmates, and have them play.

Portage & Main Press, 2017 · Hands-On Science and Technology · Grade 3 · ISBN: 978-1-55379-709-8

# Terrarium Troubleshooting: Mistakes to Avoid

1. Too much light: Keep your terrarium out of direct sunlight. Too much light can cause the glass to act like a magnifying glass—temperatures inside the terrarium will soar, and your plants could actually burn.

2. Too little light: Most plants need some light, so one of the best places for your terrarium is next to a window. You can also use artificial light— a grow light or a fluorescent light equipped with one warm bulb and one cool bulb.

3. Too close to radiators: Putting your terrarium too close to a radiator will not result in happy plants. The jar or container will heat up quickly, which can kill your plants.

4. Letting plants get gangly: Plants need to be clipped when they get gangly and untidy. If you want to keep the plants small you can also carefully prune the roots.

5. Leaving dying plants: Take dead or dying plants or leaves out of your terrarium. A diseased plant can quickly pass on the illness to other plants and should be removed as soon as you notice it. Use a small shovel or a long spoon to dig the plant out, being careful not to disturb the roots of other plants. Replace the plant you removed with another that is comparable in size and light requirements.

6. Dirty glass: Both the inside and outside of your terrarium need to be cleaned every so often. Use a damp piece of newsprint or a lint-free rag. Do not use any strong cleaning agent on the inside, as it might hurt your plants.

7. Overwatering: Do not give plants too much water. Use a spray bottle to help prevent overwatering—you give smaller amounts of water in a more controlled way than when you pour water. If you accidentally give your terrarium plants too much water, soak up extra moisture with a paper towel. Keep the top off your terrarium until the soil has dried out.

8. Overfertilizing: Your terrarium plants likely do not need fertilizer. You want your plants to remain relatively small, so they continue to fit inside the terrarium space. Feeding them fertilizer will cause them to grow more quickly.

9. Choosing the wrong plants: It is important to choose plants that will do well in the kind of terrarium you are making. If you are creating a closed terrarium, be sure to select plants that like moisture. Also, consider how much light your plants will receive, and use plants that will be happy with that level.

Portage & Main Press, 2017 · Hands-On Science and Technology · Grade 3 · ISBN: 978-1-55379-709-8

# 10 In What Other Ways Are Plants Important to Humans?

## Information for Teachers

Humans use plants to make many products other than food. For example:

- lumber
- paper
- medicine (e.g., ginseng, willow bark)
- rope
- fabric (e.g., cotton, silk, linen)
- flooring (e.g., linoleum, hardwood)
- perfume
- crayons
- rubber
- cork
- dyes

In many Indigenous cultures, plants have several important roles. For many centuries, Indigenous peoples have used local plants for spiritual and ceremonial purposes.

## 21ˢᵗ Century Competencies

**Critical Thinking, Communication, Citizenship**, and **Collaboration**: Students will brainstorm various examples of where plants and plant products are used. They will also examine careers that are related to the production or use of these products.

## Materials

- chart paper
- markers
- magazines, newspapers with pictures of products made from plants
- printer (optional)
- glue
- scissors
- computers/tablets with Internet access (optional)
- Activity Sheet A: Plant Products (1.10.1)
- Activity Sheet B: Jobs and Hobbies With Plants (1.10.2)
- resources about Indigenous Medicines (e.g., Ojibwe medicine at: <ojibweresources. weebly.com/ojibwe-medicines.html>; "The Lily Root" at: <www.aadnc-aandc.gc.ca/eng/ 1316530132377/1316530184659#chpm2> [scroll down the page to find the story]; *Relatives With Roots* by Leah Marie Dorion)
- KWHL chart (from lesson 1)
- Science and Technology Glossary (1.1.1)

## Activate

Divide the class into working groups, and give each group a sheet of chart paper and a marker. Have each group brainstorm a list of useful products that are made from plants (e.g., foods, clothing, bedding, lumber, medicines, dyes, paper, fishing poles, furniture).

Introduce the guided inquiry question: **In what other ways are plants important to humans?**

## Action: Part One

Display the groups' lists of useful products made from plants, and review the lists together. Ask:

- Which products are similar in all (or some) of the groups' lists?
- Which products are different between the groups?
- Are there any products that surprise you?

On a new sheet of chart paper, combine all of the group lists into one class list of useful products made from plants. Ask:

- Can you add any more products to the list?
- Can you sort the products into groups?

Use the Information for Teachers section to add to the list of products made from plants. This will provide a variety of topics for subsequent research. Distribute a copy of Activity Sheet A:

Portage & Main Press, 2017 · *Hands-On Science and Technology · Grade 3* · ISBN: 978-1-55379-709-8

## 10

Plant Products (1.10.1) to each student, along with magazines, newspapers, scissors, and glue. Have students cut out pictures of plant products from the magazines and newspapers. If computers/tablets with Internet access and a printer are available, students can look online for pictures; or, they may draw their own pictures. Ask students to sort their pictures, according to a rule of their choosing. Then, have them divide the circle on the activity sheet into enough parts to accommodate all groups for their sorted pictures. Finally, tell students to glue their pictures onto the activity sheet, labelling each section with their sorting rule.

### Activity Sheet A

Directions to students:

Use magazines, newspapers, and websites to find examples of products made from plants. Cut out, and sort into groups all the pictures you find. Divide the circle on the activity sheet into the same number of parts as you have groups of sorted pictures. Label each part according to your sorting rule. Glue the pictures into the appropriate sections. You may draw pictures, as well (1.10.1).

## Action: Part Two

Review with students the class list of products made from plants. Ask:

■ Which jobs or hobbies are involved in making these products?

Organize students into the same groups as before, and provide each group with a sheet of chart paper and a marker. Have each group brainstorm a list of jobs and hobbies involving plants (e.g., gardener, farmer, botanist, florist, lumber miller, artist, paper maker, doctor, traditional healer) and list them on the chart paper.

Display the groups' lists, and discuss. Ask:

■ What do you know about any of these jobs and hobbies?

■ Do you know anyone who does one of these jobs or hobbies?

Encourage students to share their experiences.

**NOTE:** This activity provides a good opportunity to invite guest speakers into the classroom to speak to students about jobs and hobbies related to plants.

Distribute a copy of Activity Sheet B: Jobs and Hobbies With Plants (1.10.2) to each student. Have students record the names of jobs and hobbies involving plants. Then, ask them to draw a picture of a person doing each job or hobby and describe the kind of work that person does with plants.

### Activity Sheet B

Directions to students:

Record the names of jobs and hobbies that involve plants. For each one, draw a picture of a person doing the job or hobby. Describe the kind of work and activities this person does with plants (1.10.2).

## Action: Part Three

Invite an Elder or a Métis Senator to share knowledge of plants that are used by Indigenous peoples for medicinal and sacred purposes.

Sweetgrass, sage, cedar, and tobacco encompass the four sacred plants for many Indigenous peoples. Burning one of these is a sign of deep spirituality in Indigenous practice, and the plants are used in both individual and group ceremonies.

Explore the Ojibwe Medicine—Mshkiki website at: <ojibweresources.weebly.com/ojibwe-medicines.html>. This website explains the four sacred medicines of the Ojibwe: tobacco, sage, sweetgrass, and cedar. The information is tied into the ceremonies that the plants would be used in, as well as teachings from the medicine wheel. There is also a video that talks about picking sage.

To further explore Indigenous medicines from plants, explore the following resources:

- *Relatives With Roots* by Leah Marie Dorion. This is a book about a Métis grandmother who takes her granddaughter out into the bush to teach her how to pick traditional medicines.

- Read or have students listen to the Anishinaabe Story "The Lily Root," found online at The Learning Circle: Classroom Activities on First Nations in Canada (Aboriginal Affairs and Northern Development Canada) at: <www.aadnc-aandc.gc.ca/eng/1316530132377/1316530184659#chpm2>. Scroll down the page to find the story. This "discovery" story will help students understand the importance of some plants as medicine for Indigenous peoples. Use the discussion questions at the end of the story to help students understand the theme.

## Consolidate and Debrief

- Revisit the guided inquiry question: **In what other ways are plants important to humans?** Have students share their knowledge, provide examples, and ask further inquiry questions.

- Add to the KWHL chart as students learn new concepts, answer some of their own inquiry questions, and ask new inquiry questions.

- Add new terms and illustrations to the class word wall. Include the words in other languages, as appropriate.

- Have students add new terms, definitions, and illustrations to their Science and Technology Glossary (1.1.1). When possible, encourage them to add words (and examples) in other languages, including Indigenous languages, reflective of the classroom population.

## Enhance

- Invite a guest speaker into the classroom to discuss their job or hobby involving plants.

- Share with students the Anishinaabe story "Winabojo and the Birch Tree" (see NativeTech: Native American Technology and Art at: <www.nativetech.org/brchbark/winabojo.htm>), and have students illustrate the story.

- Research Métis traditional uses of plants. Go to: <www.metisnation.org/media/81616/so_on_tek_darlington_report.pdf>.

- As a class, create a medicine garden. See: <www.trca.on.ca/dotAsset/149974.pdf>.

- Access the interactive activity, Importance of Plants to Humans, in the Grade 3, Unit 1 folder of the **Hands-On Interactive for Science and Technology, Grade 3** download. Find this download at: <www.portageandmainpress.com/product/hands-on-interactive-for-science-and-technology-grade-3/>.

- Have students continue their do-it-yourself projects at the Makerspace centre.

Portage & Main Press, 2017 · *Hands-On Science and Technology · Grade 3* · ISBN: 978-1-55379-709-8

# Plant Products

Name six products in your home made from plants.

1. _____   2. _____

3. _____   4. _____

5. _____   6. _____

Portage & Main Press, 2017 · Hands-On Science and Technology · Grade 3 · ISBN: 978-1-55379-709-8

# Jobs and Hobbies With Plants

| Job or Hobby | Illustration | Activities With Plants |
|---|---|---|
|  |  |  |
|  |  |  |
|  |  |  |
|  |  |  |
|  |  |  |

One job or hobby I would like to try that involves plants is

_____ , because _____

_____ .

# 11 | How Can Dye Be Made From Plants?

## Information for Teachers

Natural dyes are colorants from organisms. The majority of natural dyes are vegetable dyes from plant sources (e.g., roots, berries, bark, leaves, wood). Pioneer Thinking is a useful website for information on natural dyes (see <pioneerthinking.com/crafts/dyes>).

Colours are significant to many First Nations. For example, red, black, yellow, and white are the colours of the Medicine Wheel, a vital teaching tool among many First Nations. The interpretations of the colours vary from community to community. For some, white is associated with the North, black with the West, red with the South, and yellow with the East.

Many First Nations traditionally decorate their clothing, hunting implements, and other objects with natural colours through embroidery using dyed moose or caribou hair, beads made from coloured shells, or dyed porcupine quills. Dyes are made from plants such as:

- green: moss
- yellow: sunflowers or wild onion skins
- red: cranberries
- purple and blue: blueberries

## 21st Century Competencies

**Collaboration**, **Creativity**, **Critical Thinking**, and **Citizenship**: Students will explore how dyes can be made from plants by making their own samples of dyes. Students can also conduct research into the environmental effects of commercial dye production. Ways to increase sustainability can also be conducted, along with the possibility of students creating their own tie-dyed cloth.

## Materials

- assortment of local plants or plant parts (e.g., berries, beets, red and green cabbage, parsley, dandelions, moss, onion skin, tree leaves, flowers, beans, tree bark)
- white fabric (An old, white sheet or tablecloth works well; cut into squares [approximately 15 cm x 15 cm].)
- water
- large pot
- potato mashers or forks
- sharp knife
- bowls or containers (in which to mash plants/plant products)
- measuring cups
- heat source (stove or hot plate)
- containers for dyeing cloth
- Popsicle sticks
- scissors
- glue
- newspaper
- smocks or paint shirts
- crayons, pencil crayons, or paint
- chart paper
- markers
- graph paper (optional)
- Activity Sheet: Making Plant Dyes (1.11.1)
- Assessment as Learning Sheet: Plant Dye Reflection (1.11.2)
- KWHL chart (from lesson 1)
- Science and Technology Glossary (1.1.1)

**NOTE:** Consider having each student bring in one or two plants or plant parts, using examples from the Materials list. This would provide a wide assortment of items and will cut down on the cost of the task.

## Activate

As a class, discuss products made from plants. Ask:

- In what ways do we use plants the most to make products? (e.g., food, clothing, lumber)
- Have you ever used a plant in such a way that it left a stain on you? (e.g., sliding on the

Portage & Main Press, 2017 · Hands-On Science and Technology · Grade 3 · ISBN: 978-1-55379-709-8

grass, spilling blueberries on clothing, cutting up beets, rubbing a buttercup flower)

Have students look at their clothing and the clothing of their peers, paying special attention to the colours in the clothing. Ask:

- How do you think the different colours are created on fabrics?
- Where do you think dyes come from?

Create a tally of the colours in students' clothing—tops and bottoms. For example:

| Colour | Top | Bottom |
|---|---|---|
| white | | |
| black | | |
| red | | |
| yellow | | |
| blue | | |
| green | | |
| purple | | |
| orange | | |
| brown | | |
| grey | | |
| multi-colour | | |

Use the tally chart to read and interpret data, then have students pose questions about the information presented in it. For example:

- Which colour do we see the most in our tops?
- Which colour do we see the least in our bottoms?
- In total, how many clothing pieces are brown?

Have other students in the class respond to these questions.

Have students create bar graphs of the data in the tally chart, or they can make a pictograph using small paper cut-outs of shirts or pants.

Introduce the guided inquiry question: **How can dye be made from plants?**

## Action

**NOTE:** The following activity can be done as a whole-class experiment, or at an activity centre with an adult supervisor.

Display the variety of local plants. Have students examine, describe, and identify the plants.

 **SAFETY NOTE:** Be aware of any student allergies that may be affected by handling these plants.

Discuss the locations where these plants might be found in your local area (e.g., in nature, in gardens, on farms). Ask:

- What are these plants used for?
- Are there uses other than as food?

Introduce students to the concept of natural plant dyes. Ask:

- How do you think people coloured their clothing before clothing and fabrics were sold in stores?
- How do you think Indigenous peoples made colours?

Have students share their ideas. Have them again examine the colours of their clothing. Ask:

- Do you think any of these plants would make a similar colour if it was used for dye?

Have students share their ideas and predictions, examining specific pieces of clothing and the plants displayed.

Next, have students put on smocks or paint shirts. As a class, select one of the plants to use for dyeing. Provide each student with a copy of Activity Sheet A: Making Plant Dyes (1.11.1). Have students record the name of the plant or draw a picture of the plant they have chosen in the first row of the chart.

Portage & Main Press, 2017 · *Hands-On Science and Technology* · *Grade 3* · ISBN: 978-1-55379-709-8

**11**

Organize the class into small working groups, and distribute to each group some of the plant they have chosen, a potato masher or fork, and a bowl or container in which to mash the plant. Have students mash their portion of the chosen plant.

**NOTE:** If students are not able to mash the plant, have an adult cut it up, or leave it whole.

Distribute measuring cups, and tell students to measure 125 mL of the mashed plant. Combine all groups' portions of the mashed plant into a large pot, and add 500 mL of water. Boil the mixture for about five minutes, or until the water becomes coloured. Some plants may take longer, while others may require more water.

 **SAFETY NOTE:** For safety of all students, boiling must be done by an adult only, away from student access.

When the water is coloured, remove the pot from the heat source, and let it cool.

Now, distribute to each working group a container for dyeing and a square of white fabric, and have students place the fabric into the empty container. Have the groups pour some of the cooled, coloured water into their container. Distribute Popsicle sticks, and tell students to use them to help ensure the fabric is completely covered with coloured water.

Have students predict the colour of the fabric after ten minutes in the water by using crayons, pencil crayons, or paints to colour the appropriate box in the second column of the chart on the activity sheet.

After ten minutes, tell students to use the Popsicle stick to remove the fabric from the dye and place the fabric flat on a piece of newspaper to dry. When the fabric has dried, distribute scissors and glue, and tell the groups to cut several smaller pieces from the dried squares of

fabric. Have students glue a small piece of the dyed fabric onto the third column of the chart on their activity sheet.

Next, have students place the remaining fabric back into the container of coloured water. Ask:

- What do you think will happen to the fabric if it is left in the dye overnight?

Have students predict the colour of the fabric after it has soaked in the dye overnight by colouring the appropriate box in the fourth column of the chart on the activity sheet.

Leave the fabric pieces in the containers overnight. The next day, have the groups of students remove their fabric piece from the dye, lay it flat on newspaper to dry, and then cut the fabric into smaller pieces. Tell students to glue the new piece of fabric onto their activity sheet in the fifth column of the chart.

Repeat the dyeing process using other selected local plants.

Once all plants have been used to dye the fabric, compare how various plants produce colour on the material. Ask:

- Why were certain plants better at dyeing the fabric than others?
- Were all the pieces of fabric darker after being in the dye for a longer time?

**Activity Sheet**

Directions to students:

In the first column, write the name or draw a picture of the first plant used for dyeing. In the second column, predict the colour of the fabric after ten minutes in the dye by colouring the box with crayons, pencil crayons, or paint. In the third column, glue a small, dried piece of the fabric that has soaked in the dye for ten minutes. In the fourth column, predict the colour of the fabric after soaking in the dye overnight by

Portage & Main Press, 2017 · Hands-On Science and Technology · Grade 3 · ISBN: 978-1-55379-709-8

**11**

colouring the box with crayons, pencil crayons, or paint. In the fifth column, glue a small piece of the dried fabric that was soaked in the dye overnight. Repeat with other plants (1.11.1).

**Assessment as Learning**
Have students complete the Assessment as Learning Sheet: Plant Dye Reflection (1.11.2) to reflect on their experiences using plants to make dye.

## Consolidate and Debrief

- Revisit the guided inquiry question: **How can dye be made from plants?** Have students share their knowledge, provide examples, and ask further inquiry questions.
- Add to the KWHL chart as students learn new concepts, answer some of their own inquiry questions, and ask new inquiry questions.
- Add new terms and illustrations to the class word wall. Include the words in other languages, as appropriate.
- Have students add new terms, definitions, and illustrations to their Science and Technology Glossary (1.1.1). When possible, encourage them to add words (and examples) in other languages, including Indigenous languages, reflective of the classroom population.

## Enhance

- Have students mix several plants together to boil into dye. Encourage them to see how many different shades they can create.
- Dye pieces of wool or yarn, and use them for future art projects, such as weaving.
- Have students investigate fixators, such as vinegar and salt, which are used to set dye to fabric. Conduct experiments to explore any differences in results between using fixators with dye and using dye alone.

- Discuss and research to determine if dyes are helpful or harmful to the environment. Examine how the use and production of dyes can be sustainable.
- Use natural dyes for a tie-dye project. Be sure to use fixators, especially if students are tie-dyeing t-shirts or other clothing.
- Face painting has traditionally been an important part of Indigenous culture. Have students do online research into some examples of Indigenous face painting.
- Henna is used in both Middle Eastern and East Indian cultures for tattooing, as well as for colouring hair, hands, or feet. With permission from students' families, invite a Henna artist to visit the class to share knowledge about Henna use, as well as a tattooing experience for students. Show students samples of Henna art, and considering having students design their own tattoo patterns to use when the artist visits.
- Explore and research the use of dyes in the days of European settlement in Canada.
- Have students use a computer painting program (e.g., Microsoft Paint, Tux Paint) to match colours to the dyes they created from plants. Challenge students to determine the closest shade and hue. Students could also take digital photos, and then use Photoshop Lite or another program to get an exact RGB colour match for their colour.
- Access the interactive activity, Making Things From Plants, in the Grade 3, Unit 1 folder of the **Hands-On Interactive for Science and Technology, Grade 3** download. Find this download at: <www.portageandmainpress.com/product/hands-on-interactive-for-science-and-technology-grade-3/>.
- Have students continue their do-it-yourself projects at the Makerspace centre.

Portage & Main Press, 2017 · *Hands-On Science and Technology · Grade 3* · ISBN: 978-1-55379-709-8

Portage & Main Press, 2017 · Hands-On Science and Technology · Grade 3 · ISBN: 978-1-55379-709-8

Name: _____

# Making Plant Dyes

| Type of Plant | Colour Prediction: After Ten Minutes | Colour of Cloth: After Ten Minutes | Colour Prediction: The Next Day | Colour of Cloth: The Next Day |
|---|---|---|---|---|
|  |  |  |  |  |
|  |  |  |  |  |
|  |  |  |  |  |
|  |  |  |  |  |

# Plant Dye Reflection

| Making Dyes | How I Did √ | | |
|---|---|---|---|
| | ☺ | 😐 | ☹ |
| I enjoyed making dyes out of plants. | | | |
| I helped with the work. | | | |
| I stayed on task. | | | |
| My predictions were close. | | | |
| I wish we had used other plants to make dyes. | | | |
| I would like to learn more about making dyes. | | | |
| I would like to wear clothing that was dyed in one of the colours we made. | | | |

Draw a labelled diagram to show a conclusion you have made about using plants for dyeing.

Portage & Main Press, 2017 · Hands-On Science and Technology · Grade 3 · ISBN: 978-1-55379-709-8

# How Do Plants and Animals Depend on Each Other?

**12**

## 21st Century Competencies

**Creativity**, **Communication**, and **Character**: After looking at ways that plants and animals depend on each other, students will create and illustrate a page of a book that shows these interrelationships.

## Materials

- digital camera
- stories (including Indigenous stories) about the interdependence of plants and animals (e.g., The Anishnaubaemowin series: *Living in Harmony* by Basil Johnston; *Living Sunlight: How Plants Bring the Earth to Life* by Molly Bang; *Food Chains* by Brenda Boreham)
- computer/tablet with Internet access
- art supplies (e.g., pencil crayons, markers, oil pastels)
- drawing paper
- rulers
- Activity Sheet: How Do Plants and Animals Depend on Each Other? (1.12.1)
- Learning-Centre Task Card: I Am an Illustrator (1.12.2)
- KWHL chart (from lesson 1)
- Science and Technology Glossary (1.1.1)

## Activate

As a class, review all the things a plant needs in order to survive. Also, review (from grades 1 and 2) what animals (including humans) need in order to survive. Ask:

- Which needs are similar, and why?
- Which needs are different, and why?
- What would happen to plants if there were no animals?
- What would happen to animals if there were no plants?

Introduce the guided inquiry question: **How do plants and animals depend on each other?**

## Action: Part One

Plan a nature walk to a local park, forest, or preserve. Have students look for examples and evidence of how plants and animals are interdependent. For example:

- birds and squirrels living in trees
- worms living in soil (enriching the soil for plant life)
- bees pollinating plants
- fish feeding on water plants

Take pictures of students' examples for use back in the classroom.

Consider having an Elder or a Métis Senator guide the nature walk and share knowledge about how plants and animals depend on each other. They may be able to tell traditional stories related to these topics.

Follow up the land-based learning experience by reading Indigenous stories and other books about the interdependence of plants and animals. For example:

- The Anishnaubaemowin series: *Living in Harmony* by Basil Johnston. A story of Mother Earth and the changes in plants and animals as they balance in nature.
- *Living Sunlight: How Plants Bring the Earth to Life* by Molly Bang
- *Food Chains* by Brenda Boreham

Follow up these stories with an exploration of the Haudenosaunee Thanksgiving Address, which speaks to the interrelationship of all things. It specifically addresses plants, fish, and animals. Use the book, *Giving Thanks: A Native American Good Morning Message* by Chief Jake Swamp or go to: <www.akwesasne.ca/node/253>.

Portage & Main Press, 2017 · Hands-On Science and Technology · Grade 3 · ISBN: 978-1-55379-709-8

## Action: Part Two

Divide the class into two groups. Label one group "Plants" and the other group "Animals." Have the groups stand on opposite sides of the classroom. Explain that they are going to play a game. The goal of the game is for all students to meet in the centre of the room. In order to move from one side of the room to the centre, a student must fulfill one requirement: each "animal" must say how they can help a plant, and each "plant" must say how they can help an animal.

Have "Plants" students and "Animals" students take turns sharing ideas of how they can help each other (one student at a time). Encourage students to use first person (see examples below). As students are speaking, encourage them to show actions that represent the plant or animal's actions. Have students hold hands when they get into the centre of the room. Examples:

> **Plant:** I provide food for animals. Food gives animals energy.
> **Animal:** As a squirrel, I carry seeds (e.g., acorns) for you from one place to another, so a new tree can be planted somewhere else.
> **Plant:** As a tree (or bush), I provide shade for you on a hot summer day.
> **Animal:** I am a bee, and I help pollinate your flowers so that apples can grow.
> **Plant:** You need me to make interesting colour dyes for your clothing.
> **Animal:** I am a gardener, and I take care of plants.

If students begin to have difficulties coming up with responses, encourage them to seek help from others in their group.

## Action: Part Three

Once all students are at the centre of the room, holding hands in a circle, ask:

- Why do you think we held hands when we got to the centre of the room?

- How do plants and animals depend on each other?

Discuss the importance of plants to animals and animals to plants. The hand-holding represents the ways in which plants and animals are interconnected.

Distribute a copy of Activity Sheet: How Do Plants and Animals Depend on Each Other? (1.12.1) to each student, and have students identify how each plant depends on animals, and how each animal depends on plants.

### Activity Sheet

Directions to students:

For each animal, think of how it depends on plants to survive. For each plant, think of how it depends on animals to survive. Record your ideas in complete sentences (1.12.1).

## Learning Centre

At the learning centre, provide art supplies (e.g., pencils, crayons, markers, pencil crayons) and rulers, along with drawing paper and a copy of the Learning-Centre Task Card: I Am an Illustrator (1.12.2).

Have each student create and illustrate one page for a big class book titled *We Depend on Each Other*. Each page will depict how an animal helps a plant, or how a plant helps an animal.

Assign one student to create the cover for the book. Bind the pages together and display the book in the classroom or school library.

Alternatively, the pages can be scanned and incorporated into a slide show. In this case, students could also create their pages on the computer.

If possible, have students share the completed book (or slide show) with a grade 1 class studying "Characteristics and Needs of Living Things."

Portage & Main Press, 2017 · *Hands-On Science and Technology* · *Grade 3* · ISBN: 978-1-55379-709-8

## Consolidate and Debrief

- Revisit the guided inquiry question: **How do plants and animals depend on each other?** Have students share their knowledge, provide examples, and ask further inquiry questions.

- Add to the KWHL chart as students learn new concepts, answer some of their own inquiry questions, and ask new inquiry questions.

- Add new terms and illustrations to the class word wall. Include the words in other languages, as appropriate.

- Have students add new terms, definitions, and illustrations to their Science and Technology Glossary (1.1.1). When possible, encourage them to add words (and examples) in other languages, including Indigenous languages, reflective of the classroom population.

## Enhance

- To reinforce plant and animal interdependence, create word cycles with students. For example:

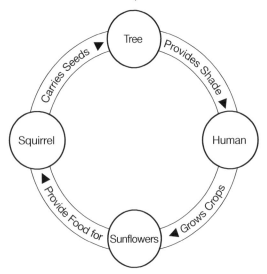

- Play a game version of the preceding word-cycle activity. Give students a deck of index cards, with plant names on some of the cards, and animal names on others. Have students manipulate the cards to make a word cycle. Ask them to explain the connections.

- Use technology to create word cycles and concept maps with connections.

- Discuss the concept of photosynthesis with students. Research and discuss the importance of plants in producing oxygen for animals.

- Read *Plantzilla* by Jerdine Nolen, to students. Have students write a letter from the perspective of Plantzilla.

- Access the interactive activity, Plants and Animals Working Together, in the Grade 3, Unit 1 folder of the ***Hands-On Interactive for Science and Technology, Grade 3*** download. Find this download at: <www.portageandmainpress.com/product/hands-on-interactive-for-science-and-technology-grade-3/>.

- Have students continue their do-it-yourself projects at the Makerspace centre.

Portage & Main Press, 2017 · *Hands-On Science and Technology · Grade 3* · ISBN: 978-1-55379-709-8

# How Do Plants and Animals
# Depend on Each Other?

depends on plants for
_____
_____
_____

depends on plants for
_____
_____
_____

depends on plants for
_____
_____
_____

depends on plants for
_____
_____
_____

depends on animals for
_____
_____
_____

depends on animals for
_____
_____
_____

Portage & Main Press, 2017 · Hands-On Science and Technology · Grade 3 · ISBN: 978-1-55379-709-8

# I Am an Illustrator

You and your classmates have been selected to be the illustrators of a new book called *We Depend On Each Other.*

Draw a picture to show how an animal helps a plant, or how a plant helps an animal.

You may use any of the art materials provided.

Portage & Main Press, 2017 · Hands-On Science and Technology · Grade 3 · ISBN: 978-1-55379-709-8

# 13 | How Do Plants Help Reduce Erosion?

## Information for Teachers

Plants perform many functions that affect both the natural and the human-made environment. For example:

- Along riverbanks, plants help reduce the effects of water on erosion, stabilizing the banks with their roots.
- Plants provide aeration for the soil due to air pockets around their roots.
- Plants provide nutrients when they die, which benefit the environment.
- Plants make gases (oxygen) that are used by animals, including humans, and use up gases (carbon dioxide, which contributes to global warming) that animals produce.
- Marsh plants filter water and improve water quality (riparian areas).

## 21st Century Competencies

**Critical Thinking** and **Communication**: Students will investigate soil erosion through a hands-on investigation, and record their results.

## Materials

- chart paper
- markers
- two aluminum baking pans (one for soil and one for sod, which is a mixture of soil and grass)
- soil
- sod
- metric ruler
- paper cup
- nail or sharp pencil
- permanent marker
- water bucket
- wood block/wedge (5-cm to 15-cm thick)
- toothpicks
- Activity Sheet: Investigating Erosion (1.13.1)
- KWHL chart (from lesson 1)
- Science and Technology Glossary (1.1.1)

## Activate

Review with students the various human uses of plants and plant products. Explain that in addition to being useful to humans, plants also help the environment in many ways. Ask:

- In what ways do plants help the environment?
- What function do trees serve in our local area? In other parts of the world?
- Do you know of any other function plants have in our local area? In other parts of the world?

Record responses on a sheet of chart paper. Ask:

- Have you ever built a sandcastle on the beach?
- What happens to the sandcastle when the waves hit it?
- If you rebuild your sandcastle, can it be exactly the same as before the water touched it?
- What does the term *soil erosion* mean?

Have students share their experiences about castle building. Record their ideas about the meaning of the term *erosion*.

Introduce the guided inquiry question: **How do plants help reduce erosion?**

## Action

**NOTE:** For this activity, you may choose to grow the sod in the pan from seed, starting a few weeks before the time this experiment is due to start. That way, students would see that pans both started with similar soil, and one is now anchored with grass roots.

Explain to students that as they study erosion, they will be looking at one particular way that plants benefit the environment. They will create a model in which tap water represents rainwater

Portage & Main Press, 2017 · *Hands-On Science and Technology · Grade 3* · ISBN: 978-1-55379-709-8

or stream water, and sod and soil represent land. They will also be doing an experiment to find out how soil erosion happens.

Distribute a copy of Activity Sheet: Investigating Erosion (1.13.1) to each student, and use it to introduce and work through the experimental process with students. Discuss the question that will guide the experiment, having students share their ideas for this question. Then, have pairs of students record, on their activity sheets, the purpose of this investigation, in the form of a testable question. For example, "How does soil erosion happen?"

Review the term *prediction*. Briefly explain that during the following experiment, they will pour water over both the soil and the sod to determine the results (what effect water has on each). Encourage students to predict what they think will happen when water is poured over a container of soil and over a container of sod. Have student pairs then record their prediction on the activity sheet.

Fill one of the aluminum baking pans with packed soil until it is two centimetres deep. Use a permanent marker to mark a line at the two-centimetre point on six toothpicks. Push the toothpicks into the soil in three rows. Tilt the pan, and place the wood block underneath it to act as a wedge. Have the bucket nearby.

---

**NOTE:** At this point, the low end of the aluminum pan is best moved to the edge of the table or surface on which it sits, and the bucket placed in position to catch any runoff when water is poured into the pan.

---

Take the paper cup, and use a nail or sharp pencil to poke several holes in the bottom. When filled with water, the cup will simulate a cloud filled with rain. Sprinkle 500 mL of water over the soil, using the bucket to catch the runoff.

Repeat the process with the pan containing the sod.

Next, have students examine the toothpicks in each pan and compare the levels of the soil and sod now to the two-centimetre point on the toothpicks (the level of the soil/sod before the simulated rain).

Have the pairs of students record their observations on their activity sheets, including a labelled diagram. Ask:

- Which eroded more, the soil or the sod?
- Why do you think this happened?
- How did the grass in the sod affect the erosion that occurred?
- Do you think plants help reduce erosion? How?

Examine the sod, focusing on the roots of the grass embedded in the soil. Discuss the role of these roots in securing the soil and reducing erosion.

As a class, have students talk about types of plants they have observed along streams or riverbanks. This can lead to a discussion about bushes, trees, grasses, and marsh plants that help to hold the soil together and slow down the water.

As a class, discuss conclusions of this experiment, as well as their applications to everyday life. Focus on the importance of plants in reducing erosion. Ask:

- How can plants reduce erosion?
- Where could plants help control erosion?

**Activity Sheet**

Directions to students:

Record details of your experiment on erosion in words and/or pictures (1.13.1).

**Assessment of Learning**

Conference with students individually. Have them refer to the erosion experiment and their activity sheets to explain ways plants can be

Portage & Main Press, 2017 · *Hands-On Science and Technology · Grade 3* · ISBN: 978-1-55379-709-8

# 13

used to inhibit erosion. Use the Anecdotal Record sheet, on page 26, to record results for each student.

## Consolidate and Debrief

- Revisit the guided inquiry question: **How do plants help reduce erosion?** Have students share their knowledge, provide examples, and ask further inquiry questions.

- Add to the KWHL chart as students learn new concepts, answer some of their own inquiry questions, and ask new inquiry questions.

- Add new terms and illustrations to the class word wall. Include the words in other languages, as appropriate.

- Have students add new terms, definitions, and illustrations to their Science and Technology Glossary (1.1.1). When possible, encourage them to add words (and examples) in other languages, including Indigenous languages, reflective of the classroom population.

## Enhance

- Use potted plants with various root systems to simulate erosion. Compare the results of the different plants.

- Invite a guest speaker from a local water conservation organization to talk about erosion and plants. Find out if it is possible to have a demonstration with a stream table so students can see how to minimize the effects of erosion. Encourage the speaker to bring any available posters or brochures, or to point out websites that show how to minimize erosion, as well as pictures of reclamation work done with planting and stream stabilization.

- Discuss how the environment is one of the sustainability pillars that must be protected, and plants help to do that.

- Access the interactive activity, Plants and Soil Erosion by Wind, in the Grade 3, Unit 1 folder of the **Hands-On Interactive for Science and Technology, Grade 3** download. Find this download at: <www.portageandmainpress.com/product/hands-on-interactive-for-science-and-technology-grade-3/>.

- Have students continue their do-it-yourself projects at the Makerspace centre.

Portage & Main Press, 2017 · Hands-On Science and Technology · Grade 3 · ISBN: 978-1-55379-709-8

Date: _____    Name: _____

# Investigating Erosion

| Question<br>(what we want to find out) | Prediction<br>(what we think will happen) |
|---|---|
| **Observations**<br>(what happened) | **Labelled Diagram**<br>(of what happened) |

Portage & Main Press, 2017 · Hands-On Science and Technology · Grade 3 · ISBN: 978-1-55379-709-8

# 14 | How Can We Protect Plants?

## 21st Century Competencies

**Creativity**, **Citizenship**, and **Communication**: Students will think about and discuss reasons why plants are important, and ways they can protect plants. Students will then help create a mural that shows the importance of plants in their local community.

## Materials

- *Grandma's Special Feeling* by Karin Clark
- *Jen and the Great One* by Peter Eyvindson
- *The Lorax* by Dr. Seuss
- butcher or mural paper
- art supplies (e.g., crayons, pastels, pencil crayons, paint, markers, glue)
- plant samples (e.g., seeds, twigs, leaves)
- pictures, magazines about jobs related to plants
- glue
- Activity Sheet: Story Map (1.14.1)
- Learning-Centre Task Card: Class Mural (1.14.2)
- KWHL chart (from lesson 1)
- Science and Technology Glossary (1.1.1)

## Activate

Discuss what all living beings need to stay alive. Ask:

- How are animals and plants the same? (Remind students that humans are animals.)
- What do all living things need to stay alive?
- Where do we get our water?
- Where do we get our food?
- Where does a plant get its water and food?

Have students share their ideas and background knowledge.

Read *Grandma's Special Feeling* by Karin Clark. In the story, Grandma takes her grandchildren out into nature to learn about how Indigenous peoples lived long ago. She talks about their cultural history and about how they respected and continue to respect plants for their contributions to humankind. The author also talks about how Indigenous peoples make sure plants will not be over-harvested.

During and after reading, have students discuss cultural practices featured in the book, as well as Indigenous beliefs about respecting and protecting plants.

Introduce the guided inquiry question: **How can we protect plants?**

## Action

Focus on the importance of plants to humans. Ask:

- What do you remember about the different ways plants help humans?
- How do plants help other animals?
- Why are plants important to us?
- How are some plants destroyed naturally? (e.g., weather disasters, forest fires, disease, bugs)
- How are some plants destroyed unnaturally? (e.g., excessive logging, forest fires, deforestation)
- What can we do to replace the plant supply in areas where damage has occurred?
- What would happen if we did not plant new plants and trees?
- What would happen if there were no plants left on Earth?
- How do humans make sure plants are well looked after?
- Who takes care of all the different kinds of plants on Earth?

Portage & Main Press, 2017 · *Hands-On Science and Technology · Grade 3* · ISBN: 978-1-55379-709-8

Portage & Main Press, 2017 · *Hands-On Science and Technology · Grade 3* · ISBN: 978-1-55379-709-8

Discuss various jobs related to plants, such as farmers, tree planters, flower growers, florists, nursery workers, and gardeners.

Read one or both of the following books:

- *Jen and the Great One* by Peter Eyvindson. The story follows Jen and her love of a giant evergreen. The author clearly speaks out against clear-cutting forests, but an equally important message is the determination of a child (Jen) who takes action along with other children.
- *The Lorax* by Dr. Seuss. This story illustrates the importance of sustainable development and how humans must manage their use of plants to ensure survival.

Discuss the characters, events, and messages in the stories. Then, distribute a copy of Activity Sheet: Story Map (1.14.1) to each student. Have students select one of the above books (or *Grandma's Special Feeling,* from the Activate section), record the events of the story, as well as its theme, on the activity sheet.

### Activity Sheet

Directions to students:

Use the story map to record the events (beginning, middle, and end) of the story you chose. Also, describe the theme or main idea of the story (1.14.1).

### Learning Centre

At the learning centre, provide mural paper, art supplies, and a copy of the Learning-Centre Task Card: Class Mural (1.14.2).

Have students create a large two-sided class mural depicting:

- what their local community looks like
- what their local community might look like if all the plants disappeared

## Consolidate and Debrief

- Revisit the guided inquiry question: **How can we protect plants?** Have students share their knowledge, provide examples, and ask further inquiry questions.
- Add to the KWHL chart as students learn new concepts, answer some of their own inquiry questions, and ask new inquiry questions.
- Add new terms and illustrations to the class word wall. Include the words in other languages, as appropriate.
- Have students add new terms, definitions, and illustrations to their Science and Technology Glossary (1.1.1). When possible, encourage them to add words (and examples) in other languages, including Indigenous languages, reflective of the classroom population.

## Enhance

- Have students interview people in the community who have hobbies or careers related to plants. Encourage students to share the results of their interviews with the class.
- Take a field trip to a wildlife centre or conservation area.
- Have students write letters to local government agencies about the importance of preserving and funding wildlife and conservation programs in your community.
- Discuss practical examples of how to protect plants and/or the environment such as tree planting (which many older students do as a summer job), planting shelter belts, or land reclamation projects (e.g., reclaiming land over a garbage dump for green space).

# 14

- Invite an Elder, Métis Senator, or another Indigenous community member to discuss how Indigenous peoples protect and conserve plants for future generations.

- Access the interactive activity, Protecting Plants, in the Grade 3, Unit 1 folder of the ***Hands-On Interactive for Science and Technology, Grade 3*** download. Find this download at: <www.portageandmainpress.com/product/ hands-on-interactive-for-science-and- technology-grade-3/>.

- Have students continue their do-it-yourself projects at the Makerspace centre.

Portage & Main Press, 2017 · *Hands-On Science and Technology · Grade 3* · ISBN: 978-1-55379-709-8

Portage & Main Press, 2017 · *Hands-On Science and Technology* · *Grade 3* · ISBN: 978-1-55379-709-8

**Date:** _____

**Name:** _____

# Story Map

**Book title:** _____

**Author:** _____

**Illustrator:** _____

Beginning

Middle

End

**The theme (main idea) of the story is:** _____

# Class Mural

Create a two-sided mural showing:

- what your local community looks like

- what the local community might look like if all the plants disappeared

Portage & Main Press, 2017 · *Hands-On Science and Technology* · Grade 3 · ISBN: 978-1-55379-709-8

# 15 Inquiry Project: What More Can I Learn About Plant Products?

## 21ˢᵗ Century Competencies

**Critical Thinking**, **Communication**, and **Creativity**: Students will research and communicate their findings about a plant product that is useful and significant to humans.

## Materials

- KWHL chart (from lesson 1)
- all charts and displays from the unit
- all student activity sheets and other work from the unit
- class word wall
- Science and Technology Glossary (1.1.1)
- chart paper
- markers
- scissors
- various books and other resources (e.g., websites) about plants and products made from plants
- computers/tablets with Internet access
- art supplies
- Activity Sheet: Research Outline (1.15.1)
- Learning-Centre Task Card: Sharing My Inquiry Research Project (1.15.2)
- Peer Assessment Slip (1.15.3)

## Activate

In preparation for this final project, revisit the KWHL chart. Discuss the knowledge and questions that students had at the beginning of the unit, as well as those they developed throughout the unit. Discuss the ways they learned new ideas and answered questions.

Also, review students' Science and Technology Glossaries (1.1.1) and the class word wall. Discuss new vocabulary, including scientific terminology, and concepts students have acquired throughout the unit. Have students cut apart the terms in their Science and Technology Glossaries, sequence terms

alphabetically, and then staple or bind the glossaries with a title page.

## Action

Display and review the class list of plant products created in lesson 10, Activate. Explain to students that they will be doing a project on a plant product of their choice.

Introduce the guided inquiry question: **What more can I learn about plant products?**

Have each student select one item from the list of plant products to research.

**NOTE:** Guide the research selections to provide a variety of plant products that are significant for various cultures, including local Indigenous cultures. See the Introduction to this unit for ideas, and consider other plant products introduced throughout lessons.

As a class, identify criteria for students' research. For example:

- Describe the product and its uses to humans.
- Provide a diagram of the plant and product.
- Use at least three sources for your research.
- Display research in an interesting way.

It is valuable for students to have examples to follow, so teachers may consider modelling the expectations by doing a short presentation on a local plant product. This can be prepared ahead of time, or even researched together as a class and presented on chart paper.

Provide resources for students to use in their information gathering. Distribute a copy of Activity Sheet: Research Outline (1.15.1) to each student. Allow students plenty of time to look for relevant resource materials and conduct their research.

Once students have completed their research, have them display their findings in an interesting

Portage & Main Press, 2017 · Hands-On Science and Technology · Grade 3 · ISBN: 978-1-55379-709-8

# 15

way, such as by creating a poster, a book, a brochure, or a slide show.

### Activity Sheet

Directions to students:

Use the research outline to guide your research on your plant product (1.15.1).

### Assessment for Learning

As students begin their research, conference with them individually. Have them share and discuss one research source they plan to use for their project. This is an opportunity to review and assess students' ability to determine the usefulness of resources for research purposes. Use the Individual Student Observations sheet, on page 27, to record results.

### Assessment of Learning

Record the established criteria for the research project on the Rubric, on page 36. When students present their inquiry projects, assess and record results.

## Learning Centre

At the learning centre, display all students' research projects, along with a copy of the Learning-Centre Task Card: Sharing My Inquiry Research Project (1.15.2) and copies of the Peer Assessment Slip (1.15.3).

Have students share their research projects with one or two classmates. Have the classmates use the peer assessment slips to provide feedback.

### Assessment as Learning

Have students complete the 21st Century Competencies Student/Teacher Reflection sheet, on page 33, to reflect on their use of the 21st Century Competencies throughout the unit. Students record their reflections in the rectangles. The sheet also includes oval spaces for teachers to provide descriptive feedback to students.

## Consolidate and Debrief

- Revisit the guided inquiry question: **What more can I learn about plant products?** Have students share their knowledge and provide examples.

- Add to the KWHL chart as students learn new concepts, answer some of their own inquiry questions, and ask new inquiry questions.

- Add new words and illustrations to the class word wall. Also, include the words in other languages, as appropriate.

- Have students add new words and pictures to their Science and Technology Glossary (1.1.1). When possible, encourage them to add words in other languages, including Indigenous languages, reflective of the classroom. Students can create a Growth and Changes in Plants vocabulary booklet by cutting apart the rows on their glossary and arranging them in alphabetical order. They can then make a cover page and bind the pages together.

## Enhance

- Have students complete their do-it-yourself projects at the Makerspace centre.

Portage & Main Press, 2017 · Hands-On Science and Technology · Grade 3 · ISBN: 978-1-55379-709-8

# Research Outline

1. The plant product I have chosen to research is: _____

   _____

2. My question about this plant product is: _____

   _____

   _____

3. Other questions to research:

   - Which plant does the product come from?

   - Where does the plant grow?

   - What part of the plant is used for this product?

   - How is the plant harvested?

   - Being sustainable means there will be enough of the plant for all people to use, now and in the future. Is this plant sustainable? Are harvesters making sure there will be enough plants for the future?

   - How is the product made?

4. You should also include:

   - a diagram of the plant

   - a diagram of the plant product

   - a list of resources you used in your research

5. Present your research in an interesting way—as a book, brochure, poster, slide show, song, game, puppet show, or another idea of your own!

Portage & Main Press, 2017 · Hands-On Science and Technology · Grade 3 · ISBN: 978-1-55379-709-8

# Sharing My Inquiry Research Project

1. Share your inquiry research project with one or two of your classmates.

2. Have your classmate(s) complete a Peer Assessment Slip about your project.

3. Collect the Peer Assessment Slip(s), and keep it (them) with your project.

Portage & Main Press, 2017 · *Hands-On Science and Technology* · Grade 3 · ISBN: 978-1-55379-709-8

# Peer Assessment Slip

My Name: _____

Researcher's Name: _____

Project: _____

What I learned: _____

_____

_____

One thing I liked about the project: _____

_____

One question I have about the project: _____

_____

# Peer Assessment Slip

My Name: _____

Researcher's Name: _____

Project: _____

What I learned: _____

_____

_____

One thing I liked about the project: _____

_____

One question I have about the project: _____

_____

Portage & Main Press, 2017 · Hands-On Science and Technology · Grade 3 · ISBN: 978-1-55379-709-8

# Unit 2

## Strong and Stable Structures

# Introduction

In this unit of *Hands-On Science and Technology, Grade 3*, students explore both human-made and natural structures. They will participate in technological problem solving as they build and test their structures for stability and strength. As students explore and work with many different kinds of materials, structures, and engineering techniques, they will be actively involved in inquiry. They will explore structures they themselves construct, and also structures already present in their own community and in communities around the world. The strength and stability of these structures are linked both to the properties of the materials used and to the particular way the materials are configured and joined together.

**NOTE:** This unit has a strong connection to mathematics, especially in the areas of geometry and measurement. Students may benefit from learning the concepts and topics from this science and technology unit concurrent to the related math strand.

## Planning Tips for Teachers

Students have many opportunities to participate in hands-on activities throughout the unit; they will benefit more from this type of experience than if you merely demonstrate the activities. Organizing the class into small working groups of three or four students is the most productive and beneficial way to manage the activities. Students will also learn from their classmates while working in cooperative groups.

- When working in cooperative groups, assign each student a role, as follows:
  - **leader:** makes sure everyone in the group has an opportunity to share their ideas and opinions
  - **recorder:** records the group's data, research, questions, and any other information on the lesson's sheets/charts
  - **reporter:** reports the group's answers back to the class

- **gopher:** collects and returns all materials needed for each activity
- Contact and set up opportunities for students to meet and interact with guest speakers involved in the fields of architecture, engineering, and/or construction.
- Collect a variety of model-building materials (see the Materials section for each lesson). To promote sustainability, ensure recycled materials are used whenever possible.
- Arrange for local Elders, Métis Senators, or other Indigenous community members to talk about traditional housing, and the tools and materials—both traditional and modern-day—used in building structures in Indigenous communities.
- Collect books, magazines, and images that represent various cultural structures (e.g., pyramids, tipis, igloos, grass huts, longhouses, sod houses), as well as tools and structural art from various cultures (e.g., totem poles, carvings, ceremonial masks). Include as many different genres as possible (e.g., fiction, nonfiction, weird-fact books, riddles, comic books, poetry). Keep these reading materials at the learning centre "Strong and Stable Structures" library where students can refer to them during activities, research, and choice time.
- Review Resources for Students (page 161), and order the books from your school, community, or local education library.
- Read through the different learning centre activities (found in most lessons), and arrange for any necessary materials ahead of time.
- Consider recording each lesson's guided inquiry question (e.g., on a sentence strip) for display throughout related investigations.
- Send a letter home to parents/guardians describing the study in which your students will be involved (structures and materials), and the kinds of materials you will need.

Portage & Main Press, 2017 · *Hands-On Science and Technology · Grade 3* · ISBN: 978-1-55379-709-8

It is recommended that this be done in advance of starting the unit, so there is sufficient time to collect all required materials.

■ Develop a Makerspace centre. Classroom Makerspaces are usually designed as centres where students learn together and collaborate on do-it-yourself projects. Students are given the opportunity to work with a variety of age-appropriate tools, as well as with everyday and recycled materials. Additionally, arts-and-crafts are often integrated into Makerspace offerings.

For this unit, set up a Makerspace centre in your classroom that encourages informal learning about materials and structures Include general materials, such as those listed in the Introduction to **Hands-On Science and Technology, Grade 3**, as well as unit-specific materials (e.g., umbrellas, nests, honeycombs, photos of animal-made structures such as beaver dams and spider webs).

⚠️ **SAFETY NOTE:** Engage in a discussion about the safety and respect of a Makerspace with students before beginning this unit. Consider small parts and potential hazards for students of all ages and abilities who will have access to the Makerspace area. At this age, this exploration needs to be supervised.

Do-it-yourself projects may include anything related to the concepts in this unit. Projects students might initiate include (but are not limited to) the following:

■ building a model structure out of sugar cubes, LEGO, and so on

■ using cardboard to build a structure that can hold the most weight possible

■ building a model of an animal's home (e.g., beaver dam, bird's nest)

■ creating a new storage structure for plastic bags

■ building the tallest structure possible out of a specified amount of supplies (e.g., LEGO, cardboard).

■ creating a structure out of cardboard that will balance on one point (such as a pencil)

■ using wood dowels and cardboard to create a truss structure (Use clay for the gussets.)

■ attempting the Marshmallow Challenge: Build the tallest freestanding structure possible out of 20 sticks of spaghetti, 90 centimetres of tape, 90 centimetres of string, and one marshmallow. The marshmallow needs to be on top.

■ constructing a shoe that will protect the soles of your feet

■ constructing something portable that will protect you from the elements (e.g., rain, sun)

Literacy connections that might inspire projects include the following:

■ *Those Shoes* by Maribeth Boelts

■ *Shoes for Me!* by Sue Fliess

■ *Pete the Cat: I Love My White Shoes* by Eric Litwin

■ *Ella's Umbrellas* by Jennifer Lloyd

■ *Iggy Peck, Architect* by Andrea Beaty

■ *Dreaming Up: A Celebration of Building* by Christy Hale

■ *If I Built a House* by Chris Van Dusen

■ *Young Frank, Architect* by Frank Viva

■ *Pop's Bridge* by Eve Bunting

■ *Twenty-One Elephants and Still Standing* by April Jones Prince

■ *The Three Little Pigs: An Architectural Tale* by Steven Guarnaccia

As inquiry questions are posed with each lesson, you will find these questions inspire other do-it-yourself projects related to the unit. Students may determine solutions to these questions through the creating they do at the Makerspace centre. It is important to not direct the learning here; simply create the conditions for the learning to happen.

Portage & Main Press, 2017 · Hands-On Science and Technology · Grade 3 · ISBN: 978-1-55379-709-8

## Indigenous Worldviews

Teachers are reminded of the value of incorporating Indigenous perspectives and worldviews into lessons whenever possible. Exploration may focus on both traditional and modern Indigenous communities in Canada and across North America, including housing and materials used in various Indigenous cultures. Students may also be exposed to modern structures and art by Indigenous architects and engineers such as Douglas Cardinal. Students may also explore other structures around the world (e.g., pyramids and other structures built by the Maya, Aztecs, Inca, mound builders).

Traditionally, people were very connected to and reliant on the natural environment to provide what they needed for shelter. Their choices in the materials they used and the structures they built reflected this—using only materials that were readily available in the local natural community, and without depleting resources. The types of homes they built also depended on the local weather from which they needed shelter, and on their own mobility. Indigenous groups that moved according to the seasons tended to build tipis or wigwams as their homes; these were made of animal skins, and were easy to dismantle and move. Other Indigenous groups that maintained more permanent villages year-round used less portable materials such as logs, bark, grass, and earth.

Modern Indigenous architecture continues to display a profound respect for nature and environmental stewardship as traditional worldviews are infused into modern building designs and structural forms. Today, an amalgamation of Indigenous and Western science bridges the gap between traditional and contemporary building practice and intelligence in Canada.

## Science and Technology Vocabulary

Throughout this unit, teachers should use, and encourage students to use, vocabulary such as:

- *balance, brace, design feature, durable, flexible, force, foundation, frame structure, function, human-built structure, joint, material, natural structure, shape, stability, strength, structure, sturdy*

In lesson 1, students start a Science and Technology Glossary in which they record new vocabulary introduced throughout the unit. Also in lesson 1, teachers create a class word wall for the unit. The word wall can be created on a bulletin board or simply on a sheet of poster paper, so as not to take up too much space. On the bulletin board or poster paper, record new vocabulary as it is introduced throughout the unit. Ensure the word wall is placed in a location where all students can see it and access the words.

Teachers should also consider including vocabulary related to scientific inquiry skills, including terms such as:

- *access, ask, brainstorm, collect, compare, connect, consider, construct, cooperate, create, describe, develop, diagram, display, draw, estimate, examine, explain, explore, find, follow, graph, improve, identify, investigate, label, measure, modify, observe, order, plan, predict, recognize, record, repeat, research, respond, retest, select, sequence, test*

These terms might be displayed in the classroom as they relate to inquiry skills used throughout the year. Students can then brainstorm which skills they are using as they work through particular lessons. They could also discuss what the skill looks and sounds like as they explore and investigate.

Portage & Main Press, 2017 · Hands-On Science and Technology · Grade 3 · ISBN: 978-1-55379-709-8

# Unit Overview

| Fundamental Concepts | Big Ideas |
|---|---|
| Structure and Function<br><br>Matter | ■ A structure has both form and function.<br><br>■ Structures are affected by forces acting on them.<br><br>■ Structures need to be strong and stable to be useful. |

## Overall Expectations

By the end of Grade 3, students will:

1. Assess the importance of form, function, strength, and stability in structures through time.
2. Investigate strong and stable structures to determine how their design and materials enable them to perform their load-bearing function.
3. Demonstrate an understanding of the concepts of structure, strength, and stability and the factors that affect them.

Portage & Main Press, 2017 · Hands-On Science and Technology · Grade 3 · ISBN: 978-1-55379-709-8

# Curriculum Correlation

| Specific Expectation | Lesson | | | | | | | | | | |
|---|---|---|---|---|---|---|---|---|---|---|---|
| | 1 | 2 | 3 | 4 | 5 | 6 | 7 | 8 | 9 | 10 | 11 |
| **1. Relating Science and Technology to Society and the Environment** | | | | | | | | | | | |
| **1.1** Assess effects of strong and stable structures on society and the environment. | | √ | | | | | √ | √ | √ | | √ |
| **1.2** Assess the environmental impact of structures built by various animals and those built by humans. | | √ | | | | | √ | √ | √ | | √ |
| **2. Developing Investigation and Communication Skills** | | | | | | | | | | | |
| **2.1** Follow established safety procedures during science and technology investigations. | √ | √ | √ | √ | √ | √ | √ | √ | √ | √ | √ |
| **2.2** Investigate, through experimentation, how various materials and construction techniques can be used to add strength to structures. | | | | √ | √ | √ | | | | | |
| **2.3** Investigate, through experimentation, the effects of pushing, pulling, and other forces on the shape and stability of simple structures. | | | | √ | √ | √ | | | | | |
| **2.4** Use technological problem-solving skills, and knowledge acquired from previous investigations, to design and build a strong and stable structure that serves a purpose. | | | | | | | | | | √ | |
| **2.5** Use appropriate science and technology vocabulary, including *compression, tension, strut, ties, strength,* and *stability*, in oral and written communication. | √ | √ | √ | √ | √ | √ | √ | √ | √ | √ | √ |
| **2.6** Use a variety of forms to communicate with different audiences and for a variety of purposes. | √ | √ | √ | √ | √ | √ | √ | √ | √ | √ | √ |
| **3. Understanding Basic Concepts** | | | | | | | | | | | |
| **3.1** Define a structure as a supporting framework, with a definite size, shape, and purpose, that holds a load. | √ | | | | | | | | | | |
| **3.2** Identify structures in the natural environment and in the built environment. | | √ | | | | | √ | √ | | | √ |
| **3.3** Identify the strength of a structure as its ability to support a load. | √ | | | | √ | | | | | | |
| **3.4** Identify the stability of a structure as its ability to maintain balance and stay fixed in one spot. | √ | | | | √ | √ | | | | | |
| **3.5** Identify properties of materials that need to be considered when building structures. | | | √ | | | | | | | | |
| **3.6** Describe ways in which the strength of different materials can be altered. | | | | √ | √ | √ | | | | | |
| **3.7** Describe ways to improve a structure's strength and stability. | | | | √ | √ | √ | | | | | |
| **3.8** Explain how strength and stability enable a structure to perform a specific function. | | | | √ | √ | √ | | | | | |
| **3.9** Describe ways in which different forces can affect the shape, balance, or position of structures. | | | | √ | √ | √ | | | | | |
| **3.10** Identify the role of struts and ties in structures under load. | | | | √ | √ | √ | | | | | |

Portage & Main Press, 2017 · *Hands-On Science and Technology · Grade 3* · ISBN: 978-1-55379-709-8

# Resources for Students

Ames, Lee J. *Draw 50 Buildings and Other Structures: The Step-by-Step Way to Draw Castles and Cathedrals, Skyscrapers and Bridges, and So Much More.* New York: Watson-Guptill Publications, 2013.

Beaty, Andrea. *Rosie Revere, Engineer.* New York: Abrams Books for Young Readers, 2013.

_____. *Iggy Peck, Architect.* New York: Abrams Books for Young Readers, 2007.

Boelts, Maribeth. *Those Shoes.* Cambridge, MA: Candlewick Press, 2009.

Brown, Margaret Wise. *The Important Book.* New York: HarperCollins, 1999.

Bunting, Eve. *Pop's Bridge.* Orlando, FL: Harcourt, 2006.

Camm, Martin and Kate Scarborough. *A Wasp Builds a Nest: See Inside a Paper Wasp's Nest and Watch It Grow.* Richmond Hill, ON: Firefly Books, 2016.

Fliess, Sue. *Shoes for Me!* New York: Amazon Children's Publishing - Two Lions, 2011.

Goble, Paul. *Tipi: Home of the Nomadic Buffalo Hunters.* Bloomington, Indiana: World Wisdom, Inc., 2007.

Guarnaccia, Steven. *The Three Little Pigs: An Architectural Tale.* New York: Abrams Books for Young Readers, 2010.

Hale, Christy. *Dreaming Up: A Celebration of Building.* New York: Lee & Low Books, 2012.

Hoberman, Mary Ann. *A House Is a House for Me.* New York: Puffin, 2007.

Hurley, Michael. *The World's Most Amazing Skyscrapers.* Landmark Top Ten series. Chicago: Raintree, 2012.

Kalman, Bobbie. *Life in a Longhouse Village.* St. Catharines, ON: Crabtree, 2001.

Knight, Margy Burns. *Talking Walls: Discover Your World.* Thomaston, ME: Tilbury House Publishers, 2014.

Litwin, Eric. *Pete the Cat: I Love My White Shoes.* New York: HarperCollins, 2010.

Lloyd, Jennifer. *Ella's Umbrellas.* Vancouver, BC: Simply Read Books, 2010.

Malam, John. *Super Structures.* Chicago: Children's Press, 2000.

Manning, Jack. *Longhouses.* North Mankato, MN: Capstone Press, 2015.

Meuse, Theresa. *L'nu'k: The People.* Nanaimo, BC: Strong Nations, 2016.

Mitcham, Allison. *Glooscap, the Beavers and the Sugarloaf Mountain.* Nanaimo, BC: Strong Nations, 2012.

Nabokov, Peter, and Robert Easton. *Native American Architecture.* New York: Oxford University Press, 1995.

Oberman, Sheldon. *The White Stone in the Castle Wall.* Montreal: Tundra, 1996.

Pettipas, Katherine, and Leo Pettipas. *Indigenous Dwellings of Canada: A Colouring Book.* Winnipeg: Manitoba First Nations Education Resource Centre, 2014.

Prince, April Jones. *Twenty-One Elephants and Still Standing.* Boston: Houghton Mifflin, 2005.

Ulmer, Michael. *The Gift of the Inuksuk.* Ann Arbor, MI: Sleeping Bear Press, 2004.

Van Dusen, Chris. *If I Built a House.* New York: Dial Books for Young Readers, 2012.

Viva, Frank. *Young Frank, Architect.* New York: Museum of Modern Art, 2013.

▶

Portage & Main Press, 2017 · *Hands-On Science and Technology · Grade 3* · ISBN: 978-1-55379-709-8

# Websites and Online Videos

## Websites

- **www.aboriginalaccess.ca/kids**
  Aboriginal Access to Engineering—Kids: Students can go to this website to play games, read about role models who are engineers, and learn more about the different areas of engineering.

- **cac.mcgill.ca/bland/building/arch101.htm**
  Canadian Architecture 101—McGill University: Canada's architectural history and its use of regional materials, including photographs. Click on different provinces and territories to read about their architectural history.

- **www.epsea.org/adobe.html**
  El Paso Solar Energy Association—Adobe: Information on the construction of adobe houses, the materials used, and the history of this type of structure. Links to straw bale homes, resources on energy efficiency, and solar heating encourage further reading.

- **www.thecanadianencyclopedia.ca/en/article/architectural-history-early-first-nations**
  Architectural History—Indigenous Peoples: This site provides information about Indigenous building traditions.

- **www.freelang.net/online/ojibwe.php**
  FREELANG—Ojibwe-English-Ojibwe online dictionary: An online dictionary to translate words between Ojibwe and English.

- **https://www.ontario.ca/environment-and-energy/find-pits-and-quarries**
  Government of Ontario—Find Pits and Quarries: This site allows you to learn about limestone pits and quarries in Ontario, using interactive maps.

- **greatstructures.info**
  Great Structures of the World: View pictures and descriptions of great structures around the world organized by continent. Information includes length of construction period, height, weight, and GPS coordinates.

- **arc.lib.montana.edu/indian-great-plains/wilber-legends.php**
  Indian Peoples of the Northern Great Plains: Stories from the Blackfoot nation about tipi design and traditions.

- **www.greatdreams.com/native/nativehsg.htm#PIT**
  Native American Housing: A rich collection of histories about North American housing among Indigenous populations.

- **www.creedictionary.com**
  NEHIYAW MASINAHIKAN Online Cree Dictionary: An online dictionary to translate words between Cree and English.

- **ojibwe.lib.umn.edu**
  The Ojibwe People's Dictionary: An online dictionary to translate words between Ojibwe and English.

- **www.ScienceU.com**
  Science U: Learn more about geometry at the geometry centre or explore the library and observatory. This website includes interactive activities (with QuickTime VR), activities for the classroom, facts and figures, and more.

- **www.exploratorium.edu/structures**
  Structures Around the World—Activities for the Elementary Classroom: Hands-on activities investigating scale and structure.

- **www.susankae.com/Tipi%20diorama%20instructions%20and%20pattern.pdf**
  Archaeology Education & Illustrations by Susan K. Nelson—Tipi diorama instructions: A template and instructions for children to create their own tipis.

Portage & Main Press, 2017 · Hands-On Science and Technology · Grade 3 · ISBN: 978-1-55379-709-8

- **www.whyzz.com/how-do-the-joints-in-our-body-work**

  Whyzz—How do the joints in our body work?: A brief explanation of the different kinds of joints in the body and their functions.

- **pbskids.org/games/engineering/**

  PBS Kids—Engineering Games: A variety of different games that focus on engineering and structures.

- **www.wisegeek.com/what-happens-to-recycled-plastic-bags.htm**

  wiseGEEK—What Happens to Recycled Plastic Bags?: Investigate how plastic bags are made into strong composite lumber.

- **www.aboriginalaccess.ca/sites/aboriginalaccess.ca/files/GRADETHREEunitPLANFINAL5.pdf**

  Aboriginal Access—Grade Three Unit Plan—Strong and Stable Structures: A unit on bridges by Aboriginal Access to Engineering at Queen's University. This unit covers the Understanding Structures and Mechanisms strand, Strong and Stable Structures, through use of culturally representative Indigenous stories and learning materials.

- **pbskids.org/designsquad/pdf/parentseducators/DS_Act_Guide_Lead_PaperTable.pdf**

  PBS Kids—Paper Table: Investigate how to make rolled-up newspapers into a sturdy paper table.

- **https://mfnerc.org/product/indigenous-dwellings-of-canada-a-colouring-book/**

  Manitoba First Nations Education Resource Centre, Inc.—Indigenous Dwellings of Canada: A Colouring Book: This resource explores the many different homes and cultures of Indigenous peoples in Canada, past and present.

- **www.djcarchitect.com/work/**

  Douglas Cardinal Architect: A website dedicated to the work of architect Douglas Cardinal. This site includes photos of different buildings that he has designed.

- **www.mohawkironworkers.com/**

  This is the website for the documentary series *Mohawk Ironworkers*. Includes trailers, video clips, and a game.

## Videos

- **https://www.youtube.com/watch?v=12Z1LD0_uaY**

  "Animal Homes (1955)." A/V Geeks (11:13).

- **https://www.youtube.com/watch?v=yJjaQExOPPY**

  "How Beavers Build Dams." PBS (2:32).

- **www.learnalberta.ca/content/wonbt/html/index.html?launch=true**

  This interactive animated video shows how to set up a tipi.

- **https://www.youtube.com/watch?v=9bKQeoNrciQ**

  "Top 10 Animal Architects And The Beautiful Homes They Build." facts@web (2:21).

- **http://www.aboriginalaccess.ca/kids/learning-modules/bear-paw-trail**

  In this video, students can listen to stories and play games to learn about engineers and natural structures.

- **https://www.pbslearningmedia.org/resource/nat15.sci.lisci.anihome/habitat-animal-homes/#.WWZ_pYjyuUl**

  Habitat: Animal Homes—Learn about how animals utilize what's in their habitat to build their homes—and how they construct their shelters to stay alive.

Portage & Main Press, 2017 · *Hands-On Science and Technology · Grade 3* · ISBN: 978-1-55379-709-8

# 1 | What Is a Structure?

## Information for Teachers

A structure is a stationary framework of interconnecting solid materials that can endure forces such as gravity and wind. Human-made structures are also generally built to withstand weight, moisture, and pressure. Whether natural or human-made, structures are all around us and include anything from footstools to beaver dams to skyscrapers to mountains. Most human-made structures have specific functions or purposes, and humans use structures every day for many different reasons.

## 21ˢᵗ Century Competencies

**Critical Thinking** and **Communication**: Students will look at similarities and differences between different structures, and develop a working definition of what a structure is.

## Materials

- Image Bank: Human-Made and Natural Structures (see Appendix, page 431)
- projection device or computer/tablet with Internet access
- large sticky notes
- pencil crayons
- chart paper
- student dictionaries
- markers (various colours)
- *Indigenous Dwellings of Canada: A Colouring Book* by Katherine Pettipas and Leo Pettipas
- Activity Sheet: Science and Technology Glossary (2.1.1)

## Activate

Display the images from Image Bank: Human-Made and Natural Structures. Have students look at the pictures without discussing them. Ask:

- What do all the pictures have in common? (There are many possible answers here

including: all are structures; all are made of materials; someone/something built them.)
- How are they different? (Some are human-made, some are found/made in nature, they are made from/of different materials, they have different shapes, they are used for different purposes.)
- What do you think you will be learning about next in science and technology?

Introduce the guided inquiry question: **What is a structure?**

## Action: Part One

Provide each student with large sticky notes. On chart paper, write: "What is a structure?" in the middle of the sheet and circle it. Brainstorm a few possible answers with students to model the activity. Encourage students to look again at the images used during the Activate activity and identify some of the characteristics of structures. Then, ask students to write or draw their answers to the question on a sticky note. If students have more than one idea, have them record or illustrate each idea or example of a structure on a separate sticky note.

When all students have completed at least one sticky note, have them come up to the chart paper one by one, affix their note to a blank area, and read aloud their written answer or interpret their drawing for the class.

Next, organize students into working groups of two or three, and ask the groups to come up to the chart paper one by one and arrange the sticky notes into groups. Allow time for students to examine the notes on the chart paper and discuss.

Have the groups report their ideas to the class. Some possibilities for organizing the information include: by materials, by examples (of structures), and by purpose.

Portage & Main Press, 2017 · *Hands-On Science and Technology · Grade 3 ·* ISBN: 978-1-55379-709-8

**Hands-On Science and Technology • Grade 3**

Have students decide together on class labels for organizing the information, and record these directly on the chart paper. Move the sticky notes into the correct locations to create a concept map. Groups of sticky notes can be circled.

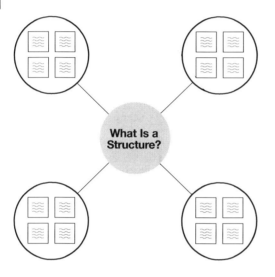

Once the concept map is complete, come up with a class definition for the term *structure*. Have students compare this definition with the one found in their dictionaries. Display the final definition in a visible area of the classroom for reference throughout the unit.

Now, ask students to write on a separate sticky note one question they have about structures. Have students share these questions with a partner or the whole class before affixing them to a separate sheet of chart paper labelled "Questions I Have About Structures."

As students share their questions, discuss ways they might find the answers to these questions. Encourage them to consider a wide variety of ways to learn new ideas or to answer scientific and technological questions. For example, they could do the following:

- Conduct experiments.
- Explore materials, and make observations.

- Use classroom resources (e.g., books, posters).
- Invite guest speakers to the classroom.
- Invite community members and family members to the classroom.
- Take field trips.
- Watch videos/DVDs.
- Research websites and blogs.
- Research library resources.
- Research resources from home (e.g., books, artifacts, family experts).
- Write letters to experts.
- Go on community walks.
- Take and/or research photographs.

Encourage students to continue to add to the concept map throughout the unit as they answer some of their own inquiry questions, ask more inquiry questions, find additional examples of structures, discover new materials from which structures can be made, learn new functions of structures, and so on.

Distribute several copies of Activity Sheet: Science and Technology Glossary (2.1.1) to each student, and have students begin their Science and Technology Glossary for the unit. Have students record the term *structure*, along with a definition and an illustration. At the end of the unit, students can cut apart the rows, alphabetize their words, and create a booklet of vocabulary related to structures and materials.

**NOTE:** The Science and Technology Glossary presents an excellent opportunity to celebrate cultural diversity by having students include words in other languages. Students may include terms in Indigenous languages or other languages spoken at home.

A variety of online dictionaries may be used as a source for translations. For example:
- ojibwe.lib.umn.edu
- www.freelang.net/online/mohawk.php

Online dictionaries are also available for other languages that may be reflective of the class population.

Portage & Main Press, 2017 · *Hands-On Science and Technology · Grade 3* · ISBN: 978-1-55379-709-8

**1**

**Activity Sheet**

Directions to students:

Begin your Science and Technology Glossary for the unit. Record the term *structure,* and include a definition and illustration (2.1.1).

## Action: Part Two

Display the Indigenous Stuctures from the Image Bank again (see Appendix, page 432). Examine each image carefully, and discuss its features. Ask:

- What do you think this structure is?
- What do you think it was used for?
- What do you think it was made of?
- How do you think it was built?

Have students share their ideas and background knowledge. Also, generate inquiry questions about these structures for further investigation.

A valuable resource for further research is *Indigenous Dwellings of Canada: A Colouring Book* by Katherine and Leo Pettipas (available at: <https://mfnerc.org/product/indigenous-dwellings-of-canada-a-colouring-book/>. This resource explores the many different homes and cultures of Indigenous peoples in Canada, past and present. The black-line illustrations include researched details and stories about various Indigenous homes.

## Consolidate and Debrief

- Revisit the guided inquiry question: **What is a structure?** Have students share their knowledge, provide examples, and ask further inquiry questions.
- Add to the concept map as students learn new concepts, answer some of their own inquiry questions, and ask new inquiry questions.
- Begin a class word wall to display new terminology (and illustrations) introduced throughout the unit. Also, include the terms

in other languages reflective of the classroom makeup when possible, including both Indigenous languages and other languages spoken at home by students' families.

## Enhance

- Explore the following website: <www.aboriginalaccess.ca/sites/aboriginalaccess.ca/files/GRADETHREEunitPLANFINAL5.pdf>. This unit, by Aboriginal Access to Engineering at Queen's University, covers the Understanding Structures and Mechanisms strand, Strong and Stable Structures, through use of culturally representative Indigenous stories and learning materials.

- Read the book, *The Gift of the Inuksuk,* by Michael Ulmer.

- Have students create digital glossaries in Google Docs or Microsoft Word. For each term introduced, have students draw a text box in a Word document, record the term and a definition for it, and then add an illustration or picture. For the latter, students may want to use a computer program such as Kid Pix to draw digital pictures, insert clip art pictures in Word, copy and paste pictures from websites, or draw their pictures by hand and have them scanned.

**NOTE:** If students are copying and pasting pictures from websites, take the opportunity to educate them about copyright with regards to photos and drawings. Explain that it is okay to copy, paste, and print online photos for personal use. However, they may not do this for mass distribution, or for selling a product in which the photo or picture is being used. The Creative Commons Canada website may also be a useful resource: <https://ca.creativecommons.org/>.

- Collect and examine photos of structures made from recycled materials (e.g., a house made with reclaimed brick, a tire swing, a tire-climbing structure, backyard decking made from recycled tire rubber). Investigate how the materials are recycled, how the structures are made, and discuss the importance of reusing and recycling.

- Have students begin their do-it-yourself projects at the Makerspace centre. (See page 18 in the Introduction to **Hands-On Science and Technology, Grade 3** and page 157 of the Introduction to this unit for details on setting up the Makerspace centre.)

Portage & Main Press, 2017 · *Hands-On Science and Technology · Grade 3* · ISBN: 978-1-55379-709-8

# Science and Technology Glossary

| Definition | Term | Illustration |
|---|---|---|
| Definition | Term | Illustration |
| Definition | Term | Illustration |
| Definition | Term | Illustration |

Portage & Main Press, 2017 · Hands-On Science and Technology · Grade 3 · ISBN: 978-1-55379-709-8

# 2 | Where Are Structures Found?

## 21ˢᵗ Century Competencies

**Critical Thinking** and **Communication:**
Students will analyze various structures in their local environment, and determine the function, materials, and design attributes of the structures.

## Materials

- chart paper
- markers
- pencils
- clipboards
- digital cameras
- chair
- Image Bank: Structures (see Appendix, page 435)
- drawing/colouring utensils (e.g., pencil crayons, markers)
- Activity Sheet: Structure Hunt (2.2.1)
- Learning-Centre Task Card: Create a Concept Web (2.2.2)
- magazines, store flyers, and catalogues that show pictures of various structures
- computers/tablets with Internet access (optional)
- printer (optional)
- scissors
- glue
- large sheets of poster or mural paper
- concept map (from lesson 1)
- Science and Technology Glossary (2.1.1)

## Activate

As a class, take a community walk to identify structures. Have students make notes about the structures they see and take photographs of the structures to use throughout the unit. Have students look at playgrounds, dwellings, businesses, bridges, and other structures.

Back in the classroom, have students share their notes and examine photographs. Have students discuss the function(s) of various structures, as well as the design features and materials used in each structure.

Introduce the guided inquiry question: **Where are structures found?**

## Action: Part One

As a class, review the previous lesson. Ask:

- What is a structure?

On chart paper, construct a chart for recording students' ideas. Title the chart as in the following example:

| Structure | Function | Material(s) | Design Feature |
|-----------|----------|-------------|----------------|
| staircase | for getting from one floor to another | steel, wood | must be sturdy |

Now, ask:

- What kinds of structures do you find inside our school?

Record students' responses in the first column under "Structure."

---

**NOTE:** It is important for students to understand that not all structures are buildings; many structures are much smaller than buildings (e.g., furniture, window and door frames, playground equipment, fences, park benches). All of these structures are designed for specific uses.

---

Discuss what the term *function* means. Ask:

- What is the function of each structure listed on the chart?

Record students' responses in the second column under "Function." Ask:

- What material(s) make up each structure?

►

---

Strong and Stable Structures

Portage & Main Press, 2017 · *Hands-On Science and Technology · Grade 3* · ISBN: 978-1-55379-709-8

Record students' responses in the third column, under "Material(s)."

## Action: Part Two

Display Image Bank: Structures (see Appendix, page 435). Also, display an actual chair, and ask students:

- What is the function of a chair?
- What material was used to make this chair?
- Do you think the chair is safe to use? Why?
- What would make the chair unsafe to use?
- Is the chair designed to meet its function?
- Is it comfortable?
- What improvements would you make to the chair, if you could?
- What are important design features to consider when building a chair? (It must be strong enough to support weight, and balanced so it does not fall over. Comfort is also an important design consideration.)

Record students' ideas in the fourth column, under "Design Feature," on the chart created in the Activate section.

Repeat these questions for the picture of a wigwam. Ask:

- What is the function of a wigwam?
- Why is it built in a dome shape?
- Why do you think Indigenous peoples living in the Eastern Woodlands built wigwams this way?
- What materials do you think they used?
- What design features do you think would have been considered when building a wigwam?
- Can you think of any problems or challenges the wigwam's structure or materials could have caused for Indigenous peoples?

Again, record students' ideas on the chart. Repeat the same questions for other structures (e.g., house, desk, play structure), recording all ideas on the chart.

## Action: Part Three

⚠ **SAFETY NOTE:** For the following activity, students will be exploring the school yard, school grounds, and areas directly adjacent to and visible from the school. It is important for teachers to find two or three other adults (e.g., parents, educational assistants) to help supervise all students and keep them in designated areas.

Explain to students that in pairs or groups of three, they will be going on a "structure hunt" outside and near the school (i.e., in the school yard, on the school grounds, and in areas directly adjacent to and visible from the school). Students will find structures, decide on the purpose(s) or function(s) of each structure, and determine materials from which each is made.

Distribute a copy of Activity Sheet: Structure Hunt (2.2.1) to each student, as well as clipboards, pencils or pens, and digital cameras. Have students record the structures they find during the structure hunt in writing, by drawing pictures, or by taking photographs. Also, have them record their ideas about the function of each structure and the materials from which it is made. Remind students that structures include more than just buildings.

**NOTE:** Teachers may consider distributing two copies of the activity sheet to each student to accommodate a greater number of structures.

At the end of the hunt, gather students together to discuss the activity. Ask:

- What structures did you find?
- Did you find anything that surprised you?
- Was it difficult to describe some of the structures you found (e.g., tool shed, sandbox, goal post)?
- What are some of the materials used to make the structures?

▶

Portage & Main Press, 2017 · Hands-On Science and Technology · Grade 3 · ISBN: 978-1-55379-709-8

- Did any group include an example of a natural structure (not built by humans)? Why or why not?

### Activity Sheet

Directions to students:

During the structure hunt, use words, draw pictures, or take digital photographs to record the structures you find. Also, record your ideas about the function of each structure you find and the materials from which it is made (2.2.1).

## Learning Centre

At the learning centre, provide magazines and store flyers, catalogues, computers/tablets with Internet access, a printer (if available), scissors, glue, large sheets of poster or mural paper, and a copy of the Learning-Centre Task Card: Create a Concept Web (2.2.2).

Have students choose a location where structures are commonly found (e.g., house, classroom, park). Then, have them look through the magazines and/or search online to find pictures of structures found in their chosen location. Tell students to print or cut out their pictures and use them to create a concept web on a sheet of poster/mural paper. Remind students to label each structure and to record the materials from which each structure is made.

### Assessment for Learning

Observe students as they work at the learning centre. Focus on their conceptual understanding of structures, and on their ability to identify structures in visual representations. Use the Individual Student Observations sheet, on page 27, to record results.

## Consolidate and Debrief

- Revisit the guided inquiry question: **Where are structures found?** Have students share their knowledge, provide examples, and ask further inquiry questions.

- Add to the concept web as students learn new concepts, answer some of their own inquiry questions, and ask new inquiry questions.

- Add new terms and illustrations to the class word wall. Also, include the words in other languages, as appropriate.

- Have students add new terms, definitions, and illustrations to their Science and Technology Glossary (2.1.1). When possible, encourage them to add words (and examples) in other languages, including Indigenous languages, reflective of the classroom population.

## Enhance

- Have students repeat the structure hunt at home. Distribute new copies of Activity Sheet: Structure Hunt (2.2.1) for them to record their findings.

- Visit other locations in the community (e.g., arena, park, corner store, theatre), and have students do another structure hunt at those places.

- Challenge students to find and/or think of structures that are made of or include recycled materials.

- Have students continue their do-it-yourself projects at the Makerspace centre.

Portage & Main Press, 2017 · *Hands-On Science and Technology · Grade 3* · ISBN: 978-1-55379-709-8

# Structure Hunt

| Structure | Function | Material(s) |
|---|---|---|
|  |  |  |
|  |  |  |
|  |  |  |
|  |  |  |
|  |  |  |
|  |  |  |
|  |  |  |
|  |  |  |

Portage & Main Press, 2017 · Hands-On Science and Technology · Grade 3 · ISBN: 978-1-55379-709-8

# Create a Concept Web

1. Choose a location where structures are found (e.g., house, bedroom, classroom, park, arena).

2. Look in magazines, flyers, and catalogues, or on the Internet for pictures of structures found in the location you have chosen.

3. Print or cut out the pictures.

4. On a large sheet of paper, draw a concept web. In the centre, record the name of your location, and circle it.

5. Glue your pictures of structures around the centre circle. Label each structure with its name.

6. Next to each structure, record the material(s) from which it is made.

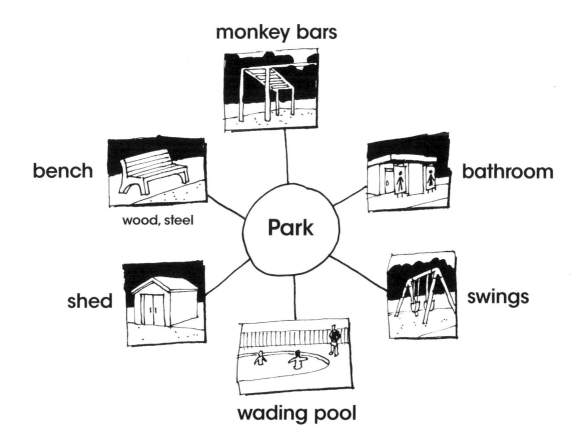

Portage & Main Press, 2017 · Hands-On Science and Technology · Grade 3 · ISBN: 978-1-55379-709-8

# 3 | Which Materials Are Stronger Than Others?

## 21st Century Competencies

**Critical Thinking**, **Collaboration**, and **Communication:** Students will examine the strength of different materials. They will also collaborate to create a poster that highlights the amazing strength of spider silk.

## Materials

- chart paper
- markers
- pencils
- drinking straws
- string
- Scotch tape
- glue
- scissors
- books (for stacking)
- drinking cups
- small weights (e.g., gram weights, coins, marbles, large washers)
- small twigs/sticks, approximately the same diameter and length as the straws (These can be collected by students anytime, or, as a class, take a walk around the community. Ensure students do not break off branches from live trees.)
- grasses, vines, and other natural materials
- writing paper (cut into 22.5-cm x 30-cm pieces)
- construction paper (cut into 22.5-cm x 30-cm pieces)
- sturdy tag board (cut into 22.5-cm x 30-cm pieces)
- masking tape
- paper plates (three for each working group of students)
- large sheets of graph paper (optional)
- rulers
- Activity Sheet A: Testing the Strength of Straws (2.3.1)

- Centimetre Graph Paper (2.3.2)
- Activity Sheet B: Testing the Strength of Paper (2.3.3)
- *Storm Maker's Tipi,* a book by Paul Goble
- "Setting up a Cree Tipi" (online interactive video available at: <www.learnalberta.ca/content/wonbt/html/index.html?launch=true>)
- materials (as determined by students) for building model tipis (e.g., sticks, twigs, bulrushes, or other plant stems as poles; grass or vines to tie the poles together; leather, suede, or other natural materials to cover the frame)
- electric fan
- watering can and access to water
- centimetre rulers
- digital camera (optional)
- computer/tablet with Internet access
- Activity Sheet C: Building a Tipi (2.3.4)
- Learning-Centre Task Card: Just How Strong Is a Spider's Web? (2.3.5)
- Reference Cards: Strong Like Spider Silk (2.3.6)
- poster paper
- construction paper
- art supplies (e.g., pencil crayons, markers, crayons)
- concept map (from lesson 1)
- Science and Technology Glossary (2.1.1)

## Activate

Engage students in a class discussion about materials. Ask:

- What is a material?
- Think about the structures you identified on your structure hunt. What types of materials were the structures made of?

Record students' answers on chart paper.

Portage & Main Press, 2017 · *Hands-On Science and Technology* · *Grade 3* · ISBN: 978-1-55379-709-8

**3**

Divide the class into working groups, and provide each group with several drinking straws. Have students examine the straws and describe them in terms of size, shape, and material. Ask:

- What material are the straws made of?
- Are the straws made of a strong material?
- Do you think a single straw could hold a lot of weight?
- What do you think would happen to the straw if you put a lot of weight on it?
- If you put a bunch of straws together, do you think they could hold more weight than a single straw could hold?

Introduce the guided inquiry question: **Which materials are stronger than others?**

## Action: Part One

In their groups, have students take a drinking cup and poke two holes across from each other near the rim. Then, have them feed a piece of string through the holes and tie the ends together to make a hanging basket. Now, have students stack several books into two even piles. The stacks should be fairly close together—when a straw spans the two piles, the ends of the straw should overlap the books by about three centimetres at each end. Have students hang their baskets at the mid-point of the straw and then place the straw so that it spans the piles of books, as in the following example:

Ask:

- If you were to add mass (weight) to the basket, how much do you think the basket would hold before the straw collapses?

Have students test their predictions by adding small weights (e.g., gram weights, coins, marbles, large washers) to the basket until the straw buckles. Distribute a copy of Activity Sheet A: Testing the Strength of Straws (2.3.1) to each student, and have students record their results from the experiment. Then, ask:

- Do you think the straw structure would be stronger if you added more straws?
- How much weight do you think two straws could hold before buckling?
- Would the result change if you used five straws, or ten straws?

Next, have students test the strength of different bundles with two to ten straws, using small pieces of masking tape to hold the straws together. Again, have students record their results on the activity sheet. When the investigation is completed, distribute a sheet of Centimetre Graph Paper (2.3.2) to each student, and have students use the experiment results to make bar graphs. Alternatively, distribute large sheets of graph paper to pairs or small groups of students, and have them use the experiment results to make bar graphs together.

### Activity Sheet A
Directions to students:
Record the results of your investigation testing the strength of straws (2.3.1).

## Action: Part Two

In working groups of three to four students, have groups repeat the above activity, but this time using natural materials. Sticks/twigs can replace the straws, and the grasses or vines can be used to tie the bundles. Students can use the same activity sheet for this task.

After groups have conducted this task, discuss and compare the human-made and natural materials used in these tasks. Focus on the

▶

Strong and Stable Structures

Portage & Main Press, 2017 · *Hands-On Science and Technology · Grade 3* · ISBN: 978-1-55379-709-8

Portage & Main Press, 2017 · *Hands-On Science and Technology* · Grade 3 · ISBN: 978-1-55379-709-8

characteristics of the materials, the advantages and disadvantages of both types of materials, and the uses of each in daily life. This activity provides an excellent opportunity to connect to Indigenous perspectives by discussing how local populations used natural materials to construct various structures.

## Action: Part Three

In their groups, have students examine the writing paper, construction paper, and Manila tag (or Bristol board). Ask:

- How are the three types of paper similar?
- How are they different?
- Which do you think is the strongest? Why do you think this?
- How might you test to see which is strongest?

Have students share their ideas. These might be used in addition to, or in place of, the suggested activity below.

Explain to students that they are going to conduct an experiment to determine which of the three types of paper is the strongest. To each group, distribute a sheet of writing paper, a sheet of construction paper, and a sheet of Manila tag or Bristol board. Each sheet should be 22.5-cm x 30-cm. Have masking tape available in an area central to all students. Also, distribute a copy of Activity Sheet B: Testing the Strength of Paper (2.3.3) to each student. Have students record a purpose for the experiment on their activity sheet.

Have the groups make cylinders from each of the three types of paper by rolling the sheets into tubes with a two-centimetre overlap, then taping the edges of the cylinder together, as shown:

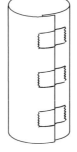

**NOTE:** On each group's set of tubes, ensure that the diameters of the tube openings are the same.

Have groups hypothesize which paper cylinder will hold the most weight when standing vertically (on one end). Have students put their cylinders in order of what they think will be the weakest to strongest. They can then record their hypotheses on Activity Sheet B (2.3.3).

Now, have students test the cylinders for strength. Distribute three paper plates to each working group, and tell students to balance a plate on top of each cylinder. Then, have them gently place small weights (e.g., gram weights, coins, marbles, large washers) onto each plate, one by one—keeping track of what they put on each plate—until each cylinder collapses. Students can record results on the activity sheet.

### Activity Sheet B
Directions to students:

Record details of your experiment as you test the strength of each paper cylinder (2.3.3).

### Assessment as Learning
Have students reflect on their ability to work with others by completing the Cooperative Skills Self-Assessment sheet, on page 34.

### Assessment of Learning
Observe students as they work together on these investigations, focusing on their group work skills. Record results on the Cooperative Skills Teacher-Assessment sheet, on page 37.

## Action: Part Four

It is important for students to understand how local Indigenous peoples (e.g., Haudenosaunee, Cree, Anishinaabe) used the resources of the land to design and build their shelters. The objective of this activity is for students to learn about one type of Indigenous housing, as well as about the tools they may have used to build the structure.

**3**

Read *Storm Maker's Tipi,* a book by Paul Goble. The author explains how the tipi was first granted to the Blackfoot people and then, in a dramatic interpretation of an old story, tells why the painted designs on tipis have come to possess their meaning and power.

As a class, watch the online video, "Setting up a Cree Tipi" at: <www.learnalberta.ca/content/wonbt/html/index.html?launch=true>. This interactive video for students explains how and why the tipi is built the way it is, including the strength of the structure and how it withstands the effects of the weather. The video also includes activities for students, lets them test out different materials to create the joint, and so on.

Have students build a freestanding tipi, using natural materials of their own choosing. If possible, take the class on a nature hike to gather materials (only taking things from the ground and not from live plants). Students may use sticks, twigs, bulrushes, or other plant stems as poles, and grass or vines to tie the poles together. Provide leather, suede, or other natural materials to cover the frame.

Have students help to co-construct the criteria for evaluating the models they build.

To test its strength, have students apply forces such as wind (from a fan) or rain (from a watering can) to see how the tipi withstands natural forces.

Distribute a copy of Activity Sheet C: Building a Tipi (2.3.4) to each student who works on this challenge. Have students use the activity sheet to record a sketch of their tipi design, as well as the results of the investigation.

**NOTE:** Provide an opportunity for students to build, test, and then redesign to make their structure stronger.

**Activity Sheet C**

Directions to students:

Before you build your tipi structure, sketch a design, including measurements of your structure and the number of sticks you will use. Once you build your structure, draw a picture or take a photo of the finished product. Be sure to include the measurements of the finished product, as well as how it withstood natural forces. Explain how your design and the resulting tipi meet the challenge (2.3.4).

## Learning Centre

At the learning centre, provide a copy of the Learning-Centre Task Card: Just How Strong Is a Spider's Web? (2.3.5), along with one copy of the Reference Cards: Strong Like Spider Silk (2.3.6). Also, provide poster paper, construction paper, and various art supplies (e.g., pencil crayons, markers, crayons), string, Scotch tape, glue, scissors.

Have small groups of students prepare informational posters about the amazing strength of spider webs. Have students take turns reading aloud the information on one of the reference cards to the rest of the group. Tell students that each member of the group must select at least one reference card and is responsible for representing one (or more) spider web fact(s) on the poster. The fact must include both a diagram and a written explanation. Students can record their facts and diagrams directly onto the poster paper, or they can use smaller, separate pieces of construction paper and glue or tape these to the poster.

## Consolidate and Debrief

■ Revisit the guided inquiry question: **Which materials are stronger than others?** Have students share their knowledge, provide examples, and ask further inquiry questions.

Portage & Main Press, 2017 · *Hands-On Science and Technology* · *Grade 3* · ISBN: 978-1-55379-709-8

- Add to the concept web as students learn new concepts, answer some of their own inquiry questions, and ask new inquiry questions.
- Add new terms and illustrations to the class word wall. Also, include the words in other languages, as appropriate.
- Have students add new terms, definitions, and illustrations to their Science and Technology Glossary (2.1.1). When possible, encourage them to add words (and examples) in other languages, including Indigenous languages, reflective of the classroom population.

### Enhance

- As a follow-up, review students' experiment testing the strength of drinking straws. Discuss purpose, hypothesis, materials, method, results, conclusion, and applications for the experiment.

  Ask students if they can think of ways to increase the strength of the straws, and then have students test their ideas (e.g., stuff straws full of Plasticine).

- Have students use decks of cards to create towers. Then, have them test the towers for strength (as in the preceding Action activities) to determine how much weight the towers can withstand.

- Have students plan and conduct experiments to test the strength of various materials they select themselves. For example:
  - wooden barbecue skewers, toothpicks, or pipe cleaners
  - different kinds of string, yarn, or thread
  - different kinds of tape (e.g., masking tape, clear tape, duct tape)

 **SAFETY NOTE:** If testing the strength of string or tape, beware of a drop/crush hazard if the string/tape snaps and a load is released.

- Investigate how plastic bags are made into strong composite lumber. Check out the article "What Happens to Recycled Plastic Bags?" on the wiseGEEK site: <www.wisegeek.com/what-happens-to-recycled-plastic-bags.htm>.

- Have students conduct Internet research to find out how materials such as rubber, plastic, and glass are made.

- Have students continue their do-it-yourself projects at the Makerspace centre.

# Testing the Strength of Straws

| Number of Straws/Sticks | Predicted Number of Weights Held | Actual Number of Weights Held |
|---|---|---|
| | | |
| | | |
| | | |
| | | |
| | | |
| | | |
| | | |
| | | |
| | | |
| | | |

Portage & Main Press, 2017 · Hands-On Science and Technology · Grade 3 · ISBN: 978-1-55379-709-8

**Date:** _____     **Name:** _____

# Centimetre Graph Paper

Portage & Main Press, 2017 · Hands-On Science and Technology · Grade 3 · ISBN: 978-1-55379-709-8

# Testing the Strength of Paper

| Question (what you want to find out): | Prediction (what you think will happen): |
|---|---|
| | |

**Method (what you did):**

**Results (what happened):**

**Conclusion (what you learned):**

**Questions you still have about the strength of paper:**

Portage & Main Press, 2017 · Hands-On Science and Technology · Grade 3 · ISBN: 978-1-55379-709-8

# Building a Tipi

| My Plan | My Finished Product |
|---|---|
| Sketch: | Sketch/Digital Picture: |
| Estimated measurements:<br>_____ | Actual measurements:<br>_____ |
| Estimated number of sticks:<br>_____ | Actual number of sticks:<br>_____ |

1. I changed the following from my original plan:

_____

_____

2. These are the reasons why my final product is different from my original plan:

_____

_____

3. Explain how your design and the structure you built meet the challenge.

_____

Portage & Main Press, 2017 · Hands-On Science and Technology · Grade 3 · ISBN: 978-1-55379-709-8

# Just How Strong Is a Spider's Web?

In your group, you are going to develop an information poster about the amazing strength of spider webs.

1. Discuss what you already know about spider webs.

2. Take turns reading aloud the information from the reference cards to the rest of your group.

3. Each member of your group is responsible for representing at least one spider-web fact on your poster. The fact must include both a diagram and a written explanation.

4. Record your fact and diagram on the poster paper or on a smaller, separate piece of construction paper, and then glue or tape it to the poster.

5. Make your poster interesting and eye-catching so that others will want to read and enjoy it!

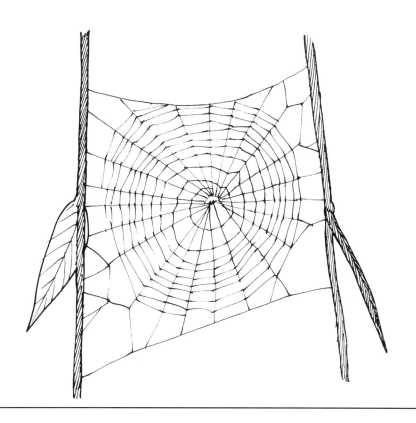

Portage & Main Press, 2017 · Hands-On Science and Technology · Grade 3 · ISBN: 978-1-55379-709-8

# Strong Like Spider Silk

1. True or false? Spiders use their own silk to build their spider webs.

   Answer: True! Spider silk is used to make spider webs.

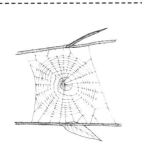

2. Scientists have done many experiments to understand why spider webs are so strong. They have tested real spider webs and have run computer simulations of spider webs surviving different forces without breaking. Results from these experiments have shown that some spider webs can withstand hurricane-force winds!

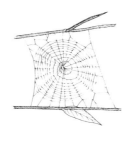

3. Spider silk is very strong, but this is not the only reason why a spider's web is so sturdy. The design is also so complex that if a single strand of a web is broken, the strength of the rest of the web actually increases! Not too many things get stronger when they break!

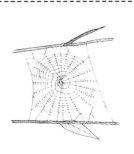

4. It takes a lot of energy for a spider to make silk that is so strong, and to build its web. Because of this, a spider cannot rebuild its web every time a thread or two breaks.

Portage & Main Press, 2017 · *Hands-On Science and Technology · Grade 3* · ISBN: 978-1-55379-709-8

# Strong Like Spider Silk (continued)

5. Scientists have discovered that different forces cause spider silk to act in different ways. For example:

| Type of Force | How Silk Reacts | Effect on Web |
|---|---|---|
| light breeze | ■ silk becomes softer<br>■ silk becomes more flexible | ■ web does not break |
| moderate (medium) breeze | ■ silk becomes softer<br>■ silk becomes more flexible | ■ web does not break |
| larger force acting on part of web | ■ silk becomes stiff in the part of the web affected | ■ one or two threads break in affected part of web<br>■ the rest of web does not break |

6. Spiders use their webs to catch food. The flexibility of the silk from which the spider spins its web allows the web to stretch when an insect lands on it. But it is strong enough not to break, and sticky enough to trap the insect.

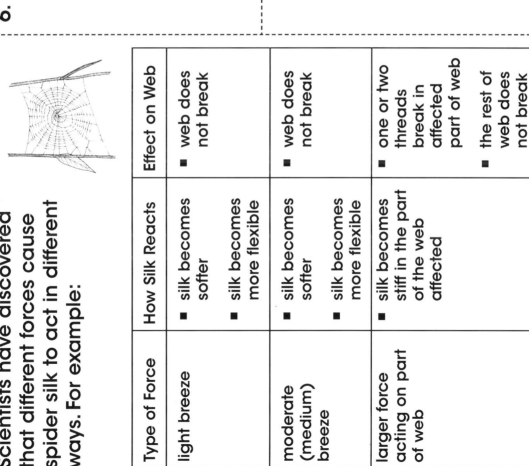

Portage & Main Press, 2017 · Hands-On Science and Technology · Grade 3 · ISBN: 978-1-55379-709-8

# 4 | What Are Joints?

## Information for Teachers

A joint is a point at which two or more pieces of building material are joined together. If joints are sturdy and resistant to change, then structures for which they are used can withstand the many forces acting on them. Often, some joints need to be more flexible than other joints (e.g., the human hip joint).

**NOTE:** In the human body, joints are dynamic, which means they move. Static joints are those that do not move (e.g., joints connecting a table leg to the tabletop).

## 21st Century Competencies

**Critical Thinking** and **Creativity**: Students will explore various ways to join materials and examine examples of joints in structures found in their immediate environment.

## Materials

- interactive whiteboard, or other projection device (optional)
- pictures or X-rays of a knee, a femur (upper leg bone), an elbow, and a humerus (upper arm bone) (optional)
- clipboards
- classroom furniture with joints
- drinking straws
- Popsicle sticks
- spaghetti (or linguine, fettuccini)
- round toothpicks
- construction paper
- items to use as joint connectors (e.g., paper clips, pipe cleaners, Plasticine or play dough [various colours], mini-marshmallows, butterfly fasteners)
- white glue
- Activity Sheet: Constructing Shapes With Joints (2.4.1)
- Diagram: Joints (2.4.2)
- Learning-Centre Task Card: The Hip Bone Is Connected to the Thigh Bone (2.4.3)
- Chart: Human Body Joints (2.4.4)
- pencils
- digital camera
- concept map (from lesson 1)
- Science and Technology Glossary (2.1.1)

## Activate

As a class, examine several pieces of classroom furniture to look at how parts are joined.

Have students identify where different joints are on the furniture structures, and, as a class, discuss how they are joined together. Ask:

- What materials are used to join parts together?

Take a walk around the school looking for other examples of furniture structures, and examine the ways in which the parts are joined together.

Introduce the guided inquiry question: **What are joints?**

## Action: Part One

Give each student a clipboard, then, as a class, walk around the community to explore how joints work in other structures. Have students record notes to identify structures and how parts are joined together. Also, take photographs for use throughout the unit.

Back in the classroom, ask:

- What are some structures in our community?
- Do these structures have joints?
- What are some examples of joints on structures in our community?
- What sorts of materials are used to make joints in these structures? (e.g., wood, steel, concrete)
- How do you think joints are made in these structures? What kinds of tools might be

**Hands-On Science and Technology • Grade 3**

Portage & Main Press, 2017 · Hands-On Science and Technology · Grade 3 · ISBN: 978-1-55379-709-8

used to make them? (e.g., glue, screwdriver and screw, welding, slot and key)

## Action: Part Two

Provide each student with two drinking straws, and ask:

- How can you join these two straws together at the ends?
- What "connectors" could you use?
- How could you make different kinds of joints?

Have students offer suggestions.

Next, introduce the engineering challenge: joint construction. Provide students with drinking straws, Popsicle sticks, spaghetti (or linguine, fettuccini), or round toothpicks, along with any of the available joint connectors provided (e.g., paper clips, pipe cleaners, Plasticine or play dough, mini-marshmallows, butterfly fasteners) to make a variety of two-dimensional shapes.

Have all students make the same shape. Ask:

- Using the available materials, how many different ways can you build a triangle?

Have students use the materials to build various triangles. Encourage them to work on their own shapes, but seat students together in small groups for this activity.

Now, challenge students to make other shapes (e.g., squares, diamonds, parallelograms). Provide plenty of time for investigation, experimentation, and testing. As students work, encourage them to discuss with one another the ways they are making joints. Distribute a copy of Activity Sheet: Constructing Shapes With Joints (2.4.1) to each student. Have students use it to record their designs as they create their shapes.

Have students display their shapes on their desks/tables and circulate around the classroom to look at other students' designs. Discuss the various ways that students made the joints and shapes.

### Activity Sheet

Directions to students:

Draw and label a diagram for each shape you made, and record the materials you used to make each shape and its joints (2.4.1).

## Action: Part Three

Project the Diagram: Joints (2.4.2), or distribute a copy of this sheet to each student.

**NOTE:** This is a two-page activity sheet.

As a class, discuss the different types of joints presented on the sheet. Ask:

- Did you use any of these joints when you built your shapes?
- Which ones did you use?
- Which did you not use?

Provide an opportunity for students to make more shapes, using the techniques presented on this sheet. If they have used all of these joints, challenge them to find other ways to make joints.

Discuss students' choices of materials used to make each shape, including the material used for the joints. Based on the samples collected, ask questions such as:

- Why did you use Popsicle sticks and tape to make a hexagon?
- Why did you use toothpicks and marshmallows to make a hexagon?

Focus on the sturdiness of the joints. Ask:

- Are the joints you constructed sturdy?
- How could you make them sturdier?

Discuss, and record students' ideas on chart paper.

Portage & Main Press, 2017 · *Hands-On Science and Technology · Grade 3* · ISBN: 978-1-55379-709-8

**4**

## Action: Part Four

Explore dynamic (movable) joints. Invite three student volunteers to take part in the following demonstration:

Ask one volunteer to point to their upper arm bone (humerus). Ask another volunteer to point to their lower arm bones (radius and ulna). Now, have the third volunteer point to their elbow. Ask students:

- How are these parts of the body similar? How are they different?
- What is the function of the elbow?

Discuss students' responses. Now, ask the first volunteer to point to their upper leg bone (femur), and another to point to their lower leg bones (tibia and fibula). Have the third volunteer point to their knee. Ask students:

- How are these parts of the body similar? How are they different?
- How are elbows and knees similar? How are the femur and the humerus similar?

Discuss that the knee and elbow are joints, whereas the femur, tibia, fibula, humerus, radius, and ulna are bones.

As an optional additional activity, use an interactive whiteboard or other projection device to project images or X-rays of a knee, a femur, an elbow, and a humerus. Ask students:

- What are these pictures of? (possible answers: X-rays, parts of the human body, bones and joints)
- How are they similar? (all are parts of the body, made of bone)
- How are they different? (knee and femur are from the leg, elbow and humerus are from the arm, elbows and knees bend, leg bone [femur] and arm bone [humerus] do not bend)

## Learning Centre

At the learning centre, provide a copy of the Learning-Centre Task Card: The Hip Bone Is Connected to the Thigh Bone (2.4.3) and copies of the Chart: Human Body Joints (2.4.4), Plasticine or play dough in various colours, construction paper, pencils, and a digital camera.

Students can use the chart to explore human joints. Then, they can build four of these joints out of Plasticine or play dough and explain where the joints are found in the human body and how each moves. Students may refer to the chart and their own body joints to answer how the joints move. Have them take photos of their finished project for display at the centre.

## Consolidate and Debrief

- Revisit the guided inquiry question: **What are joints?** Have students share their knowledge, provide examples, and ask further inquiry questions.
- Add to the concept web as students learn new concepts, answer some of their own inquiry questions, and ask new inquiry questions.
- Add new terms and illustrations to the class word wall. Also, include the words in other languages, as appropriate.
- Have students add new terms, definitions, and illustrations to their Science and Technology Glossary (2.1.1). When possible, encourage them to add words (and examples) in other languages, including Indigenous languages, reflective of the classroom population.

## Enhance

- Have students join together all of the two-dimensional shapes created during the lesson to build a larger structure. They may

Portage & Main Press, 2017 · *Hands-On Science and Technology · Grade 3* · ISBN: 978-1-55379-709-8

join the shapes together using any of the methods and materials they have learned about in this lesson.

- Have a guest speaker present to the class about joint replacement in humans— specifically knee or hip.

- Have students continue their do-it-yourself projects at the Makerspace centre.

Portage & Main Press, 2017 · *Hands-On Science and Technology · Grade 3* · ISBN: 978-1-55379-709-8

Date: _____     Name: _____

# Constructing Shapes With Joints

| Shape (labelled diagram) | Material Used to Make the Shape | Material Used to Make the Joints |
|---|---|---|
| | | |
| | | |
| | | |
| | | |
| | | |

What do you think is the best method to make a sturdy joint? Explain.

_____

_____

Portage & Main Press, 2017 · Hands-On Science and Technology · Grade 3 · ISBN: 978-1-55379-709-8

# Joints

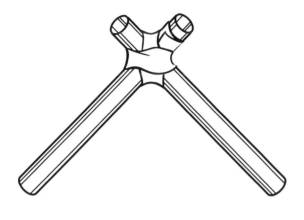

masking-tape joint

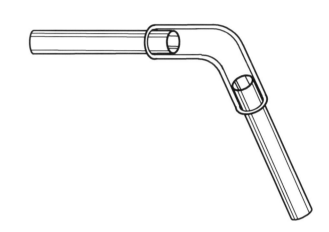

sleeve joint

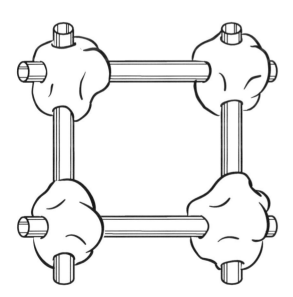

straws and play dough

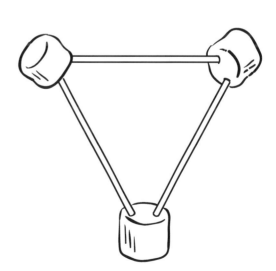

toothpicks and
mini-marshmallow joint

Portage & Main Press, 2017 · Hands-On Science and Technology · Grade 3 · ISBN: 978-1-55379-709-8

# Joints (continued)

**straws and paper-clip joint**

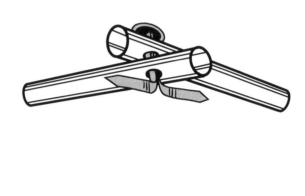

**butterfly fastener joint**

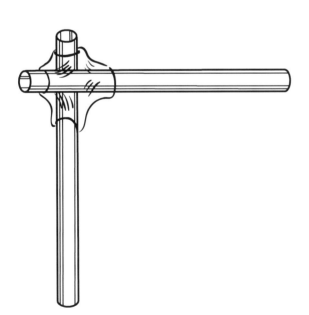

**Plasticine joint**

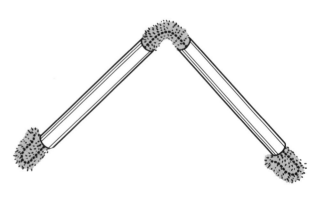

**pipe-cleaner joint**

Portage & Main Press, 2017 · *Hands-On Science and Technology* · *Grade 3* · ISBN: 978-1-55379-709-8

# The Hip Bone Is Connected to the Thigh Bone

Today, you are going to learn more about some of the joints in the human body.

1. Select two different colours of Plasticine or play dough to create four human-body joint models.

   ■ As you study the chart, Human Body Joints, you will discover each joint has two main parts.

   ■ Use a different colour of Plasticine or play dough for each main part of each joint you create.

2. Use the chart, Human Body Joints, to help you create your model joints.

3. Display your finished joints on a sheet of construction paper.

4. Beside each joint, print its name, and write one or two sentences explaining where the joint is found in the human body and how it moves. (Look at the chart to help you, and also look at your own joints!)

5. Use a digital camera to take a picture of your finished project.

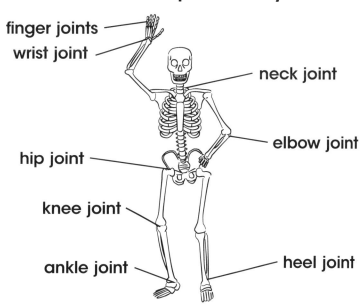

finger joints

wrist joint

neck joint

elbow joint

hip joint

knee joint

ankle joint

heel joint

Portage & Main Press, 2017 · Hands-On Science and Technology · Grade 3 · ISBN: 978-1-55379-709-8

# Human Body Joints

Synovial joints are the most common joints in the human body.

- They are very movable.

- The bones creating the joints are padded with cartilage and held in place with muscles and tendons.

Here are four different types of synovial joints:

| Joint Type | Example | Model |
|---|---|---|
| hinge | knee | |
| pivot | top of neck | |
| ball and socket | hip | |
| saddle | thumb | |

Portage & Main Press, 2017 · Hands-On Science and Technology · Grade 3 · ISBN: 978-1-55379-709-8

# How Can We Build Structures to Be Stronger and More Stable?

**5**

## Information for Teachers

Structural engineers use knowledge of geometry and stable shapes when designing structures. Engineers have developed numerous techniques to make structures more stable. Some of these stabilizing techniques include building beams, columns, braces, and trusses in strategic places throughout the structure.

A truss is a rigid framework, usually of wood or metal, designed to support a structure. A truss is most often designed as a triangle for strength.

A brace is a component that provides additional support to a structure with fasteners and beams.

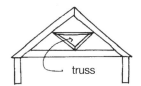 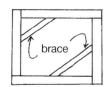

truss    brace

**NOTE:** During the following activity, students use drinking straws and butterfly fasteners, as well as newspaper and masking tape to build various two-dimensional shapes. Students are then challenged to stabilize the shapes (make them sturdier) by adding straws or newspaper to act as braces, as in the following examples:

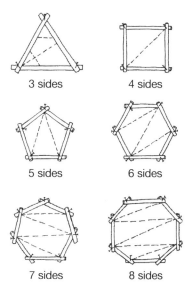

3 sides    4 sides

5 sides    6 sides

7 sides    8 sides

## 21st Century Competencies

**Critical Thinking** and **Communication:**
Students will examine different ways to make structures stronger and more stable.

## Materials

- drinking straws
- butterfly fasteners
- newspaper
- masking tape
- string
- plastic drinking cup
- small weights (e.g., gram weights, coins, marbles, large washers)
- scissors
- *Life in a Longhouse Village* by Bobbie Kalman and/or *Longhouses* by Jack Manning
- Longhouses from Image Bank: Indigenous Structures (see Appendix, page 432)
- natural materials for building model longhouses, as suggested by students
- Activity Sheet: How Can We Make Shapes Stronger? (2.5.1)
- Learning-Centre Task Card: Build Your Own Cabinet! (2.5.2)
- art supplies (e.g., paint, markers, stickers)
- glue
- tape
- pipe cleaners
- cardboard
- cardboard boxes
- concept map (from lesson 1)
- Science and Technology Glossary (2.1.1)

## Activate

Display a piece of newspaper, and ask students:

- What can be done to this newspaper to make it stronger without cutting it, tearing it, or adding other materials to it? (fold, crumple, roll)

Portage & Main Press, 2017 · *Hands-On Science and Technology · Grade 3* · ISBN: 978-1-55379-709-8

**5**

Depending on the answers, demonstrate each action/example mentioned above. Then, have students test the strength of each example in the same way other types of paper were tested in lesson 3 (Action: Part One).

Once students have conducted the three experiments—folding, crumpling, and rolling newspaper—to test for sturdiness, they will likely have come to the conclusion that rolling is the best way to make a piece of newspaper (or any paper) stronger, and the tighter the roll made, the sturdier the paper becomes.

Introduce the guided inquiry question: **How can we build structures to be stronger and more stable?**

## Action: Part One

Distribute drinking straws and butterfly fasteners, and have each student use the materials to build a square.

**NOTE:** Also distribute scissors, and tell students they may cut the straws to shorter lengths if this helps with construction.

Have students examine their squares and test their stability by standing the squares up on one side, and pressing gently onto the opposite side. Ask:

- Is the square sturdy?
- How could you make it sturdier?

Challenge students to make their squares stable enough so their shape will not change easily when a force is applied to it. Ask:

- Examine your square structure. If you apply pressure to the joints, can you change its shape?
- Where could you place another straw to help the structure keep its shape?

Discuss students' ideas and strategies for making their squares sturdier.

Once students have experimented, discuss the various solutions students discovered.

## Action: Part Two

Distribute a copy of Activity Sheet: How Can We Make Shapes Stronger? (2.5.1) to each student. Divide the class into working groups of students, and give each group some newspaper and some masking tape. Have the groups use the materials to make shapes with three, four, five, six, or more sides. Then, challenge them to make their shapes more stable, record the results on the activity sheet, and draw diagrams of their final shapes.

Have students record their solutions in diagrams on the activity sheet.

Afterward, invite students to share how they made their geometric shapes sturdier. Compare and contrast the strategies used.

**Activity Sheet**
Directions to students:

Draw a diagram of each geometric shape you make. Label each diagram (2.5.1).

## Activity: Part Three

Explore the design of the longhouse, a long and narrow structure that was home to several related families. The longhouse was a rectangular structure made from a frame of saplings driven into the ground, bent toward each other, and tied at the top to form an arch. This created a flexible barrel-vaulted (deeply arched) frame. The frame was covered with bark, and then more saplings were attached horizontally on the outside for added strength. Sheets of bark were fastened between the poles, and additional saplings were attached horizontally on the outside for reinforcement.

Portage & Main Press, 2017 · Hands-On Science and Technology · Grade 3 · ISBN: 978-1-55379-709-8

**5**

Usually, sturdy posts were positioned down the centre to provide support for the roof.

Invite a local Elder or Métis Senator to present to the class about the construction of the longhouse. Or, in addition to the guest speaker, explore resources about this structure. For example, have students read *Life in a Longhouse Village,* by Bobbie Kalman, which includes information about how a longhouse was built and/or *Longhouses,* by Jack Manning, which includes information about the tools and materials used to build longhouses and about the people who lived in them.

Also, examine the visuals of longhouses included in the Image Bank: Indigenous Structures (see Appendix, page 432).

As students learn about the design and materials used to build longhouses, challenge them to construct their own models, using natural materials as much as possible. Their growing knowledge of structures, joints, and stability will provide them with a foundation for this task. As a class, co-construct criteria for the project and assess final products accordingly.

## Learning Centre

At the learning centre, provide a large selection of cardboard boxes, scrap cardboard, butterfly fasteners, pipe cleaners, scissors, glue, tape, and various art supplies (e.g., paint, markers, stickers). Also, provide a copy of the Learning-Centre Task Card: Build Your Own Cabinet! (2.5.2).

Have students use the boxes and cardboard scraps to build a miniature cabinet with shelves. Remind students to make joints strong and sturdy.

## Assessment of Learning

Conference with students individually. Have students present their miniature cabinets and reflect on the experiments to strengthen geometric shapes. Encourage students to share how they made each structure sturdier. Use the Individual Student Observations sheet, on page 27, to record results.

## Consolidate and Debrief

- Revisit the guided inquiry question: **How can we build structures to be stronger and more stable?** Have students share their knowledge, provide examples, and ask further inquiry questions.

- Add to the concept web as students learn new concepts, answer some of their own inquiry questions, and ask new inquiry questions.

- Add new terms and illustrations to the class word wall. Also, include the words in other languages, as appropriate.

- Have students add new terms, definitions, and illustrations to their Science and Technology Glossary (2.1.1). When possible, encourage them to add words (and examples) in other languages, including Indigenous languages, reflective of the classroom population.

## Enhance 🖥️

- Have students examine bookshelves in the classroom and/or school library. Ask:
  - How are the bookshelves attached to the wall?
  - How many braces or supports does a bookshelf have?
  - How much mass/weight (books) can a bookshelf hold before you notice the shelves sagging?

Portage & Main Press, 2017 · *Hands-On Science and Technology · Grade 3* · ISBN: 978-1-55379-709-8

**5**

- How does the size of book affect the number of books a bookshelf can hold before the shelves sag?
- If the shelves are sagging, what could you do to fix them?

■ Investigate how to make rolled-up newspapers into a sturdy paper table. See the article "Paper Table" on the PBS kids website at: <pbskids.org/designsquad/pdf/parentseducators/DS_Act_Guide_Lead_PaperTable.pdf>.

■ Have students continue their do-it-yourself projects at the Makerspace centre.

Portage & Main Press, 2017 · Hands-On Science and Technology · Grade 3 · ISBN: 978-1-55379-709-8

# How Can We Make Shapes Stronger?

| | |
|---|---|
| Number of sides _____ <br><br> Name of shape _____ <br><br><br><br><br><br> | Number of sides _____ <br><br> Name of shape _____ <br><br><br><br><br><br> |
| Number of sides _____ <br><br> Name of shape _____ <br><br><br><br><br><br> | Number of sides _____ <br><br> Name of shape _____ <br><br><br><br><br><br> |
| Number of sides _____ <br><br> Name of shape _____ <br><br><br><br><br><br> | Number of sides _____ <br><br> Name of shape _____ <br><br><br><br><br><br> |

Portage & Main Press, 2017 · Hands-On Science and Technology · Grade 3 · ISBN: 978-1-55379-709-8

# Build Your Own Cabinet!

Today, pretend you are a carpenter!

1. Using cardboard scrap and a cardboard box, build a miniature cabinet with shelves to hold your personal items.

2. Remember to make your cabinet's joints strong and sturdy.

3. What can you do to prevent the shelves from sagging when weight is added?

Portage & Main Press, 2017 · Hands-On Science and Technology · Grade 3 · ISBN: 978-1-55379-709-8

# How Can We Build a Frame That Is Strong and Stable?

**6**

## Information for Teachers

All structures have at least a few important components. One of these is the foundation, on which the entire structure sits or stands. Another is the frame, which is the structure's basic support system—built before the walls or sides or borders are added. The frame constitutes what is referred to as a "skeleton" in mathematical terms. So, a cube shape that shows only beams and columns (but no sides) is one example of a frame. It might help students to think of a frame as a skeleton of a geometric solid.

## 21st Century Competencies

**Critical Thinking:** Students will design and build a stable frame and test its strength with a predetermined load.

## Materials

- sample cubes (e.g., wooden blocks, cube tissue boxes)
- drinking straws
- round toothpicks
- Popsicle sticks
- Plasticine or play dough
- pipe cleaners
- paper clips
- butterfly fasteners
- masking tape
- mini-marshmallows
- cardboard
- scissors
- natural materials to build model wigwams, as suggested by students
- paper plates
- timer
- gram weights
- digital camera
- uncooked spaghetti
- cardboard tubes
- paper rolls

- *L'nu'k* by Theresa Meuse and/or the article, "Architectural History: Indigenous Peoples," which can be found at: <www.thecanadianencyclopedia.ca/en/article/architectural-history-early-first-nations/>
- wigwams from Image Bank: Indigenous Structures (see Appendix, page 433)
- computers/tablets with Internet access (optional)
- materials to build model wigwams
- Diagram: Frames (2.6.1)
- Activity Sheet: Blueprint for a Frame (2.6.2)
- Learning-Centre Task Card: Designing and Building for Strength and Stability (2.6.3)
- concept map (from lesson 1)
- Science and Technology Glossary (2.1.1)

## Activate

Review the materials students used to make joints in the previous lesson (e.g., tape, butterfly fasteners, mini-marshmallows). Also, review various ways to make sturdy shapes.

Display the sample cubes for students to manipulate and examine. Ask:

- What shape is this object?
- From what material is it made?
- How could you make a cube shape out of drinking straws, Popsicle sticks, or toothpicks?

Introduce the guided inquiry question: **How can we build a frame that is strong and stable?**

## Action: Part One

Display Diagram: Frames (2.6.1) to ensure students are clear about the design of a frame.

---

**NOTE:** For the purpose of this lesson, students will work with rectangular prism frames, in order to test strength and add storeys. However, be sure they understand that they are not limited to cubes.

---

▶

Portage & Main Press, 2017 · *Hands-On Science and Technology · Grade 3* · ISBN: 978-1-55379-709-8

**6**

Explain to students that they will each build their own frame from drinking straws, toothpicks, or Popsicle sticks. For joints, they will use materials of their own choice (e.g., Plasticine or play dough, pipe cleaners, paper clips, butterfly fasteners, masking tape, mini-marshmallows). Explain that they will also create a plan for their frame, which builders refer to as a *blueprint*. Ask:

■ How many straws, toothpicks, or Popsicle sticks will you need to make a frame?
■ How many joints will you make?

Challenge students to design and build a frame that is strong enough to stand on its own. As a class, discuss and identify four criteria for the design project. For example:

■ Create an accurate blueprint.
■ Construct the frame.
■ Test the design.
■ Identify improvements.

Also, identify criteria for the frame itself. For example:

■ uses selected materials
■ is a 3D frame
■ can stand freely
■ can hold 20 grams of mass for 20 seconds

**NOTE:** If students choose to use drinking straws for construction of their frames, they may cut the straws first if they want. Full-length straws can be awkward to work with and make for an unstable structure. Straws about the same length as Popsicle sticks are an ideal size.

Distribute a copy of Activity Sheet: Blueprint for a Frame (2.6.2) to each student. On it, have students record details of their plan for a frame.

**Activity Sheet**
Directions to students:

Draw a blueprint for your frame structure. At the bottom of the page, list the materials you will use to make your frame (2.6.2).

## Action: Part Two

Once students have completed their blueprints, review each student's plan. Ask:

■ Why did you choose these materials to make your frame?
■ Why did you choose these materials for the joints?
■ How will you make your frame sturdy enough to stand alone?

When all students' blueprints have been approved, distribute pieces of cardboard for them to use as a foundation, and have students collect the necessary materials and then build their own frame structures. They can add reinforcing beams and braces to their frames as they see fit.

When each student has completed their frame structure and is satisfied with its sturdiness, have students test the strength of their frames, according to the criteria, by placing a paper plate with 20 gram weights on it and timing for 20 seconds. If frames do not meet the criteria, students can modify their frame structure to improve its strength and stability. Take photographs of each student's final product.

## Action: Part Three

Challenge students to add second storeys to their frames and then third storeys. Remember to take a picture after each storey is completed.

After all students have built their structures, discuss the activity as a class. Ask:

■ What made your frames strong?
■ Did you add any extra beams to strengthen your frame?
■ What happened when you added a second and a third storey?
■ Did the structure lose some of its sturdiness?
■ What do you think engineers do when they build very tall buildings?

Portage & Main Press, 2017 · Hands-On Science and Technology · Grade 3 · ISBN: 978-1-55379-709-8

- How do you think they strengthen the buildings?

Display students' frame structures, along with their blueprints and their photographs.

### Assessment of Learning

On the Rubric, on page 36, list the criteria identified by students for the frame structure design project, and record results as you observe students working.

---

**NOTE:** From the list of criteria for the frame structure and the list of criteria for the design project, the class can select four to include on this assessment.

---

## Action: Part Four

Explore the designs of wigwams, both conical and dome-shaped. Usually meant for smaller groups of one or two families, the wigwam had either a circular or rectangular base and was about four metres in diameter.

In the conical wigwam, a frame was first constructed with four poles that were driven into the ground and tied together at the top, similar to a tipi. Smaller saplings were then added between these main ones. Additional branches were positioned horizontally around the frame for strength. The frame was covered with sheets of birch bark sewn together. Animal hides, reed mats, and evergreen boughs were also used. When people moved from one place to another, they removed the exterior sheathing and took it with them, leaving the poles standing, to be re-used later either by themselves or by others.

Domed wigwams were often used for winter settlements. Saplings were pounded into the ground and bent toward the centre to form the dome. The top ends were then tied together, and horizontal branches were added for support and strength. Sheets of bark covered the frame, although sometimes mats of cattails covered the bottom area of the structure. A smoke hole was left at the top.

Invite a local Elder or Métis Senator to present to the class about the construction of the wigwams. Alternately, or in addition to the guest speaker, explore resources on this structure. Have students read *L'nu'k*, by Theresa Meuse, which tells a story about the traditional daily life of the Mi'kmaq, including details on constructing wigwams and canoe building. Students can also read the article "Architectural History: Indigenous Peoples" at: <www.thecanadianencyclopedia.ca/en/article/architectural-history-early-first-nations/>. It explains the different types of homes Indigenous peoples in Canada used and includes detailed visuals and useful information on construction.

Also, have students examine the visuals of wigwams included in the Image Bank: Indigenous Structures (see Appendix, page 433).

As students learn about the design and materials used to build the wigwam, they may be challenged to construct models using natural materials as much as possible. Their growing knowledge of structures, joints, and stability will provide them with a foundation for this task. As a class, co-construct criteria for the project and assess final products accordingly.

## Learning Centre

At the learning centre, provide the same types of materials used in the Action activity (e.g., drinking straws, round toothpicks, Popsicle sticks, Plasticine or play dough, pipe cleaners, paper clips, butterfly fasteners, tape, mini-marshmallows), as well as new materials (e.g., uncooked spaghetti, cardboard tubes, paper rolls). Also, provide a copy of the Learning-Centre Task Card: Designing and Building for Strength and Stability (2.6.3) and a digital camera.

Have students explore the materials and then design and build other structures for strength and stability. Have them also consider wind

---

Portage & Main Press, 2017 · *Hands-On Science and Technology · Grade 3* · ISBN: 978-1-55379-709-8

**6**

and vibration factors. Encourage students to try using materials different from the ones they used in the Action activity. Have them take photographs of the frame structures they build to display at the centre.

## Consolidate and Debrief

- Revisit the guided inquiry question: **How can we build a frame that is strong and stable?** Have students share their knowledge, provide examples, and ask further inquiry questions.

- Add to the concept web as students learn new concepts, answer some of their own inquiry questions, and ask new inquiry questions.

- Add new terms and illustrations to the class word wall. Also, include the terms in other languages, as appropriate.

- Have students add new terms, definitions, and illustrations to their Science and Technology Glossary (2.1.1). When possible, encourage students to add words (and examples) in other languages, including Indigenous languages, reflective of the classroom population.

## Enhance

- Have students use various materials to build other three-dimensional frames (e.g., pyramids, prisms). Encourage them to improve the stability of their structures.

- Visit the school playground to study the play structures as frames. Before students play on the equipment, explore it, discuss it, and make connections.

- Access the interactive activity, Altering the Strength of Objects, in the Grade 3, Unit 2 folder of the **Hands-On Interactive for Science and Technology, Grade 3** download. Find this download at: <www.portageandmainpress.com/product/hands-on-interactive-for-science-and-technology-grade-3/>.

- Have students continue their do-it-yourself projects at the Makerspace centre.

Portage & Main Press, 2017 · *Hands-On Science and Technology · Grade 3* · ISBN: 978-1-55379-709-8

# Frame

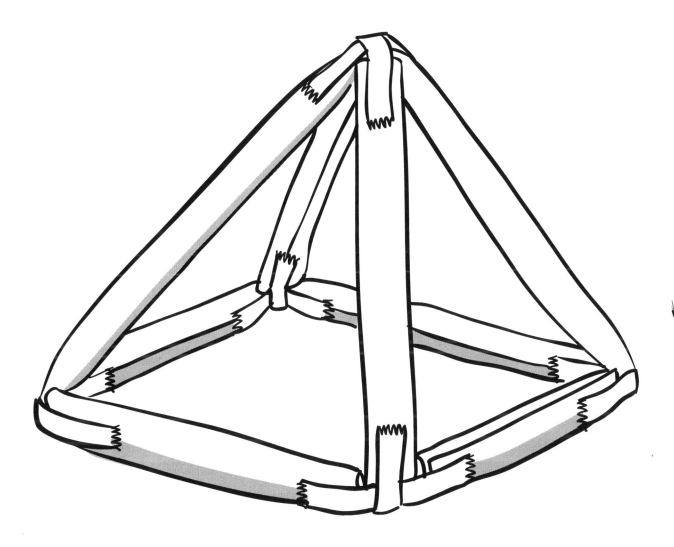

Portage & Main Press, 2017 · *Hands-On Science and Technology · Grade 3* · ISBN: 978-1-55379-709-8

# Blueprint for a Frame

**This is a diagram of my frame:**

**Materials I will use to make my frame:**

_____   _____

_____   _____

_____   _____

_____   _____

Portage & Main Press, 2017 · Hands-On Science and Technology · Grade 3 · ISBN: 978-1-55379-709-8

# Designing and Building for Strength and Stability

You are a building engineer, and you have been hired to design and build frame structures!

1. You are to use materials that are different from those you used to build earlier frame structures.

2. Be sure to design and construct for strength and stability. Consider factors such as wind, vibration, and gravity.

3. Be prepared to explain the steps you took to construct your structure and why you designed it the way you did.

4. Take a picture of your design and completed structure, and display it at the centre along with an explanation.

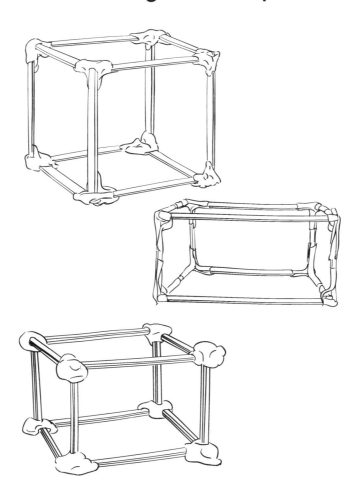

# 7 | What Structures Has Nature Engineered?

## Information for Teachers

Engineers have long considered nature a valuable source of ideas. The shapes and structures found in nature are not accidental. They are tried, tested, and perfected results of thousands of years of evolution. Copying designs from nature is called *biomimicry* and is seen in many different fields of engineering and architecture. Look, for example, at the hexagonal shapes in a honeycomb, which may have inspired hexagonal gazebos or decks; examine the spiral design of seashells, which may have been the inspiration for some spiral staircases and towers. The oval shape of an egg, cut in half, could have provided the idea for the dome shape used in many buildings and in household utensils such as the spoon and the bowl.

 **SAFETY NOTE:** Eggs are used in Action: Part Two. Teachers should check for any student allergies in the class.

It is also useful to note that a dome is an extremely strong structure. In fact, the dome-shaped egg is very difficult to break when squeezing it between two hands, top and bottom. This is because the force applied is spread out over the surface of the egg, meaning that the shells can withstand more pressure. Domes are often used for buildings that cannot have pillar supports (e.g., arenas, wigwams, igloos).

## 21st Century Competencies

**Creativity**, **Critical Thinking**, **Communication**, and **Collaboration**: Students will examine various structures and shapes found in nature, and build a model of a specific structure of their choice.

## Materials

- *Glooscap, the Beavers and the Sugarloaf Mountain* by Allison Mitcham
- 3D solids
- 2D shapes (e.g., pattern blocks)
- masking tape
- Image Bank: Human-Made and Natural Structures (see Appendix, page 431)
- chart paper
- markers
- clipboards
- pencils
- digital camera
- whole raw eggs
- sharp knife (teacher use only)
- stacks of books
- Activity Sheet: Shapes, Solids, and Structures in Nature (2.7.1)
- *A Wasp Builds a Nest: See Inside a Paper Wasp's Nest and Watch It Grow* by Martin Camm and Kate Scarborough, and/or *A House Is a House for Me* by Mary Ann Hoberman
- Learning-Centre Task Card: Human-Made or Natural Structure? (2.7.2)
- computer/tablet with Internet access
- printer and paper
- magazines with pictures of both human-made and natural structures
- scissors
- glue
- natural materials for building models of natural structures
- concept map (from lesson 1)
- Science and Technology Glossary (2.1.1)

## Activate

Divide a sheet of chart paper into two columns, "Geometric Shape" and "Example." Have students brainstorm a list of two-dimensional geometric shapes and three-dimensional geometric solids. Display the pattern blocks and geometric solids to ensure students are familiar with all the shapes and solids. Record students' ideas in the first column of the chart.

Portage & Main Press, 2017 · *Hands-On Science and Technology · Grade 3* · ISBN: 978-1-55379-709-8

**7**

Ask:

- Can you see any of these shapes in the classroom?

Record students' responses in the second column of the chart. Ask:

- Do you think you will be able to find more examples of geometric shapes and solids in the playground and in the community?
- Can these shapes be found in nature?

Introduce the guided inquiry question: **What structures has nature engineered?**

## Action: Part One

Read *Glooscap, the Beavers and the Sugarloaf Mountain* by Allison Mitcham. This Mi'kmaw story is about beavers that build a huge dam across a river, preventing the fish from swimming upstream and, in turn, preventing the fishers from catching their food. The Mi'kmaq call on Glooscap for help.

After reading and discussing the book, ask:

- Is the dam in this story a structure? How do you know?
- Is it natural or human-made?
- What materials is it made from?
- How does the beaver build the dam?
- What is the dam used for?
- What other structures might we find in nature?

Have students share their ideas and background knowledge.

Also, review Image Bank: Human-Made and Natural Structures (see Appendix, page 431). This will help students as they prepare for the land-based learning experience in the next part of the lesson.

## Action: Part Two

As a class, walk to a local park, forest, or nature preserve. On the walk, encourage students to look for geometric shapes and solids in nature. For example:

- oval on a flower petal
- circle shape of a bird's nest
- cylindrical shape of a tree trunk
- triangles on pine cone seeds

Also, have students look for natural structures such as:

- beaver dams
- bird nests
- shells
- spider webs
- cocoons
- anthills

Have students take photos of these shapes, solids, and structures for use back in the classroom.

Invite a local Elder or Métis Senator to guide the nature walk. They can share knowledge about structures, shapes, and solids in nature and may be able to tell traditional stories related to these topics.

After the walk, have students discuss their observations and recordings. Add these to the chart started at the beginning of the lesson.

Follow up the land-based learning experience by reading stories about structures in nature: *A Wasp Builds a Nest: See Inside a Paper Wasp's Nest and Watch It Grow* by Martin Camm and Kate Scarborough and/or *A House Is a House for Me* by Mary Ann Hoberman.

### Activity Sheet
Directions to students:

Record your observations of geometric shapes, solids, and structures in nature (2.7.1).

▶

Portage & Main Press, 2017 · *Hands-On Science and Technology · Grade 3* · ISBN: 978-1-55379-709-8

Portage & Main Press, 2017 · Hands-On Science and Technology · Grade 3 · ISBN: 978-1-55379-709-8

# 7

## Action: Part Three

 **SAFETY NOTE:** Eggs are used in the following two experiments. Before beginning the activities in Action: Part Three and Action: Part Four, be sure to check for any student allergies to eggs. In addition, raw eggs pose a salmonella risk, especially if they break. For this reason, the following activities should be conducted as demonstrations.

Display the whole raw eggs (point out that they are not cooked). Ask:

- What shape is this?
- Is this a natural or a human-made structure? What is the difference between a natural and a human-made structure?
- Do you think the egg is a strong structure? Why or why not?

Test students' prediction by placing your hands on either end of the egg, squeezing the egg, and trying to break it. Ask:

- Why did the egg not break?
- Why does an egg need to be strong?

**NOTE:** The egg's dome-like shape makes it very difficult to break when squeezing it between two hands, top and bottom, because the force applied is spread out over the surface of the egg.

## Action: Part Four

**NOTE:** It is recommended that preparation of the eggshell halves be done in advance, following these procedures:

1. Rinse the shell with soap and warm water (for salmonella risk).
2. Gently tap the small end of the egg on a table to break it open, and make a small hole at that end of the egg.
3. Pour out the raw egg.
4. Wrap a piece of masking tape around the middle of the eggshell. This will prevent the shell from cracking when you cut it.
5. Use a knife to carefully cut around the eggshell in the middle, with a straight (non-jagged) cut. Do this

with all four eggs, keeping the four pieces without holes, and discarding the pieces with holes.

Display the four eggshell halves. Place the eggshells on a table, open-end down, in a square shape that is just smaller than the book at the bottom of a stack of books.

Now, test the strength of the eggshells. Ask:

- Do you think the eggshells will break if I place a book on top of them?
- How many books do you think I can add before the eggshells break?

Test students' predictions by placing books on top of the eggshells, one by one in a stack, until the shells break. Tell students to keep track of the number of books that can be stacked before the shells break.

Discuss the strength of these natural structures, focusing on the fact that eggshells are shaped like domes, which are extremely strong structures. The weight or force put on the eggshells is spread out over the entire surface of the dome, meaning that the shells can withstand considerable pressure.

## Action: Part Five

Discuss the similarities and differences in human-made structures and those found in nature. Ask:

- What kinds of materials are used to build homes? (e.g., bricks, cement, wood, steel)
- What kinds of materials do animals use to build their homes?
- Create a chart to record students' ideas, as in the following example:

| Animal | Home | Materials |
|--------|------|-----------|
| bird | nest | twigs, grass |
| | | |
| | | |

**7**

Brainstorm a list of animals, and then identify the name of each animal's home and the materials of which each home is made. Record ideas on the chart.

After students have shared background knowledge, expand their understanding of this topic by watching videos such as:

- "Top 10 Animal Architects And The Beautiful Homes They Build." facts@web (2:21). Go to: <https://www.youtube.com/watch?v=9bKQeoNrciQ>.
- "Animal Homes (1955)." A/V Geeks (11:13). Go to: <https://www.youtube.com/watch?v=12Z1LD0_uaY>.

As you watch the videos, add information to the chart.

Discuss these natural structures. Ask:

- How do animal structures compare to those of humans?
- Do you think animal structures are easier or more difficult to build than human structures?

Have students attempt to build models of specific natural structures or animal homes (e.g., beaver dams, bird nests). Challenge students to use natural materials as much as possible, collecting whatever is needed for their plan.

Students can also help co-construct criteria for evaluating their projects.

## Activity: Part Six

As a class, discuss the environmental impact of structures built by humans. Ask:

- What happens to the natural environment when humans build in that area?
- How does building affect plants and animals in a natural environment? Would they survive? Where would they go?

- How are a lake and a forest affected by new cottage construction?
- How does it affect plants and animals in that area?

Discuss how construction of structures by humans affects the environment, and have students suggest ways negative impacts might be addressed.

Now, discuss the impact of structures built by animals. Ask:

- What is the impact on the environment of a dam built by a beaver?
- What is the impact on the environment of a nest built by a tent caterpillar in a tree?
- What is the impact on the environment of an anthill built in a backyard?

Have students share their ideas and background experiences.

---

**NOTE:** This is an excellent opportunity to invite guests to discuss these ideas with the class. For example, invite:
- a city planner to discuss the impact of development on nature
- a construction company owner to discuss how the company will protect the environment when building
- a local Elder or Métis Senator to discuss how beaver dams and hydro dams affect communities
- an entomologist to discuss the impact of tent caterpillars on communities

---

## Learning Centre

At the learning centre, provide chart paper, markers, magazines, computer/tablet with Internet access and a printer, scissors, and glue, along with a copy of the Learning-Centre Task Card: Human-Made or Natural Structure? (2.7.2).

Have students create t-charts on chart paper that show examples of human-made structures on one side and natural structures on the other.

Portage & Main Press, 2017 · Hands-On Science and Technology · Grade 3 · ISBN: 978-1-55379-709-8

Portage & Main Press, 2017 · Hands-On Science and Technology · Grade 3 · ISBN: 978-1-55379-709-8

**7**

Label one column "Human-Made Structures" and the other "Natural Structures." Ask students to find pictures in magazines and online of both human-made and natural structures. Have students cut out the pictures and paste them under the appropriate column on their charts. Remind them to include the name of the structure beside each example.

**NOTE:** Teachers may want to encourage students to use Internet sites that are part of Creative Commons, so that visuals are copyright-free. Google Image Search allows you, under Search Tools, to select "Usage Rights." There are lots of images that are labelled for non-commercial reuse.

## Consolidate and Debrief

- Revisit the guided inquiry question: **What structures has nature engineered?** Have students share their knowledge, provide examples, and ask further inquiry questions.
- Add to the concept web as students learn new concepts, answer some of their own inquiry questions, and ask new inquiry questions.
- Add new terms and illustrations to the class word wall. Also, include the words in other languages, as appropriate
- Have students add new terms, definitions, and illustrations to their Science and Technology Glossary (2.1.1). When possible, encourage students to add words (and examples) in other languages, including Indigenous languages, reflective of the classroom population.

### Assessment for Learning
Using geometric solids and pattern blocks, ask individual students the names of the three-dimensional solids and the two-dimensional shapes to ensure they are familiar with all the names. Use the Anecdotal Record sheet, on page 26, to record results.

## Enhance

- Explore the Aboriginal Access to Engineering site, specifically, the learning module "Bear Paw Trail," which deals with natural structures. Go to: <www.aboriginalaccess.ca/Kids/learning-modules/bear-paw-trail>.
- Together with students, examine a variety of pictures of buildings and other structures. Encourage students to identify geometric shapes and solids that have been incorporated into the buildings.
- Challenge students to build structures that will provide a protective casing for an egg. Then, have students drop their structures with the egg inside to find out if it helps the egg withstand the impact.
- Have students sort the photographs, taken during the class walk, based on two or more attributes. Tell them to look at shape and materials used, or shape and stability. Later, have them chart or graph that data, considering an electronic option for doing so.
- Access the interactive activity, Structures in Their Environments, in the Grade 3, Unit 2 folder of the **Hands-On Interactive for Science and Technology, Grade 3** download. Find this download at: <www.portageandmainpress.com/product/hands-on-interactive-for-science-and-technology-grade-3/>.
- Have students continue their do-it-yourself projects at the Makerspace centre.

Date: _____  Name: _____

# Shapes, Solids, and Structures in Nature

On our walk we went _____

| Object | Geometric Shape Observed | Diagram/ Photo (√) |
|--------|--------------------------|--------------------|
|        |                          |                    |
|        |                          |                    |
|        |                          |                    |
|        |                          |                    |
|        |                          |                    |
|        |                          |                    |
|        |                          |                    |
|        |                          |                    |

Other structures I observed on our walk were _____

_____

_____

Portage & Main Press, 2017 · Hands-On Science and Technology · Grade 3 · ISBN: 978-1-55379-709-8

# Human-Made or Natural Structure?

1. Create a t-chart on chart paper.

   - Label one column "Natural Structures" and the other column "Human-Made Structures."

2. Find pictures of each type of structure in magazines and on websites.

   - Cut out or print all the pictures you find.

3. Glue the pictures in the appropriate column.

4. Label the name of each structure.

5. On the back of the chart paper, answer this question:

   - How do humans use what they learn from nature to make their lives better?

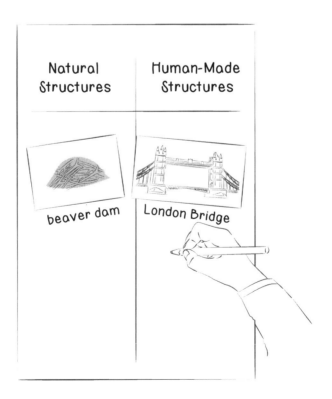

Portage & Main Press, 2017 · Hands-On Science and Technology · Grade 3 · ISBN: 978-1-55379-709-8

# 8 | How Are Structures Around the World Similar and Different?

## Information for Teachers

Building materials used in any given community depend largely on availability, suitability, and era of construction. Several Canadian provinces have a forestry industry, making wooden structures prevalent. Other areas may be rich in Tyndall stone or limestone, so this material may be widely used in the region.

The wealth of a community also plays a major role in determining which materials are used. The more affluent a community, the greater its ability to import specialized materials and/or use more expensive materials such as steel and glass.

In many countries where wood is scarce but sand is plentiful, brick structures are common. In developing countries and poverty-stricken areas, homes are often built from materials that are found and hand-hewn.

Climate is also a major factor in the construction of homes and other buildings, and in the materials used in an area. Compare buildings found in northern Canada to buildings found in South America. Structures are often designed and built to withstand natural disasters or, at least, in such a way that their collapse would be less hazardous to the overall community.

Different cultures use different shapes for their structures. For example:

tipi

igloo

Zulu hut

Berber tent

pioneer wooden-frame house

## 21st Century Competencies

**Critical Thinking**, **Communication**, and **Citizenship:** Students will analyze various structures from around the world, focusing on how the availability of materials and culture may affect the design.

Portage & Main Press, 2017 · Hands-On Science and Technology · Grade 3 · ISBN: 978-1-55379-709-8

**8**

## Materials

- Image Bank: Important Structures Around the World (see Appendix, page 435)
- projection device (optional)
- world map
- sticky notes
- Image Bank: Homes Around the World (Print copies of these images.) (see Appendix, page 437)
- chart paper
- markers
- library books, magazines, and images with famous buildings and landmarks
- computer/tablet with Internet access
- printer
- construction paper or Manila tag
- wool or string
- Scotch tape
- scissors
- glue
- clipboards
- pencils
- Activity Sheet: Buildings in Our Community (2.8.1)
- Learning-Centre Task Card: Create a Puzzle (2.8.2)
- white construction paper or Manila tag (11 x 14 in./28 cm x 35.5 cm)
- art supplies (e.g., pencil crayons, charcoal, paint)
- access to a photocopier
- large envelopes
- concept map (from lesson 1)
- Science and Technology Glossary (2.1.1)

## Activate

Take students on a field trip around the neighbourhood. Encourage students to pay particular attention to structural features, use of geometric shapes, and the types of materials used in the construction of the buildings and structures.

Stop at several locations for students to observe and discuss the structures and buildings they see. Along the walk, select three building/structure sites for students to sketch and record their features.

Back in the classroom, distribute a copy of Activity Sheet: Buildings in Our Community (2.8.1) to each student. Review the class word wall and student Science and Technology glossaries for vocabulary that students can use on the activity sheet to communicate their observations.

### Activity Sheet

Directions to students:

Draw a diagram of a building or structure at three different sites. Name the building, list some of the materials that were used to build it, and describe the building (2.8.1).

Introduce the guided inquiry question: **How are structures around the world similar and different?**

## Action: Part One

Have students discuss their diagrams and descriptions on the activity sheet. Ask:

- What kinds of buildings did you see in our community?
- Were they mostly one-storey buildings or multiple-storey buildings?
- What are most of the buildings you saw used for?
- What structural or geometric shapes did you see in our community?
- Did you see any columns or arches?
- What kinds of materials were used in the construction of the buildings in our community?

- Where do you think these materials came from?
- Is there anything that all or many of the buildings in our community have in common?
- Were there any specialized buildings in our community (e.g., tower, very modern building, very old or heritage building)?
- How are the specialized buildings similar to/different from the other buildings in our neighbourhood?

Have students share their diagrams and ideas.

## Action: Part Two

Display the images from Image Bank: Important Structures Around the World. Work as a class to identify each structure, and locate its country of origin on the world map. Use sticky notes to mark the location of each structure on the map. Discuss the designs of the various structures, highlighting interesting features and materials.

## Action: Part Three

Display the images from Image Bank: Homes Around the World. As a class, discuss the various structures. Compare and contrast them to homes in your local community.

For each picture, provide information on the location of the homes, and have students identify these places on the world map.

Provide each student with a printed copy of one of the homes. Have students mount the pictures on construction paper. Display the images. As a class, discuss how the pictures could be sorted and classified in various ways. Some examples are:

- by continent
- by material
- by shape
- by any other sorting rule determined by students

Sort the images in a variety of ways, discussing features during the process.

Attach the images around the world map, and use wool or string to connect the image to its country. Ask:

- How are homes from around the world similar?
- How are homes from around the world different?
- How do the homes in our community compare to those in another community or in another country?

Encourage students to generate their own inquiry questions from the display. Record their questions on chart paper for further exploration and research.

## Learning Centre

At the learning centre, provide sheets of white construction paper or Manila tag (28 cm x 35.5 cm), art supplies, scissors, glue, and a copy of the Learning-Centre Task Card: Create a Puzzle (2.8.2). Display books and images of famous structures as well.

Have students sketch and colour a picture of a famous structure on the construction paper and then cut the picture apart into different shapes to create a puzzle.

---

**NOTE:** Before students cut apart their pictures into puzzles, photocopy the pictures, and have them use the photocopy version for their puzzle. Keep the original pictures in a large envelope at the centre; students visiting the centre can use these as additional support when putting together other students' puzzles.

---

## Consolidate and Debrief

- Revisit the guided inquiry question: **How are structures around the world similar and different?** Have students share their

Portage & Main Press, 2017 · *Hands-On Science and Technology · Grade 3* · ISBN: 978-1-55379-709-8

Portage & Main Press, 2017 · *Hands-On Science and Technology · Grade 3* · ISBN: 978-1-55379-709-8

knowledge, provide examples, and ask further inquiry questions.

- Add to the concept web as students learn new concepts, answer some of their own inquiry questions, and ask new inquiry questions.
- Add new terms and illustrations to the class word wall. Also, include the words in other languages, as appropriate
- Have students add new terms, definitions, and illustrations to their Science and Technology Glossary (2.1.1). When possible, encourage students to add words (and examples) in other languages, including Indigenous languages, reflective of the classroom population.

## Enhance

- To further reinforce concepts from the unit, have students choose a particular structure and explain how its shape and materials help it to withstand various forces. Also, challenge students to find two similar structures and explain how they are the same or find two different structures and explain how they differ.

- Have students select a world-famous (or a less known) structure, and challenge them to build a miniature version of it. Encourage students to decide, as a group, what type of material to use (e.g., LEGO, construction paper, drinking straws, fabrics, precut wood pieces).

- Have students continue their do-it-yourself projects at the Makerspace centre.

# Buildings in Our Community

| Diagram of building | Materials used: _____ |
|---|---|
| | _____ |
| | _____ |
| | Description: _____ |
| Name of building: | _____ |
| _____ | _____ |
| | _____ |
| Diagram of building | Materials used: _____ |
| | _____ |
| | _____ |
| | Description: _____ |
| | _____ |
| Name of building: | _____ |
| _____ | _____ |
| Diagram of building | Materials used: _____ |
| | _____ |
| | _____ |
| | Description: _____ |
| Name of building: | _____ |
| _____ | _____ |

Portage & Main Press, 2017 · Hands-On Science and Technology · Grade 3 · ISBN: 978-1-55379-709-8

# Create a Puzzle

1. Choose a famous building to sketch and colour.

2. Have your picture photocopied.

3. Cut the photocopied picture into different shapes to create a puzzle.

4. Place the puzzle and your original picture in a large envelope labelled with your name and the number of pieces in your puzzle.

5. Trade puzzles with another student.

6. Try to complete your classmate's puzzle, and figure out what famous building it is!

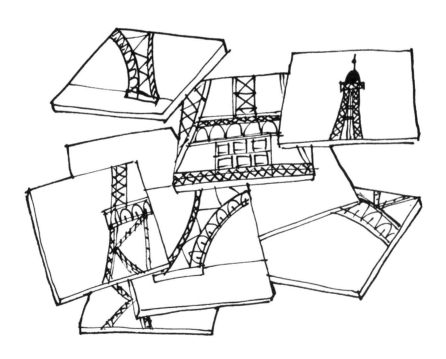

Portage & Main Press, 2017 · Hands-On Science and Technology · Grade 3 · ISBN: 978-1-55379-709-8

# 9 | What Are Some Careers in Design and Building?

## Information for Teachers

Most human activity depends on engineers of all kinds. Houses, televisions, video games, and toys are some of the smaller-scale products designers and engineers have created. On a larger scale, engineers are responsible for designing bridges, airports, factories, highways, airplanes, and rockets.

People who have careers in design and building are problem solvers. They collect information, make plans, conduct experiments, and build models before they begin actual on-site construction. They must find and choose the safest and most effective solution to a design problem by applying science and technology concepts, as well as engineering and design techniques. These careers occur in a challenging and ever-changing environment, and the individuals make far-reaching contributions to our communities.

**NOTE:** Of special interest to Indigenous students and teachers, see the information from Aboriginal Access to Engineering at Queen's University on First Nations engineers: <www.aboriginalaccess.ca/kids>.

## 21st Century Competencies

**Citizenship** and **Character**: Students will explore various careers related to engineering and construction trades, and determine some of the skills and attitudes required to be successful.

## Materials

- paper
- pencils
- chart paper
- markers
- resources about architect Douglas Cardinal (including access to: <www.djcardinal.com/work/>)

- resources about the Mohawk iron workers (including access to: <www.mohawkironworkers.com/rivetrampage/>)
- computers/tablets with Internet access
- Learning-Centre Task Card: We Are Composers (2.9.1)
- writing paper
- audio-recording device(s) (optional)
- reproductions, on chart paper, of the KWL chart (see Action: Part Two)
- concept map (from lesson 1)
- Science and Technology Glossary (2.1.1)

## Activate

As a class, discuss the types of jobs related to construction, engineering, architecture, and design. On a sheet of paper, record a list of careers, which may include engineer, architect, millwright, draftsperson, designer, and others in the building field, as well as artisans and hobbyists who build model airplanes, furniture, or toys. Do not forget to mention high-school teachers who provide technical/vocational education (e.g., metal, woodworking), and college and university instructors in the fields of design and architecture.

Introduce the guided inquiry question: **What are some careers in design and building?**

## Action: Part One

Invite guests into the classroom who have jobs related to construction, engineering, architecture, and design. Involve students in the invitation process by having them write letters requesting visits.

**NOTE:** Teachers should contact the guests to be approached by students before students send their own letters.

Portage & Main Press, 2017 · *Hands-On Science and Technology* · Grade 3 · ISBN: 978-1-55379-709-8

Portage & Main Press, 2017 · Hands-On Science and Technology · Grade 3 · ISBN: 978-1-55379-709-8

## Action: Part Two

Before any guest speaker presents to the class, create a KWL chart to complete with students based on the career or hobby of the presenter.

| What We <u>Know</u> | What We Want to Know | What We Learned |
|---|---|---|
| | | |

Have students discuss what they already know about that field, and record it in the first (K) column of the chart. Also, have them brainstorm a list of questions they have for the presenter, and record these in the second (W) column of the chart. Be sure to display some of the structures students have built during the unit so the presenter can examine them, discuss students' designs, and perhaps suggest new construction techniques.

When the guest arrives, invite them to review the chart and discuss the information students already know about in their field. Ask the guest to confirm the information or point out ideas that are not accurate.

Have students also refer to the chart when asking the guest questions.

After the presentation, complete the final column of the chart with students by recording new ideas and concepts students learned (L) from the guest speaker.

### Assessment as Learning

Have students reflect on what they learned about careers in design and building by completing a Science and Technology Journal sheet, on page 28.

## Action: Part Three

Learn about Indigenous peoples with careers in design and building. Do the following activities as a class, or divide the class into working groups and assign a different activity to each group.

- Invite a local Indigenous person with a career in design and building to present to the class. Have students prepare questions for the speaker ahead of time. Send the questions to the guest, and have students ask their questions during the presentation. Follow up with thank-you letters to the guest, ensuring that students explain what they learned from the presentation.

- Explore the work of architect Douglas Cardinal. His website includes a collection of images of buildings he has designed. Go to: <www.djcarchitect.com/work/>.

- Research architect Étienne-Joseph Gaboury.

- Explore the Aboriginal Access to Engineering site from Queen's University, especially the learning module, A Day in the Life of an Engineer. Go to: <www.aboriginalaccess.ca/kids/learning-modules/a-day-in-the-life-of-an-engineer>.

- Learn about the Mohawk iron workers who specialize in working high above the ground building sky scrapers. A video series on their website includes an episode on Women of Steel that focuses on breaking stereotypes in construction. Go to: <www.mohawkironworkers.com/>. There is also a website for children that will put them in the role of a Mohawk iron worker. Go to: <www.mohawkironworkers.com/rivetrampage/>.

## Learning Centre

At the learning centre, provide writing paper and pencils, audio-recording device(s) (optional), and a copy of the Learning-Centre Task Card: We Are Composers (2.9.1).

Have pairs of students create poems, raps, riddles, or songs based on information gained from the guest presenter. The details of the

**9**

poem, rap, riddle, or song can be a summary of the presentation, the answer to (a) class question(s), or (b) new question(s) students still have about the career. Have student pairs perform their creation for the rest of the class.

## Consolidate and Debrief

- Revisit the guided inquiry question: **What are some careers in design and building?** Have students share their knowledge, provide examples, and ask further inquiry questions.

- Add to the concept web as students learn new concepts, answer some of their own inquiry questions, and ask new inquiry questions.

- Add new terms and illustrations to the class word wall. Also, include the words in other languages, as appropriate.

- Have students add new terms, definitions, and illustrations to their Science and Technology Glossary (2.1.1). When possible, encourage students to add words (and examples) in other languages, including Indigenous languages, reflective of the classroom population.

## Enhance

- Have individual, pairs, or groups of students research a career related to construction, engineering, architecture, or design that is different from that of any of the guest presenters.

- Invite a guest speaker from an architectural (or engineering) firm who has worked with/ has experience with Indigenous architecture or design. Ask the guest to speak to students about career opportunities, as well as inspirations for the firm's designs. Encourage an avenue for students to learn about structures throughout your city, town, or community that are inspired by Indigenous values, arts, and design.

- Take students on a field trip to one or more sites of Indigenous architecture or design, so they can learn firsthand about the buildings and how they were made.

- Have students continue their do-it-yourself projects at the Makerspace centre.

# We Are Composers

1. With a partner, create a poem, rap, riddle, or song based on information given by

_____

(presenter's name and title)

_____

2. Your poem, rap, riddle, or song can be a summary of the presentation, answers to class questions, or questions you still have about the career.

3. With your partner, perform your poem, rap, riddle, or song for the class.

# 10 | What Other Structures Can We Build?

## Information for Teachers

The seven designing/building challenges presented in Action: Part One of this lesson incorporate all the learning outcomes for this unit. They provide students with enriching experiences and build on the skills they have acquired. Teachers may choose to have students do all seven challenges or a select few. Students can do the challenges individually, in pairs, or in groups.

## 21ˢᵗ Century Competencies

**Creativity**, **Critical Thinking**, **Collaboration**, and **Communication:** Students will engage in challenges that use the skills and knowledge that they have developed in this unit. They will reflect on their designs and share successes and challenges they faced.

## Materials

- construction paper
- digital camera (optional)
- audio- or video-recording device
- drawing paper
- drawing pencils
- pencil crayons
- small weights (e.g., gram weights, coins, marbles, large washers)
- stacks of books
- masking tape
- paper clips
- paper plates
- Plasticine or play dough
- newspaper
- rulers
- scissors
- sets of dominoes
- decks of playing cards
- drinking straws
- stopwatch (optional)
- computer/tablet with Internet access (optional)

- resources about building birdhouses
- variety of building materials for constructing birdhouses, traps, or other structures of various shapes, as specified by students
- tape measures or metre sticks
- paper (30 cm x 22.5 cm)
- Activity Sheet A: Balanced Structures (2.10.1)
- Activity Sheet B: Building a Birdhouse (2.10.2)
- Activity Sheet C: Building a Trap (2.10.3)
- Activity Sheet D: Building a Straw Tower (2.10.4)
- Activity Sheet E: Building Newspaper Structures (2.10.5)
- Activity Sheet F: Designing a Paper Tower (2.10.6)
- Activity Sheet G: Designing a Construction-Paper Structure (2.10.7)
- Learning-Centre Task Card: How Would You Build It? (2.10.8)
- concept map (from lesson 1)
- Science and Technology Glossary (2.1.1)

## Activate

As a class, review some of the big ideas from the unit, referring to the class concept map created in the first lesson and used throughout the unit. Ask:

- What is a structure?
- What are the forces acting upon a structure?
- Where are structures found?
- Which materials are stronger than others?
- What are joints, and how are they made?
- How can structures be built stronger?
- How is a frame structure built?
- What are the similarities and differences between human-made and natural structures?
- How are structures found in different parts of the world similar to and different from one another?

Portage & Main Press, 2017 · *Hands-On Science and Technology · Grade 3* · ISBN: 978-1-55379-709-8

- What are some careers in design and building, and what sorts of skills do these jobs require?

Introduce the guided inquiry question: **What other structures can we build?**

## Action: Part One

**NOTE:** Remember to have students draw a sketch or take a photograph of any structure they build before they attempt to test it for sturdiness/strength (i.e., by adding mass/weight until it collapses). Remind students to do this with each challenge, so they can build a complete record of their work. Also, consider videotaping as structures are tested.

### Challenge 1: Balanced Structures

Challenge students to use playing cards or dominoes to build balanced, stable structures within a certain time frame. Have them predict and investigate to determine how high or wide they can make their structure.

Distribute a copy of Activity Sheet A: Balanced Structures (2.10.1) to each student who works on this challenge. Have students use it to record their results.

**NOTE:** If using playing cards, have students first build and test, and then expand on the task, by thinking of ways they could change it/add materials to make it better. Then, have a second attempt where cards could be folded, cut, or joined using play dough or Plasticine to create more friction/adhesion at the joints.

### Activity Sheet A

Directions to students:

Predict how high and/or wide you can build your playing-card or domino structure, while also keeping it stable and balanced. After you have built your structure, measure its height and/or width. Determine how close your estimate was. Draw a picture or take a photo of the finished product. Explain how your design and

the structure you built best meet the challenge (2.10.1).

### Challenge 2: Building a Birdhouse

Have students use technological problem solving to build a birdhouse for a local species of bird. Have them research what type of house would be best for the particular bird, where the house should be located, and materials that should be used to build the birdhouse.

Other design considerations might be:

- size of entry hole—large enough for desired bird species to enter but small enough to keep out predators
- ways to prevent squirrels from climbing up to the house
- paint the birdhouse with light colours to keep it cooler on hot days
- solutions to other practical problems in bird homes

Distribute a copy of Activity Sheet B: Building a Birdhouse (2.10.2) to each student who works on this challenge. Have students use it to plan their birdhouses.

**NOTE:** The research is an important component of this project, as birds have specific needs for their homes. Purple martins, for example, prefer large houses that are at high elevations. Robins and sparrows prefer houses lower to the ground.

### Activity Sheet B

Directions to students:

Decide which bird you will build a birdhouse for. Research what type of house is best for this bird, including where the birdhouse should be located, and what materials you should use to build it. Sketch a design of your birdhouse, and include measurements. Build your birdhouse. Draw a picture or take a photo of the finished product. Include measurements. Explain how your design and the birdhouse you built best meet the challenge (2.10.2).

Portage & Main Press, 2017 · Hands-On Science and Technology · Grade 3 · ISBN: 978-1-55379-709-8

## 10

### Challenge 3: Building a Trap

Challenge students to use technological problem solving to build a trap for a goblin, ogre, troll, or another mystical creature.

Distribute a copy of Activity Sheet C: Building a Trap (2.10.3) to each student who works on this challenge. Have students use it to plan their traps.

#### Activity Sheet C

Directions to students:

Use technological problem solving to help you build a trap for a goblin, ogre, troll, or another mystical creature of your choice. Before you build your trap, sketch a design that includes measurements. Once built, draw your finished trap, or take a photo. Include measurements for the finished product. Explain how your design and the trap you built meet the challenge (2.10.3).

### Challenge 4: Building a Straw Tower

Have students use 25 drinking straws and Plasticine or play dough to make the tallest tower that can hold coins or other small weights without collapsing. To test the strength of their towers, tell students to place a paper plate at the top of the tower and add coins as mass/weights (keeping track of the quantity added) until the tower collapses.

Distribute a copy of Activity Sheet D: Building a Straw Tower (2.10.4) to each student who works on this challenge. Have students use it to record results of the experiment.

**NOTE:** Provide an opportunity for students to build, test, and then redesign to make their structure stronger.

#### Activity Sheet D

Directions to students:

Use 25 drinking straws and Plasticine or play dough to make the tallest tower that can hold coins or other small weights without collapsing.

Before you build your tower, sketch a design and include measurements. Estimate how many coins or weights the tower will hold before it collapses. Draw a picture or take a photo of the finished product. Include measurements and the quantity of coins or weights it actually held. Explain how your design and the tower you built meet the challenge (2.10.4).

### Challenge 5: Building Newspaper Structures

Have students create beams: Roll single sheets of newspaper into long, tight tubes and secure with tape. Then, challenge students to build structures that will stand freely, using only the beams and tape. Beginning with a cube-shape frame, encourage students to design without restraint and to see how high they can build their structures. Encourage them to add extra beams to support or strengthen the structures.

Also, challenge students to use newspaper and tape to make chairs or stools. Have them roll the newspaper into beams for the main frame and then layer paper for the seat or back of the chair/stool. They can then test the structures for strength by piling books on them. Extend the challenge by having students build a chair or stool they can actually sit on without it collapsing.

Distribute a copy of Activity Sheet E: Building Newspaper Structures (2.10.5) to each student who works on one of the newspaper challenges. Have students use it to plan and record the results of their newspaper structures.

**NOTE:** Provide an opportunity for students to build, test, and then redesign to make their structure stronger.

#### Activity Sheet E

Directions to students:

Create beams by rolling single sheets of newspaper into long, tight tubes that are taped secure. Then, build freestanding structures using

Portage & Main Press, 2017 · Hands-On Science and Technology · Grade 3 · ISBN: 978-1-55379-709-8

only the beams and tape. Try building a chair or stool by rolling the newspaper into beams for the main frame and then layering paper for the seat or back of the chair/stool. Before you build your newspaper structure, sketch a design, and include measurements. Once built, draw a picture or take a photo of the finished product, being sure to include measurements. Explain how your design and the structure you built meet the challenge (2.10.5).

## Challenge 6: Designing a Paper Tower

Have students build freestanding towers using 20 sheets of paper (30 cm x 22.5 cm), 30 centimetres of masking tape, and 10 paper clips. Challenge students to see how high they can build their towers. To test the strength of the towers, have students place a paper plate at the top of the tower, and add coins as mass/weights (keeping track of the quantity) until the tower collapses.

Distribute a copy of Activity Sheet F: Designing a Paper Tower (2.10.6) to each student who works on this challenge. Have students use it to plan their paper towers and record their results of the experiment.

**NOTE:** Provide an opportunity for students to build, test, and then redesign to make their structure stronger.

### Activity Sheet F

Directions to students:

Use 20 sheets of paper, 30 centimetres of masking tape, and 10 paper clips to build a freestanding tower. Before you build your tower, sketch a design for it. Include measurements, and estimate the number of coins or weights it will hold. Draw a picture or take a photo of the finished product. Be sure to include the measurements of the finished product and the number of coins or weights it held. Explain how your design and the tower you built meet the challenge (2.10.6).

## Challenge 7: Designing a Construction-Paper Structure

Have students use construction paper and masking tape to build structures of various shapes. Students can determine the shapes to be built. Have them test the strength of each structure built by placing a paper plate on top and adding weight until the structure collapses. Challenge students to determine the shape that has the most strength.

Distribute a copy of Activity Sheet G: Designing a Construction-Paper Structure (2.10.7) to each student who works on this challenge. Have those students use it to sketch a design and record results of the shape and strength experiment.

**NOTE:** Provide an opportunity for students to build, test, and then redesign to make their structure stronger.

### Activity Sheet G

Directions to students:

Use construction paper and masking tape to build a structure. Before you build your structure, sketch a design. Include measurements, and estimate the number of coins or weights the structure will hold. Once you build your structure, draw a picture or take a photo of the finished product. Be sure to include the measurements of the finished product, as well as the number of coins or weights it held. Explain how your design and the structure you built meet the challenge (2.10.7).

### Assessment of Learning

Observe students as they work at the various challenges, noticing their ability to use problem-solving steps and strategies. Assess their ability to understand the problem/challenge, make a plan/design, carry out the plan, and then evaluate it. Use the Anecdotal Record sheet, on page 26, to record results.

Portage & Main Press, 2017 · *Hands-On Science and Technology* · Grade 3 · ISBN: 978-1-55379-709-8

## 10

### Action: Part Two

Engage students in a whole-class discussion about the building of the different structures. Ask:

- What were your successes?
- What kinds of challenges did you have?
- Which challenges were easier to solve than others?
- Which challenges did you find more difficult to solve?
- How did your final product differ from your original plan and sketch?

### Learning Centre

At the learning centre, provide a copy of the Learning-Centre Task Card: How Would You Build It? (2.10.8), as well as an audio- or video-recording device, drawing paper, pencils, markers, and pencil crayons.

Ask students to reflect on the value of (1) using their imagination to design and build structures, and (2) following instructions when designing and building structures. Have them use an audio- or video-recording device to record their responses, and also draw a picture of a structure they would build.

### Consolidate and Debrief

- Revisit the guided inquiry question: **What other structures can we build?** Have students share their knowledge, provide examples, and ask further inquiry questions.
- Add to the concept web as students learn new concepts, answer some of their own inquiry questions, and ask new inquiry questions.
- Add new words and illustrations to the class word wall. Also, include the words in other languages, as appropriate.
- Have students add new terms, definitions, and illustrations to their Science and

Technology Glossary (2.1.1). When possible, encourage students to add words (and examples) in other languages, including Indigenous languages, reflective of the classroom population.

### Enhance

- Have students continue their do-it-yourself projects at the Makerspace centre.

Portage & Main Press, 2017 · *Hands-On Science and Technology · Grade 3* · ISBN: 978-1-55379-709-8

# Balanced Structures

1. I will use _____ to build my structure.

2. I predict the height of my structure will be _____.

3. I predict the width of my structure will be _____.

4. The actual height of my structure is _____.

5. The actual width of my structure is _____.

6. Use the space below to calculate the difference between predicted and actual measurements.

| Height | Width |
|---|---|
| | |
| The difference in predicted and actual height is:<br><br>_____ | The difference in predicted and actual width is:<br><br>_____ |

7. Explain how your design and the structure you built meet the challenge.

_____

_____

Portage & Main Press, 2017 · Hands-On Science and Technology · Grade 3 · ISBN: 978-1-55379-709-8

# Building a Birdhouse

I will be building a structure for _____.

My research:

| | |
|---|---|
| **My Plan** | **My Finished Product** |
| Sketch: | Sketch/Photo: |
| Materials used: _____ | Materials used: _____ |
| _____ | _____ |
| Estimated measurements: | Actual measurements: |
| _____ | _____ |
| _____ | _____ |

Explain how your design and the structure you built meet the challenge.

_____

_____

Portage & Main Press, 2017 · Hands-On Science and Technology · Grade 3 · ISBN: 978-1-55379-709-8

**Date:** _____     **Name:** _____

# Building a Trap

| My Plan | My Finished Product |
|---|---|
| Sketch: | Sketch/Photo: |
| Estimated measurements: <br><br>_____ <br><br>_____ | Actual measurements: <br><br>_____ <br><br>_____ |
| Estimated number of coins/ weights held: <br><br>_____ | Actual number of coins/ weights held: <br><br>_____ |

1. I changed the following from my original plan: _____

_____

2. These are the reasons why my final product is different from my original plan:

_____

_____

3. Explain how your design and the structure you built meet the challenge.

_____

_____

Portage & Main Press, 2017 · Hands-On Science and Technology · Grade 3 · ISBN: 978-1-55379-709-8

Date: _____ Name: _____

# Building a Straw Tower

Diagram of design (include measurements):

Estimate: I think the tower will hold _____ coins.

Final tower (with measurements):

Result: The tower held _____ coins.

How did your tower meet the challenge?

_____

_____

_____

_____

Portage & Main Press, 2017 · Hands-On Science and Technology · Grade 3 · ISBN: 978-1-55379-709-8

Date: _____   Name: _____

# Building Newspaper Structures

Diagram of design (include measurements):

Final chair/stool (with measurements):

How did your structure meet the challenge?

_____

_____

_____

_____

Portage & Main Press, 2017 · Hands-On Science and Technology · Grade 3 · ISBN: 978-1-55379-709-8

# Designing a Paper Tower

Diagram of design (include measurements):

Estimate: I think the tower will hold _____ coins.

Final tower (with measurements):

Result: The tower held _____ coins.

How did your tower meet the challenge?

_____

_____

_____

_____

Portage & Main Press, 2017 · Hands-On Science and Technology · Grade 3 · ISBN: 978-1-55379-709-8

# Designing a Construction-Paper Structure

Diagram of design (include measurements):

Estimate: I think the tower will hold _____ coins.

Final structure (with measurements):

Result: The structure held _____ coins.

How did your structure meet the challenge?

_____

_____

_____

_____

Portage & Main Press, 2017 · Hands-On Science and Technology · Grade 3 · ISBN: 978-1-55379-709-8

# How Would You Build It?

Pretend you have been given a new box of LEGO containing 50 assorted pieces. The set comes with a booklet of instructions for various things you can build with the LEGO.

Read the questions below and audio/video record your answers to them.

1. What kind of structure would you build with your LEGO? Explain your answer.

   - Would you use the instruction booklet to find something to build?

   - Would you use your imagination to create something from the LEGO?

   - Would you use the instruction booklet to find something to construct, but then make some personal changes to the design as you build?

2. Why is it important to have an imagination when building a structure?

3. Why is it important to be able to follow the instructions when building a structure?

4. Use your imagination: Draw a picture of the structure you would build with the LEGO.

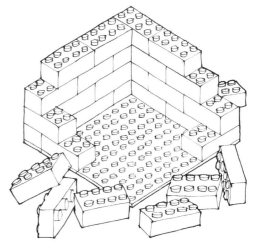

Portage & Main Press, 2017 · Hands-On Science and Technology · Grade 3 · ISBN: 978-1-55379-709-8

# Inquiry Project: What More Can I Learn About Important Buildings and Structures?

**11**

## 21st Century Competencies

**Critical Thinking**, **Communication**, **Creativity**, and **Collaboration:** Students will research a topic of their choice related to structures, and will communicate their findings in a format of their choice.

## Materials

- chart paper
- markers
- Image Bank: Indigenous Architecture (see Appendix, page 439)
- projection device
- wall map of Canada
- sticky notes
- print and Internet resources related to important structures
- stapler and staples
- scissors
- computers/tablets with Internet access
- Activity Sheet A: Research Project (2.11.1)
- Activity Sheet B: Research Outline (2.11.2)
- art supplies (e.g., pencil crayons, crayons, Scotch tape, glue, scissors)
- poster paper
- construction materials for model structure
- concept map (from lesson 1)
- Science and Technology Glossary (2.1.1)

## Activate

As a class, make a list of important buildings and structures in the community and around the world (e.g., City Hall or Town Hall, provincial legislative building, Parliament Buildings of Canada, CN Tower, Calgary Tower [Husky Tower], Rogers Centre [SkyDome], Empire State Building, Willis Tower [Sears Tower], White House, Hoover Dam, Golden Gate Bridge, London Bridge, Big Ben, Tower of London, Eiffel Tower, Sydney Opera House, Taj Mahal, Burj Khalifa, Petronas Towers, Leaning Tower of Pisa).

**NOTE:** Ensure that any structures of interest to students are included on this list. For example, a student might have a rich question about bridges, the Chunnel, or Indigenous structures, based on personal experience. There is no limit to what is explored.

Record this list on chart paper.

Project Image Bank: Indigenous Architecture, and discuss each image. Provide the names and locations of the buildings. Have students find these places on the map of Canada and mark them with sticky notes. Discuss the structures, asking:

- What designs are used?
- What materials are used?
- Who do you think designed these structures?
- How are they similar to traditional Indigenous structures?
- How are they different from traditional Indigenous structures?

Add the names of these structures to the chart paper list.

Introduce the guided inquiry question: **What more can I learn about important buildings and structures?**

## Action: Part One

Have students work individually, in pairs, or in small groups to select one structure from the class list to research (or any other structure of personal interest). Provide a variety of resources for students to use to gather their information (e.g., books, brochures, bookmarked Internet sites).

Provide each student with a copy of Activity Sheet A: Research Project (2.11.1), and review expectations. As a class, identify criteria for the project. Have students record these on their activity sheet.

### Activity Sheet A

Directions to students:

Read the questions. Record the questions you want to answer. List the criteria for the research project (2.11.1).

▶

Portage & Main Press, 2017 · Hands-On Science and Technology · Grade 3 · ISBN: 978-1-55379-709-8

## Action: Part Two

Provide support as students look for relevant resource materials and conduct their research. Also, collaborate with students as they gather materials for their final projects (e.g., poster paper, materials for constructing a model of the structure, art supplies).

Distribute a copy of Activity Sheet B: Research Outline (2.11.2) to each student, and have students record four questions they will answer about the structure. Also, have students include both a diagram and a model of the structure, a map to show where it is located, and a list of resources used in their research.

### Activity Sheet B

Directions to students:

Record four questions about your structure that you will answer, two from Activity Sheet A and two more of your own. Include a diagram of your structure, a model of your structure, a map to show where it is located, and a list of resources you used (2.11.2).

## Action: Part Three

Once students have completed the research, have them plan and present their research in a way that they have chosen (e.g., poster, song, puppet show, game). Presentations must also include a display of the diagram, model, map, and research reference list.

Display the research projects in the classroom or the school library.

### Assessment as Learning

Have students reflect on their success in meeting the criteria of the inquiry project by completing a Student Self-Assessment sheet, on page 31.

### Assessment of Learning

On the Rubric, on page 36, record the criteria identified for the inquiry project. Record results as students present their projects to the class.

### Assessment as Learning

Have students complete the 21st Century Competencies Student/Teacher Reflection sheet, on page 29, to reflect on their use of the 21st Century Competencies throughout the unit. Students record their reflections in the squares. The sheet also includes oval spaces for teachers to provide descriptive feedback to students.

## Consolidate and Debrief

■ Revisit the guided inquiry question: **What more can I learn about important buildings and structures?** Have students share their knowledge, provide examples, and ask further inquiry questions.

■ Add to and review the concept web as students learn new concepts and/or answer some of their own inquiry questions.

■ Add new terms and illustrations to the class word wall, and review the final representation of unit concepts and vocabulary.

■ Have students add new terms, definitions, and illustrations to their Science and Technology Glossary (2.1.1). Students can then cut apart the rows, alphabetize the words, and complete the glossary with a cover and binding.

## Enhance

■ Access the interactive activity, Designing and Constructing Bridges, in the Grade 3, Unit 2 folder of the **Hands-On Interactive for Science and Technology, Grade 3** download. Find this download at: <www.portageandmainpress.com/product/hands-on-interactive-for-science-and-technology-grade-3/>.

■ Have students complete their do-it-yourself projects at the Makerspace centre.

Portage & Main Press, 2017 · Hands-On Science and Technology · Grade 3 · ISBN: 978-1-55379-709-8

**Date:** _____      **Name:** _____

# Research Project

Choose one structure that interests you. You may work by yourself or with a partner. Using the different resources at school or at home (e.g., nonfiction books, brochures, bookmarked Internet sites). Choose two of the questions below to answer.

- Where is the structure located?

- What materials were used to build the structure?

- How old is the structure?

- How long did it take for the structure to be built?

- What is the purpose of the structure?

My two questions:

1. _____ ?

2. _____ ?

Criteria for the project:

1. _____

2. _____

3. _____

4. _____

Portage & Main Press, 2017 · Hands-On Science and Technology · Grade 3 · ISBN: 978-1-55379-709-8

Date: _____     Name: _____

# Research Outline

1. The structure I have chosen to research is  _____

   _____ .

2. The four questions about the structure I will answer are:

   _____ **?**

   _____ **?**

   _____ **?**

   _____ **?**

3. Also include:

   - diagram of the structure

   - model of the structure

   - map of where the structure is located

   - list of resources used in your research

4. Once you have completed the research, display and share your findings in an interesting way (e.g., poster, song, puppet show, game, electronic presentation).

Portage & Main Press, 2017 · Hands-On Science and Technology · Grade 3 · ISBN: 978-1-55379-709-8

# Unit 3

## Forces Causing Movement

# Introduction

This unit introduces students to two types of forces and their effects. The first type of force involves pushes and pulls with direct interaction. The second type involves a push or pull at a distance, such as magnetic or gravitational forces. In essence, a force is any push or pull, whether with contact or at a distance. Students will explore the effects of different forces including muscular force, magnetism, static electricity, and gravitational force. They will investigate ways in which forces create movement in objects and will expand their understanding by designing and making devices that use force to create controlled movement.

The concept of force can be a difficult topic for students this age to understand. When possible, provide hands-on examples of devices or pictures of devices that use various forms of energy to function and create movement (e.g., windup toys, paper airplanes, remote-control toys, small household appliances).

## Planning Tips for Teachers

- Collect a variety of magnets (e.g., bar, horseshoe, cylinder). Test them for their magnetic strength before the start of the unit.

- Collect shoeboxes and cardboard boxes. Students can bring these from home, as well.

- Proper storage of magnets is very important. If stored incorrectly, magnets can lose their charge. Store horseshoe magnets end-to-end, with opposite poles touching. Store bar magnets so the opposite poles are beside each other—the north pole of one magnet should be next to the south pole of the other. Also, ensure magnets are stored away from computers and cell phones, as they can cause damage to these items.

- Ensure electrical outlets are accessible and in working order before beginning the unit. Teachers will be using a kettle, vaporizer, or humidifier during the unit.

- A hygrometer is useful for this unit. With a hygrometer, the class can take accurate humidity readings, and conduct experiments when humidity readings are below 30 percent. This will result in more successful experiments, because humidity affects static electricity.

---

**NOTE:** Hygrometers are often included in home thermostats for reading humidity along with temperature. Scientific hygrometers may be available through local high schools.

---

- Consider recording each lesson's guided inquiry question (e.g., on a sentence strip) for display throughout related investigations.

- Develop a Makerspace centre. Classroom Makerspaces are usually designed as centres where students learn together and collaborate on do-it-yourself projects. Students are given the opportunity to work with a variety of age-appropriate tools, as well as everyday and recycled materials. Additionally, arts-and-crafts are often integrated into Makerspace offerings.

For this unit, set up a Makerspace centre in your classroom that encourages informal learning about forces causing movement. Include general materials, such as those listed in the Introduction to *Hands-On Science and Technology, Grade 3*, as well as unit-specific materials. For example, collect a large variety of materials and equipment, including toy cars, elastics, Slinkies, springs, and magnets, as well as various devices that incorporate magnets in their design.

Do-it-yourself projects may include anything related to the concepts within this unit. Projects that students might initiate include (but are not limited to):

- designing and building a model catapult
- designing and building a hoist
- investigating the use of magnets in a specific device

Portage & Main Press, 2017 · Hands-On Science and Technology · Grade 3 · ISBN: 978-1-55379-709-8

**Hands-On Science and Technology** • Grade 3

- using an elastic to create something that moves using tension
- creating a stage and using magnets to move characters from underneath
- creating a device that launches a paper airplane
- creating a crane that moves to lift blocks
- creating a display, structure, or device that uses magnetism to perform a task
- creating a display, structure, or device that uses gravitational force to move a ping pong ball through a series of obstacles

Literacy connections that might inspire projects include:

- *Oscar and the Cricket: A Book About Moving and Rolling* by Geoff Waring
- *And Everyone Shouted, "Pull!": A First Look at Forces and Motion* by Claire Llewellyn and Simone Abel
- *Stuck in the Mud* by Jane Clarke
- *Magnet Max* by Monica L. Hughes
- *Newton And Me* by Lynne Mayer and Sherry Rogers
- *Toy Stories* by Gabriele Galimberti

As inquiry questions are posed with each lesson, you will find these questions inspire other do-it-yourself projects related to the unit. Students may determine solutions to these questions through the creating they do at the Makerspace centre. Remember to not direct the learning here; simply create conditions for learning to happen.

## Indigenous Worldviews

Teachers are reminded of the value of incorporating Indigenous perspectives and worldviews into lessons, whenever possible. Indeed, forces that cause movement are infused into Indigenous perspectives as part of daily life, such as the Earth/Sun relationship or the phenomenon of the Northern Lights

(Aurora borealis) being more brilliant during the winter season.

Traditionally, Indigenous peoples understood there was an unknown force in nature that affected things on Earth, whether it was a projectile in hunting, or running bison off a cliff (bison jump), and they used this knowledge to their advantage.

Indigenous peoples often have a special relationship with and connection to Mother Earth, guiding them to practise respect and to revere the unknown forces within their environment.

## A Note About Materials

The materials needed to complete some activities are extensive. Teachers should review the materials lists for each lesson ahead of time and make a note of items students may be able to bring from home (e.g., plastic containers, paper plates and/or cups, spoons, pie plates, fabric samples, balls of wool). Then, before beginning the unit, teachers can send a letter home with students asking parents/guardians to donate some of these materials.

## A Note About Safety

During their exploration of forces and movement, students should be able to identify and understand the importance of some fundamental practices that will ensure their own safety, as well as the safety of others. This includes knowing why it is important that they protect their faces and eyes from materials they are manipulating through stretching and twisting. Students should also protect their feet from loads that may drop.

Portage & Main Press, 2017 · *Hands-On Science and Technology · Grade 3* · ISBN: 978-1-55379-709-8

## Science and Technology Vocabulary

Throughout the unit, teachers should use, and encourage students to use, vocabulary such as:

- *attract, charge/charged, compass, direct force, discharge, distance, electroscope, electrostatic charge, electrostatic force, force, friction, function, geographical poles, gravity, humidity, indirect force, load, magnet, magnetic field, magnetic poles, magnetism, magnetize, motion, movement, muscular force, neutral, north pole, pull, push, repel, south pole, speed, static charge, static electricity*

In lesson 1, students start a Science and Technology Glossary in which they record new vocabulary introduced throughout the unit. Also in lesson 1, teachers create a class word wall for the unit. The word wall can be created on a bulletin board or simply on a sheet of poster paper, so as not to take up too much space. On the bulletin board or poster paper, record new vocabulary as it is introduced throughout the unit. Ensure the word wall is placed in a location where all students can see it and access the words.

Teachers should consider including vocabulary related to scientific inquiry skills. Vocabulary related to scientific inquiry skills include terms such as:

- *access, ask, brainstorm, collect, compare, connect, consider, construct, cooperate, create, describe, develop, diagram, display, draw, estimate, examine, explain, explore, find, follow, graph, identify, improve, investigate, label, measure, observe, order, plan, predict, recognize, record, repeat, research, respond, select, sequence, test*

These terms might be displayed in the classroom as they relate to inquiry skills used throughout the year. Students can then brainstorm which skills they are using as they work through particular lessons. They could also discuss what the skill looks and sounds like as they explore and investigate.

Portage & Main Press, 2017 · Hands-On Science and Technology · Grade 3 · ISBN: 978-1-55379-709-8

# Unit Overview

| Fundamental Concepts | Big Ideas |
|---|---|
| Energy | ■ There are several types of forces that cause movement. |
| Change and Continuity | ■ Forces cause objects to speed up, slow down, or change direction through direct contact or through interaction at a distance.<br>■ Forces in nature, such as high winds or water, can have a significant impact on humans and the environment, and need to be regarded with respect. |

## Overall Expectations

By the end of Grade 3, students will do the following:

1. Assess the impact of various forces on society and the environment.
2. Investigate devices that use forces to create controlled movement.
3. Demonstrate an understanding of how forces cause movement and changes in movement.

Forces Causing Movement

Portage & Main Press, 2017 · Hands-On Science and Technology · Grade 3 · ISBN: 978-1-55379-709-8

# Curriculum Correlation

| Specific Expectation | Lesson | | | | | | | | | | | | | | | | |
|---|---|---|---|---|---|---|---|---|---|---|---|---|---|---|---|---|---|
| | 1 | 2 | 3 | 4 | 5 | 6 | 7 | 8 | 9 | 10 | 11 | 12 | 13 | 14 | 15 | 16 | 17 |
| **1. Relating Science and Technology to Society and the Environment** | | | | | | | | | | | | | | | | | |
| 1.1 Assess the effects of the action of forces in nature (natural phenomena) on the natural and built environment, and identify ways in which human activities can reduce or enhance this impact. | | | | | | | √ | | | √ | | | √ | √ | | | |
| 1.2 Assess the impact of safety devices that minimize the effects of forces in various human activities. | | | | | | | | | | | | | | | | √ | |
| **2. Developing Investigation and Communication Skills** | | | | | | | | | | | | | | | | | |
| 2.1 Follow established safety procedures during science and technology investigations. | √ | √ | √ | √ | √ | √ | √ | √ | √ | √ | √ | √ | √ | √ | √ | √ | √ |
| 2.2 Investigate forces that cause an object to start moving, stop moving, or change direction. | √ | | | √ | | √ | | | √ | √ | √ | √ | √ | √ | √ | √ | √ |
| 2.3 Conduct investigations to determine the effects of increasing or decreasing the amount of force applied to an object. | | | √ | √ | | √ | | | √ | √ | √ | √ | √ | √ | | | √ |
| 2.4 Use technological problem-solving skills, and knowledge acquired from previous investigations, to design and build devices that use forces to create controlled movement. | | | | | √ | | | | | | | √ | | | √ | | √ |
| 2.5 Use appropriate science and technology vocabulary, including *push, pull, load, distance*, and *speed*, in oral and written communication. | √ | √ | √ | √ | √ | √ | √ | √ | √ | √ | √ | √ | √ | √ | √ | √ | √ |
| 2.6 Use a variety of forms to communicate with different audiences and for a variety of purposes. | √ | √ | √ | √ | √ | √ | √ | √ | √ | √ | √ | √ | √ | √ | √ | √ | √ |
| **3. Understanding Basic Concepts** | | | | | | | | | | | | | | | | | |
| 3.1 Identify a force as a push or a pull that causes an object to move. | √ | √ | | √ | | | | | | | | | | | | √ | √ |
| 3.2 Identify different kinds of forces. | | | | √ | | | | √ | | | | | √ | | | √ | √ |
| 3.3 Describe how different forces applied to an object at rest can cause the object to start, stop, attract, repel, or change direction. | | | √ | √ | | √ | | √ | | | √ | √ | √ | | | | √ |
| 3.4 Explain how forces are exerted through direct contact or through interaction at a distance. | | √ | √ | √ | | √ | | √ | | | √ | √ | √ | | | √ | √ |
| 3.5 Identify ways in which forces are used in their daily lives. | | | | √ | | √ | | √ | | | √ | | √ | | | √ | √ |

Portage & Main Press, 2017 · Hands-On Science and Technology · Grade 3 · ISBN: 978-1-55379-709-8

# Resources for Students

Alexie, Sherman. *Thunder Boy Jr.* New York, NY: Little, Brown Books, 2016.

Alpert, Barbara. *A Look at Magnets*. Mankato, MN: Capstone Press, 2012.

Anderson, Margaret Jean. *Isaac Newton: Greatest Genius of Science*. Revised ed. Berkeley Heights, NJ: Enslow Publishers, 2015.

Anderson, Teddy. *Medicine Wheel: Stories of a Hoop Dancer*. Victoria, BC: Medicine Wheel Education, 2014.

Asch, Frank. G*ravity Buster: Journal #2 of a Cardboard Genius*. Toronto, ON: Kids Can Press, 2007.

Barnard, Bryn. *Dangerous Planet: Natural Disasters That Changed History*. New York, NY: Crown Publishers, 2003.

Bedard, Michael. *The Nightingale*. New York, NY: Clarion Books for Young Readers, 2015.

Bradley, Kimberly Brubaker. *Forces Make Things Move*. New York, NY: HarperCollins Publishers, 2005.

Branley, Franklyn M. *Gravity is a Mystery*. New York, NY: HarperCollins, 2007.

_____. *What Makes a Magnet?*. New York, NY: HarperCollins Publishers, 2016.

Bruchac, J. B. *Native American Games and Stories*. Golden, CO: Fulcrum Publishing, 2000.

Bruchac, Joseph, and Michael J. Caduto. *Native Stories from Keepers of the Earth*. Markham, ON: Fifth House, 1994.

Chin, Jason. *Gravity*. New York: Roaring Brook Press, 2014.

Clarke, Jane. *Stuck in the Mud.* London: Puffin, 2007.

Claybourne, Anna. *Gut-Wrenching Gravity and Other Fatal Forces*. St. Catharines, ON: Crabtree Publishing Company, 2013.

Cobb, Vicki. *I Fall Down*. New York, NY: HarperCollins, 2004.

Cole, Joanna. *The Magic School Bus and the Electric Field Trip*. St. Louis, MO: Turtleback Books, 1999.

Colson, Mary. *Crumbling Earth Erosion and Landslides.* Chicago, IL: Raintree, 2006.

Confederated Salish and Kootenai Tribes. *Beaver Steals Fire: A Salish Coyote Story.* Lincoln, NE: Bison Books, 2008.

Cooper, Christopher. *The Basics of Magnetism.* New York, NY: Rosen Publishing Group, 2015.

Dwyer, Mindy. *Aurora: A Tale of the Northern Lights.* Portland, OR: Alaska Northwest Books, 2001.

Fowler, Allan. *What Magnets Can Do.* Chicago, IL: Children's Press, 1995.

Galimberti, Gabriele. *Toy Stories: Photos of Children from Around the World with Their Favorite Things.* New York, NY: Abrams Image, 2014.

Gianopoulos, Andrea. *The Attractive Story of Magnetism with Max Axiom, Super Scientist.* Mankato, MN: Capstone Press, 2008.

Gilman, Phoebe. *The Balloon Tree.* Reprint ed. New York, NY: Sky Pony Press, 2011.

Goldsworthy, Katie. *Magnetism.* New York, NY: Weigl Education, 2012.

Gray, Leon. *Forces and Motion.* New York, NY: Gareth Stevens Publishing, 2014.

_____. *Magnetism.* New York, NY: Gareth Stevens Publishing, 2014.

Hamilton, Richard. *Cal and the Amazing Anti-Gravity Machine.* New York, NY: Bloomsbury Children's Books, 2006.

Hewitt, Sally. *Amazing Forces and Movement.* New York, NY: Crabtree Publishing, 2008.

Portage & Main Press, 2017 · *Hands-On Science and Technology* · Grade 3 · ISBN: 978-1-55379-709-8

Hewitt, Sally. *Forces Around Us.* New York, NY: Children's Press, 1998.

Hughes, Monica Lozano. *Magnet Max.* Dallas, TX: Brown Books Publishing Group, 2015.

Hyde, Natalie. *What is Motion?* St. Catharines, ON: Crabtree Publishing Company, 2014.

Ives, Rob. *Fun Experiments with Forces and Motion: Hovercrafts, Rockets, and More.* Minneapolis, MN: Learner Publications, 2018.

Kusugak, Michael. *Northern Lights: The Soccer Trails.* Toronto: Annick Press, 1993.

Lewis, Paul Owen. *Frog Girl.* Vancouver, BC: Whitecap Books, 2001.

Lionni, Leo. *Alexander and the Wind-up Mouse.* New York, NY: Random House, 2017.

Llewellyn, Claire. *And Everyone Shouted, "Pull!": A First Look at Forces and Motion.* Minneapolis, MN: Picture Window Books, 2005.

Mason, Adrienne. *Move It!: Motion, Forces and You.* Toronto: Kids Can Press, 2005.

Mayer, Lynne. *Newton and Me.* Mount Pleasant, SC: Abordale Publishing, 2010.

Miller, Bruce. *Our Original Games: A Look at Aboriginal Sport in Canada.* Owen Sound, ON: Ningwakwe Learning Press, 2002.

Royston, Angela. *Forces and Motion.* Mankato, MN: Capstone, 2014.

Rumbolt, Paula Ikuutaq. *The Legend of Lightning and Thunder.* Iqaluit, NU: Inhabit Media, 2013.

Samatte, Sandra. *Grandfather, What is A Medicine Wheel?* Winnipeg, MB: Native Reflections, 2009.

_____. *The Medicine Wheel.* Winnipeg, MB: Native Reflections, 2013.

Sohn, Emily. A *Crash Course in Forces and Motion with Max Axiom, Super Scientist.* Mankato, MN: Captstone, 2016.

_____. *Experiments in Forces and Motion with Toys and Everyday Stuff.* Mankato, MN: Captstone, 2016.

Spilsbury, Louise. *The Science of Magnetism.* New York: Gareth Stevens Publishing, 2016.

Stiefel, Chana. *The Weather Channel: Forces of Nature.* New York: Scholastic, 2010.

Stott, Jon C. *Quests for Fire: Tales from Many Lands.* Victoria, BC: Heritage House Publishing, 2012.

Syliboy, Alan. *The Thundermaker.* Halifax, NS: Nimbus, 2015.

Swanson, Jennifer. *Explore Forces and Motion with 25 Great Projects.* White River Junction, VT: Nomad Press, 2016.

Taylor, C.J. *How We Saw the World: Nine Native Stories of the Way Things Began.* Toronto: Tundra Books, 1999.

Thomas, Isabel. *Experiments with Forces.* Mankato, MN: Capstone, 2015.

Trumbauer, Lisa. *What Is Gravity?* New York, NY: Children's Press, 2004.

Van Allsburg, Chris. *The Wreck of the Zephyr.* 30th Anniversary ed. Boston, MA: Houghton Mifflin Books for Children, 2013.

Waboose , Jan Bourdeau. *SkySisters.* Toronto: Kids Can Press, 2002

Waboose, Jan Bourdeau. *Morning on the Lake.* Toronto: Kids Can Press, 1999.

Waring, Geoff. *Oscar and the Cricket: A Book About Moving and Rolling.* Cambridge, MA: Candlewick Press, 2008.

Portage & Main Press, 2017 · *Hands-On Science and Technology · Grade 3* · ISBN: 978-1-55379-709-8

# Websites and Online Videos

## Websites

- **www.spiritsd.ca/learningresources/ FNM%20Resources/GR5%20Forces%20 and%20Simple%20Machines%20(2).pdf**
  Integrating First Nations and Métis Content and Perspective—Physical Sciences—Forces and Simple Machines: A Grade Five unit from Saskatchewan demonstrating how to integrate First Nations and Métis perspectives into a unit about simple machines and forces.

- **researchonline.jcu.edu.au/34480/1/ Simple%20Machines-for%20students.pdf**
  Forces and Simple Machines—An Integrated Science Learning Unit for Yukon Grade 5 Students: Another model unit for integrating Indigenous perspectives in a unit about forces and simple machines.

- **www.enchantedlearning.com/Home.html**
  Enchanted Learning—Curriculum Material Online: 35,000 pages of content covering a wide range of educational topics. The materials and lessons provided are intended to emphasize creativity and enjoyment of learning.

- **lightning.nsstc.nasa.gov/**
  Global Hydrology Resource Center and NASA—Lightning and Atmospheric Electricity Research: An introduction to lightning and how it affects space craft, lightning properties, characteristics of a storm, types of lightning, and more.

- **www.fi.edu/exhibit/electricity**
  The Franklin Institute—Electricity Exhibit: This is a permanent exhibit dedicated to Benjamin Franklin. A good site for students doing research on Benjamin Franklin, and includes information on his important contributions to science, especially in the area of electricity. Extensive links.

- **eskimo.com/~billb/emotor/sticky.html**
  Sticky Electrostatics: To help explain electricity, this site provides two experiments using plastic tape. These interesting activities provide information about static, positive and negative attraction, and charges. Included is a reference section to help students learn more.

- **www.howstuffworks.com**
  HowStuffWorks: Type "gravity" in the search box and find the answers to many questions on this or any topic. The information is accessible and the site provides many helpful links.

- **www.nyelabs.com/**
  Bill Nye—The Official Website for Bill Nye the Science Guy: The Educational Resources section of the website includes episode guides to find information on different topics, demonstrations that can be done at home or with students, and printable one-page PDF instructions for multiple experiments.

- **scienceworld.wolfram.com/biography/ Newton.html**
  Wolfram Research—Newton, Isaac: Learn more about the father of physics, Sir Isaac Newton. This site has useful information about his life, work, and many extensions and explanations.

- **www.storyjumper.com/book/ index/11697072/Force-and-Motion**
  Story Jumper—Force and Motion: Create your own book to explain force and motion using the tools on this website.

- **history.alberta.ca/headsmashedin/ default.aspx**
  Alberta Culture and Tourism —Head-Smashed-In Buffalo Jump World Heritage Site: Use the "View from the Jump" link on the right side of the page to see a live feed from a webcam at the site.

Portage & Main Press, 2017 · *Hands-On Science and Technology · Grade 3* · ISBN: 978-1-55379-709-8

- **history.alberta.ca/headsmashedin/ docs/Head-Smashed-In-Information- Guide-2015.pdf**
  Alberta Tourism and Culture—Head-Smashed-In Buffalo Jump World Heritage Site Information Guide: Describes one of the world's oldest, largest, and best-preserved buffalo jumps; explains how Indigenous peoples ran buffalo off cliffs for hunting, using gravity to their advantage. It also includes information about the archaeology found at the site.

- **www.enwin.com/kids/electricity/history.cfm**
  Kids Zone—The History of Electricity: An excellent, student-friendly website detailing the history of electricity and four pioneers in the field. It also includes information about electricity in general and a game related to electricity.

- **www.internet4classrooms.com/science_ elem_magnets.htm**
  Internet4Classrooms – Magnets for Elementary Science: A long list of useful resources for teachers on this topic.

- **www.nasa.gov/offices/education/about/ index.html**
  NASA Education: This site contains numerous short videos related to electromagnets, static electricity, and lightning. Use the search bar to find information and videos on a specific topic.

- **www.nasa.gov/audience/forstudents/ index.html**
  NASA for Students: This site is user-friendly, is continuously updated with new information, and has information on a variety of topics. Use the search bar to find electricity-related information.

- **iroquoisnationals.org/the-iroquois/ the-story-of-lacrosse/**
  Iroquois Nationals—The Story of Lacrosse: This article captures the oral traditions of the Haudenosaunee people as they relate to lacrosse.

- **www.fourdirectionsteachings.com**
  Four Directions Teachings: Audio-narrated information to celebrate Indigenous oral traditions that includes information about the importance of the cardinal directions to Indigenous peoples, and a lesson plan targeting grades 7–9 (which teachers can easily adapt to younger grades.

- **nces.ed.gov/nceskids/createagraph**
  NCES Kids' Zone—Create A Graph: A website to walk students through the steps of creating their own graphs. Five different graphs and chart styles are available, as well as tutorial material.

- **mathcentral.uregina.ca/RR/database/ RR.09.00/treptau1/**
  Games from the Aboriginal people of North Americ: This site contains a list of games (and their rules) played by Indigenous peoples across North America. These games can be used to demonstrate math and science concepts in the classroom.

- **www.na.fs.fed.us/fire_poster/nativeamer.htm**
  How the Coyote Stole Fire—A story about how Indigenous peoples in North America used fire as a tool. Includes a lesson plan and historical background information.

## Videos

- **www.teachingchannel.org/videos/ science-lesson-magnets**
  Teaching Channel—Journaling to Master Magnets: A science teacher delivers his lesson about magnetism through story.

- **https://www.youtube.com/ watch?v=zyWX3VRsk38**
  "St. Elmo's fire in airplane cockpit Elmsfeuer im Airbus Cockpit." AirplaneTVcom (0:46) When flying close to thunderstorms, there

Portage & Main Press, 2017 · Hands-On Science and Technology · Grade 3 · ISBN: 978-1-55379-709-8

is often increased static electricity in the air. As we can see in this video, the extra static electricity can lead to static discharges on window frames. The phenomenon is known as St. Elmo's fire.

- **https://www.youtube.com/watch?v=3XhhMAxsyOU**
  "St. Elmo's fire on aircraft windscreen." stratfordhens. (0:19).

- **https://www.youtube.com/watch?v=P1luqXNqC1c**
  "737 Jumpseat Takeoff & St. Elmo's Fire!!!" PilotsTubeHD (3:08).

- **https://www.youtube.com/watch?v=5C-RM4fh5Xg**
  "Magnets for Kids." The Science Bucket (3:00).

- **https://www.youtube.com/watch?v=dJpIU1rSOFY**
  "What Is an Earthquake | The Dr. Binocs Show | Educational Videos For Kids." Peekaboo Kidz. (3:42.)

- **https://www.youtube.com/watch?v=-s3UwOq1P1E**
  "What is a Tornado?" SciShow Kids (3:46).

- **https://www.youtube.com/watch?v=IAmqsMQG3RM**
  "Volcano | The Dr. Binocs Show | Learn Videos For Kids." Peekaboo Kidz (2:50).

- **https://www.youtube.com/watch?v=J2__Bk4dVS0**
  "Hurricane | The Dr. Binocs Show | Educational Videos For Kids." Peekaboo Kidz (3:17).

- **https://youtu.be/sZBX5KLp4gk**
  "Medicine Game—Lacrosse." Richard Powless (4:38).

- **https://youtu.be/iSoR9oGGpOc**
  "The Stickmaker – Alf Jaques "Unstrung" Handmakes Wood Lacrosse Sticks." Stylin Strings (3:32).

- **https://www.youtube.com/watch?v=Bhfw5R2U5mE**
  "Physics of a Lacrosse Shot." Jennthoomas (6:30).

- **https://www.youtube.com/watch?v=eYSG5aeTy-Y**
  "Magnets & Magnetism for kids. " makemegenius (5:03).

- **https://www.youtube.com/watch?v=NZlfxWMr7nc**
  "Relax Music & Stunning Aurora Borealis-Northern Polar Lights – 2 Hours." BaLu: Relaxing Nature (1:57:10).

- **https://www.youtube.com/watch?v=fVsONlc3OUY**
  "Nights of the Northern Lights." Maciej winiarczyk (2:22).

- **https://www.youtube.com/watch?v=fVMgnmi2D1w**
  "NASA UHD Video: Stunning Aurora Borealis from Space in Ultra-High Definition Space." Space Videos (4:36).

Portage & Main Press, 2017 · *Hands-On Science and Technology · Grade 3* · ISBN: 978-1-55379-709-8

# 1 | What Is a Force?

## Information for Teachers

Invisible forces are constantly acting upon objects in our surroundings. A force is any push or pull on an object. There are two basic types of forces that cause movement. Contact forces involve direct interaction (pushes and pulls between surfaces that are in direct contact). Non-contact forces include magnetic and gravitational forces and involve interaction at a distance. Magnets (magnetism), static electricity, and gravity are all examples of forces. When objects are pulled together, they are attracted to each other; when objects are pushed apart by forces, they are repelling each other.

## 21st Century Competencies

**Communication**: Students will explore the concept of force, and communicate their current understanding of concepts related to force.

## Materials

- book
- chart paper
- markers
- Activity Sheet: Science and Technology Glossary (3.1.1)
- resources with information covering a variety of topics related to forces and magnetism (e.g. fiction and nonfiction books, magazines, brochures, posters, weird-fact books, riddles)
- Learning-Centre Task Card: Reading About Forces (3.1.2)
- Learning-Centre Activity Slips (3.1.3)

## Activate

Place a book (or an eraser, a marker, or a pencil) on a table, and ask students:

- How can the book be moved closer to me?

Once students have responded, demonstrate by using your hand to pull the book toward you.

Now, ask students:

- How can the book be moved away from me?

Again, once students have responded, demonstrate by using your hand to push the book away.

Next, hold a book with two hands at chest height in front of you. Ask:

- What will happen if I let go of the book?

Have students provide predictions, and then demonstrate.

Ask:

- Why did the book fall down?
- What stopped the book from falling farther?
- What would happen if I threw the book up in the air?
- What keeps objects from floating away?
- How would you describe a force to a younger student?
- How else might you demonstrate a force?

Introduce the guided inquiry question: **What is a force?**

## Action

Explain to students that during this unit, they will be learning about different forces that act upon objects, particularly muscular force, magnetic force, gravity, and static electricity. On chart paper, create a herringbone chart by drawing a horizontal line with slanted lines above and below it, as shown below:

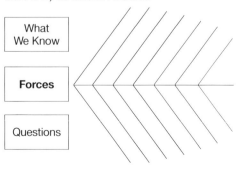

Portage & Main Press, 2017 · Hands-On Science and Technology · Grade 3 · ISBN: 978-1-55379-709-8

Ask students:

- What do you already know about forces?

On the diagonal blanks above the horizontal line of the herringbone chart, record students' responses. On diagonal blanks below the horizontal line, record any questions students have about forces. Encourage students to brainstorm a variety of questions (from basic knowledge to more complex analysis).

During the unit, a second horizontal line should be added below the questions section, with more diagonal blanks running in the opposite direction. Students' answers to the questions will be recorded in these blanks.

Have each student begin their own Science and Technology Glossary for the unit. Distribute several stapled copies of Activity Sheet: Science and Technology Glossary (3.1.1) to each student. Explain to students they will be recording terms, definitions, and examples in their glossaries throughout the unit. At the end of the unit, students can cut apart the rows, alphabetize their words, and create booklets of vocabulary related to Forces Causing Movement.

**NOTE:** The Science and Technology Glossary presents an excellent opportunity to celebrate cultural diversity by having students include words in other languages. Students may include terms in Indigenous languages or other languages spoken at home.

A variety of online dictionaries may be used as a source for translations. For example:

- ojibwe.lib.umn.edu/
- www.freelang.net/online/mohawk.php

Online dictionaries are also available for other languages that may be reflective of the class population.

**Activity Sheet**
Directions to students:

Record the term *force* in your glossary, along with your own definition and an example. You can include other new vocabulary, definitions, and examples (3.1.1).

## Learning Centre

At the learning centre, set up a Forces library. Provide a copy of the Learning-Centre Task Card: Reading About Forces (3.1.2) and copies of the Learning-Centre Activity Slips (3.1.3) along with fiction and nonfiction books, magazines, brochures, posters, weird-fact books, riddles, and other resources with information covering a variety of topics related to forces and magnetism. Ensure the resources provided at the centre include a wide range of reading levels to engage all students.

Have students choose anything they want to read from the Forces library.

Have students complete one of the following written tasks on Learning-Centre Activity Slips (3.1.3):

1. Book Recommendation. For example:
   Title: *What Magnets Can Do*
   Author: Allan Fowler
   I recommend this book because it has many cool facts about magnets in it!
2. Write a "Did You Know?" fact slip.
   For example: Did you know a push or pull is called a "force"?
3. Write a forces riddle. For example:
   I have a north pole and a south pole.
   What am I?

Display students' work in the library for everyone to enjoy, and keep a range of writing samples to share with students at a later time. Teachers are encouraged to keep track of which writing tasks students complete. A goal might be for students to complete all three writing tasks by the end of the unit.

**Forces Causing Movement**

Portage & Main Press, 2017 · *Hands-On Science and Technology · Grade 3* · ISBN: 978-1-55379-709-8

**1**

## Consolidate and Debrief

- Revisit the guided inquiry question: **What is a force?** Have students share their knowledge, provide examples, and ask further inquiry questions.
- Add to the herringbone chart as students learn new concepts, answer some of their own inquiry questions, and ask new inquiry questions.
- Begin a class word wall for the unit to display new terms and illustrations that students learn throughout the unit. Also, include the words in other languages, as appropriate.

---

**NOTE:** Include terminology in other languages on the class word wall. This is a way of acknowledging and respecting students' cultural backgrounds, while enhancing learning for all students.

---

## Enhance

- Have students create digital glossaries in Google Apps for Education (GAFE) or Microsoft Word. For each term introduced, have them draw a text box in a Word document, record the term and its definition, and then add an illustration or picture. For the latter, students may want to use a computer program such as Kid Pix to draw digital pictures, insert clip art pictures in Word, copy and paste pictures from websites, or draw their pictures by hand and have them scanned.

---

**NOTE:** If students are copying and pasting pictures from websites, take the opportunity to educate them about copyright with regards to photos and drawings. Explain that it is okay to copy, paste, and even print online photos for personal use. However, they may not do this for mass distribution, or for selling a product in which the photo or picture is being used.

---

- Have students begin their do-it-yourself projects at the Makerspace centre (See page 244 in the Introduction to this unit and page 18 in the Introduction to **Hands-On Science and Technology, Grade 3** for details on setting up the Makerspace centre).

Portage & Main Press, 2017 · *Hands-On Science and Technology · Grade 3* · ISBN: 978-1-55379-709-8

# Science and Technology Glossary

| Word | Definition |
|---|---|
| **Example** | |

| Word | Definition |
|---|---|
| **Example** | |

| Word | Definition |
|---|---|
| **Example** | |

| Word | Definition |
|---|---|
| **Example** | |

Portage & Main Press, 2017 · Hands-On Science and Technology · Grade 3 · ISBN: 978-1-55379-709-8

# Reading About Forces

Welcome to the Forces Library. The entire library is for you to enjoy!

1. Choose anything you want to read from the library.

2. Read your selection.

3. Decide how you want to share something you have learned with your classmates. You can:

   - Recommend a book.

   - Write a "Did You Know?" fact about forces.

   - Write a riddle about forces.

FRICTION

FORCES AND MUSCLES

STATIC ELECTRICITY

Portage & Main Press, 2017 · Hands-On Science and Technology · Grade 3 · ISBN: 978-1-55379-709-8

# Learning-Centre Activity Slips

## Book Recommendation

Title: _____

Author: _____

I recommend this book because _____

_____

This book is recommended by: _____

## Did You Know?

Did you know _____

_____

_____

_____

Fact written by: _____

## Forces Riddle

_____

_____

_____

Answer: _____

Riddler writer: _____

Portage & Main Press, 2017 · Hands-On Science and Technology · Grade 3 · ISBN: 978-1-55379-709-8

# 2 | How Is a Force a Push or a Pull?

## Information for Teachers

In this lesson, students will explore the newton as the unit used to measure force (symbol N).

## 21st Century Competencies

**Critical Thinking** and **Communication**: Students will examine the scientific meaning of the word *force*, and explore the newton as the metric unit used to measure force.

## Materials

- Image Bank: Forces in Traditional Indigenous Daily Life (see Appendix, page 441)
- cardboard box filled with light objects
- cardboard box filled with heavy objects
- backpack filled with books
- chart paper
- markers
- spring scales that measure in newtons (one for each working group)
- various everyday objects (e.g., keys, water bottle, scissors)
- small paper bags with handles
- toy cars (one for each student)
- student dictionaries
- Activity Sheet: Investigating Forces: Push and Pull (3.2.1)
- Learning-Centre Task Card: Measuring Force! (3.2.2)
- herringbone chart (from lesson 1)
- Science and Technology Glossary (3.1.1)

## Activate

To introduce the lesson, provide each student with a toy car. Challenge students to move the toy cars in as many ways as they can. Invite them to discuss the ways in which they were able to move the cars.

Now, place the cardboard boxes and the backpack on the floor in the classroom. Have students make a circle around the boxes and backpack. Ask students:

- If I want to move the backpack from one side of the circle to the other without picking it up off the floor, how would I do it?

Select a student to move the backpack. Ask:

- What direction did the backpack move?
- Was the backpack pushed or pulled?

Select another student to move the cardboard box filled with light objects. Give a number of specific instructions as to how the box should be moved (e.g., push the box to the left, pull the box to the right, push the box slowly forward, pull the box quickly backward). Repeat using the box filled with heavy objects. Discuss the difference in moving the box filled with light objects versus the box filled with heavy objects.

Ask students:

- How did you move the backpack and the boxes?
- What did you need in order to move the boxes and backpack from one spot to another?
- What is a force?

Introduce the guided inquiry question: **How is a force a push or a pull?**

## Action: Part One

Conduct the following activity with students, which highlights the many meanings of the term *force*. Have students brainstorm to create sentences using the word *force* such as, "May the force be with you" or "I will force you to do it." After students have made up several sentences, have them look up the term *force* in the dictionary. Co-construct a class definition for the term, based on their own sentences,

Portage & Main Press, 2017 · *Hands-On Science and Technology · Grade 3* · ISBN: 978-1-55379-709-8

experiences, and the review of references. Record the definition on an anchor chart for future reference.

Focus on the scientific definition of the word. Explain to students that a force is a push or a pull. Forces often produce movement. Things stay still unless a force pushes or pulls them.

Have students brainstorm other examples of force in the classroom. Record these on chart paper (e.g., pushing a door open, pulling a book from a shelf, pushing a pencil across a piece of paper, dragging or pulling a gym bag along the floor).

## Action: Part Two

Display Image Bank: Forces in Traditional Indigenous Daily Life. Examine each picture. Have students role-play each activity and ask related questions. For example, have students pretend to be using a bow and arrow. Ask:

- What do you do to the string on the bow? (pull it back)
- What force are you using? (a pull)
- What happens when you do this? (the arrow is pushed forward)

Repeat this process with the other traditional Indigenous activities. Discuss how:

- the spear is pushed forward
- the paddle is pulled back through the water, which causes the canoe to push forward
- the travois is pulled
- the dog sled is pulled

Students can also compare these activities to others with which they are familiar. For example:

- pulling on a slingshot
- pulling a toboggan up a hill
- pushing a toboggan down a hill
- pulling a wagon

Focus on pushes and pulls as forces on the objects discussed.

## Action: Part Three

Ask students:

- How do you measure the length of an object?
- How do you measure the mass of an object?
- Do you think you can measure the force of an object?

Introduce the newton spring scale. Explain to students that a unit of force was given the name *newton* in honour of Sir Isaac Newton, who discovered the nature of forces.

Divide the class into groups of three or four students. Give them time to experiment with the newton spring scale. Have one student sit in a chair. Have another student hook the scale onto the chair and hold the scale in place. Encourage students to use the spring scale to get a feel for 1 newton, 5 newtons, 10 newtons, and 15 newtons of force by pulling on the hook of the scale.

Once students have had an opportunity to experiment with the newton scale, distribute a small paper bag with handles and an everyday object (e.g., keys, water bottle, scissors) to each group. Also distribute a copy of Activity Sheet: Investigating Forces: Push and Pull (3.2.1) to each student. Have students record their results of the following investigations.

Have students place the handles of the bag onto the hook of the spring scale. (The bag should be resting on the ground.) Ask students to place the everyday object into the bag, record the name of the object on the activity sheet, estimate how many newtons will be necessary to lift the bag, and record their estimate on the activity sheet. Then, have students lift the bag with the object and record the actual number of newtons required to lift the bag.

Portage & Main Press, 2017 · *Hands-On Science and Technology · Grade 3* · ISBN: 978-1-55379-709-8

Portage & Main Press, 2017 · Hands-On Science and Technology · Grade 3 · ISBN: 978-1-55379-709-8

**2**

Now, have students place the bag on the floor and hook the scale onto its handles (students should leave the same everyday object inside the bag.) Have them estimate how many newtons it will take to pull the bag along the floor. Make sure students record their estimates on their activity sheet. Once they have recorded their estimates, have students pull the bag along the floor and record the actual number of newtons required.

Have students repeat the activity with a variety of everyday objects inside the bag.

### Activity Sheet
Directions to students:

Record the names of the objects measured, as well as your estimates and results (3.2.1).

## Learning Centre

At the learning centre, provide spring scales, additional copies of Activity Sheet: Investigating Forces: Push and Pull (3.2.1), and a copy of the Learning Centre Task Card: Measuring Force! (3.2.2). Encourage students to collect objects from home and from around the classroom. Have students use the spring scale to measure the force, in newtons, needed to lift or pull the various objects collected.

### Assessment for Learning
As students work with the spring scale, observe their ability to estimate and measure amounts of force. Ask students to describe force and to use the materials from the lesson to provide examples of force. Use the Anecdotal Record sheet, found on page 26, to record results.

## Consolidate and Debrief

- Revisit the guided inquiry question: **How is a force a push or a pull?** Have students share their knowledge, provide examples, and ask further inquiry questions.

- Add to the herringbone chart as students learn new concepts, answer some of their own inquiry questions, and ask new inquiry questions.

- Add new terms and illustrations to the class word wall. Include the words in other languages, as appropriate.

- Have students add new terms, definitions, and illustrations to their Science and Technology Glossary (3.1.1). When possible, encourage them to add words (and examples) in other languages, including Indigenous languages, reflective of the class.

## Enhance

- Have students use the spring scale to pull a one-kilogram weight. They will see that gravity acting on 1 kg produces about 10 N of force. This is a very useful reference for further study on forces, gravity, and newtons.

- Have students research the life of Sir Isaac Newton.

- Have students continue their do-it-yourself projects at the Makerspace centre.

Date: _____     Name: _____

# Investigating Forces: Push and Pull

| Object | Action | Estimate Force (N) | Actual Force (N) |
|---|---|---|---|
| | lifting | | |
| | pulling | | |
| | lifting | | |
| | pulling | | |
| | lifting | | |
| | pulling | | |
| | lifting | | |
| | pulling | | |

What did you learn from this activity? _____

_____

_____

Portage & Main Press, 2017 · Hands-On Science and Technology · Grade 3 · ISBN: 978-1-55379-709-8

# Measuring Force!

1. Collect objects from home and from around the classroom.

2. Use the spring scale to measure the force, in newtons, needed to lift or pull the various objects collected.

3. Record your work on the activity sheet.

Portage & Main Press, 2017 · Hands-On Science and Technology · Grade 3 · ISBN: 978-1-55379-709-8

# 3 | What Is Friction?

## 21st Century Competencies

**Critical Thinking** and **Communication**:
Students will examine the concept of friction by estimating and measuring the amount of force required to pull objects across different surfaces.

## Materials

- Image Bank: Traditional Indigenous Fire Starters (see Appendix, page 441)
- wooden blocks with a screw eye in one end
- weights or heavy objects
- chart paper
- markers
- spring scales that measure in newtons (one for each working group)
- surfaces on which to test friction (e.g., smooth flooring, carpeting, large pieces of sandpaper)
- Activity Sheet: Friction (3.3.1)
- herringbone chart (from lesson 1)
- Science and Technology Glossary (3.1.1)

## Activate

Begin the activity by having students rub their hands together firmly. Ask students:

- What do you notice when you rub your hands together rapidly? (feel warm)
- Why do you think your hands started to feel warm? (rubbing)
- Does anyone have an idea what you have created by rubbing your two hands together?

Introduce the guided inquiry question: **What is friction?**

## Action: Part One

Explain to students that when they rubbed their hands together, they created friction. Friction is created when two surfaces rub together. Friction can be increased or reduced depending on the surfaces of the two objects that come in contact with each other.

Tell students they are going to conduct an experiment to find out the amount of force needed to pull a block across different kinds of surfaces (e.g., a smooth surface, like tile or linoleum; a carpeted surface; sandpaper). Ask:

- What device did you use to measure forces during the previous activity?
- What unit is used to measure force?

Distribute a copy of Activity Sheet: Friction (3.3.1) to each student. Divide the class into working groups, and review the procedure for the investigation. As you are explaining these procedures, record simple directions on chart paper for students to refer to during their investigations.

1. Attach the spring scale to the screw eye in the end of the wooden block.
2. Place the wooden block onto a smooth surface on the floor (if it is a tile floor, students should place the block directly on the floor). Estimate the number of newtons required to pull the block across the smooth surface.
3. Pull the block gently, at a constant speed, over the smooth surface. Record the number of newtons required on Activity Sheet: Friction (3.3.1).
4. Repeat with the carpeted surface and the sandpaper surface.
5. Record the results on the activity sheet.
6. Place a weight on top of the wooden block, and repeat the experiment using all three surfaces. Record the results.

Once they have completed the investigation, have students share their findings in a large group. Ask:

- What type of surface increased the amount of friction?
- What type of surface decreased the amount of friction?
- Did your results vary when you placed the weight on the wooden block? If so, how?

Portage & Main Press, 2017 · Hands-On Science and Technology · Grade 3 · ISBN: 978-1-55379-709-8

Discuss and relate this back to rubbing hands together, either lightly or with more force. More friction when pressing hard is similar to more weight on the wooden block.

### Activity Sheet

Directions to students:

Record your results on the chart, and answer the questions at the bottom of the page (3.3.1).

### Assessment of Learning

As students investigate friction, observe their ability to work together as a group. Use the Cooperative Skills Teacher Assessment sheet, found on page 37, to record results.

### Assessment as Learning

Have students complete a Cooperative Skills Self-Assessment sheet, found on page 34, to reflect on their own cooperative skills.

## Action: Part Two

Display the Image Bank: Traditional Indigenous Fire Starters. Have students examine and describe each image. Ask:

- What do you think these tools are used for?

Have students share their ideas. Discuss the various tools and how they work.

- A fire drill consists of a wooden stick and a piece of wood with a hole carved into it. The wooden stick is twirled rapidly around in the hole, and eventually, the friction heats the stick and makes a spark, which lights dried grass or bark.
- A bow and drill consists of a wooden bow attached to a stick. The stick is placed on a fire-starting board with a hole in the bottom. The bow acts like a saw to push and twist the stick against the fire-starting board, creating enough friction to start a fire.

 **SAFETY NOTE:** Stress that students should never attempt to start fires.

Follow up this discuss by reading Indigenous stories about fire. For example:

- "How the Coyote Stole Fire" go to: <www. na.fs.fed.us/fire_poster/nativeamer.htm>
- *Quests for Fire: Tales From Many Lands* by Jon C. Stott
- *Beaver Steals Fire: A Salish Coyote Story* by Confederated Salish and Kootenai Tribes

## Consolidate and Debrief

- Revisit the guided inquiry question: **What is friction?** Have students share their knowledge, provide examples, and ask further inquiry questions.
- Add to the herringbone chart as students learn new concepts, answer some of their own inquiry questions, and ask new inquiry questions.
- Add new terms and illustrations to the class word wall. Include the words in other languages, as appropriate.
- Have students add new terms, definitions, and illustrations to their Science and Technology Glossary (3.1.1). When possible, encourage them to add words (and examples) in other languages, including Indigenous languages, reflective of the class population.

## Enhance

- Have students design and construct a maze or obstacle course on a surface that will allow the wooden block to be pulled using the least or the most newtons.
- Collect pictures from car magazines that show cars being driven on various road surfaces. Have students identify the safest and most dangerous road surfaces. Also, discuss how tires help create the friction necessary to drive and stop cars on slippery surfaces.
- Have students continue their do-it-yourself projects at the Makerspace centre

Portage & Main Press, 2017 · *Hands-On Science and Technology · Grade 3* · ISBN: 978-1-55379-709-8

# Friction

| Item | Surface | Force to Pull (N) |
|---|---|---|
| wooden block | smooth | |
| wooden block | carpet | |
| wooden block | sandpaper | |
| wooden block + weight | smooth | |
| wooden block + weight | carpet | |
| wooden block + weight | sandpaper | |

What type of surface increased the friction?

_____

_____

How do you know the surface increased the friction?

_____

_____

What type of surface decreased the friction?

_____

_____

How do you know the surface decreased the friction?

_____

_____

Portage & Main Press, 2017 · *Hands-On Science and Technology* · Grade 3 · ISBN: 978-1-55379-709-8

# 4 | Which Objects Do Magnets Attract?

## Information for Teachers

Earth is a giant magnet, and like all magnets, it has a north pole and a south pole. In fact, Earth's magnetic poles are not in the same geographical position as the North Pole and the South Pole, but the same terms are used.

All magnets also have a north pole and a south pole. Long bar magnets usually have the poles marked. If like poles meet, they will repel each other. If unlike poles meet, they will attract each other.

Some metals are attracted to the magnetic pull or force. Other metals do not react. Objects made from iron, cobalt, nickel, and some steel are attracted to magnets, while objects made from aluminum, copper, and tin are not affected.

Teachers should ensure students use proper scientific vocabulary to describe how objects react when they are near a magnet; verbs such as *attract* and *repel* are correct, but students may be tempted to use verbs like *stick*, which is not proper terminology.

## 21st Century Competencies

**Critical Thinking** and **Communication**: Students will explore various aspects of magnetism and make predictions and then test to see which materials are magnetic and non-magnetic.

## Materials

- chart paper
- markers
- variety of magnets (e.g., bar, horseshoe, cylinder) You will need several of each type.
- several of each type of the following small objects: coins (nickels, dimes, quarters), buttons, pencils, pens, combs, erasers, paper clips, nails, tacks, rocks, rulers, staples and safety pins

- glasses of water
- small pieces of cloth
- plastic wrap
- wax paper
- tissue paper
- red pens
- Activity Sheet: Magnetic Attraction (3.4.1)
- True or False? Cards (3.4.2)
- Learning-Centre Task Card: Going Fishing (3.4.3)
- Sorting Mat: Materials and Magnets (3.4.4)
- scissors
- glue
- large paper clips
- string
- construction paper
- metre sticks
- large basin
- digital camera
- pencils
- writing paper
- herringbone chart (from lesson 1)
- Science and Technology Glossary (3.1.1)

## Activate

Divide the class into working groups of two to three students, and provide each group with various magnets. Give students time to examine and discuss the magnets. Ask:

- What are these objects?
- What do you know about magnets?
- What kinds of objects do they attract?
- How are magnets used in everyday life?

On the chart paper, record students' responses.

Introduce the guided inquiry question: **Which objects do magnets attract?**

Portage & Main Press, 2017 · *Hands-On Science and Technology · Grade 3* · ISBN: 978-1-55379-709-8

**4**

## Action: Part One

Provide the groups of students with several small objects to examine. Tell students they will be using the objects to test how each reacts to magnets (make sure students do not start testing until you tell them to begin). Distribute a copy of Activity Sheet: Magnetic Attraction (3.4.1) and a red pen to each student. Have students discuss the characteristics of the objects, including the material from which each one is made. On the activity sheet, have students record the name of each object and the material from which it is made.

Now, have the groups discuss how they think each object will react to the magnets. Ask:

- Which objects do you think will be attracted to the magnets?
- Why?

Have students use red pens to record their predictions on the activity sheet.

---

**NOTE:** Students may want to use verbs like *stick* when describing how objects react when near a magnet. Remind them to use proper scientific vocabulary, including the verbs *attract* and *repel*.

---

Now, have the groups test all items and record their results, using a pen or pencil in a colour other than red, to distinguish their results from their predictions.

## Action: Part Two

Have students return to their working groups. Provide each group with a glass of water, a safety pin, a paper clip, a staple, and a tack. Have students place the items in their glass of water. Now, ask students to move a magnet up and down along the outside of the glass. Ask:

- Are the objects attracted to the magnet at the side of the glass?

- Do they follow the magnet as you move it up and down the side of the glass?

Discuss students' observations and inferences.

## Action: Part Three

To the groups, distribute small pieces of cloth, plastic wrap, wax paper, and tissue paper. Have students use these materials to wrap around the objects from Action: Part One that were attracted to magnets. Ask:

- Do you think these objects will still be attracted to the magnets?

Have students test the objects with a magnet.

## Action: Part Four

Engage students in a whole-class follow-up discussion, to provide students with ideas of how magnets work, and what materials are attracted to magnets. Ask:

- What characteristics do the objects that were attracted to the magnets have in common?
- What characteristics do the objects that were not attracted to the magnets have in common?
- Why do you think some objects are attracted to the magnets?
- Could you pick up a nickel with the magnets? Why not? (The Canadian nickel is made from an alloy—a combination of metals—so even though the metal nickel is attracted to magnets, there is not enough nickel in the coin for it to be attracted to the magnets.)
- Which part of the magnet attracts the best?

On chart paper, together with students, record a class statement that answers the question: What kinds of objects do magnets attract?

Have students use their conclusions to complete the activity sheet.

Portage & Main Press, 2017 · *Hands-On Science and Technology · Grade 3* · ISBN: 978-1-55379-709-8

**4**

Follow this discussion by watching the following video, to enhance understanding of how magnets work, go to: <https://www.youtube.com/watch?v=5C-RM4fh5Xg>.

### Activity Sheet

Directions to students:

Record the name of each object you test and the material from which it is made. Predict which objects will be attracted to magnets and which ones will not be attracted to magnets. Test each object, and record the results. Sort the objects into two groups: those attracted to magnets and those that are not (3.4.1).

## Learning Centre

At the learning centre, create a Magnet Fishing Pond with 12 construction paper fish and metre stick fishing rods. Also include a digital camera, writing paper, pencils, and a copy of the Learning-Centre Task Card: Going Fishing (3.4.3).

To make the construction paper fish, cut apart the True or False Cards (3.4.2). Then create a construction paper fish template that is slightly larger than the individual cards and make a total of 12 fish. Glue a card onto one side of each fish and a paper clip onto the other side. Make the fishing rods by tying string to metre sticks and then tying a magnet to the end of each string. Place all fish into a large basin, paper-clip side up.

Have students use one of the fishing rods to catch a fish. Tell students to read the true or false question on the fish they catch and say whether the statement is true or false. Have students repeat this action until they have sorted all the fish into two groups: true and false. Then, have students use the digital camera to take a picture of the two groups of fish.

Once all fish are caught, sorted, and a picture has been taken, have students select one of

the fish and write an explanation of why they said true or false for that statement. Finally, tell students to take a digital photo of that individual fish card along with their explanation.

### Assessment of Learning

Have students use copies of Sorting Mat: Materials and Magnets (3.4.4) to show which objects from the lesson are attracted to magnets and which are not. Ask students to either write the words for or draw pictures of the objects attracted to magnets in the left circle and write the words or draw pictures of those objects not attracted to magnets in the right circle.

## Consolidate and Debrief

■ Revisit the guided inquiry question: **Which objects do magnets attract?** Have students share their knowledge, provide examples, and ask further inquiry questions.

■ Add to the herringbone chart as students learn new concepts, answer some of their own inquiry questions, and ask new inquiry questions.

■ Add new terms, including *attract* and *repel*, and illustrations to the class word wall. Include words in other languages, as appropriate. Have students add new words, definitions, and examples to their Science and Technology Glossary (3.1.1). When possible, encourage students to add the words in other languages, including Indigenous languages, reflective of the class population.

## Enhance

■ Have students take home a magnet and a new copy of Activity Sheet: Magnetic Attraction (3.4.1). Ask them to test 10 items in their home for attraction to the magnet and record their predictions and results on the activity sheet. The next (or another) day, have students share their findings with the class.

**4**

- Rare-earth magnets are strong permanent magnets made from alloys of rare earth elements. They are the strongest type of permanent magnets made. If teachers have a strong, rare-earth magnet, they can use it to push small metal objects away. This shows that magnetism is a type of force—metals are moved by the attractive or repulsive forces within a magnetic field.

- Fill a basin with sand or uncooked rice. Place at least 20 magnetic items in the basin (e.g., nails, paper clips, screws, steel teaspoons, steel thimbles), and mix them in the sand or rice so they are hidden. Challenge students to find the "buried treasures" using only magnets and explain why the game would not work the same if the treasures were plastic or made of other non-magnetic materials.

- Access the interactive activity, Magnetic Force, in the Grade 3, Unit 3 folder of the **Hands-On Interactive for Science and Technology, Grade 3** download. Find this download at: <www.portageandmainpress.com/product/hands-on-interactive-for-science-and-technology-grade-3/>.

- Have students continue their do-it-yourself projects at the Makerspace centre.

Portage & Main Press, 2017 · Hands-On Science and Technology · Grade 3 · ISBN: 978-1-55379-709-8

**Date:** _____     **Name:** _____

# Magnetic Attraction

| Object | Material | Prediction | | Result | |
|---|---|---|---|---|---|
| | | Attracted | Not Attracted | Attracted | Not Attracted |
| | | | | | |
| | | | | | |
| | | | | | |
| | | | | | |
| | | | | | |
| | | | | | |
| | | | | | |
| | | | | | |
| | | | | | |
| | | | | | |
| | | | | | |
| | | | | | |

Portage & Main Press, 2017 · Hands-On Science and Technology · Grade 3 · ISBN: 978-1-55379-709-8

# True or False?

A magnet is attracted
to plastic.

True or False?

A magnet is attracted
to iron.

True or False?

A magnet does not
attract paper.

True or False?

A magnet does not
attract steel.

True or False?

Every magnet has a north pole
and a south pole.

True or False?

A magnet is the weakest at its
north and south poles.

True or False?

A force is a push or a pull.

True or False?

The force of a magnet can
pass through another object.

True or False?

When objects are pulled
together, they are repelled.

True or False?

When objects are pulled
together, they are attracted.

True or False?

Magnets can be different
shapes and sizes.

True or False?

Window decorations that cling
to glass are magnetic.

True or False?

Portage & Main Press, 2017 · Hands-On Science and Technology · Grade 3 · ISBN: 978-1-55379-709-8

# Going Fishing

You are going fishing!

1. Without looking, lower your fishing rod into the basin, and catch a fish.

2. When you catch one, reel it up, and read what it says.

3. Decide if the statement is true or false.

4. Sort all the fish in this same way, as you catch them, adding each one to either a "true" group or a "false" group.

5. Write your name on a small piece of paper, and place it near your sorted fish.

6. Use a digital camera to take a picture of your day's catch.

7. Choose one fish, and write an explanation for why you sorted it into the "true" group or the "false" group.

8. Take a photo of this fish, your explanation, and your name.

Portage & Main Press, 2017 · Hands-On Science and Technology · Grade 3 · ISBN: 978-1-55379-709-8

# Materials and Magnets

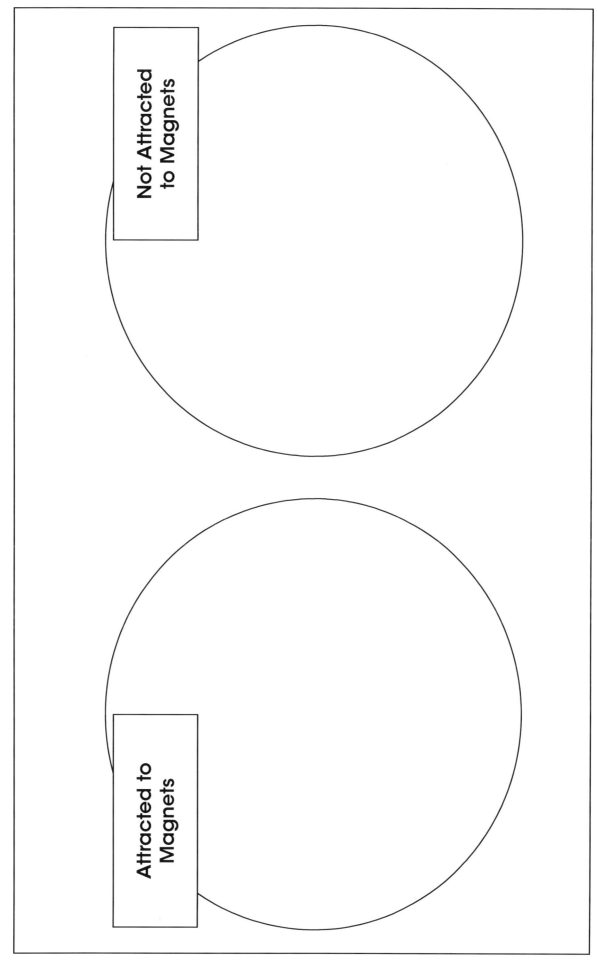

Not Attracted
to Magnets

Attracted to
Magnets

Portage & Main Press, 2017 · Hands-On Science and Technology · Grade 3 · ISBN: 978-1-55379-709-8

# 5 | How Is a Magnet Made?

## Information for Teachers

The first magnets were pieces of rock. Called "lodestones," these rocks contain magnetite, which is naturally attracted to iron. Magnetic induction occurs when a piece of metal, such as iron, touches a magnet. Then, the metal becomes a magnet itself. When a magnet rubs against a metal object containing iron or steel, the object becomes magnetized, meaning charged particles within the object take on a particular alignment. Iron will act like a magnet for a short period of time when treated like this. Steel (made from iron) will hold its magnetism for a long period of time. The length of time depends on how well the metal is able to maintain the new alignment of the charged particles. Also, the more the metal is stroked with a magnet, and the stronger the magnet, the longer the magnetism will last.

## 21st Century Competencies

**Critical Thinking** and **Communication**: Students will learn how to magnetize metal objects. They will predict how many objects can be picked up by a magnetized object, and examine how the number of strokes with the magnet affects the size of magnetic force in the magnetized object.

## Materials

- large bowl or basket
- objects attracted to magnets (e.g., nails, screws, staples, tacks, safety pins). You will need several of each type of object.
- objects not attracted to magnets (e.g., plastic buttons, elastic bands, small pieces of fabric, marbles, small erasers, pen caps, nickels, small squares of paper) You will need several of each type of object.
- scissors (one pair for each working group of students)
- bar magnets (one for each working group of students)
- red pens
- pencils
- paper clips
- audio-recording device
- Activity Sheet: Making a Magnet (3.5.1)
- Learning-Centre Task Card: Magnet Minstrels (3.5.2)
- Learning-Centre Song Template #1 (3.5.3)
- Learning-Centre Song Template #2 (3.5.4)
- herringbone chart (from lesson 1)
- Science and Technology Glossary (3.1.1)

## Activate

Review the previous lesson by asking students to identify objects attracted to magnets and objects not attracted to magnets. Combine the objects attracted to magnets and the objects not attracted to magnets into a large bowl or basket. Hold up one object at a time, and have students show a "thumbs-up" sign if they think it is attracted to magnets, and a "thumbs-down" sign if they think it is not attracted to magnets. If students are unsure about the magnetism of any object shown, have them show a "thumbs-sideways" sign. Note any students who are unsure about any objects, or who are incorrect about the magnetism of the objects.

Divide the class into working groups of two to four students. Provide each group with several objects attracted to magnets (e.g., nails, screws, metal needles, paper clips, staples, tacks, safety pins), several objects not attracted to magnets (e.g., plastic buttons, elastic bands, small pieces of fabric, marbles, small erasers, pen caps, nickels, small squares of paper), a pair of scissors, and a bar magnet. Have students examine the scissors and the paper clips or staples. Ask:

Portage & Main Press, 2017 · *Hands-On Science and Technology · Grade 3* · ISBN: 978-1-55379-709-8

**5**

- Do you think the scissors could pick up paper clips or staples the way a magnet would, right now?
- What can you do to the scissors so they pick up paper clips or staples the way a magnet would?

If necessary, guide students to the response that the scissor blades could be magnetized by rubbing the magnet 15 times across them in the same direction (not back and forth). This will charge the scissors. Ask:

- Do you think the scissors will be able to pick up the paper clips after charging it?

Introduce the guided inquiry question: **How is a magnet made?**

## Action

Ask:

- Once the scissors are magnetized, how many paper clips do you think the scissors will be able to pick up? (How many paper clips will be attracted to the scissors?)

Distribute a copy of Activity Sheet: Making a Magnet (3.5.1) to each student, and have students record their predictions. Next, ask them to test their predictions by rubbing the magnets across the blades of their scissors, and then counting how many paper clips are attracted to the scissors as a magnet. Have them record the results on the activity sheet. Ask:

- How many paper clips were attracted to the scissors?

Now, tell students they are going to magnetize the nail, the safety pin, the screw, and so on. Have them repeat the steps above by first predicting how many paper clips will be attracted to the magnetized object, recording the prediction, magnetizing the object, and then recording the results on the activity sheet.

Discuss this investigation. Ask:

- How many paper clips were attracted to each of these objects?
- Which object worked best as a magnet?
- Do you think it would make a difference if you rubbed the object with the magnet twice as many times (30 times)?

Have students choose one or two of the objects to rub 30 times with the magnet and record their predictions and results on the activity sheet. Ask students to complete the activity sheet by answering the questions on it.

Engage students in a class discussion about the activity. Ask:

- How can you tell when an object is charged or magnetized?
- Why did you rub the magnet against the object in only one direction?
- When you rub a magnet across an object to magnetize the object, does the number of rubs across the object make a difference to the charge of the object?

### Activity Sheet

Directions to students:

Record the name of each object and the number of rubs it takes to magnetize it (15 or 30). Then, use a red pen to record a prediction of how many paper clips the object will attract. Test your prediction, and use a pencil (or colour other than red) to record how many paper clips your object actually picks up/attracts. Answer the questions at the bottom of the page (3.5.1).

### Learning Centre

At the learning centre, provide a copy of the Learning-Centre Task Card: Magnet Minstrels (3.5.2), copies of the Song Template #1 (3.5.3) and the Song Template #2 (3.5.4), an audio-recording device, and pencils.

▶

Portage & Main Press, 2017 · *Hands-On Science and Technology · Grade 3* · ISBN: 978-1-55379-709-8

Portage & Main Press, 2017 · Hands-On Science and Technology · Grade 3 · ISBN: 978-1-55379-709-8

**5**

Have pairs of students use a familiar tune (e.g., "Three Blind Mice," "Mary Had a Little Lamb") and one of the song templates to create and record a song about magnets. Students may also create an original tune for their song.

Once all students have created a song, have students share their songs with each other.

## Consolidate and Debrief

- Revisit the guided inquiry question: **How is a magnet made?** Have students share their knowledge, provide examples, and ask further inquiry questions.
- Add to the herringbone chart as students learn new concepts, answer some of their own inquiry questions, and ask new inquiry questions.
- Add new terms, including *magnetize*, and illustrations to the class word wall. Add the words in other languages, as appropriate.
- Have students add new words, definitions, and examples to their Science and Technology Glossary (3.1.1). When possible, encourage students to add the words in other languages, including Indigenous languages, reflective of the class population.

### Assessment as Learning
Have students complete the Student Self-Assessment sheet, on page 31, to reflect on what they have learned about how magnets are made.

## Enhance

- Provide paper clips (or staples), bar magnets, and objects to test (e.g., nails, pens, pencils, scissors). Have students make temporary magnets by touching the bar magnet to the head of the nail. Instruct them to use the nail's point to try to pick up the paper clips or staples. Ask:
  - How many paper clips can you pick up?

Now, have them gradually move the nail away from the magnet. Ask:

- What happens to the paper clips?

Experiment with other objects (e.g., scissors, screws, washers, bolts, sewing needles, jewellery, small kitchen utensils).

- Have students continue their do-it-yourself projects at the Makerspace centre.

# Making a Magnet

| Object | Number of Rubs | Number of Paper Clips Attracted | |
| --- | --- | --- | --- |
| | | Prediction | Result |
| | | | |
| | | | |
| | | | |
| | | | |
| | | | |
| | | | |

How can you tell when an object is charged or magnetized?

_____

_____

When you rub an object with a magnet, does the number of rubs make a difference to the charge?

_____

_____

Portage & Main Press, 2017 · Hands-On Science and Technology · Grade 3 · ISBN: 978-1-55379-709-8

# Magnet Minstrels

Today, you are a musician!

1. Create a song about magnets.

2. For your song you may:

   - Use a tune that is familiar to you ("Mary Had a Little Lamb" or "Three Blind Mice") along with one of the templates at the centre.

   - Use the tune of a song that plays currently on the radio.

   - Make up your own tune.

3. Be sure to use new vocabulary from the lesson in your song, such as *magnet*, *attract*, and *magnetize*.

4. Use the audio-recording device to record your song.

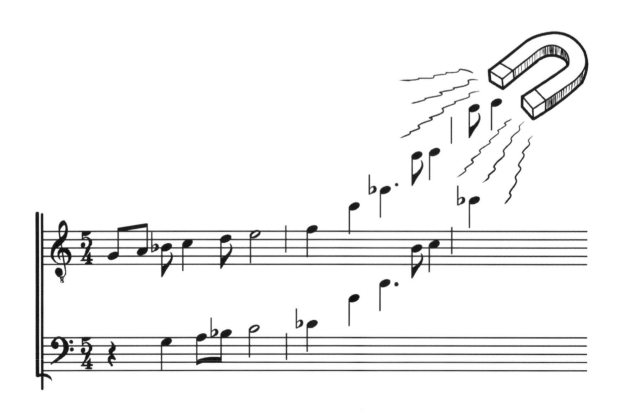

Portage & Main Press, 2017 · *Hands-On Science and Technology · Grade 3* · ISBN: 978-1-55379-709-8

# Song Template #1

## (sung to the tune of "Three Blind Mice")

Magnets, magnets, magnets.

Magnets, magnets, magnets.

They are _____ .

They are _____ .

Magnets pick up _____ and _____ .

But they repel _____ and _____ .

We know a lot about magnets now.

Oh, magnets, magnets, magnets!

Portage & Main Press, 2017 · Hands-On Science and Technology · Grade 3 · ISBN: 978-1-55379-709-8

**Date:** _____     **Name:** _____

# Song Template #2

### (sung to the tune of "Mary Had a Little Lamb")

If you have a mag-net, a mag-net, a mag-net,

If you have a mag-net, _____.

Touch it to a _____, _____,

_____.

Touch it to a _____, and it will _____.

(attract/repel)

Portage & Main Press, 2017 · *Hands-On Science and Technology · Grade 3* · ISBN: 978-1-55379-709-8

# 6 | How Can a Magnetic Force Be Altered?

## 21st Century Competencies

**Critical Thinking** and **Communication**:
Students will experiment to see if cardboard strips placed between a magnet and an object alter the strength of the magnetic force of attraction.

## Materials

- large graph paper
- markers
- horseshoe magnets (one for each working group of students)
- bar magnets (one for each working group of students)
- paper clips
- small steel ball bearings (Available online or from retailers such as Lee Valley Tools.)
- rulers (plastic or wooden, not metal)
- cardboard strips (Strips should be 0.5 cm thick. Length and width are not important.) (five or six for each working group of students)
- Activity Sheet: Magnetic Force (3.6.1)
- Centimetre Graph Paper (Photocopy two sheets for each working group of students.) (3.6.2)
- Learning-Centre Task Card: Floating Paper-Clip Experiment (3.6.3)
- Learning-Centre Activity Sheet: How Many Paper Clips? (3.6.4)
- pencils
- white paper
- coloured paper
- construction paper
- tissue paper
- thin cardboard
- thick cardboard
- newspaper
- plastic
- glass
- Styrofoam
- herringbone chart (from lesson 1)
- Science and Technology Glossary (3.1.1)

## Activate

Divide the class into working groups of two to four students, and provide each group with a bar magnet, a pile of paper clips, and a number of small steel ball bearings.

Have students use the magnet to pick up a paper clip. Then, challenge students to make a chain of paper clips by continuing to pick up the paper clips end to end. Have students predict how many paper clips the bar magnet will hold in a chain. Tell students to continue adding paper clips until no more can be added without falling off the chain. Have the groups compare their results. Repeat the task with the steel ball bearings instead of the paper clips. Ask students:

- Do you think the magnet will hold more or fewer ball bearings than paper clips? Why?
- How many ball bearings do you think can be held in a chain?
- Why does a chain form?

---

**NOTE:** The magnetic pull will travel through both the paper clips and the ball bearings. At a certain point, however, there still might be attraction, but the force of attraction will not be as strong as the force of gravity acting on the paper clip or ball bearing, so the paper clip and ball bearing will no longer be attracted.

---

As a class, on the large graph paper, create two bar graphs to show each group's results for the two investigations: (1) how many paper clips a magnet attracts, and (2) how many ball bearings a magnet attracts. Each bar on each graph will show results from one group for that material (paper clips or ball bearings).

Portage & Main Press, 2017 · Hands-On Science and Technology · Grade 3 · ISBN: 978-1-55379-709-8

Portage & Main Press, 2017 · Hands-On Science and Technology · Grade 3 · ISBN: 978-1-55379-709-8

# 6

Discuss the graphs with students. Ask:

- How could we have changed the results to attract more or fewer paper clips or ball bearings?

Introduce the guided inquiry question: **How can a magnetic force be altered?**

## Action: Part One

Have students work in the same groups as before. Distribute to each group five or six cardboard strips, a paper clip, a ruler, and both a bar magnet and a horseshoe magnet. Also, distribute a copy of Activity Sheet: Magnetic Force (3.6.1) to each student. Have students place the bar magnets on the table, then place the ruler on the table with the 0-cm mark almost touching one end of the magnet. Tell students to slide the paper clip along the edge of the ruler (without touching the ruler), and bring the paper clip close to the magnet until a pull is felt. Ask students to measure the distance between the paper clip and the magnet (as shown in the figure below) and record this on their activity sheet. Have students repeat the same task using the horseshoe magnet.

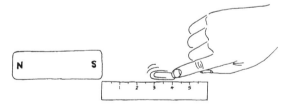

Now, have students examine one of the cardboard strips. Ask:

- If you placed the cardboard strip flat against the end of the magnet, do you think the magnet would still attract a paper clip through the strip of cardboard?
- What do you think would happen if you added two, three, four, or five strips of cardboard to the end of the magnet? Do you

think the magnet would still attract a paper clip through the stack of cardboard?

- How many cardboard strips do you think you could place between the magnet and the paper clip before you observed no more attraction?

Have students test their predictions, repeating the activity with a second strip of cardboard between the magnet's end and the paper clip, then three, four, five, and six strips of cardboard, recording all results on the activity sheet.

Ask:

- Does the magnet attract the paper clip through the cardboard?
- Does the strength of the attraction change when the amount of cardboard is increased?

Have students repeat the investigation using the horseshoe magnet. Again, have them predict, test, measure, and record the results on the activity sheet.

**NOTE:** Different magnets vary in strength. Test results will vary when different magnets are tested.

### Activity Sheet
Directions to students:

Measure and record the distance between the paper clip and the bar magnet as soon as you notice an attraction/pull. Then, place a piece of cardboard flat against the end of the magnet, between the magnet and the paper clip, to see if the paper clip is still attracted to the magnet (through the cardboard). Do the same with up to six strips of cardboard. Repeat the activity with the horseshoe magnet (3.6.1).

## Action: Part Two

Engage students in a discussion about the construction of bar graphs, assessing their background knowledge. Identify criteria for bar graphs, such as title, labelled x-axis, labelled

**Hands-On Science and Technology** · Grade 3

y-axis, accurate data, and separated bars. Discuss dependent and independent variables.

**NOTE:** In this investigation, the independent variable is the number of cardboard strips insulating the magnet. The dependent variable is the distance before an attraction/pull is experienced.

Have students use Centimetre Graph Paper (3.6.2) to create two bar graphs that show the results for the two investigations—one for the bar magnets and one for the horseshoe magnets. Have each group of students compare results with other groups. Ask:

- Did the number of cardboard strips have an effect on the distance between the paper clip and the bar magnet when an attraction/pull was first noticed? Why or why not?

- Did the type of magnet have an effect on the distance between the paper clip and the bar magnet when an attraction/pull was first noticed? Why or why not?

### Assessment for Learning

Observe students as they construct bar graphs. Focus on their ability to transfer data from charts to graphs. Also, focus on the agreed-on criteria for the graphs (e.g., title, labelled x-axis, labelled y-axis, accurate data, separated bars). Provide descriptive feedback as appropriate. Use the Anecdotal Record sheet, on page 26, to record results.

### Learning Centre

At the learning centre, provide a copy of the Learning-Centre Task Card: Floating Paper-Clip Experiment (3.6.3), along with copies of the Learning-Centre Activity Sheet: How Many Paper Clips? (3.6.4), pencils, paper clips, horseshoe magnets, white paper, coloured paper, construction paper, tissue paper, thin cardboard, thick cardboard, newspaper, plastic, glass, and Styrofoam.

Have students investigate various materials to determine what happens when each material is placed between a magnet and an attracted object. Students can first hold a horseshoe magnet over some paper clips and count how many paper clips the magnet picks up. Then, have them investigate what happens with each of the other materials when placed between the magnet and the paper clips. Students can record the results on the activity sheet (3.6.4).

## Consolidate and Debrief

- Revisit the guided inquiry question: **How can a magnetic force be altered?** Have students share their knowledge, provide examples, and ask further inquiry questions.

- Add to the herringbone chart as students learn new concepts, answer some of their own inquiry questions, and ask new inquiry questions.

- Add new terms and illustrations to the class word wall. Include the words in other languages, as appropriate.

- Have students add new words, definitions, and examples to their Science and Technology Glossary (3.1.1). When possible, encourage students to add the words in other languages, including Indigenous languages, reflective of the class.

## Enhance

- Have students use technology to create bar graphs of their investigation results. Go to NCES Kids' Zone Create A Graph: <nces.ed.gov/nceskids/createagraph>). Have students start with raw data, then construct hand-drawn graphs, and, finally, use technology to create new graphs to enhance students' understanding of data representation.

- Have students follow these instructions to make magnet testers. (Teachers may also

Portage & Main Press, 2017 · *Hands-On Science and Technology* · Grade 3 · ISBN: 978-1-55379-709-8

choose to make one magnet tester ahead of time, and have students test it with various materials.)

1. Gather the following materials:
   - one piece of wood, 15 cm long x 10 cm wide x 2.5 cm deep
   - two pieces of wood, 7 cm long x 10 cm wide x 2.5 cm deep
   - nails
   - hammer
   - small magnet
   - paper clip
   - thread
   - tape

2. Using a hammer and nails, attach the two smaller pieces of wood to each end of the longer piece to form the letter C. Tape the magnet to the underside of the top piece of wood. Tie one end of a 16-centimetre piece of thread to a paper clip. Tape the other end of thread to the base of the tester. Hold the paper clip upright under the magnet (there should be a gap of one or two centimetres between the magnet and the paper clip). It should now be suspended and appear to be free floating.

3. Have students predict, then test, a variety of materials to find out whether or not the materials affect the magnetism. Have students place each material (one at a time) in the space between the paper clip and the magnet. Materials might include strips of paper, wax paper, aluminum foil, metal, plastic overhead transparency sheets, and glass microscope slides. Have students record their predictions and results on the Enhance Activity Sheet: Floating Magnet (3.6.5).

- Have students continue their do-it-yourself projects at the Makerspace centre.

Portage & Main Press, 2017 · *Hands-On Science and Technology · Grade 3* · ISBN: 978-1-55379-709-8

**Date:** _____  **Name:** _____

# Magnetic Force

| Number of Cardboard Pieces | Distance From Bar Magnet (cm) | Distance From Horseshoe Magnet (cm) |
|:---:|:---:|:---:|
| 0 | | |
| 1 | | |
| 2 | | |
| 3 | | |
| 4 | | |
| 5 | | |

Now, use your results to make two bar graphs on the graph paper.

Portage & Main Press, 2017 · Hands-On Science and Technology · Grade 3 · ISBN: 978-1-55379-709-8

**Date:** _____  **Name:** _____

# Centimetre Graph Paper

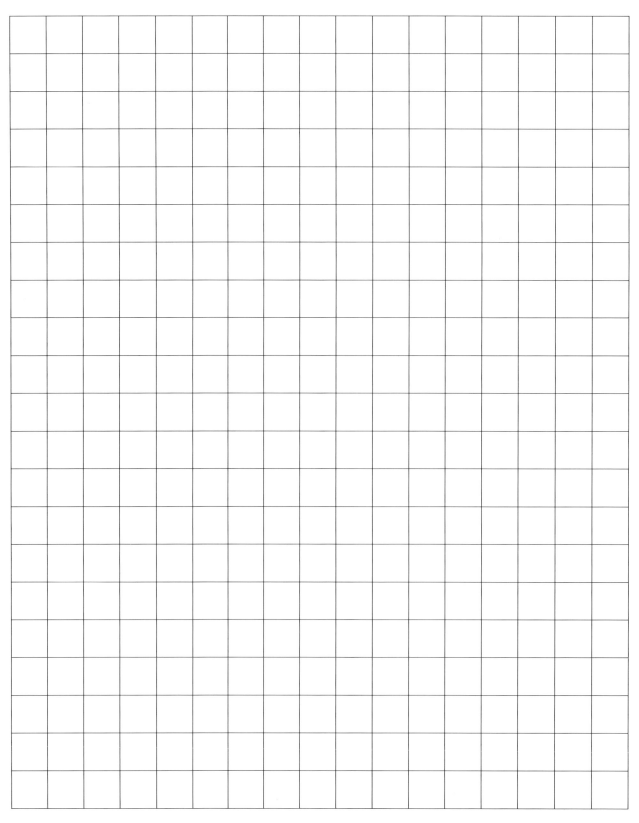

Portage & Main Press, 2017 · *Hands-On Science and Technology* · *Grade 3* · ISBN: 978-1-55379-709-8

# Floating Paper-Clip Experiment

Find out what happens when you place each of the materials provided between a horseshoe magnet and an attracted object (paper clips).

1. Place about a dozen paper clips on a flat surface, and hold a horseshoe magnet above the paper clips. Count and record how many paper clips the magnet attracts.

2. Choose a material (white or coloured paper, construction paper, tissue paper, thin or thick cardboard, newspaper, plastic, glass, or Styrofoam), note it on the recording sheet, and then place it between the paper clips and the magnet. Predict whether or not the magnetic force will pass through the material. Record your prediction.

3. Test to see if the magnetic force passes through the material to the paper clips. Record how many paper clips the magnet picks up now.

4. If there is a difference between your prediction and the result, work out the difference by recording the number sentence.

5. Test all the materials in the same way.

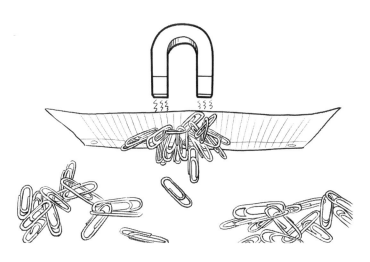

Portage & Main Press, 2017 · Hands-On Science and Technology · Grade 3 · ISBN: 978-1-55379-709-8

# How Many Paper Clips?

| Material | Prediction: Number of paper clips still attracted to magnet | Result: Number of paper clips still attracted to magnet | Difference |
|---|---|---|---|
|  |  |  |  |
|  |  |  |  |
|  |  |  |  |
|  |  |  |  |
|  |  |  |  |
|  |  |  |  |
|  |  |  |  |

Portage & Main Press, 2017 · Hands-On Science and Technology · Grade 3 · ISBN: 978-1-55379-709-8

**Date:** _____     **Name:** _____

# Floating Magnet

| Material | Number of Strips | Effects – Paper Clip Floats (yes/no) | |
| --- | --- | --- | --- |
| | | Prediction | Result |
| | | | |
| | | | |
| | | | |
| | | | |
| | | | |
| | | | |
| | | | |
| | | | |
| | | | |
| | | | |
| | | | |
| | | | |

Portage & Main Press, 2017 · Hands-On Science and Technology · Grade 3 · ISBN: 978-1-55379-709-8

# 7 | How Is Earth Like a Giant Magnet?

## Information for Teachers

Earth has a north pole and a south pole, just as a magnet does. Earth's magnetism is created in its core. Deep under its surface, Earth has an inner core made of solid iron metal surrounded by a thick outer core of molten iron-nickel. This liquid is always flowing, causing electric currents that generate magnetic fields. The result is one giant magnetic field around Earth. A compass will almost always line up in the direction of the magnetic field of Earth (strong magnets or electrical fields may interfere).

## 21st Century Competencies

**Critical Thinking** and **Communication**: A model will be created to show how Earth is like a giant magnet.

## Materials

- index cards (Print the names of the cardinal directions [north, east, south, west] on the cards, one per card.)
- sticky notes (four for each student)
- globe
- compasses (one for each student)
- orange or grapefruit
- toothpicks
- sharp knife (adult use only)
- bar magnet (slim and at least 15 cm long)
- Activity Sheet: The Earth's Poles (3.7.1)
- Learning-Centre Task Card: Magnetic North and South Poles (3.7.2)
- Learning-Centre Activity Sheet: The Magnetic Poles (3.7.3)
- herringbone chart (from lesson 1)
- Science and Technology Glossary (3.1.1)

### Assessment for Learning

Ask students the names of the cardinal directions. For each direction said, show the student the corresponding index card.

## Activate

Give each student four sticky notes, and on each note ask them to record one of the four abbreviations for the four cardinal directions (N, E, S, W). Then, ask students to affix each of their four sticky notes to what they think to be the corresponding wall in the classroom.

Now, show students the globe, and have them identify the North Pole. Explain that Earth actually has two north poles and two south poles, the geographical ones and the magnetic ones. The poles on the globe show the geographic North Pole and South Pole, which is the axis on which Earth turns. The magnetic poles are very close to the geographic poles, with the difference called the "declination." The only way to find the magnetic north pole, however, is to use a compass.

We use a compass to guide us in the correct direction. The needle of a compass is actually a small magnet.

Introduce the guided inquiry question: **How is Earth like a giant magnet?**

## Action: Part One

As a demonstration, cut an incision straight through an orange or a grapefruit, and push the bar magnet through so the ends of the magnet show on either side. The fruit now represents Earth, with the magnet identifying the magnetic north and south poles.

---

**NOTE:** For a true representation, the south end of the bar magnet should be at the north end of the model.

---

Add toothpicks to the orange to represent the geographic North Pole and South Pole. Have students investigate the effects of bringing a compass near the "Earth" orange.

Portage & Main Press, 2017 · Hands-On Science and Technology · Grade 3 · ISBN: 978-1-55379-709-8

NOTE: The compass will always align itself with the magnetic north and south poles.

Distribute a copy of Activity Sheet: The Earth's Poles (3.7.1) to each student, and have students show the geographic North Pole and South Pole and the magnetic north pole and south pole. Also, have students record a sentence describing something they know about each of the poles.

### Activity Sheet

Directions to students:

Show the geographic North Pole and South Pole, and the magnetic north pole and south pole. Also, write a sentence to show what you have learned about each of Earth's poles (3.7.1).

## Action: Part Two

Take students outside, and provide each student with a compass. Show them how to use the compass and how to find the magnetic north pole.

To show that a compass is affected by magnetism, bring a bar magnet close to a compass, and watch how the needle follows the magnet as it is rotated.

Challenge students to use the compass to find the other three directions.

## Action: Part Three

Discuss, from an Indigenous perspective, the importance of the cardinal directions to everyday living in terms of travel, hunting, and ceremonies. As a class, visit the Four Directions Teachings website, which includes information on the four directions and their relationship to the Medicine Wheel. Go to: <www.fourdirectionsteachings.com>.

Consider having a local Elder or Métis Senator speak to the class to share their knowledge of how the cardinal directions play a role in traditional Indigenous life. They may also share stories on the topic.

Follow up with related Indigenous books such as:

- *Medicine Wheel: Stories of a Hoop Dancer* by Teddy Anderson
- *The Medicine Wheel* by Sandra Samatte
- *Grandfather, What Is A Medicine Wheel?* by Sandra Samatte

## Action: Part Four

Learn about the Auroras, which is a phenomenon related to the concept of Earth's magnetic traits. Auroras are made when energetic gas particles from the Sun create a solar wind. These particles could be dangerous to us, but we are protected by an invisible shield around our planet. This magnetic shield, called the magnetosphere, sometimes traps these particles. Auroras are most likely to be found at the poles of the planet due to their strong magnetic force, which attracts the gas particles. When these particles collide with the gases in Earth's atmosphere (mainly oxygen and nitrogen), the aurora's colourful displays of light occur.

Many videos offer the opportunity to view the Northern Lights, or Aurora borealis. For example:

- **www.youtube.com/watch?v=NZlfxWMr7nc** "Relax Music & Stunning Aurora Borealis— Northern Polar Lights." BaLu-Relaxing Nature (1:57:10).

- **www.youtube.com/watch?v=fVsONlc3OUY** "Night of the Norther Lights." Maciej Winiarczyk (2:22).

- **www.youtube.com/watch?v=fVMgnmi2D1w** "NASA UHD Video: Stunning Aurora Borealis from Space in Ultra-High Definition." Space Videos (4:36).

Consider having a local Elder or Métis Senator speak to the class to share their knowledge of how the Northern Lights play a role in

Portage & Main Press, 2017 · *Hands-On Science and Technology · Grade 3* · ISBN: 978-1-55379-709-8

Portage & Main Press, 2017 · Hands-On Science and Technology · Grade 3 · ISBN: 978-1-55379-709-8

**7**

Indigenous life. There are many stories about the Northern Lights from different Indigenous peoples, which can be shared by Indigenous guests. As an alternative, students can research these stories to share with the class.

As a class, read an Indigenous story about the Aurora Borealis:

- *Northern Lights: The Soccer Trails* by Michael Kusugak
- *Aurora: A Tale of the Northern Lights* by Mindy Dwyer
- *SkySisters* by Jan Bourdeau Waboose

## Learning Centre

At the learning centre, provide a copy of the Learning-Centre Task Card: Magnetic North and South Poles (3.7.2), copies of the Learning-Centre Activity Sheet: The Magnetic Poles (3.7.3), bar magnets, and pencils. Have students place a bar magnet on the X in the middle of the activity sheet, following the instructions about north-south cardinal directions. Then, at each number, have students place a compass directly on the number and draw an arrow to the direction the needle is pointing.

## Consolidate and Debrief

- Revisit the guided inquiry question: **How is Earth like a giant magnet?** Have students share their knowledge, provide examples, and ask further inquiry questions.
- Add to the herringbone chart as students learn new concepts, answer some of their own inquiry questions, and ask new inquiry questions.
- Add new terms, including *magnetic north pole*, *magnetic south pole*, and *compass*, and illustrations to the class word wall. Add the words in other languages, as appropriate.
- Have students add new words, definitions, and examples to their Science and

Technology Glossary (3.1.1). When possible, encourage students to add the words in other languages, including Indigenous languages, reflective of the class population.

## Enhance

- Have students make their own compasses in one of two different ways. Divide the class into four equal groups, and have two groups create one design and the other two groups create the second design.

### Compass 1

This simple compass requires the following materials:

- bar magnet
- bowl
- water
- half a drinking straw
- sewing needle
- tape

1. Rub the sewing needle with the magnet several times. Make sure you rub in the same direction, and not back and forth.
2. Place the needle inside half a drinking straw. Fold the ends of the straw, or seal them with tape.
3. Place the straw in a bowl of water, where it will float. Once the straw settles, it should point to the north and south. Have students rotate the bowl to see if the needle/straw always points the same way.

### Compass 2

This simple compass requires the following materials:

- water
- bowl
- cork
- thumbtack
- bar magnet
- sewing needle

1. Rub the sewing needle with the bar magnet at least 10 times. Make sure you rub in the same direction, and not back and forth.

2. Stick the thumbtack into one end of the cork, and then float the cork in a bowl of water, thumbtack side down.

3. Lay the needle on top of the cork. Allow the cork to turn. When it stops, it will be pointing north-south.

4. Give the cork a little push, and the needle will begin to turn again. When it stops, it will again be pointing north-south.

■ Connect with the physical education teacher/program at your school to plan some outdoor orienteering activities, which will help to develop students' compass skills.

■ Watch the video "Magnets & Magnetism." Go to: <www.youtube.com/watch?v=eYSG5aeTy-Y>

■ Show students visuals about Earth's magnetism to enhance their understanding of this rather abstract idea.

■ Have students continue their do-it-yourself projects at the Makerspace centre.

Portage & Main Press, 2017 · Hands-On Science and Technology · Grade 3 · ISBN: 978-1-55379-709-8

**Date:** _____     **Name:** _____

# The Earth's Poles

View from the
North Pole

View from the
South Pole

Earth's geographic poles _____

_____

Earth's magnetic poles _____

_____

# Magnetic North and South Poles

1. Place a bar magnet on the **X** in the middle of the activity sheet. Be sure to follow the north-south instructions.

2. Then, at each number, place a compass directly on the number and draw an arrow in the direction the compass needle is pointing.

3. Repeat the task for all numbers.

Portage & Main Press, 2017 · Hands-On Science and Technology · Grade 3 · ISBN: 978-1-55379-709-8

Portage & Main Press, 2017 · Hands-On Science and Technology · Grade 3 · ISBN: 978-1-55379-709-8

# The Magnetic Poles

Place the bar magnet on the X, with the north and south poles as shown.
Place the compass on circle 1. Draw an arrow beside the compass to show the
direction that the needle is pointing. Continue for all numbers.

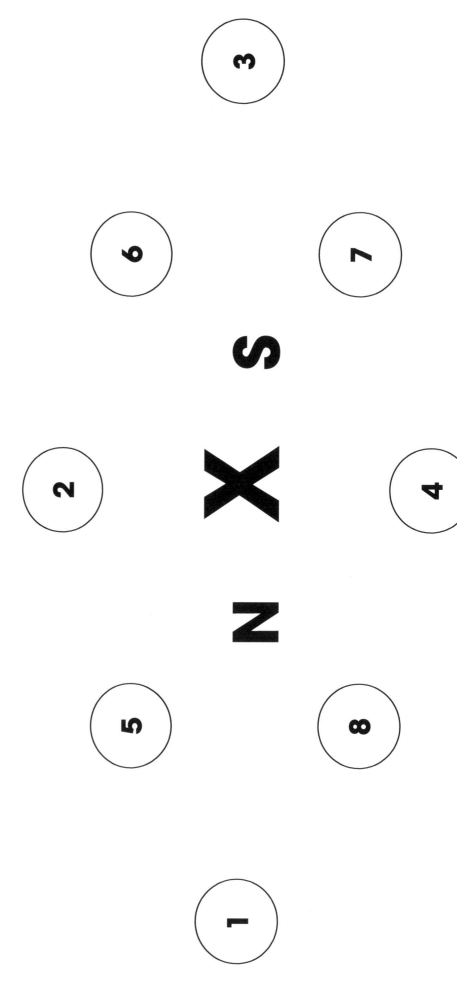

# 8 | What Are Helpful Uses and Harmful Effects of Magnets?

## Information for Teachers

Magnets are used in many ways. In a home, magnets can be found within magnetic knife holders, and magnets keep the fridge door and many cupboard doors closed. Magnets are also used in many kinds of machines. They are found in stereo speakers, computers, and telephones. Magnets can be helpful if used properly. If used incorrectly, they can cause serious problems. Powerful magnets can actually erase the picture on a television screen by rearranging the atoms. Magnets can also cause damage to computers and other technological devices.

## 21st Century Competencies

**Critical Thinking**, **Communication**, and **Creativity**: Students will research how devices that use magnets work, and some possible harmful effects of magnets. Students will choose a way in which to share their research findings.

## Materials

- chart paper
- markers
- resources about magnets (e.g., nonfiction books, specific bookmarked Internet sites)
- computers/tablets with Internet access
- pencils
- Activity Sheet: Magnet Inquiry Research Project (3.8.1)
- Learning-Centre Task Card: Assessing a Peer (3.8.2)
- Learning-Centre Activity Sheet: Two Stars and One Wish—Peer Assessment Form (3.8.3)
- herringbone chart (from lesson 1)
- Science and Technology Glossary (3.1.1)

## Activate

As a class, discuss the helpful uses of magnets. Brainstorm a list of devices that use magnets, and record these on a sheet of chart paper.

Also, have students share their background knowledge about possible harmful effects of magnets. Record these ideas on a second sheet of chart paper.

Explain to students they will be participating in an inquiry project to research one helpful use for magnets and one harmful effect of using magnets. Students may work individually or in pairs.

Introduce the guided inquiry question: **What are helpful uses and harmful effects of magnets?**

## Action

Before students select their inquiry topics, have them conduct some informal research into the helpful uses of magnets, as well as their potential harmful effects. Encourage students to look through books and review appropriate websites, with the goal of selecting, for further research, one helpful use and one harmful effect of using magnets.

Brainstorm for good questions based on ideas on the word wall, in the student Science and Technology Glossary, and on the herringbone chart. For example:

- How does a device that uses magnets work?
- How can magnets cause damage to a device?

Have students also include two questions of their own choice.

Distribute a copy of Activity Sheet: Magnet Inquiry Research Project (3.8.1) to each student, and have students record their inquiry questions.

Portage & Main Press, 2017 · Hands-On Science and Technology · Grade 3 · ISBN: 978-1-55379-709-8

**8**

Also, co-construct criteria for the inquiry project. As a class, discuss the characteristics of a successful project. These criteria should be directly related to the inquiry questions. Record class criteria on chart paper, and display during project development.

Provide students with information from a variety of sources to use for their research, including bookmarked websites. Encourage students to also seek out information on their own, assisting them in discovering information, but helping only as much as necessary. Teachers are encouraged to ask questions that will guide students in the right direction rather than to tell them how to find the answer. Model for students how to look for information in a nonfiction text.

Once students have gathered sufficient information to answer their inquiry questions, have them choose a way to present their research. Brainstorm and discuss various ideas for presentation, and have students choose one format. Guide and model the process of transferring research findings to a presentation format. Provide time, support, and specific materials as students work to present the answers to their questions.

### Activity Sheet
Directions to students:

Record your inquiry questions, any information you find that might help you answer your questions, sketches of your experiments and activities, and so on (3.8.1).

**NOTE:** This is a two-page activity sheet.

### Assessment of Learning
Record the class criteria for the research project on the Rubric, on page 36. When students present their projects, use the criteria to help assess them, and record results.

## Learning Centre

At the learning centre, provide a copy of the Learning-Centre Task Card: Assessing a Peer (3.8.2), copies of the Learning-Centre Activity Sheet: Two Stars and One Wish—Peer Assessment Form (3.8.3), and pencils. After each presentation of an inquiry project, have students use the activity sheet to provide feedback. Ask students to record a peer reflection based on the other student's project and include two things they liked about the project (stars), and one thing the student could work on for next time (a wish).

## Consolidate and Debrief

- Revisit the guided inquiry question: **What are helpful uses and harmful effects of magnets?** Have students share their knowledge, provide examples, and ask further inquiry questions.

- Add to the herringbone chart as students learn new concepts, answer some of their own inquiry questions, and ask new inquiry questions.

- Add new terms and illustrations to the class word wall. Add the words in other languages, as appropriate.

- Have students add new words, definitions, and examples to their Science and Technology Glossary (3.1.1). When possible, encourage students to add the words in other languages, including Indigenous languages, reflective of the class.

## Enhance

- Research and investigate with students the harmful effects of magnets when magnets erase credit card data and computer hard drives.

- Have students continue their do-it-yourself projects at the Makerspace centre.

Portage & Main Press, 2017 · Hands-On Science and Technology · Grade 3 · ISBN: 978-1-55379-709-8

# Magnet Inquiry Research Project

Working by yourself or with a partner, choose one helpful use of magnets and one harmful effect of magnets.

- How does a device that uses magnets work?

- How can magnets cause damage to a device?

My two questions:

1. _____

_____

_____

2. _____

_____

_____

Use the following resources from your home, school, and/or community for your research:

- nonfiction books

- brochures

- bookmarked Internet sites

# Magnet Inquiry Research Project (continued)

Decide how you will present the information gained from your research. Here are some ideas:

- Write a song.

- Create a 3D model.

- Write a play/skit.

- Draw or paint or create a digital picture.

- Record your information in essay or brochure style.

- Write a poem.

- Video record a news report.

- Use an idea of your own.

Describe how you will present your inquiry project and what you will need for your presentation.

Your project is due: _____

Portage & Main Press, 2017 · Hands-On Science and Technology · Grade 3 · ISBN: 978-1-55379-709-8

# Assessing a Peer

1. Choose a classmate's project, and provide feedback on it.

2. After listening to your classmate's presentation, complete a copy of the "Two Stars and One Wish" peer assessment form. Include:

   - Two stars—Two things you like about the presentation or content

   - One wish—One thing for your classmate to work on for next time

Portage & Main Press, 2017 · Hands-On Science and Technology · Grade 3 · ISBN: 978-1-55379-709-8

**Date:** _____     **Name:** _____

# Two Stars and One Wish—
# Peer Assessment Form

Portage & Main Press, 2017 · *Hands-On Science and Technology · Grade 3* · ISBN: 978-1-55379-709-8

# 9 | What Is Static Electricity, and How Is It Created?

## Information for Teachers

All matter is made up of atoms. Atoms are made up of smaller particles called *protons*, which carry positive charge; *electrons*, which carry negative charge; and *neutrons*, which have no charge.

Static electricity is electricity that builds up on an object due to an imbalance of negative and positive charges. Static electricity can be produced when one object rubs against another. When you rub a cloth against a balloon, some electrons are transferred from the cloth to the balloon, which becomes negatively charged. As in magnets, negative charges repel negative charges. If you take a negatively charged balloon and bring it in contact with an uncharged balloon, the balloons attract each other. If you bring a charged balloon in contact with another similarly charged balloon, the balloons will repel each other.

Do the activities in this lesson on cold, dry winter days, when it is easier to produce static electricity. Moisture in the air allows static electricity buildup to discharge, making it more difficult to achieve good results from the experiments.

## 21st Century Competencies

**Critical Thinking**, **Communication**, and **Collaboration**: Students will work collaboratively to explore the concept of static electricity and how it is produced.

## Materials

- combs (one for each working group)
- wool mittens (one mitten for each working group)
- tissue paper
- paper
- aluminum foil
- various materials to test with static electricity (e.g., copper wire, wax pieces, sawdust, thread, Styrofoam chips)
- scissors (one pair for each student)
- Activity Sheet: Static Electricity (3.9.1)
- herringbone chart (from lesson 1)
- Science and Technology Glossary (3.1.1)

## Activate

Ask students if they have ever experienced a shock when they touched something after walking in socks on carpet or if their hair has ever stood up on end after brushing it or wearing a toque. Let students discuss these events and elaborate on other similar incidents. Ask:

- Why do you think this happens?

Introduce the guided inquiry question: **What is static electricity, and how is it created?**

## Action

In working groups of three or four students, have students cut up the paper, aluminum foil, and tissue paper into small bits, about the size of a dime or a caramel. Provide each group with a comb and a mitten. Also, distribute a copy of Activity Sheet: Static Electricity (3.9.1) to each student. Ask the groups to spread the tissue paper bits onto another sheet of paper. Have one student from each group use the wool mitten to rub the comb briskly, about 10 times back and forth. This should produce a static electricity charge.

Now, have students hold the charged comb near the tissue paper bits, without touching either the bits or the sheet of paper the tissue paper bits are on, and observe what occurs. Ask:

- What happened to the pieces of tissue paper?
- Why do you think this happened?

Portage & Main Press, 2017 · *Hands-On Science and Technology · Grade 3* · ISBN: 978-1-55379-709-8

■ What effect do you think rubbing the comb with the mitten had on the tissue paper?

Have students record their results on their activity sheet. Ask:

■ What do you think will happen if you do the same test using small bits of regular paper or aluminum foil, rather than the tissue paper?

Have students test their predictions by rubbing the comb with the wool mitten and observing its effects on the paper and on the aluminum foil. Again, have students record results on their activity sheet.

Have students prepare other materials to test. Cut thread into one-centimetre lengths, break up wax into pea-size pieces, strip copper wire and cut into one-centimetre pieces, and so on. Students can test any and all materials to see how each reacts to the charged comb. Encourage students to make predictions before they test the materials then record results on the activity sheet.

Following the investigation, ask:

■ How did the different materials react to the charged comb?

■ Which materials jumped onto the comb and stayed there?

■ Which materials attached themselves to the comb, fell off, and then reattached themselves?

■ Did any materials try to attach themselves but could not actually be attracted?

■ Why do you think that happened?

■ Which materials did not react to the charged comb?

■ How was the comb like a magnet?

■ What do you think caused certain materials to be attracted to the comb?

■ What caused the comb to attract materials?

■ Do you think that rubbing the comb with the mitten did anything to the comb? What?

**Activity Sheet**

Directions to students:

During your investigations, use the chart to record your observations about each material, including the number of pieces attracted to the comb (3.9.1).

## Consolidate and Debrief

■ Revisit the guided inquiry question: **What is static electricity, and how is it created?** Have students share their knowledge, provide examples, and ask further inquiry questions.

■ Add to the herringbone chart as students learn new concepts, answer some of their own inquiry questions, and ask new inquiry questions.

■ Add new terms, including *charged* and *static electricity*, and illustrations to the class word wall. Add the words in other languages, as appropriate.

■ Have students add new words, definitions, and examples to their Science and Technology Glossary (3.1.1). When possible, encourage students to add the words in other languages, including Indigenous languages, reflective of the classroom.

## Enhance

■ Have students experiment with charged balloons. Ask them to spread out small pieces of tissue paper across a table. Tell them to rub the balloon briskly for 10 seconds with the wool mitten. Have them bring the balloon close to the tissue paper pieces and observe the reaction. Then, have students neutralize the balloon by wiping it with a damp cloth (make sure no water remains on the balloon). Now, ask students to test the balloon using materials other than the mitten (e.g., fake fur, a cotton or silk cloth, burlap, hair). Tell students to record

▶

Portage & Main Press, 2017 · *Hands-On Science and Technology · Grade 3* · ISBN: 978-1-55379-709-8

how much tissue paper is attracted each time and create a bar graph of their results.

- Using the same materials to charge the balloons as in the preceding activity, have students try to attach the balloon to the wall, a ceiling tile, and window glass.

- Access the interactive activity, Static Electrical Force, in the Grade 3, Unit 3 folder of the *Hands-On Interactive for Science and Technology, Grade 3* download. Find this download at: <www.portageandmainpress.com/product/hands-on-interactive-for-science-and-technology-grade-3/>.

- Have students continue their do-it-yourself projects at the Makerspace centre.

Portage & Main Press, 2017 · *Hands-On Science and Technology · Grade 3* · ISBN: 978-1-55379-709-8

# Static Electricity

## Charging a Comb

| Material Tested | Observations | Number of Pieces Attracted |
|---|---|---|
|  |  |  |
|  |  |  |
|  |  |  |
|  |  |  |
|  |  |  |
|  |  |  |
|  |  |  |
|  |  |  |

## Draw a diagram to show how you charged the comb.

Portage & Main Press, 2017 · Hands-On Science and Technology · Grade 3 · ISBN: 978-1-55379-709-8

# 10 | How Does Humidity Affect Static Electricity?

## Information for Teachers

Static electricity is affected by the level of humidity in the air. The less humidity, the greater the potential for static electricity to be evident. As such, it is helpful to check the humidity in your classroom prior to conducting experiments with static electricity. A hygrometer can be used to measure humidity in the air. Experiments will be much more successful if humidity is less than 30 percent.

## 21ˢᵗ Century Competencies

**Critical Thinking** and **Communication**: Students will experiment to see how humidity affects the ability of objects to build up and maintain a static charge.

## Materials

- hygrometer
- chart paper
- markers
- classroom clock or stopwatches
- balloons (at least one for each student)
- permanent markers
- kettle, vaporizer, and/or humidifier
- water
- Activity Sheet A: How Long Will a Balloon Stay on the Wall? (3.10.1)
- *The Balloon Tree* by Phoebe Gilman
- Learning-Centre Task Card: Balloon-apalooza (3.10.2)
- computers/tablets with Internet access
- resources about balloons
- paper
- pencils
- herringbone chart (from lesson 1)
- Science and Technology Glossary (3.1.1)

## Activate

**NOTE:** The following activity takes a full school day to complete, starting at the beginning of the day.

Ask students if they experience static electricity more in the winter or in the summer.

In order to understand humidity, conduct a demonstration with a kettle or misting spray bottle to show water 'disappearing' into the air. Then, ask:

- Which time of year is usually drier?

Show students the hygrometer. Ask:

- Do you know what this is?
- What do you think it is used for?
- Why would we use this instrument when studying static electricity?
- How does the name of this instrument tell us what it measures?

Record students' responses on the chart paper.

Explain to students that the device is a hygrometer. It is an instrument that measures the amount of moisture or humidity in the air. Have students read the hygrometer to determine the level of humidity in the classroom. Distribute a copy of Activity Sheet A: How Long Will a Balloon Stay on the Wall? (3.10.1) to each student. Have students record the information about hygrometers on their activity sheet.

Introduce the guided inquiry question: **How does humidity affect static electricity?**

## Action

Give each student a balloon to blow up and tie closed. Have students use permanent markers to print their names on the balloons. Ask:

- Is your balloon charged or uncharged right now?
- How can you charge this balloon?

Portage & Main Press, 2017 · *Hands-On Science and Technology · Grade 3* · ISBN: 978-1-55379-709-8

- Do you think you can charge it so it is attracted to a surface like the wall?
- How long do you think it would stay charged and stick to the wall?

Tell students to record on their activity sheet their predictions of how long the balloon will stick to the wall.

Have students rub the balloon on their hair for 10 seconds and stick the balloon on the wall.

Ask:

- Why do you think the balloon sticks to the wall?

**NOTE:** Rubbing the balloon against hair transfers electrons (negative charge) to the surface of the balloon. The balloon is then attracted to the more positively charged wall, because opposites attract.

Have students use the classroom clock or a stopwatch to time how long it takes for the balloon to lose its charge and fall off the wall (continue with other classroom activities while this test is being conducted). Have students record results on the activity sheet.

This investigation provides a good opportunity to discuss variables. Engage students in such a conversation, having them determine control variables—what they keep the same during the experiment (e.g., rubbing the balloon on their hair for 10 seconds).

**NOTE:** If the humidity level of the room is very low, the balloons may stay on the wall for a day or longer. Usually the balloons fall down after 15 or 20 minutes (depending on the size and weight of the balloon).

Now, ask students if they can think of ways to increase the humidity level in the classroom. Give students a chance to brainstorm, and then show them the humidifier, the vaporizer, and/ or the kettle. Use one of the devices for a few hours to add humidity to the classroom. Keep

the classroom door closed to maintain the moisture. Ask:

- Do you think increasing the humidity will affect the charge of a balloon?
- If you rubbed the balloon again on your hair, would it stick to the wall for a longer or shorter period of time, now that there is more humidity in the room?

Have students record their predictions on the activity sheet. After a few hours, once the humidity level in the room has increased, have students record the new humidity level on their activity sheet. Conduct the same investigation as before, having students measure how long the balloons stick to the wall. Have them record the results. Ask:

- How did the increased humidity in the room affect the charge of the balloon?

This second part of the investigation presents another opportunity to discuss variables. Because humidity is the one variable that is being changed, it is possible to talk about cause and effect.

### Activity Sheet
Directions to students:

Record your predictions and the results of your investigation (3.10.1).

### Assessment for Learning
Conference with students individually to discuss the investigation. Encourage them to use the materials provided in the activity to demonstrate their understanding of the investigation. Use the Individual Student Observations sheet, on page 27, to record results.

### Learning Centre

At the learning centre, include the book, *The Balloon Tree* by Phoebe Gilman, along with a copy of the Learning-Centre Task Card: Balloon-apalooza (3.10.2). Also, have computers or

Portage & Main Press, 2017 · Hands-On Science and Technology · Grade 3 · ISBN: 978-1-55379-709-8

tablets with Internet access available, along with any other resources about balloons, and paper and pencils. Have small groups of students read the book, *The Balloon Tree*. Then, have them research balloons' uses and explore how life would change if balloons did not exist. Guide students to online encyclopedias or other appropriate websites such as the following: <www.enchantedlearning.com/Home.html>.

## Consolidate and Debrief

- Revisit the guided inquiry question: **How does humidity affect static electricity?** Have students share their knowledge, provide examples, and ask further inquiry questions.

- Add to the herringbone chart as students learn new concepts, answer some of their own inquiry questions, and ask new inquiry questions.

- Add new terms and illustrations to the class word wall. Add the words in other languages, as appropriate.

- Have students add new words, definitions, and examples to their Science and Technology Glossary (3.1.1). When possible, encourage students to add the words in other languages, including Indigenous languages, reflective of the class.

## Enhance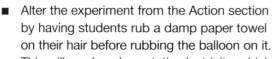

- Alter the experiment from the Action section by having students rub a damp paper towel on their hair before rubbing the balloon on it. This will produce less static electricity, which will affect the results of the experiment in terms of how long (or if) the balloon sticks to the wall.

- Have students continue their do-it-yourself projects at the Makerspace centre.

Portage & Main Press, 2017 · *Hands-On Science and Technology · Grade 3* · ISBN: 978-1-55379-709-8

# How Long Will a Balloon Stay on the Wall?

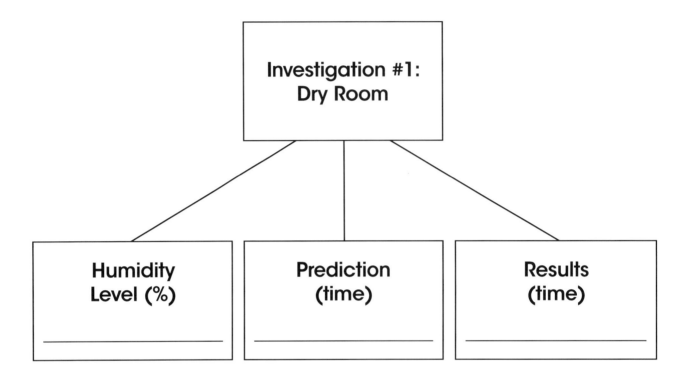

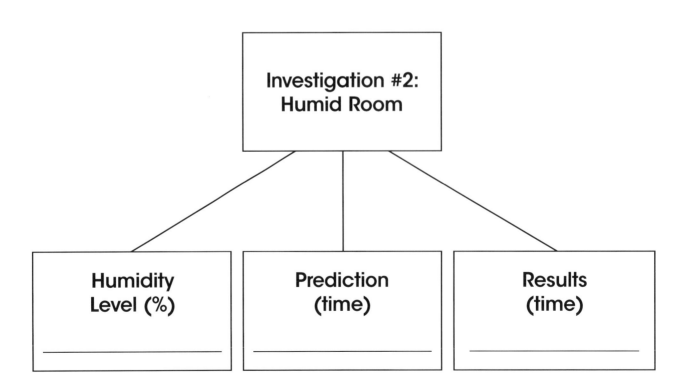

Portage & Main Press, 2017 · *Hands-On Science and Technology · Grade 3* · ISBN: 978-1-55379-709-8

# Balloon-apalooza

1. Read the book *The Balloon Tree,* by Phoebe Gilman.

2. As a group, make a list of all the ways balloons are used.

3. Do more research to find out other ways balloons are used.

4. Think about what would happen if all of the balloons on Earth were popped, just like in the story, *The Balloon Tree.*

   - How would life be different if all balloons disappeared?

   - What would we not be able to do?

5. Discuss your ideas as a group.

6. Record your answer in pictures and words.

Portage & Main Press, 2017 · *Hands-On Science and Technology* · Grade 3 · ISBN: 978-1-55379-709-8

# 11 | How Can the Force of Static Electricity Be Demonstrated Safely?

## Information for Teachers

Normally, objects are neutral—with their positive and negative charges balanced.

Rubbing various objects with certain materials produces an imbalance between the negative and positive charges on the surface of those materials. Substances end up more negatively charged or more positively charged when electrons move between surfaces. Like charges repel each other; unlike charges attract each other, so some sort of action can result when objects become charged. Even the flow of water can be attracted to charged objects. This push or pull is caused by static electric force.

When you walk across a carpet, for example, the negative charge on your body builds up, because your feet rub the carpet. Those extra electrons will try to leave you when they get a chance, forming a spark. Reach out to touch a metal light switch or doorknob, and you will see that happen. Once this occurs, your body is discharged (back in balance), and you can touch that object again without receiving a shock.

Similarly, rubbing can also occur as air masses move in a cloud. Warm air moves up through a cloud where it is cooler on top, and its water vapour turns to ice particles. The particles bump into each other as they fall, creating static electricity. In stormy conditions, clouds can become positively charged on top and negatively charged on the bottom. The cloud is discharged when lightning (a stream of electrons) jumps between the areas of the cloud or to the ground. It is the same principle as the spark from your hand to the doorknob. Lightning will not occur again until the same conditions in the cloud are recreated.

## 21ˢᵗ Century Competencies

**Critical Thinking** and **Communication**: Students will observe static electricity as it acts on water, and then examine static electricity in a real-life setting.

## Materials

- access to a sink and faucet
- silk cloth
- wool cloth
- comb
- two glass rods
- string
- two sealing wax rods
- access to YouTube
- Activity Sheet: Charged Rods and Flowing Water (3.11.1)
- Learning-Centre Task Card: St. Elmo's Fire (3.11.2)
- books and other reference material related to St. Elmo's fire
- pencils
- watercolour paints and painting supplies (e.g. brushes, paper)
- computers/tablets with Internet access
- herringbone chart (from lesson 1)
- Science and Technology Glossary (3.1.1)

## Activate

**NOTE:** The following activity works best as a demonstration, since it is unlikely there will be enough sinks and taps for cooperative groups of students to work on this themselves. Use a tablet or phone to video record the demonstration, and then project it on a screen so it is easier to see and can be reviewed during discussion.

Turn on the water faucet so a thin stream of water is flowing. Place the uncharged glass rod near, but not touching, the flow of water. Ask:

- Is the rod affecting the water flow?

Now, rub the glass rod with the silk cloth. Ask

- Is the rod now charged or uncharged?
- What do you think will happen if the rod is brought close to the water stream?

Portage & Main Press, 2017 · Hands-On Science and Technology · Grade 3 · ISBN: 978-1-55379-709-8

Test students' predictions by bringing the charged rod near, but not touching, the flowing water. Observe and discuss the results.

---

**NOTE:** The water stream will bend toward the rod, because it is attracted to the charged object.

---

Repeat this investigation using a wool cloth to charge a comb, and compare results.

Introduce the guided inquiry question: **How can the force of static electricity be demonstrated safely?**

## Action: Part One

Tell students the story of St. Elmo's fire, which is a phenomenon named after St. Erasmus, the patron saint of sailors. A long time ago, sailors were frightened at night by a strange bluish light that danced on the masts of their ships. The light was often accompanied by crackling noises. Airplane pilots sometimes see the same lights dance on the wings and propellers of their planes, usually when flying near a thunderstorm or cumulonimbus clouds.

St. Elmo's fire is actually a discharge of static electricity and is usually seen or heard before or during a thunderstorm. Static electricity often builds up on tall objects when the atmosphere is full of electrical charges. This produces the lights and the crackling noises seen and heard by sailors and pilots.

Static electricity can also produce problems. For example, the hydrogen-filled airship, the *Hindenburg*, is believed to have exploded because of a discharge of static electricity near a hydrogen gas leak.

There are several YouTube videos that capture St. Elmo's fire sightings. Show some of these to students to visually enhance their understanding of the concept.

For example:

- **www.youtube.com/watch?v=3XhhMAxsyOU** "St. Elmo's fire on aircraft windscreen." stratfordhens (00:00:19)

- **www.youtube.com/watch?v=zyWX3VRsk38** "St. Elmo's fire in airplane cockpit—Elmsfeuer im Airbus Cockpit." AirplanetvCOM (00:00:46).

- **www.youtube.com/watch?v=P1luqXNqC1c** "737 Jumpseat Takeoff & St. Elmo's Fire !!!" PilotsTubeHD (00:03:08).

After watching the videos, discuss how St. Elmo's Fire might be dangerous for pilots who experience it.

## Action: Part Two

Present the following demonstration to students:

Tie a loop at each end of a piece of string. Charge two glass rods by rubbing them with a piece of silk cloth. Have a student hold the string at the centre, and place one of the glass rods through the loops in the string, as shown in the diagram below:

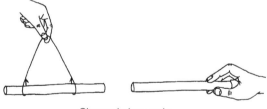

Charged glass rods

Now, have a second student bring the other rod near one end of the suspended rod. While students observe carefully, ask:

- What happens? (Since the rods have the same charge, they repel each other.)

Repeat the experiment with the wax rods instead of the glass ones. Finally, try it with one glass rod and one wax rod. Discuss and compare the results of this investigation with students.

---

Portage & Main Press, 2017 · *Hands-On Science and Technology* · Grade 3 · ISBN: 978-1-55379-709-8

Portage & Main Press, 2017 · *Hands-On Science and Technology · Grade 3* · ISBN: 978-1-55379-709-8

Distribute a copy of Activity Sheet: Charged Rods and Flowing Water (3.11.1) to each student. Have students complete the activity sheet.

### Activity Sheet

Directions to students:

Draw diagrams of the two demonstrations completed during the lesson. Explain each diagram (3.11.1).

## Action: Part Three

Explore the role of static electricity in producing lightning. Lightning consists of huge static electric sparks that jump from cloud to cloud or from a cloud to an object on Earth. Lightning usually occurs during a heavy rainstorm. Turbulence in storm clouds creates static electric charges that build up until they are released as a stream of electrons that create a bolt of lightning and a shock wave that is the sound of thunder.

Consider having a local Elder or Métis Senator speak to the class to share traditional stories about lightning and thunder. Also consider reading books on the topic, such as:

- *The Legend of Lightning and Thunder* by Paula Ikuutaq Rumbolt
- *The Thundermaker* by Alan Syliboy
- *Thunder Boy Jr.* by Sherman Alexie

After reading these stories, discuss the dangers of lightning with students and what they can do to stay safe during a storm.

## Learning Centre

At the learning centre, provide books and other reference material related to St. Elmo's fire, a copy of the Learning-Centre Task Card: St. Elmo's fire (3.11.2), watercolour paints, other painting supplies (e.g., brushes, paper), pencils, and computers or tablets with Internet access. Have students use all available resources to find pictures and other illustrative examples of

St. Elmo's fire. Then, ask each student to first draw and then paint a watercolour picture of this natural phenomenon.

## Consolidate and Debrief

- Revisit the guided inquiry question: **How can the force of static electricity be demonstrated safely?** Have students share their knowledge, provide examples, and ask further inquiry questions.
- Add to the herringbone chart as students learn new concepts, answer some of their own inquiry questions, and ask new inquiry questions.
- Add new terms and illustrations to the class word wall. Add the words in other languages, as appropriate.
- Have students add new words, definitions, and examples to their Science and Technology Glossary (3.1.1). When possible, encourage students to add the words in other languages, including Indigenous languages, reflective of the class.

## Enhance

- Organize students in pairs. Have each student blow up a balloon and attach a string to it. Then, have the pairs of students predict what will happen when they bring their two balloons together, holding them by the strings. Now, have students rub one of the balloons against their hair 10 times, predict what will happen when the balloons are brought together again, then test what does happen when the two balloons are brought together. Finally, have students rub both balloons against their hair 10 times, predict what will happen when the balloons are brought together, and then test.
- Have students continue their do-it-yourself projects at the Makerspace centre.

# Charged Rods and Flowing Water

## Demonstration #1

| Diagram | Explanation |
|---|---|
|  | _____ <br><br> _____ <br><br> _____ <br><br> _____ <br><br> _____ <br><br> _____ <br><br> _____ |

## Demonstration #2

| Diagram | Explanation |
|---|---|
|  | _____ <br><br> _____ <br><br> _____ <br><br> _____ <br><br> _____ <br><br> _____ |

Portage & Main Press, 2017 · Hands-On Science and Technology · Grade 3 · ISBN: 978-1-55379-709-8

# St. Elmo's Fire

1. Use books and images from the Internet to study what St. Elmo's fire looks like.

2. Observe the colours and shapes.

3. Use a pencil to draw a picture of St. Elmo's fire.

4. Use watercolours to paint your picture.

Portage & Main Press, 2017 · Hands-On Science and Technology · Grade 3 · ISBN: 978-1-55379-709-8

# 12 | How Does an Electroscope Work?

## Information for Teachers

An electroscope is a device used to detect and identify static electricity.

## 21st Century Competencies

**Critical Thinking** and **Communication**: Students will build and test an electroscope, using it to measure the static charge on various objects.

## Materials

- aluminum foil
- corks (cork balls work better than wine corks, but both will work)
- 30-cm pieces of coat-hanger wire
- 15-cm pieces of thread
- Plasticine
- 2.5 cm x 10 cm x 10 cm blocks of wood, with a small pre-drilled hole in the centre (Hole should be slightly larger than the diameter of the coat-hanger wire.)
- thumbtacks
- wax rods
- combs
- glass rods
- balloons
- pieces of silk cloth
- pieces of wool cloth
- plastic wrap
- rulers
- pieces of scrap cloth
- bowls of water
- pliers
- interactive whiteboard or other projection device
- Information Sheet: Making an Electroscope (3.12.1)
- Activity Sheet: Testing the Electroscope (3.12.2)
- Learning-Centre Task Card: Making Another Electroscope (3.12.3)
- Learning-Centre Activity Sheet: Testing Electroscope #2 (3.12.4)
- herringbone chart (from lesson 1)
- Science and Technology Glossary (3.1.1)

## Activate

Discuss with students how the force of static electricity has been demonstrated in previous lessons. Review that a force is a push or pull that causes a change in motion.

Explain to students they will be making a device that can be used to detect and identify static electricity. The device is called an *electroscope*.

Introduce the guided inquiry question: **How does an electroscope work?**

## Action

Organize students into working groups of four. Provide each group with all the materials needed to build an electroscope: aluminum foil, a cork, thread, a thumbtack, coat-hanger wire, a block of wood with a hole in it, Plasticine, and access to a pair of pliers. Also, provide each student with a copy of Information Sheet: Making an Electroscope (3.12.1) (or use an interactive whiteboard to project the instructions) and a copy of Activity Sheet: Testing the Electroscope (3.12.2).

In their groups, have students follow the instructions (3.12.1) to make their electroscopes.

**NOTE:** Depending on the class, teachers may choose to give verbal step-by-step instructions to students instead of having students follow the instructions on their own.

Once all groups have built their electroscope, have students test several objects (e.g., wax rods, glass rods, balloons, comb). Have students rub each object with a variety of materials (e.g., plastic wrap, wool cloth, silk cloth). Ask students to record their predictions of what they think will happen, as well as the actual results, on their activity sheet (3.12.2).

Portage & Main Press, 2017 · *Hands-On Science and Technology* · *Grade 3* · ISBN: 978-1-55379-709-8

Portage & Main Press, 2017 · Hands-On Science and Technology · Grade 3 · ISBN: 978-1-55379-709-8

**NOTE:** Students using their electroscopes to measure static electricity provides an excellent opportunity to encourage them to repeat measurements, checking for accuracy.

### Activity Sheet

Directions to students:

On the chart, record both your predictions and your results of the investigations with your electroscope (3.12.2).

## Learning Centre

At the learning centre, provide a copy of the Learning-Centre Task Card: Making Another Electroscope (3.12.3), copies of the Learning-Centre Activity Sheet: Testing Electroscope #2 (3.12.4), glass rods, pieces of silk and scrap cloth, corks, thumbtacks, blocks of wood with holes, coat hangers, rulers, and bowls of water. Also, have pliers available. Have students use the materials to make electroscopes. Then, have them use their electroscopes to measure whether or not the number of times a glass rod is rubbed with a silk cloth affects its charge.

Explain to students they will conduct five trials of rubbing a silk cloth against a glass rod, each time changing how many times they rub the cloth against the rod (2, 4, 6, 8, and 10 times). With each trial, ask students to start with the charged rod 20 centimetres from the cork, then slowly close the distance until the cork is attracted to the rod. Tell students to carefully measure the distance at which the cork is attracted to the rod. After each trial, have students use a damp cloth to neutralize the charge. Have them record the results on the activity sheet (3.12.4).

## Consolidate and Debrief

- Revisit the guided inquiry question: **How does an electroscope work?** Have students share their knowledge, provide examples, and ask further inquiry questions. As a class,

discuss static electricity as a force, focusing on the meaning of the term *force*. Connect this back to what students have learned about magnetism as a force.

- Add to the herringbone chart as students learn new concepts, answer some of their own inquiry questions, and ask new inquiry questions.

- Add new terms and illustrations to the class word wall. Add the words in other languages, as appropriate.

- Have students add new words, definitions, and examples to their Science and Technology Glossary (3.1.1). When possible, encourage students to add the words in other languages, including Indigenous languages, reflective of the class.

### Assessment of Learning

Have individual students demonstrate how the electroscope works. Through questioning, assess each student's ability to explain the concepts and use related vocabulary (*charge*, *attract*, *repel*). Use the Individual Student Observations sheet, on page 27, to record results.

## Enhance

- Have students graph the results of the learning-centre investigation, presenting data on the number of times the glass rod was rubbed and the distance at which attraction was observed.

- Have students research technologies that use electrostatics and how to use them safely. For example, they can investigate electrostatic air cleaners. This is an excellent opportunity to have a guest presenter demonstrate this technology.

- Have students continue their do-it-yourself projects at the Makerspace centre.

# Making an Electroscope

1. Wrap aluminum foil around the cork.

2. Loop one end of the thread several times around the thumbtack. Press the thumbtack into one end of the cork wrapped in foil.

3. Bend a coat hanger to look like a streetlight. (You may need to use pliers to bend the top end into a hook.) Put the other end of the hanger into the hole in the block of wood. Secure with Plasticine.

4. Hang the cork from the coat-hanger hook, and tie a knot in the thread to secure.

5. The electroscope is now ready to be tested:

   ■ To identify static electricity, bring objects close to the foil-wrapped cork.

   ■ As you bring a charged object near the cork, the cork will be attracted to it.

   ■ If the cork and the object repel each other, this means that both are charged.

   ■ You can get rid of the charge on the cork by touching it with your hand to ground it after every test.

   ■ If there is no reaction between the object and the cork, neither is charged.

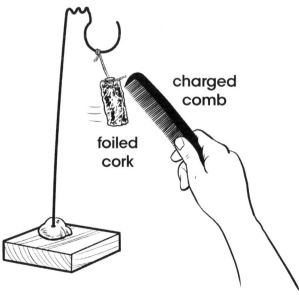

charged comb

foiled cork

Portage & Main Press, 2017 · Hands-On Science and Technology · Grade 3 · ISBN: 978-1-55379-709-8

# Testing the Electroscope

| Object | Material Used for Rubbing | Prediction | Result |
|---|---|---|---|
| | | | |
| | | | |
| | | | |
| | | | |
| | | | |
| | | | |
| | | | |
| | | | |
| | | | |
| | | | |
| | | | |
| | | | |
| | | | |
| | | | |

**What did you learn from this investigation with the electroscope?**

_____

_____

Portage & Main Press, 2017 · Hands-On Science and Technology · Grade 3 · ISBN: 978-1-55379-709-8

# Making Another Electroscope

1. Use the materials at the centre to make another electroscope with your group.

2. Use your electroscope to find out if the number of times you rub the rod affects the attraction of the charged object.

3. Conduct five trials, changing the number of times you rub a glass rod with a silk cloth each time (two, four, six, eight, and ten times).

4. With each trial, begin with the charged rod 20 centimetres from the cork, then slowly move it closer until the cork is attracted to the rod.

5. For each trial, measure the distance between the charged glass rod and the cork at the point where you noticed attraction.

6. Use a damp cloth on the glass rod after each trial to get rid of the charge.

7. Record your results on the activity sheet provided.

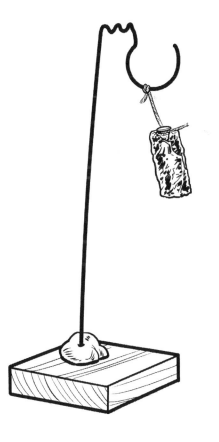

Portage & Main Press, 2017 · Hands-On Science and Technology · Grade 3 · ISBN: 978-1-55379-709-8

# Testing Electroscope #2

| Charging: Number of Rubs | Distance (cm) |
|:---:|:---:|
| 2 | |
| 4 | |
| 6 | |
| 8 | |
| 10 | |

## Draw a diagram of your electroscope. Label the parts.

Portage & Main Press, 2017 · Hands-On Science and Technology · Grade 3 · ISBN: 978-1-55379-709-8

# 13 | What Effect Does Gravity Have on Different Objects?

## Information for Teachers

Gravity is another force that attracts objects to each other. All masses exert gravitational attraction. However, the effect is usually unnoticeable except for very large masses. We are most familiar with the gravitational attraction of Earth—the force that pulls objects (including humans) toward the centre of Earth. To lift an object off the ground, you must exert an upward force because gravity is pulling the object down. To lift a sheet of paper, you only need to exert a small force. To lift a book, however, you must exert greater force, because the book's mass is greater than the mass of the sheet of paper.

Gravity affects other masses beyond Earth, which have consequences for us here on Earth. It is because of the Sun's gravity that Earth orbits the Sun. It is because of the moon's gravity that ocean tides ebb and flow. On the moon, gravitational pull is not as great as it is on Earth; the moon's mass is not as great as Earth's mass. This is why the astronauts who walked on the moon wore special weighted suits and boots that held them near the moon's surface. Even then, the astronauts tended to float or bounce when they walked because of the limited gravitational force pulling them downward.

Gravitational force is a rather complex concept and should be introduced to students through simplified activities and discussion. At the same time, the force of gravity is quite possibly the single most influential force in the lives of our students in terms of their safety. Falls from playground equipment, falls off bikes, falls off stairs, tripping—all of these are injury hazards that are a result of gravity.

### 21st Century Competencies

**Critical Thinking**, **Creativity**, **Collaboration**, and **Communication**: Students will explore the concept of gravitational force. They will graph the amount of time they can hold different masses in front of them to see how gravity combines with different sized masses to generate a force.

## Materials

- heavy books (one per student)
- sheets of paper
- classroom clock or stopwatches
- computer/tablet with Internet access
- Activity Sheet A: The Force of Gravity (3.13.1)
- Centimetre Graph Paper (3.13.2)
- Activity Sheet B: Save the Eggs! (3.13.3)
- shoeboxes
- various materials for building dioramas (as specified by students)
- raw eggs
- materials identified by students for designing protective coverings for the eggs
- Learning-Centre Task Card: Making a Parachute (3.13.4)
- access to a local park, forest, or nature preserve
- small plastic figurines
- plastic garbage bags
- tape
- string
- scissors
- rulers
- tissue paper
- newsprint
- cheesecloth
- thick wool
- thread
- dental floss
- herringbone chart (from lesson 1)
- Science and Technology Glossary (3.1.1)

## Activate

Gather students in a circle on the floor. Give each student a heavy book, and have students hold the books level in front of themselves with their arms extended. Ask:

Portage & Main Press, 2017 · *Hands-On Science and Technology · Grade 3* · ISBN: 978-1-55379-709-8

# 13

- Do you think you can hold the book out like that for a long time?

Have students test their predictions by holding the books out until their arms can no longer bear the weight. Ask:

- Why was it difficult to hold the book for a long time?
- Did you feel a pull downward as you held the book?

Discuss this downward pull, explaining that the force of gravity pulls all objects toward the ground. Have students hold their books in front of themselves again, with their arms extended.

Ask:

- What do you think will happen if you let go of the book?
- Will the book stay in the air?
- Will it fall to the ground?
- What do you think causes the book to fall to the ground?

Again, focus on gravity as the force that will pull the book toward the ground after it has been released.

Now, provide each student with a piece of paper. Ask:

- Do you think you could hold a piece of paper for a longer period of time than you could hold the book?

Have students test their predictions by holding a sheet of paper level with their arms extended. Ask:

- Why do you think it is easier to hold the paper than it is to hold the book?

Introduce the guided inquiry question: **What effect does gravity have on different objects?**

## Action: Part One

Take a walk to a local park, forest, or nature preserve. On the walk, encourage students to look for examples that demonstrate the effects of gravity on different objects in nature. For example:

- a leaf falling from a tree
- an acorn on the ground
- twigs on the ground

Have students take photos of these objects for use back in the classroom.

Also observe and identify examples of how animal movements counteract the force of gravity. For example:

- A bird uses its wings to fly. If it could not fly, the force of gravity would pull it to the ground.
- A squirrel uses muscular force to climb a tree. If it did not use muscular force, the pull of gravity would not allow it to climb upward.

Have students take photos of these examples for use back in the classroom.

Use natural objects to review the effects of gravity. Take photos of the following activities for use back in the classroom.

Have each students find a heavy rock or a fallen piece of wood. Have students hold the rock or wood level in front of themselves with their arms extended. Ask:

- Do you think you can hold the rock/wood out like that for a long time?

Have students test their predictions by holding the rocks/wood out until their arms can no longer bear the weight. Ask:

- Why was it difficult to hold the rock/wood for a long time?

Portage & Main Press, 2017 · Hands-On Science and Technology · Grade 3 · ISBN: 978-1-55379-709-8

■ Did you feel a pull downward as you held the rock/wood?

Discuss this downward pull, explaining that the force of gravity pulls all objects toward the ground. Have students hold their rock/wood in front of themselves again, with their arms extended.

Ask:

■ What will happen if you let go of the rock/wood?

■ Will the rock/wood stay in the air?

■ Will it fall to the ground?

■ What causes the rock/wood to fall to the ground?

Again, focus on gravity as the force that will pull the rock/wood toward the ground after it has been released.

Now, have students find a natural object of a lighter mass, such as a leaf or blade of grass. Ask:

■ Do you think you could hold a leaf/grass for a longer period of time than you could hold the rock/wood?

Have students test their predictions by holding leaf/grass level with their arms extended. Ask:

■ Why do you think it is easier to hold the leaf/grass than it is to hold the rock/wood?

Consider having a local Elder or Métis Senator guide the nature walk. They can share knowledge about the effects of gravity in nature. They may be able to tell traditional stories related to this topic, including stories about ocean tides or the Earth's orbit around the Sun.

## Action: Part Two

Discuss gravity in terms of the mass of objects. Explain that heavier objects are pulled toward Earth with greater force than lighter objects,

which is why a book is more difficult to hold than a paper.

Divide the class into working groups, and provide each group with several books and several sheets of paper. Also, provide each student with a copy of Activity Sheet A: The Force of Gravity (3.13.1). Have students complete the activity sheet by recording how long they are able to hold each item listed on the chart. Tell students to use the classroom clock, or distribute stopwatches for measuring time.

### Activity Sheet A

Directions to students:

Predict, and then measure, the amount of time you are able to hold out in front of you each item (or collection of items) listed on the chart (3.13.1).

## Action: Part Three

When students have completed the activity sheet, gather them as a class to discuss their findings. Ask:

■ How long were you able to hold a sheet of paper out in front of you?

■ How long were you able to hold four books out in front of you?

■ Why were you able to hold the sheet of paper longer than you were able to hold the four books?

■ What force was pulling the books downward toward the ground?

Now, distribute a copy of Centimetre Graph Paper (3.13.2) to each student, and have students use the results from their activity sheet to create bar graphs. Be sure to first review with students the criteria for bar graphs.

### Assessment of Learning

Observe students as they construct their bar graphs. Focus on their ability to transfer data from charts to graphs. Also, focus on criteria

Portage & Main Press, 2017 · *Hands-On Science and Technology · Grade 3* · ISBN: 978-1-55379-709-8

Portage & Main Press, 2017 · Hands-On Science and Technology · Grade 3 · ISBN: 978-1-55379-709-8

**13**

such as title, labelled x-axis, labelled y-axis, accurate data, and separated bars. Use the Anecdotal Record sheet, on page 26, to record results.

### Action: Part Four

Have students analyze the effects of gravity on the movement of objects. Explain that traditionally, Indigenous peoples such as the Kainai, Piikuni, Cree, and Tsuu T'ina used these effects to their advantage when hunting bison. A bison (buffalo) jump is an example of direct and indirect forces on an object. A group of hunters would frighten the bison herd toward a cliff. The bison at the front of the herd would try to stop at the edge of the cliff, but the stampeding herd behind them would push them over the edge. The direct force is the buffalo behind bumping the ones in front. Once they are bumped off the cliff, indirect force (gravity) takes over. So, both direct and indirect forces are at work.

Explore Head-Smashed-In Buffalo Jump online with students by visiting the following site, go to: <www.history.alberta.ca/headsmashedin/default.aspx>.

Have groups of students design a plan for their own bison jump diorama. Have them start with a shoebox and find other materials they will need in the classroom and/or at home. Then, have students create their diorama based on their design. Ask the groups to present their plans, as well as their dioramas, to the rest of the class.

### Action: Part Five

Students will now take on a challenge involving technological problem solving, as they design a protective covering to keep an egg from breaking when it is dropped.

To demonstrate the impact of gravitational force, tell students you are going to drop a raw egg from a height of one metre. Ask:

- What will happen to the egg?
- Which force causes it to fall?

Have students observe as you drop the egg. Ask:

- Why did the egg break?
- Is there any way that you could stop the egg from breaking?

Divide the class into working groups, and provide each group with a copy of Activity Sheet B: Save the Eggs! (3.13.3). Review the instructions together. Give groups time to discuss options, make plans, collect materials, construct, and test their prototypes.

Plan an event to test their final prototypes and discuss successful designs.

**Activity Sheet B**
Directions to students:
Use the sheet to design and test your egg protector. (3.13.3)

### Learning Centre

At the learning centre, provide string, plastic garbage bags, scissors, tape, rulers, small plastic figurines and a copy of the Learning-Centre Task Card: Making a Parachute (3.13.4). Also, provide other materials, which students can use later to experiment with their parachute designs (e.g., tissue paper, newsprint, cheesecloth, thick wool, thread, dental floss).

To further investigate gravity, have students design, construct, and test parachutes.

First, have students build parachutes according to the specifications on the task card. Then, challenge them to experiment with parachute designs: encourage students to change the material used, the shape of their parachute, the length of strings, or the mass of the objects tied to the string. Tell students to be sure to record any changes they make to the original

# 13

specifications (e.g., if they use cheesecloth rather than plastic, different lengths of string, change the diameter of the circle used as the parachute).

**NOTE:** Before students work at this centre, take time to discuss technological problem solving with them, which involves seeking solutions to practical problems and includes specific steps:

1. Identify a need: Recognize a problem and the need to solve it (in this case, making a parachute). As a class, determine a question for the task such as "How can we make parachutes that will affect the force of gravity?" Co-construct criteria for the parachute.

2. Create a plan: Seek various solutions to a given problem, create a plan based on a chosen solution, and record the plan using writing and labelled diagrams. (Discuss students' ideas for their designs.)

3. Develop a product: Construct an object that solves the given problem and meets criteria.

4. Communicate the results: Identify and make improvements to the product.

### Assessment for Learning

Meet with students individually. Interview them on their understanding of the force of gravity, their parachute design, and how they tested their design. Use the Individual Student Observations sheet, on page 27, to record results.

## Consolidate and Debrief

■ Revisit the guided inquiry question: **What effect does gravity have on different objects?** Have students share their knowledge, provide examples, and ask further inquiry questions.

■ Add to the herringbone chart as students learn new concepts, answer some of their own inquiry questions, and ask new inquiry questions.

■ Add new terms, including *gravity, gravitation,* and *gravitational force*, and illustrations to the class word wall. Add the words in other languages, as appropriate.

■ Have students add new words, definitions, and examples to their Science and Technology Glossary (3.1.1). When possible, encourage students to add the words in other languages, including Indigenous languages, reflective of the class population.

## Enhance

■ Have students measure their exact height in centimetres just before they go to bed at night and again when they first get up in the morning (family members can help with this). Ask students to record the results and bring them to school. Create a class chart of the results.

**NOTE:** The human backbone is made up of separate bones called *vertebrae*, with liquid-filled discs between each vertebra. As we stand and walk during the day, gravity pulls the bones down and squeezes the discs. While we sleep, the vertebrae separate again as the discs take their original form. As a result, we are slightly taller first thing in the morning than we are at day's end. Astronauts actually grow a few centimetres taller when they are in space because there is less gravitational force pulling on the bones of their spines.

■ Show students videos of astronauts in space, to observe how they are affected by limited gravitational force or zero gravity.

■ Access the interactive activity, Gravitational Force, in the Grade 3, Unit 3 folder of the ***Hands-On Interactive for Science and Technology, Grade 3*** download. Find this download at: <www.portageandmainpress.com/product/hands-on-interactive-for-science-and-technology-grade-3/>.

■ Have students continue their do-it-yourself projects at the Makerspace centre.

Portage & Main Press, 2017 · *Hands-On Science and Technology · Grade 3* · ISBN: 978-1-55379-709-8

# The Force of Gravity

| Object | Time Held in Seconds | |
| --- | --- | --- |
| | Estimate | Result |
| sheet of paper | | |
| 1 book | | |
| 2 books | | |
| 3 books | | |
| 4 books | | |

1. How long do you think you could hold 10 books? _____

   _____

2. What force would make it difficult for you to hold the books for a long time?

   _____

   _____

   _____

   _____

3. Use your results to make a bar graph on the graph paper.

Portage & Main Press, 2017 · Hands-On Science and Technology · Grade 3 · ISBN: 978-1-55379-709-8

**Date:** _____   **Name:** _____

# Centimetre Graph Paper

Portage & Main Press, 2017 · *Hands-On Science and Technology · Grade 3* · ISBN: 978-1-55379-709-8

# Save the Egg!

Design a way to protect a raw egg from breaking when it is dropped from a height of one metre.

1. In your group, discuss different plans to solve this problem.

2. Choose a plan and draw a labelled blueprint below.

3. Collect materials and list them below.

_____    _____    _____

_____    _____    _____

_____    _____    _____

4. Test your egg-protector. Record your observations.

_____

_____

_____

Portage & Main Press, 2017 · Hands-On Science and Technology · Grade 3 · ISBN: 978-1-55379-709-8

## Save the Egg! (continued)

5. Make improvements to your design. Draw a labelled diagram of your final prototype. Include measurements.

6. Test your final prototype and record your results.

_____

_____

_____

7. Think about the egg-protector prototypes designed by different groups. What have you learned about successful designs?

_____

_____

_____

Portage & Main Press, 2017 · Hands-On Science and Technology · Grade 3 · ISBN: 978-1-55379-709-8

# Making a Parachute

You will need a plastic garbage bag, tape, string, scissors, small plastic figurine (and other materials available at centre).

1. Cut a 30-centimetre square piece of plastic from a garbage bag.

2. Tape four pieces of string, each 30 centimetres long, to each corner of the plastic.

3. Tape or tie the four pieces of string to the small plastic figurine.

4. Stand on a chair, spread out the parachute, and drop it. Time how long it takes to get to the floor, and compare this with another student's parachute.

   Gravity will pull the parachute toward the ground. It will catch air, however, which will slow it down as it travels to the ground. This is called *air resistance*.

5. Experiment with other designs by making parachutes of different materials, different shapes, and using different types and lengths of string and different masses of objects tied to the string.

6. Compare how the different parachutes fall. Which parachute has the most air resistance?

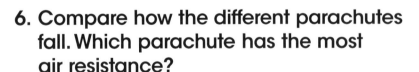

Portage & Main Press, 2017 · *Hands-On Science and Technology · Grade 3 ·* ISBN: 978-1-55379-709-8

# 14 | What Are Some Forces of Nature?

## Information for Teachers

If you have ever felt the rumble of an earthquake or seen the eruption of a volcano, you have witnessed a force of nature. For scientists, the term *force* is defined as a "push" or "pull" that causes a change in motion. Forces of nature, then, are the pushing and pulling in the core, crust, or water of Earth that cause motion such as eruptions, quakes, or floods. The Earth's atmosphere also produces forces. Wind, for example, is a hugely destructive force.

Landslides can happen anywhere and are triggered by rains, floods, earthquakes, and other natural events. Humans contribute to landslides when they change the land to put in roads, houses, lawns, and gardens. Landslides can destroy houses, transportation routes, and utilities. They can cause flooding and pollute water. They can carry trees and other plants away with them.

## 21ˢᵗ Century Competencies

**Critical Thinking** and **Communication**: Students will examine different ways landslides can occur and demonstrate how excessive water can create a landslide. They will then research various forces in nature and their effects on the natural and human-built environment.

## Materials

- *Landslide* by Anne Ylvisaker

**NOTE:** If *Landslide* is not available, you can use other books or videos about landslides and forces of nature.

- *How We Saw the World: Nine Native Stories of the Way Things Began* by C.J. Taylor
- *Frog Girl* by Paul Owens Lewis

- *Native Stories from Keepers of the Earth* by Michael J Caduto and Joseph Bruchac
- two-litre cardboard milk cartons (with one side and one end cut away)
- sand
- soil
- pebbles
- diatomaceous earth (fine, powdery, chalk-like substance found from the skeletal remains of diatoms, available online or at garden centres)
- clay
- graduated cylinder
- books
- watering can or empty pop bottle
- newspaper (to cover tables or floor)
- balance scale (optional)
- cookie sheets
- Activity Sheet: Video Viewing Guide (3.14.1)
- herringbone chart (from lesson 1)
- Science and Technology Glossary (3.1.1)

## Activate

Review with students the meaning of the term *force*, focusing on the idea that force is defined as a push or pull that causes a change in motion. Ask:

- Can forces happen in nature?
- When have you seen a push or pull on an object caused by nature?

Have students share ideas (e.g., wind blowing trees, waves on the lake, a volcano, a hurricane, lightning striking a tree). Record their ideas on an anchor chart for reference.

Introduce the guided inquiry question: **What are some forces of nature?**

Portage & Main Press, 2017 · *Hands-On Science and Technology · Grade 3* · ISBN: 978-1-55379-709-8

# 14

## Action: Part One

Read aloud the book *Landslides* by Anne Ylvisaker (or another book on this topic). Discuss the different types of landslides that can occur. Discuss the different conditions that trigger each type and the resulting damage wrought by each type.

Tell students they will be doing their own investigation to test different types of landslides. Show students the materials they will be using to simulate a small-scale landslide. Discuss the different variables that trigger landslides, such as slope, material, and amount of water.

Divide the class into working groups, and have the groups discuss how they will simulate different types of landslides.

Have groups construct a model landslide. Use a milk carton that has one side and one end cut away. Set it on its side on a cookie sheet. Place newspaper under the cookie sheet for easier clean-up. Add one-centimetre layers of sand, soil, pebbles, and diatomaceous earth to the bottom of the carton. Prop up the uncut end of the carton with two books. This model now represents a hill.

Put a measured amount of water into a watering can or an empty pop bottle. Have one student from each group pour the water slowly onto the higher end of the model until all of the soil mixture is soaked. Have all students observe the patterns formed on the "hill."

When the mixture has been soaked with water but has not moved, have students use a graduated cylinder filled with water to create a "landslide." To do this, tell students to carefully measure the amount of water they add to the stream table. Have students note the exact amount of water they added to instigate the landslide. Once the landslide has occurred, ask students to use the balance scales to measure, by weight, the amount of mixture involved in the slide. Have each group share its results with the class.

## Action: Part Two

Read books related to other forces of nature, such as hurricanes, tornadoes, volcanoes, and earthquakes. Discuss how these forces of nature cause motion and affect humans and the environment.

Select videos on these topics to show students. For example:

- **www.youtube.com/watch?v=dJpIU1rSOFY** "What is an Earthquake?—The Dr. Bincos Show Educational Videos for Kids." Peek-a-boo Kids (3:42).

- **www.youtube.com/watch?v=-s3UwOq1P1E** "What is a Tornado?" SciShow Kids (3:46).

- **www.youtube.com/watch?v=IAmqsMQG3RM** "Volcano—The Dr. Bincos Show Educational Videos for Kids." Peek-a-boo Kidz (2:50)

- **www.youtube.com/watch?v=J2__Bk4dVS0** "Hurricane—The Dr. Bincos Show Educational Videos for Kids." Peek-a-boo Kidz (3:17).

Distribute a copy of Activity Sheet: Video Viewing Guide (3.14.1) to each student. As students watch the videos, have them complete the Video Viewing Guide to record new ideas.

**Activity Sheet**
Directions to students:

Complete the sheet as you watch videos about the forces of nature. (3.14.1)

Portage & Main Press, 2017 · *Hands-On Science and Technology · Grade 3* · ISBN: 978-1-55379-709-8

## Action: Part Three

Consider having a local Elder or Métis Senator share traditional stories about forces of nature. These stories can include themes related to weather, storms, floods, and so on.

Follow up by reading Indigenous stories on the topic. For example:

- *How We Saw the World: Nine Native Stories of the Way Things Began* by C.J. Taylor. Includes a story about the origin of tornadoes.
- *Frog Girl* by Paul Owen Lewis. The story of a young girl during an earthquake and the impact of human activity on the environment.
- *Native Stories from Keepers of the Earth* by Michael J. Caduto and Joseph Bruchac. Includes stories about Earth, Wind, Water, and Weather.

## Consolidate and Debrief

- Revisit the guided inquiry question: **What are some forces of nature?** Have students share their knowledge, provide examples, and ask further inquiry questions.
- Add to the herringbone chart as students learn new concepts, answer some of their own inquiry questions, and ask new inquiry questions.
- Add new terms and illustrations to the class word wall. Add the words in other languages, as appropriate.
- Have students add new words, definitions, and examples to their Science and Technology Glossary (3.1.1). When possible, encourage students to add the words in other languages, including Indigenous languages, reflective of the class.

## Enhance

- Encourage students to repeat the landslide activity and experiment with increased amounts of water, different materials, or different slope. Remind students to experiment with one variable at a time—and to carefully record the variable with each experiment.
- Have students continue their do-it-yourself projects at the Makerspace centre.

Portage & Main Press, 2017 · *Hands-On Science and Technology · Grade 3* · ISBN: 978-1-55379-709-8

Date: _____     Name: _____

# Video Viewing Guide

Name of Video: _____

| New terms used: | Diagrams: | Main idea: |
| --- | --- | --- |
| | | |
| **Interesting facts:** | | **New questions I have:** |

Portage & Main Press, 2017 · Hands-On Science and Technology · Grade 3 · ISBN: 978-1-55379-709-8

# 15 | How Are Forces Used to Move Toys?

## Information for Teachers

Action: Part Two of this lesson deals with forces in lacrosse. Lacrosse, also called the Creator's game, is one of Canada's two national sports; the other is hockey. Lacrosse was first played by the Haudenosaunee.

Forces are a major component of a good lacrosse shot. Factors such as length of stick, point of release, and muscle power all affect the motion of the ball.

## 21$^{st}$ Century Competencies

**Critical Thinking**, **Communication**, and **Creativity**: Students will experiment with a simple windup toy that uses an elastic band to store potential energy.

## Materials

- toys that require muscular or gravitational force for movement (e.g., toy cars)
- toys that store energy to create movement (e.g., jack-in-the-box, elastic band-propelled plane, windup toys)
- pencils
- empty thread spools (with a groove cut into the bottom)
- nails
- large beads
- elastic bands
- rulers or metre sticks
- lacrosse sticks
- lacrosse ball
- Activity Sheet: Elastic-Band Motor (3.15.1)
- herringbone chart (from lesson 1)
- Science and Technology Glossary (3.1.1)

## Activate

Have students sit in a circle. As a class, sort the toys into groups according to how they move (e.g., pushing, winding, twisting). Place the different toys in the centre of the circle. Ask individual students to find a way to make each toy move (e.g.,they can push a toy car, wind up the windup toy, twist the elastic band on the propeller of the airplane to make it fly). Ask students:

- How did the objects move?
- What did you need to do to make the objects move?

Introduce the guided inquiry question: **How are forces used to move toys?**

## Action: Part One

Explain to students they are going to make their own elastic-band motor. Divide the class into working groups. Give each group the required materials: elastic band, spool, nail, large bead, and pencil. Write the instructions on chart paper, or work through the instructions orally.

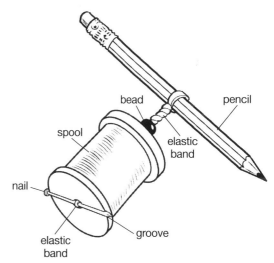

Instructions for Making an Elastic-Band Motor:

1. Thread an elastic band through the centre hole of the spool.
2. Put a nail through the elastic band, and fix it into the groove.
3. Thread the other end of the elastic band through a large bead.
4. Fix a pencil to the end of the elastic band.

Portage & Main Press, 2017 · *Hands-On Science and Technology · Grade 3* · ISBN: 978-1-55379-709-8

# 15

Explain to students that they are going to wind the pencil, then use a ruler or metre stick to measure how far the spool travels. The distance will depend on the number of times the pencil is wound. Distribute a copy of Activity Sheet: Elastic-Band Motor (3.15.1) to each student. Have students record their findings on the activity sheet.

### Activity Sheet

Directions to students:

Use the chart to record the movement of your elastic-band motor (3.15.1).

## Action: Part Two

Display the lacrosse sticks and ball for students to examine. Ask:

- What are these?
- What are they used for?
- What do you know about the game of lacrosse?
- Do you know who invented the game and the equipment?

Have students visit the following website to learn about the Haudenosaunee story about the creation of lacrosse: <iroquoisnationals.org/the-iroquois/the-story-of-lacrosse/>. Then have students watch videos to learn about the history of lacrosse:

- **www.youtube.com/watch?v=sZBX5KLp4gk**
  "Mind Medicine: Lacrosse." Richard Powless (4:38).

- **www.thecanadianencyclopedia.ca/en/article/lacrosse/**
  "The Stickmaker - Alf Jaques "Unstrung" Handmakes Wood Lacrosse Sticks." Stylin Strings (3:32).

  A short video on the making of a traditional lacrosse stick showing the use of various tools and techniques.

Have students consolidate their learning by writing a paragraph about the origins of lacrosse.

Now, watch a video that talks about the physics of how the force works:

- **www.youtube.com/watch?v=Bhfw5R2U5mE**
  "Physics of a Lacrosse Shot." Jenn Thoomas (6:30).

After watching the video, take students outside or to the gym to have them practice the lacrosse shot, and discuss the forces used.

## Consolidate and Debrief

- Revisit the guided inquiry question: **How are forces used to move toys?** Have students share their knowledge, provide examples, and ask further inquiry questions.
- Add to the herringbone chart as students learn new concepts, answer some of their own inquiry questions, and ask new inquiry questions.
- Add new terms and illustrations to the class word wall. Add the words in other languages, as appropriate.
- Have students add new words, definitions, and examples to their Science and Technology Glossary (3.1.1). When possible, encourage students to add the words in other languages, including Indigenous languages, reflective of the class.

## Enhance

- Have students experiment with different sized elastic bands and different sized spools to design another elastic band motor. What other things can they change about their elastic band motor?
- Have students bring in other toys that can be moved using muscular energy or stored energy. Provide students with opportunities to use force to create movement of the toys.

Portage & Main Press, 2017 · Hands-On Science and Technology · Grade 3 · ISBN: 978-1-55379-709-8

Have them use appropriate vocabulary, such as *force*, *push*, *pull*, *direction*, *distance*, and *speed*, as they discuss their investigations.

■ Bug in the Envelope: Bend a bobby pin into a V-shape. Thread a button onto an elastic band, and stretch the elastic band over the two ends of the bobby pin (this is the "bug"). Wind up the button by twisting it on the elastic band. The bobby pin will close. Place the button in an envelope, ensuring that it stays wound up. When the envelope is opened, energy will be released, causing the "bug" to move.

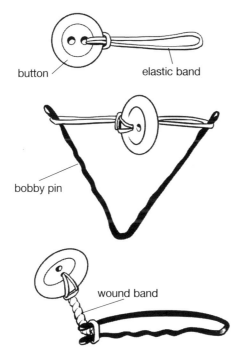

button                 elastic band

bobby pin

wound band

■ Research the use of forces when using traditional Indigenous tools, such as bow and arrow, spears, canoe/kayak paddles, knives, axes, and clubs.

■ Have students continue their do-it-yourself projects at the Makerspace centre.

Portage & Main Press, 2017 · *Hands-On Science and Technology · Grade 3* · ISBN: 978-1-55379-709-8

**Date:** _____     **Name:** _____

# Elastic-Band Motor

| Number of Winds | Distance Travelled | Observations |
|---|---|---|
| 10 | | |
| 20 | | |
| 30 | | |
| 40 | | |
| 50 | | |

In your own words, explain how the spool travelled.
From where did it get its energy? _____

_____

_____

Portage & Main Press, 2017 · Hands-On Science and Technology · Grade 3 · ISBN: 978-1-55379-709-8

# 16 | How Can Safety Devices Be Used to Reduce the Effects of Forces?

## 21st Century Competencies

**Critical Thinking**, **Communication**, **Character**, and **Citizenship**: Students will examine their home environment to assess various safety devices, and understand their role in staying safe.

## Materials

- inline skates
- chart paper
- felt markers
- magazines, catalogues, and newspaper flyers
- glue
- printer
- computer/tablet with Internet access
- scissors
- mural paper
- Activity Sheet: Reducing the Effects of Forces on Humans (3.16.1)
- herringbone chart (from lesson 1)
- Science and Technology Glossary (3.1.1)

## Activate

Begin the lesson by displaying the inline skates. Ask students:

- What are these?
- What are they used for?
- How do you use force when you inline skate?
- What kind of force is used? (muscular force)
- When might you use gravitational force when you inline skate? (going downhill)
- Are there any dangers involved in inline skating?
- How can the forces involved in inline skating harm you?
- What can you use to stay safer when inline skating?

Discuss students' ideas.

Introduce the guided inquiry question: **How can safety devices be used to reduce the effects of forces?**

## Action

On chart paper, recreate the following table:

| Activity | Harmful Forces | Safety Device |
|---|---|---|
|  |  |  |
|  |  |  |
|  |  |  |
|  |  |  |

As a class, discuss everyday activities that might involve forces that could harm a person (e.g., cycling, skating, skiing, riding in a car, using power tools, working in construction). Have students share ideas of such activities, the harmful forces that might result from such activities, and the safety devices used to minimize force on humans. Complete the chart during this discussion.

Divide the class into working groups. Provide each group with magazines, catalogues, access to the Internet and printers, flyers, scissors, and glue. Have students find pictures of safety devices that help keep humans safe from forces. Create a class collage on mural paper. Display the collage mural along with the chart.

Distribute a copy of Activity Sheet: Reducing the Effects of Forces on Humans (3.16.1) to each student. Have students complete the activity sheet at home. Students will find safety devices at home that are used to reduce the effects of forces on humans.

### Activity Sheet

**NOTE:** The activity sheet is to be completed by students at home as a follow-up to the classroom activity.

Directions to students:

Look around your home, and find safety devices that are used to reduce the effects of forces on humans. Draw a diagram of each device and describe how and when it is used (3.16.1).

Forces Causing Movement

Portage & Main Press, 2017 · *Hands-On Science and Technology* · *Grade 3* · ISBN: 978-1-55379-709-8

# 16

## Consolidate and Debrief

- Revisit the guided inquiry question: **How can safety devices be used to reduce the effects of forces?** Have students share their knowledge, provide examples, and ask further inquiry questions.

- Add to the herringbone chart as students learn new concepts, answer some of their own inquiry questions, and ask new inquiry questions.

- Add new terms and illustrations to the class word wall. Add the words in other languages, as appropriate.

- Have students add new words, definitions, and examples to their Science and Technology Glossary (3.1.1). When possible, encourage students to add the words in other languages, including Indigenous languages, reflective of the class.

## Enhance

- Have students design and create posters to encourage others to use safety devices to reduce the impact of forces (e.g., helmets, seat belts, sports equipment)

- Have students continue their do-it-yourself projects at the Makerspace centre.

Portage & Main Press, 2017 · Hands-On Science and Technology · Grade 3 · ISBN: 978-1-55379-709-8

# Reducing the Effects of Forces on Humans

| Safety Device | Diagram | How and When it Is Used |
|---|---|---|
|  |  |  |
|  |  |  |
|  |  |  |
|  |  |  |
|  |  |  |
|  |  |  |

Portage & Main Press, 2017 · Hands-On Science and Technology · Grade 3 · ISBN: 978-1-55379-709-8

# Inquiry Project: How Can I Design a Toy or Game That Uses Forces?

## 21st Century Competencies

**Communication**, **Creativity**, and **Critical Thinking**: Students design and construct a game, toy, or device that uses forces.

## Materials

- chart paper
- scissors
- stapler and staples
- paint
- paintbrushes
- markers
- objects or materials necessary to students for building their games, toys, or devices (e.g., cardboard boxes [with or without lids], cardboard, poster board, paper, string or yarn, tape, glue, paint, paintbrushes, pencil crayons, ball bearings, paper clips, magnets)
- Activity Sheet: Blueprint for a Game (3.17.1)
- Learning-Centre Task Card: Designing a Game (3.17.2)
- digital camera
- herringbone chart (from lesson 1)
- Science and Technology Glossary (3.1.1)

## Activate

Have students compare muscular, magnetic, electrostatic, and gravitational forces. On chart paper, create a chart like the one below to record students' knowledge:

| Force | Description | Examples |
|---|---|---|
| muscular | | |
| gravitational | | |
| electrostatic | | |
| magnetic | | |

Use the various activities conducted throughout the unit to complete the chart.

Explain to students they will be demonstrating their knowledge about muscular, gravitational, magnetic, or electrostatic forces by designing a game, toy, or device that uses one or more of those forces.

Introduce the guided inquiry question: **How can I design a toy or game that uses forces?**

## Action: Part One

For this activity, students can work individually, in pairs, or in groups of three or four to design and create a game, toy, or device that uses at least one of the forces studied: gravitational, magnetic, muscular, or electrostatic. Some examples may include:

- pull toy (muscular)
- catapult (muscular)
- yo-yo (muscular)
- Chinese checkers (muscular)
- maze (magnetic)
- fishing game (magnetic)
- car or boat race (magnetic)
- ball toss (gravitational)
- paper plane contest/game (gravitational)
- balloon game (electrostatic)
- spear toss (muscular)
- bow and arrow/archery game (muscular)

 **SAFETY NOTE:** Ensure designs are not made with pointed arrow heads.

Distribute a copy of Activity Sheet: Blueprint for a Game (3.17.1) to each student. Have students use the activity sheet to help them plan their game and create a blueprint for construction.

As a class, identify criteria for the project. For example:

- game includes one or more of the forces learned about (gravitational, magnetic, muscular, and/or electrostatic)

Portage & Main Press, 2017 · *Hands-On Science and Technology* · Grade 3 · ISBN: 978-1-55379-709-8

- game uses a variety of materials, including recycled items
- rules for playing the game are written
- game developers explain how forces are used in the game

Give students ample time and opportunity to work on creating their games (or toys or devices). The specific amount of time can be discussed and decided upon together by the teacher and students.

### Activity Sheet

Directions to students:

Create a blueprint of your toy/game idea. Include the materials you will need, a drawing of how your game will look, and an outline of the rules to playing your game. Also, record the criteria for the project (3.17.1).

## Action: Part Two

Have students and groups present their projects to the rest of the class, demonstrating how it is played and explaining the rules for playing the game. Be sure each student or group of students reports about:

- which force(s) their game uses
- what they learned
- what they would change in their model
- what things worked best
- what was the hardest part of the construction

Have students take digital photos of their completed games and attach the printed photos to their activity sheet. Students can compare these to their original designs to see what changed as they were constructing their game (or toy or device).

### Assessment of Learning

Meet with students individually. Interview them about the process they went through to address all steps of the technological problem-solving process, and how they met all project criteria.

Use the Individual Student Observations sheet, on page 27, to record results.

### Assessment of Learning

For all students working in pairs or groups, complete a copy of the Cooperative Skills Teacher Assessment sheet, on page 37, to record observations of their skills in working together.

### Assessment as Learning

Have students who worked in pairs or groups complete the Cooperative Skills Self-Assessment sheet, on page 34, reflecting on their own skills working with others.

## Learning Centre

At the learning centre, provide a copy of the Learning-Centre Task Card: Designing a Game (3.17.2). Have all students/groups of students set up their games so they are ready to be played by others, including all game parts and written rules. Have small groups of students visit the centre together to explore and play with the other games, toys, and devices made by their classmates.

### Assessment as Learning

Have students complete the 21st Century Competencies Student/Teacher Reflection sheet, on page 33, to reflect on their use of the 21st Century Competencies throughout the unit. Students record their reflections in the squares. The sheet also includes oval spaces for teachers to provide descriptive feedback to students.

## Consolidate and Debrief

- Revisit the guided inquiry question: **How can I design a toy or game that uses forces?** Have students share their knowledge, provide examples, and ask further inquiry questions.
- Add to the herringbone chart as students learn new concepts, answer some of their

▶

Portage & Main Press, 2017 · Hands-On Science and Technology · Grade 3 · ISBN: 978-1-55379-709-8

**17**

own inquiry questions, and ask new inquiry questions. Review the herringbone concept map from the beginning of the unit. Engage students in conversation about the concepts learned and any unanswered questions.

- Add new terms and illustrations to the class word wall. Add the words in other languages, as appropriate.

- Have students add new words, definitions, and examples to their Science and Technology Glossary (3.1.1). When possible, encourage students to add the words in other languages, including Indigenous languages, reflective of the class. Have students cut apart the pages, sequence terms alphabetically, and then staple or bind the glossaries with a title page.

## Enhance

- As a class, research and play traditional Indigenous games. Some valuable resources on this topic are:
  - *Native American Games and Stories* by J.B. Bruchac
  - *Our Original Games: A Look at Aboriginal Sport in Canada* by Bruce Miller
  - mathcentral.uregina.ca/RR/database/ RR.09.00/treptau1/
    A Search engine for Aboriginal Games.

- Have students complete their do-it-yourself project at the Makerspace Centre.

Portage & Main Press, 2017 · *Hands-On Science and Technology · Grade 3* · ISBN: 978-1-55379-709-8

**Date:** _____    **Name:** _____

# Blueprint for a Game or Toy

Name(s) of creator(s): _____

Materials needed: _____

_____

Diagram of design:

How to play: _____

_____

_____

_____

_____

_____

# Designing a Game or Toy

1. Set up your game or toy so it is ready to be played by others.

2. Include all the parts and written rules.

3. Play with other toys and games at the centre.

4. Think about how each game or toy uses forces.

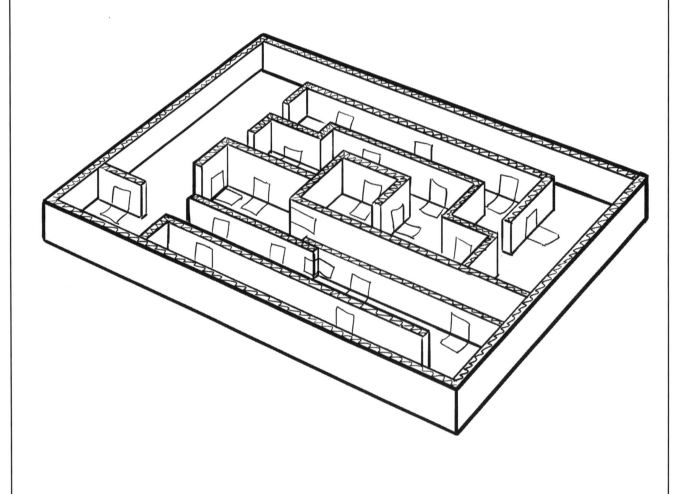

Portage & Main Press, 2017 · Hands-On Science and Technology · Grade 3 · ISBN: 978-1-55379-709-8

# Unit 4

## Soils in the Environment

# Introduction

In this unit of **Hands-On Science and Technology, Grade 3**, students will focus on soil, which is an important source of life and nourishment for many organisms. Soil provides a base for gardens, forests, fields, and farms, and supports different plant and animal life, as well as human activities. There is a significant dependence by humans and other living things on soil, which is an important source of materials for making useful objects.

Soil is a combination of different earth materials and various living things, and there are similarities and differences between various soils. Moving water has an effect on these soils, and erosion by water presents significant ramifications for soil management.

Students will have been introduced to some of the concepts in this unit while studying the first unit of **Hands-On Science and Technology, Grade 3**, Growth and Changes in Plants, so they may already be familiar with some of the ideas and vocabulary. Teachers are encouraged to assist students in making connections between soils and plants.

## Planning Tips for Teachers

- This unit relies on outdoor activities and should be taught during seasons when the ground is soft and the soil can be easily turned. Be sure to identify locations near the school where investigations can take place.

- Collect pictures, books, and videos depicting different types of soil, growing environments for different plants, and organisms that live in the soil. Sources for photographs and drawings include:
    - websites
    - old calendars and magazines
    - department of agriculture
    - local garden nurseries
    - gardening magazines
    - forestry or environmental associations

- local farming, gardening, or naturalist societies

- Before beginning the unit, teachers are encouraged to send letters home to students' parents or guardians requesting large, old shirts students can wear as "soil smocks" for many of the experiments conducted during the unit. Many of the activities will get messy, particularly when students are handling the soil. Teachers are encouraged to liberally have students use the smocks, to keep clothing clean during any of this unit's lessons.

- Study of this unit presents an opportunity to work with community members such as:
    - local farmers
    - greenhouse personnel
    - water conservation district personnel
    - university or government agriculture soil specialists
    - community garden groups
    - local Elders or Métis Senators
    - representatives of Communities-in-Bloom programs, a nonprofit Canadian organization committed to fostering civic pride, environmental responsibility, and beautification through community involvement and the challenge of a national program, with focus on enhancing green spaces in communities

- Consider recording the guided inquiry question (e.g., on a sentence strip) for display throughout related investigations.

- Develop a Makerspace centre. Classroom Makerspaces are usually designed as centres where students learn together and collaborate on do-it-yourself projects. Students are given the opportunity to work with a variety of age-appropriate tools, as well as everyday and recycled materials. Additionally, arts-and-crafts are often integrated into Makerspace offerings.

Portage & Main Press, 2017 · Hands-On Science and Technology · Grade 3 · ISBN: 978-1-55379-709-8

For this unit, set up a Makerspace centre in your classroom that encourages informal learning about soils in the environment. Include general materials, such as those listed in the Introduction to **Hands-On Science and Technology, Grade 3**, as well as unit-specific materials. For example, collect a large variety of soil, clay, and rock samples, as well as clear containers, sieves, and magnifying glasses.

Do-it-yourself projects may include anything related to the concepts within this unit. Projects that students might initiate include (but are not limited to):

- constructing a three-dimensional cross section model of soil layers
- creating a mosaic or diorama using earth materials
- building a balloon greenhouse (go to: <www.education.com/activity/article/balloon-greenhouse/>)
- making objects from earth materials (e.g., clay pots, bricks to build a structure, sand castles, mud houses)

Literacy connections that might inspire projects include:

- *Mud Paperback* by Mary Lyn Ray
- *Stuck in the Mud* by Jane Clarke
- *Dirt Boy* by Eric Jon Slangerup
- *Dirt: The Scoop on Soil* by Natalie M. Rosinsky
- *Dig In!* by Cindy Jenson-Elliott
- *Compost Stew: An A to Z Recipe for the Earth* by Mary McKenna Siddals
- *Wiggling Worms at Work* by Wendy Pfeffer
- *Yucky Worms: Read and Wonder* by Vivian French

As inquiry questions are posed with each lesson, you will find these questions inspire other do-it-yourself projects related to the unit. Students may determine solutions to these questions through the creating they do at the Makerspace centre. Remember to not direct the learning here; simply create conditions for learning to happen.

## Indigenous Worldviews

The unit also gives rise to many possibilities for incorporating Indigenous perspectives and worldviews into science and technology lessons. Indigenous peoples often refer to Mother Earth when speaking about the land or soil, which is essential for growing plants for food, medicines, and other uses, thereby providing sustenance important for survival. Traditionally, Indigenous peoples understood the different types of soil, which plants were best suited to grow in those soils, and how to replenish nutrients in the soil by returning unused plant or animal products back to the land as a form of composting. This unit provides opportunity to learn about the different types of soil, as well as how forces such as water and wind can impact or change how people use the land and soil for their survival. Moreover, a study of soil with an Indigenous mindset is infused with the understanding of the interconnectedness of all living things, and of our dependency on nature for all aspects of life.

## Science and Technology Vocabulary

Throughout this unit, teachers should use, and encourage students to use, vocabulary such as:

- *absorption, capacity, clay, compost, decay, humus, loam, organic matter, pebble, rocks, sand, sedimentation, sieving, soil, soil compost, water-holding*

In lesson 1, students start a Science and Technology Glossary in which they record new vocabulary introduced throughout the unit. Also in lesson 1, teachers create a class word wall

Portage & Main Press, 2017 · *Hands-On Science and Technology · Grade 3* · ISBN: 978-1-55379-709-8

for the unit. The word wall can be created on a bulletin board or simply on a sheet of poster paper, so as not to take up too much space. On the bulletin board or poster paper, record new vocabulary as it is introduced throughout the unit. Ensure the word wall is placed in a location where all students can see it and access the words.

Teachers should consider including vocabulary related to scientific inquiry skills. Vocabulary related to scientific inquiry skills include terms such as:

- *access, ask, brainstorm, collect, compare, connect, consider, construct, cooperate, create, describe, develop, diagram, display, draw, estimate, examine, explain, explore, find, follow, graph, identify, improve, investigate, label, measure, observe, order, plan, predict, recognize, record, repeat, respond, research, select, sequence, test*

These terms might be displayed in the classroom as they relate to inquiry skills used throughout the year. Students can then brainstorm which skills they are using as they work through particular lessons. They could also discuss what the skill looks and sounds like as they explore and investigate.

Portage & Main Press, 2017 · *Hands-On Science and Technology · Grade 3* · ISBN: 978-1-55379-709-8

# Unit Overview

| Fundamental Concepts | Big Ideas |
|---|---|
| Systems and Interactions | ■ Soil is made up of living and non-living things. |
| Change and Continuity | ■ The composition, characteristics, and condition of soil determine its capacity to sustain life.<br>■ Soil is an essential source of life and nutrients for many living things. |
| Sustainability and Stewardship | ■ Living things, including humans, interact with soils and can cause positive or negative changes. |

## Overall Expectations

By the end of Grade 3, students will do the following:

1. Assess the impact of soils on society and the environment, and of society and the environment on soils.
2. Investigate the composition and characteristics of different soils.
3. Demonstrate an understanding of the composition of soils, the types of soils, and the relationship between soils and other living things.

Portage & Main Press, 2017 · Hands-On Science and Technology · Grade 3 · ISBN: 978-1-55379-709-8

# Curriculum Correlation

| Specific Expectation | Lesson | | | | | | | | | |
|---|---|---|---|---|---|---|---|---|---|---|
| | 1 | 2 | 3 | 4 | 5 | 6 | 7 | 8 | 9 | 10 |
| **1. Relating Science and Technology to Society and the Environment** | | | | | | | | | | |
| **1.1** Assess the impact of soils on society and the environment, and suggest ways in which humans can enhance positive effects and/or lessen or prevent harmful effects. | | | √ | √ | √ | √ | √ | | √ | √ |
| **1.2** Assess the impact of human action on soils, and suggest ways in which humans can affect soils positively and/or lessen or prevent harmful effects on soils. | | | √ | | | | √ | √ | √ | √ |
| **2. Developing Investigation and Communication Skills** | | | | | | | | | | |
| **2.1** Follow established safety procedures during science and technology investigations. | √ | √ | √ | √ | √ | √ | √ | √ | √ | √ |
| **2.2** Investigate the components of soil, the condition of soil, and additives found in soil, using a variety of soil samples from different local environments, and explain how the different amounts of these components in a soil sample determine how the soil can be used. | | √ | √ | | √ | | √ | | √ | √ |
| **2.3** Use scientific inquiry/experimentation skills, and knowledge and skills acquired from previous investigations, to determine which type(s) of soil will sustain life. | | | | √ | √ | | √ | | | |
| **2.4** Investigate the process of composting, and explain some advantages and disadvantages of composting. | | | | | | | | √ | | |
| **2.5** Use appropriate science and technology vocabulary, in oral and written communication. | √ | √ | √ | √ | √ | √ | √ | √ | √ | √ |
| **2.6** Use a variety of forms to communicate with different audiences and for a variety of purposes. | √ | √ | √ | √ | √ | √ | √ | √ | √ | √ |
| **3. Understanding Basic Concepts** | | | | | | | | | | |
| **3.1** Identify and describe the different types of soils. | √ | √ | √ | √ | √ | | | | √ | |
| **3.2** Identify additives that might be in soil but that cannot always be seen. | | | √ | | | | | | | |
| **3.3** Describe the interdependence between the living and non-living things that make up soil. | | | √ | | | √ | | | | |
| **3.4** Describe ways in which the components of various soils enable the soil to provide shelter/ homes and/or nutrients for different kinds of living things. | | | √ | | √ | | | | | |

Portage & Main Press, 2017 · Hands-On Science and Technology · Grade 3 · ISBN: 978-1-55379-709-8

# Resources for Students

Ahenakew, Freda. *Wisahkecahk Flies to the Moon*. Winnipeg, MB: Pemmican Publications, 2015.

Aloian, Molly. *Different Kinds of Soil*. St. Catharines, ON: Crabtree Publishing, 2010.

Anderson, Jean. *Amazing Mud*. Logan, IA: Perfection Learning, 2006.

Bourgeois, Paulette. *The Dirt on Dirt*. Toronto: Kids Can Press, 2008.

Caduto, Michael J. and Joseph Bruchac. *Native American Gardening: Stories, Projects and Recipes for Families*. Golden, CO: Fulcrum Publishing, 1996.

Clarke, Jane. *Stuck in the Mud*. London: Puffin, 2007.

Cohen, Caron Lee. *The Mud Pony: A Traditional Skidi Pawnee Tale*. New York, NY: Scholastic, 1989.

Cronin, Doreen. *Diary of a Worm*. New York, NY: HarperCollins, 2003.

Davis, Barbara J. *Minerals, Rocks and Soils*. Mankato, MN: Capstone, 2017.

Ditchfield, Christin. *Soil*. New York, NY: Children's Press, 2002.

Dixon, Norma. *Lowdown on Earth Worms*. Markham, ON: Fitzhenry & Whiteside, 2005.

Downey, Shirley. *Mud Muddelicious Mud – Verse for the Very Young*. Halifax, NS: Nimbus Publishing, 2017.

French, Vivian. *Yucky Worms*. Somerville, MA: Candlewick Press, 2012.

Gurney, Beth. *Sand and Soil: Earth's Building Blocks*. New York, NY: Crabtree Publishing Company, 2005.

Hyde, Natalie. *Micro Life in Soil*. New York, NY: Crabtree Publishing Company, 2010.

_____. *Soil Erosion and How to Prevent It*. St. Catharines, ON: Crabtree Publishing Company, 2010.

James, Betsy. *The Mud Family*. Markham, ON: Fitzhenry & Whiteside ,1994.

Jenson-Elliott, Cindy. *Dig in!* New York, NY: Beach Lane Books, 2016.

Lee, Ji-hyeon. *We Need Soil!* Big & Small Publishing, 2016.

Love, Hallie N. *Watakame's Journey: The Huichol Myth of the Great Flood and the New World*. Santa Fe, NM: Clear Light Publishers, 1999.

Mack, Dave. *In the Soil. Rocks and Soil*. New York: Rosen Publishing, 2016.

MacAulay, Kelley. *Why Do We Need Soil?* St. Catharines, ON: Crabtree Publishing, 2014.

Montgomery, Heather L. *How Is Soil Made?* St. Catharines, ON: Crabtree Publishing Company, 2010.

Munsch, Robert. *Mud Puddle*. Toronto: Annick Press, 2012.

Oxlade, Chris. *Soil*. Chicago: Heinemann-Raintree, 2016.

Pfeffer, Wendy. *Wiggling Worms at Work*. New York, NY: HarperCollins, 2003.

Ray, Mary Lyn. *Mud*. Boston, MA: Houghton Mifflin Harcourt, 2001.

Reilly, Kathleen M. *Explore Soil! With 25 Great Projects*. White River Junction, VT: Nomad Press, 2015.

Riley, Peter. *Rocks and Soil*. New York: Rosen Publishing, 2017.

Rosinsky, Natalie M. *Dirt: The Scoop on Soil*. Minneapolis, MN: Picture Window Books, 2003.

▶

Portage & Main Press, 2017 · *Hands-On Science and Technology · Grade 3* · ISBN: 978-1-55379-709-8

Santella, Andrew. *The Hopi: A True Book.* Danbury, CT: Children's Press, 2002.

Schuh, Mari. *From Soil to Garden.* Lerner Publications, 2017.

Siddals, Mary McKenna. *Compost Stew: An A to Z Recipe for the Earth.* Berkeley, CA: Tricycle Press, 2010.

Tomecek, Steve. *Jump into Science: Dirt.* Washington, DC: National Geographic Society, 2016.

Vickers, Roy Henry and Robert Budd. *Peace Dancer.* Madeira Park, BC: Harbour Publishing, 2016.

Walker, Sally M. *Studying Soil.* Lerner Publications, 2013.

Portage & Main Press, 2017 · *Hands-On Science and Technology · Grade 3* · ISBN: 978-1-55379-709-8

# Websites and Online Videos

## Websites

- **www.aitc-canada.ca/en/ontario.html**
  Agriculture in the Classroom: Curriculum-based programs, activities, and tools for teachers and students to learn more about agriculture and the role it plays in Ontario. The website offers a variety of downloadable resources (many of them free) and programs such as Little Green Thumbs, Healthy Kids Quest, Lunch Box for Plants, and more.

- **forces.si.edu/soils/index.html**
  Smithsonian Environmental Research Center —Dig it! The Secrets of Soil: Discover the amazing world of soils with images and information from an exhibit from the Smithsonian's National Museum of Natural History. The site includes a video tour of the original exhibit, as well as interactive activities and educational materials.

- **www.kidcyber.com.au/earthworms/?rq=earthworms**
  KidCyber—Earthworms: Informational site for students about earthworms, with links to videos, information about the worm's anatomy, how to make a worm farm, and more.

- **extension.illinois.edu/gpe/case2/case2.html**
  The Great Plant Escape—Case #2 Soiled Again: Students try to complete a soils adventure by helping Detective Le Plant dig for clues in the soil. To solve the case, you must find out what soil is, why it is important, and in what kinds of soil plants grow.

- **www.wonderville.ca/asset/kelvin-adventures-the-dirt-on-soil**
  Kelvin Adventures—The Dirt on Soil (Wonderville): A 3D online farm game where the goal is to grow as many crops as you can. Students learn how to balance factors that affect crop growth for farmers.

- **www.harcourtschool.com/activity/dirt/compostion.html**
  Harcourt School Publishers—Soil Formation Activity 1—Soil Composition: An interactive game where players can test their knowledge about the different layers of soil and what the layers are made of.

- **studyjams.scholastic.com/studyjams/jams/science/rocks-minerals-landforms/soil.htm**
  Scholastic Study Jams—Soil—Landforms, Rocks & Minerals: Students can watch a slide show and read about how soil is formed, as well as different types of soil. Then, they can test their knowledge by answering review questions.

- **www.letthechildrenplay.net/2011/08/10-reasons-why-we-should-let-children.html**
  "10 reasons why we should let children play in the mud"—Let the Children Play: Brief article about why playing in the mud is beneficial to children.

- **www.education.com/activity/article/balloon-greenhouse/**
  Education.com—Balloon Greenhouse: In this activity, students see firsthand how a greenhouse works by creating their own.

- **www.naturetracking.com/getting-started/**
  Nature Tracking—Getting Started Identifying Animal Tracks: This resource covers the basics of identifying animal tracks, with examples and what to look for to help identify a set of tracks.

- **www.gardeningknowhow.com/composting/vermicomposting/worms-for-vermicomposting.htm**
  Gardening Know How—Worms and Vermicomposting—Best Types of Worms for Vermicomposting: This article provides a quick summary for vermicomposting.

▶

Portage & Main Press, 2017 · *Hands-On Science and Technology · Grade 3* · ISBN: 978-1-55379-709-8

Portage & Main Press, 2017 · Hands-On Science and Technology · Grade 3 · ISBN: 978-1-55379-709-8

- **www.cathyscomposters.com/**
  Cathy's Crawly Composters—Worm Away Your Garbage: A useful resource for setting up vermicomposting yourself.

- **snpolytechnic.com/search/node/clay%20pots**
  Six Nations Polytechnic—Clay Pots: This site provides excellent examples and background on Indigenous clay pots and pottery designs.

- **www.wordle.net**
  Wordle—Use this easy-to-navigate website to generate word clouds from text that you provide. Words that appear more frequently in the source text are emphasized in the word cloud.

- **www.inspiration.com/Kidspiration**
  Inspiration Software—Kidspiration: a way to visually explore and understand words, numbers, and concepts.

- **www.archaeological.org/pdfs/education/digs/Digs_shoebox.pdf**
  Shoebox Dig—A guide to creating a small-scale excavation for your students.

- **school.discoveryeducation.com/schooladventures/soil**
  Discovery Education—The Dirt on Soil: Students get "down and dirty" exploring the many layers of soil. The Field Guide helps students discover what is alive under their feet, while the Soil Safari takes students on a journey underground.

- **www.historymuseum.ca/cmc/exhibitions/archeo/ceramiq/cerart1e.shtml**
  Canadian Museum of History: Take the virtual tour titled *Gather Around This Pot*. This tour provides stunning visuals and descriptions of pottery made by Indigenous peoples from across Canada. The virtual exhibit tour can be projected on an interactive whiteboard, so the pottery can be discussed and examined together as a class.

- **www.virtualmuseum.ca/sgc-cms/expositions-exhibitions/esprits-spirits/English/Dig/index.html**
  Virtual Museum—This site includes tools to help students prepare as though they were doing a real archaeological dig, and gives some of the basics of archaeology.

## Videos

- **pbskids.org/dragonflytv/show/wormfarm.html**
  PBS Kids—Dragonfly TV. "Worm Farm (by Kevin)."

- **https://youtu.be/CcdXCVbeD4U**
  "Soil Pollution and Its Impact on Environment—Part 3." Iken Edu (13:35)

- **https://youtu.be/nGaONJ05UJc**
  "Soil Pollution." Flexiguru (0:28)

- **https://www.youtube.com/watch?v=UaVuLlwYEvA**
  "Soil Pollution (Causes, effects and solutions)" Thanhh Nguyeen (3:53)

- **https://www.youtube.com/watch?v=Njbn34JrKnE**
  "Compost Kids What Is Back Yard Composting?" Hamilton County Recycling (4:04)

- **https://www.youtube.com/watch?v=hOSHlv__Vro**
  "The Mud Pony by Caron Lee Cohen." Nicholas Kemper (6:10)

# 1 | What Do We Know About Soil?

## Information for Teachers

Soil is loose, broken-down rock and organic material in which plants can grow. Soil is a mixture of four components: mineral grains (sand, silt, and clay), organic matter or humus (the remains of once-living things), water, and air.

## 21st Century Competencies

**Communication** and **Collaboration**: In pairs, students will examine a word splash related to soil, and determine their level of understanding of various words. They will also add words they know that relate to soil.

## Materials

- various soil samples, bagged (e.g., from a garden, woods, roadside)

**NOTE:** It is very useful to also have a photo of the site from which each soil sample is gathered (e.g., soil from Toronto Beaches, from your backyard, from a forest, and from the Rouge River creek bed).

- newspaper or paper plates
- magnifying glasses
- chart paper
- markers
- Activity Sheet A: Word Splash (4.1.1)
- sand
- white glue
- spoons
- small containers with lids (e.g., yogurt containers)
- small pebbles
- water
- Learning-Centre Task Card: Reading About the World of Soils (4.1.2)
- Learning-Centre Library Resource Report (4.1.3)
- Activity Sheet B: Science and Technology Glossary (4.1.4)

## Activate

Place each different soil sample on a separate piece of newspaper or a different paper plate. Organize students into as many groups as you have soil samples. Have the groups rotate through the stations, encouraging students to use magnifying glasses as they examine each sample. When all groups have looked at each soil sample, bring students back together as a class, and ask:

- What kinds of samples were you just observing?
- How do you know what they were?
- What is the soil made of?
- Does soil change as you dig deeper into the Earth?
- Why is soil important to plant growth?

On chart paper, record students' responses.

Introduce the guided inquiry question: **What do we know about soil?**

**NOTE:** Keep the soil samples from this activity for future activities. Do not disclose to students the locations from which the soil samples have been taken. This will be disclosed in the next lesson.

## Action: Part One

Provide each student with a copy of Activity Sheet A: Word Splash (4.1.1), and reproduce a copy onto chart paper. Give students time to look over each word and mark a check mark (√) next to any words they can read. Circle all the words they understand. Underline any words they can use in a sentence.

Tell students not to mark anything on words they cannot read.

Now, organize students into pairs, and have them share their word splashes with each other. Then, ask:

▶

Portage & Main Press, 2017 · Hands-On Science and Technology · Grade 3 · ISBN: 978-1-55379-709-8

- What do all the words on our word splash have in common?
- What other words about soil can you add to the word splash?

With their partners, have students discuss other words they could add to their word splashes. Then, bring the class back together, and have the pairs share the words they have added to their word splashes. Add these to the class word splash.

Have students use their underlined words to make sentences to share with the rest of the class.

### Activity Sheet A

Directions to students:

Look at all the words on your word splash. Mark a check mark (√) next to any words you can read. Circle all the words you understand. Underline any words you can use in a sentence. Do not mark anything on words you cannot read (4.1.1).

## Action: Part Two

Soil is a mixture of four components: mineral grains, organic material, water, and air. To help students understand how soil is formed, have them conduct an investigation involving the breakdown of rocks.

Begin the activity by asking students if they have ever built a sandcastle at the beach. Ask:

- Do you think your sandcastle is still there now? Why not?
- What happens to the sand as the waves roll in?
- Do you think the waves have the same effect on rocks on the beach?

Have students share their ideas.

Divide the class into working groups. Provide each group with newspaper or a paper plate, sand, a spoon, and white glue. Have each group mix about eight spoonfuls of sand with about four spoonfuls of white glue. The mixture should be the consistency of clay or dough in order to shape. Add more sand if too runny or more glue if too dry. Have students shape the mixture into a cube. Allow each cube to dry for two days.

After two days, have students observe their cube. Then, ask each group to put its cube inside a small container with a lid, along with some small pebbles and about 2cm of water. Have students take turns shaking the container. Shake each container for approximately five minutes.

After five minutes, have students remove the lid and observe the changes to the cube and the water. Ask:

- Is the cube smaller than when you put it in the container? Why?
- What does the water in the container look like now?
- How are these results similar to what you would see in nature (e.g., at a beach, in a river or stream)?
- Over time, what happens to rocks and pebbles in a river?

Discuss with students how rocks are broken down by water, and then those small particles mix with natural materials, air, and water to form soil.

## Action: Part Three

Distribute several copies of Activity Sheet B: Science and Technology Glossary (4.1.4) to each student. Tell students to record any new terms they learn while studying the unit, as well as a definition, and then use the term in a sentence. At the end of the unit, students will cut apart the rows, alphabetize their words, add a title page, and create booklets of terminology related to soils in the environment.

Portage & Main Press, 2017 · Hands-On Science and Technology · Grade 3 · ISBN: 978-1-55379-709-8

**NOTE:** The Science and Technology Glossary presents an excellent opportunity to celebrate cultural diversity by having students include words in other languages. Students may include terms in Indigenous languages or other languages spoken at home.

**NOTE:** A variety of online dictionaries may be used as a source for translations. For example:

■ ojibwe.lib.umn.edu/

■ www.freelang.net/online/mohawk.php

Online dictionaries are also available for other languages that may be reflective of the class population.

### Activity Sheet B

Directions to students:

Record any new words on the sheet. Include a definition and a sentence using the word. (4.1.4)

## Learning Centre

At the learning centre, set up a World of Soils library. Provide books, magazines, brochures, catalogues (e.g., seed), articles from the Internet, posters, and any other resources found on a variety of topics related to soils. Also, include a copy of the Learning-Centre Task Card: Reading About the World of Soils (4.1.2) and copies of the Learning-Centre Library Resource Report (4.1.3). Have students read whatever interests them at the centre and create a library report on one of the resources.

**NOTE:** Ensure the resources are at a variety of reading levels to engage all learners.

## Consolidate and Debrief

■ Revisit the guided inquiry question: **What do we know about soil?** Have students share their knowledge, provide examples, and ask further inquiry questions.

■ Add to the class word splash as students learn new concepts, answer some of their own inquiry questions, and ask new inquiry questions.

■ Begin a class word wall to display new terminology students learn throughout the unit. Add illustrations.

**NOTE:** Include terminology in other languages on the class word wall. This is a way of acknowledging and respecting students' cultural backgrounds, while enhancing learning for all students.

## Enhance

■ Have students create digital word splashes using Microsoft Word or a website such as Wordle (<www.wordle.net>) or Kidspiration (<www.inspiration.com/Kidspiration>). Students may want to add pictures or illustrations using a computer program (e.g., they may use Word to add clip art, or draw using Kid Pix), or they can copy and paste a picture from a website or draw a picture by hand and have it scanned. Continue to add to the digital word splace throughout the unit.

■ Have students begin their do-it-yourself projects at the Makerspace centre (See page 18 in the Introduction to **Hands-On Science and Technology, Grade 3** and page 352 to this unit for details on setting up the Makerspace centre).

Portage & Main Press, 2017 · *Hands-On Science and Technology · Grade 3* · ISBN: 978-1-55379-709-8

Date: _____    Name: _____

# Word Splash

sand

soil

leaf/leaves

loam

clay

pebble

mud

rock

insect

humus

compost

absorb

Portage & Main Press, 2017 · Hands-On Science and Technology · Grade 3 · ISBN: 978-1-55379-709-8

# Reading About the World of Soils

Welcome to the World of Soils library.

1. Choose anything you want to read from the library.

2. Read your selection.

3. After you have read your selection, complete a copy of the Learning-Centre Library Resource Report.

4. Share your report with a classmate.

ROCKS & SAND
DIRT
SOIL
WORMS
MUD PIES

Portage & Main Press, 2017 · Hands-On Science and Technology · Grade 3 · ISBN: 978-1-55379-709-8

Date: _____          Name: _____

# Learning-Centre Library
# Resource Report

Resource title: _____

Author: _____

## 1. Explain what the resource is about.

_____

_____

_____

_____

_____

## 2. Redraw one of the pictures or photographs from the resource.

## 3. One question I have about the topic of this resource is:

_____

_____

Portage & Main Press, 2017 · *Hands-On Science and Technology · Grade 3* · ISBN: 978-1-55379-709-8

# Science and Technology Glossary

| Word | Definition |
|------|------------|
|      |            |

## Sentence

| Word | Definition |
|------|------------|
|      |            |

## Sentence

| Word | Definition |
|------|------------|
|      |            |

## Sentence

Portage & Main Press, 2017 · Hands-On Science and Technology · Grade 3 · ISBN: 978-1-55379-709-8

# 2 | What Are the Different Types of Soil?

## Information for Teachers

The observable characteristics of some types of soil are:

### Sandy Soil

- falls apart easily
- feels gritty
- mostly sand, mixed with a little silt, clay, and humus

### Silt

- fine soil with grains smaller than sand but larger than clay

### Loam (garden soil)

- forms clods (lumps of earth or clay)
- feels like velvet
- about half sand, a third clay, and the rest is silt and humus

### Clay

- sticks together
- feels greasy
- at least half clay, and the rest is sand, silt, and humus

### Humus

- soft and spongy
- falls apart quite easily
- composed of decayed organic material

### Peat

- brown/black earth material created when plants decay in water
- can be dried and used as fertilizer
- traditionally, was cut, dried, and used as fuel instead of wood

## 21st Century Competencies

### Critical Thinking and Communication:
Students will go on a community soil gathering walk, and then analyze their samples. They will compare their samples to those used in the previous activity, and discuss whether samples from different sites could have similar profiles.

## Materials

- soil samples from lesson 1 (label these with numbers)
- plastic zipper-lock bags
- garden trowels
- rulers
- digital camera
- chart paper
- markers
- world map
- tacks or other markers for the map
- string or yarn
- resources related to animal tracks
- Plasticine
- plastic wrap
- several dish basins or large plastic containers
- permanent markers
- newspaper
- magnifying glasses
- tweezers
- containers of water
- clear plastic cups
- variety of materials for modelling soil profiles (e.g., pebbles, clay, humus, top soil; broken cookies, cookie crumbs, brown sugar, rock candy, gummy worms, coconut, pudding, crushed chocolate sandwich cookies, coloured sprinkles; marbles, Styrofoam chips, rice, beans, beads; recyclables such as cardboard, paper, plastic, aluminum)
- computers/tablets with Internet access
- Activity Sheet: Soil Search (four copies for each student) (4.2.1)
- *Wisahkecahk Flies to the Moon* by Freda Ahenakew
- Learning-Centre Task Card: Creating a Model Soil Profile (4.2.2)
- word splash (from lesson 1)
- Science and Technology Glossary (4.1.4)

Portage & Main Press, 2017 · *Hands-On Science and Technology · Grade 3* · ISBN: 978-1-55379-709-8

**2**

## Activate

As a class, discuss what soil is. Display soil samples, labelled with numbers, from lesson 1. Allow students to examine the soil, encouraging them to feel the different soils. Ask:

- From where do you think each of these soil samples came?
- Why do you think that?

Record students' responses on chart paper.

---

**NOTE:** If you have photos of the sites from where soil samples were gathered, have students look at soils and their composition and try to match the location.

---

Introduce the guided inquiry question: **What are the different types of soil?**

## Action: Part One

---

**NOTE:** Before doing this activity with students, locate at least four different areas near the school where students can examine soil and collect samples (e.g., school garden, field, along a sidewalk, near a creek, in a vacant lot).

---

Explain to students that you are going to take them on a soil search. Distribute a plastic zipper-lock bag to each student. Divide the class into groups of four students and distribute a trowel, a ruler, and a permanent marker to each group. Take students on a walk to at least four different locations around the school neighbourhood. Demonstrate the proper technique for retrieving a soil sample (use the trowel to dig below the surface to get at the soil; scoop up a sample and deposit it in the bag).

Have each student within each group select a different location (from the designated areas) from which to take a soil sample, use the trowel to collect the soil, and deposit it into the bag. Also, have the groups decide (within their groups) on different depths from which to take their samples, using the rulers to measure the

depth of the hole from which their soil sample came. Make sure students label their bags to show where each sample came from and record the depth measurement on the bag. At the end of the soil search, each group should have four different soil samples.

Take photographs of each site.

Back in the classroom, have the groups examine the bags of soil samples. To help them analyze each sample, ask them to brainstorm a list of descriptive words about the soil, and record these on chart paper. Help guide students by asking:

- What words could you use to describe the texture of the different soils?
- What words could you use to describe the smell of the different soils?
- What words could you use to describe how different soils look?

Now, have each group empty its soil samples into separate piles on newspaper. For each sample, have groups record on the newspaper the location and the depth of the hole from which it came.

Distribute a magnifying glass, tweezers, and four copies of Activity Sheet: Soil Search (4.2.1), to each student. Have students use the tools to analyze their soil samples. They may be able to recognize many different materials in the soil (e.g., bits of rock, sticks, leaves, seeds, sand, clay). Encourage students to identify as many of these components as possible, sharing their discoveries with others in their group, and then recording their observations on the corresponding activity sheet.

Next, have students wet a small amount of soil from each sample by dipping their hands into a container of water and then picking up a handful of soil. Ask:

▶

Portage & Main Press, 2017 · *Hands-On Science and Technology* · *Grade 3* · ISBN: 978-1-55379-709-8

- What are the different parts of soil?
- How does the soil hold together?
- Can you roll it into a ball?
- Does it stick together or fall apart?
- Can you squeeze some of the water out?
- What does the soil feel like when you rub it between your fingers?

Continue having students record their observations on their activity sheets.

**NOTE:** Keep the soil samples from this activity for future activities.

### Activity Sheet

Directions to students:

Record your observations about each soil sample your group collected on a separate sheet (4.2.1).

**NOTE:** Each student will need four copies of this activity sheet.

### Assessment of Learning

Observe students as they examine and describe the soil types. Focus on their ability to describe the texture, appearance, and malleability of the soil samples. Use the Anecdotal Record sheet, on page 26, to record results.

## Action: Part Two

As a class, discuss the soil samples and students' observations. On chart paper, record the similarities and differences students observed.

Refer back to students' responses from the beginning of the lesson about the locations from which the original soil samples (from lesson 1) came. Ask:

- Which of your present soil samples look like the original samples?
- Could the soil samples look similar and be from different locations? Why?

Disclose the locations where the original soil samples were collected.

## Action: Part Three

In this activity, students will learn about animal tracks, and will identify characteristics of soil that would make it more likely for visible tracks to be made and to endure.

Consider inviting a local Elder or Métis Senator to guide students on a nature walk to learn about animal tracks. This will provide background knowledge for further investigation.

Back in the classroom, have students study a variety of animal tracks, from large and small animals. Use reference material, as well as websites such as: <www.naturetracking.com/getting-started/>.

Have students select an animal track, and make a model of it from Plasticine. They can then make track patterns in various soil samples to determine how well the tracks are imprinted.

Have soil samples in several large dish basins or containers. Have students place a small piece of plastic wrap over the soil, and then press their animal track model into the soil until it is level with the soil surface. Remove the model and plastic wrap, then examine the tracks.

Have students examine tracks made in different types of soil, as well as different tracks made by other students. Discuss their observations, drawing conclusions with regard to the types of soil that best allow tracks to be imprinted.

## Action: Part Four

Read *Wisahkecahk Flies to the Moon* by Freda Ahenakew, a Cree story about how muskeg came to be. The term *muskeg* comes from the Cree word *maskek*, meaning low-lying marsh.

Portage & Main Press, 2017 · *Hands-On Science and Technology · Grade 3* · ISBN: 978-1-55379-709-8

As a class, research muskeg to find out its characteristics and locations in Ontario, in Canada, and in other parts of the world. Have students mark locations on a world map. Connect photographs of muskeg to the map using yarn or string to show examples of muskeg in different locations.

## Learning Centre

 **SAFETY NOTE:** Various foods are suggested as materials for the following activity. Before providing any foods for students' use or access, review any allergies students have.

At the learning centre, provide clear plastic cups, permanent markers, and a variety of materials students can use to design and construct models of soil profiles such as:

- pebbles, clay, humus, top soil
- broken cookies, cookie crumbs, brown sugar, pudding, rock candy, gummy worms, coconut, crushed chocolate sandwich cookies, coloured sprinkles
- marbles, Styrofoam chips, rice, beans, beads
- recyclables such as cardboard, paper, plastic, and aluminum

Also, provide a copy of the Learning-Centre Task Card: Creating a Model Soil Profile (4.2.2). As well, students will need access to computers/tablets and the Internet.

Explain to students they are going to create 3D model soil profiles. Have students examine the soil profile diagrams on the Learning-Centre Task Card and conduct research to access simple soil profiles online. Then, they can use the materials at the centre to create their own soil profiles in plastic cups and use a permanent marker to label each horizon (layer), to describe what each layer of their model represents.

## Consolidate and Debrief

- Revisit the guided inquiry question: **What are the different types of soil?** Have students share their knowledge, provide examples, and ask further inquiry questions.
- Add to the class word splash as students learn new concepts, answer some of their own inquiry questions, and ask new inquiry questions.
- Add new terms, including *loam*, *humus*, *clay*, *peat*, and *horizon*, and illustrations to the class word wall. Include the words in other languages, as appropriate.
- Have students add new terms and definitions, as well as sentences that include the terms, to their Science and Technology Glossary (4.1.4). When possible, encourage students to use the words in other languages, including Indigenous languages, reflective of the class population.

## Enhance

- One way we know about peoples of the past is through archeology. When archeologists explore the land looking for historical sites, they look for signs that the soil has been disturbed in the past. Signs of this are soils of different colours or textures that form discernible patterns. Have students conduct a shoebox dig to explore the idea of archeology and soil layers. Fill shoeboxes in the following manner:
  - bottom layer: 3 cm of gravel. Place several artifacts on top of this layer (e.g., plastic fish or insects)
  - third layer: 3 cm of sand. Place several artifacts on top of this layer (e.g., beads).
  - second layer: 3 cm of soil. Place several artifacts on top of this layer (e.g., coins)
  - top layer: 3 cm of grass, leaves, and twigs

▶

Portage & Main Press, 2017 · *Hands-On Science and Technology · Grade 3* · ISBN: 978-1-55379-709-8

As a class, explore the Virtual Archaeological Dig though the Virtual Museum of Canada website. Go to: <www.virtualmuseum.ca/sgc-cms/expositions-exhibitions/esprits-spirits/English/Dig/index.html>. This site includes tools to help students prepare as though they are doing a real dig, and gives some of the basics of archaeology.

Have students conduct digs in which they attempt to examine the characteristics of each soil layer, and locate the artifacts found in each layer. Conduct a follow-up discussion in which students infer who or what might have lived in the area where this soil was found during different times. For more detail on shoebox digs go to: <www.archaeological.org/pdfs//education/digs/Digs_shoebox.pdf>.

- Many communities have had some archeological exploration nearby. Teachers could find photos or visit these digs as they occur.

- Invite a horticulturist to speak to students about different types of soils, the importance of soil for growing plants, and the different types of plants that grow in various soils.

- Visit a local nursery or botanical garden to observe the different types of soils used to grow different types of plants.

- Investigate how different communities or regions have different types of soil (e.g., prairie soil is different from coastal region soil). Then, to make an excellent language arts and social studies connection, have students write letters to various schools or other organizations in different regions, requesting a soil sample from the region.

- Have students research the difference between soil and dirt. This concept is explained well in the online article "The Dirt on Soil," found on the Discovery Education website at <school.discoveryeducation.com/schooladventures/soil/down_dirty.html>. In essence, dirt/mud is displaced soil components that cannot do their jobs alone. They need to be working with the other soil components either in the ground or in a carefully constructed soil mix. Soil relies on the interaction of its components to support life; dirt cannot support life, it is just bits of soil that have been separated out from the other soil components.

- Have a soil specialist demonstrate what a soil pit tells us about the composition of soil. Students can compare their soil profile models or diagrams of soil layers found at the learning centre to those in a soil pit. Encourage discussion about the depth of various layers of soil, which can then lead into discussion about protection of soil by farmers.

- Access the interactive activity, Different Types of Soil, in the Grade 3, Unit 4 folder of the ***Hands-On Interactive for Science and Technology, Grade 3*** download. Find this download at: <www.portageandmainpress.com/product/hands-on-interactive-for-science-and-technology-grade-3/>.

- Have students continue their do-it-yourself projects at the Makerspace centre.

Portage & Main Press, 2017 · *Hands-On Science and Technology · Grade 3* · ISBN: 978-1-55379-709-8

**Date:** _____        **Name:** _____

# Soil Search

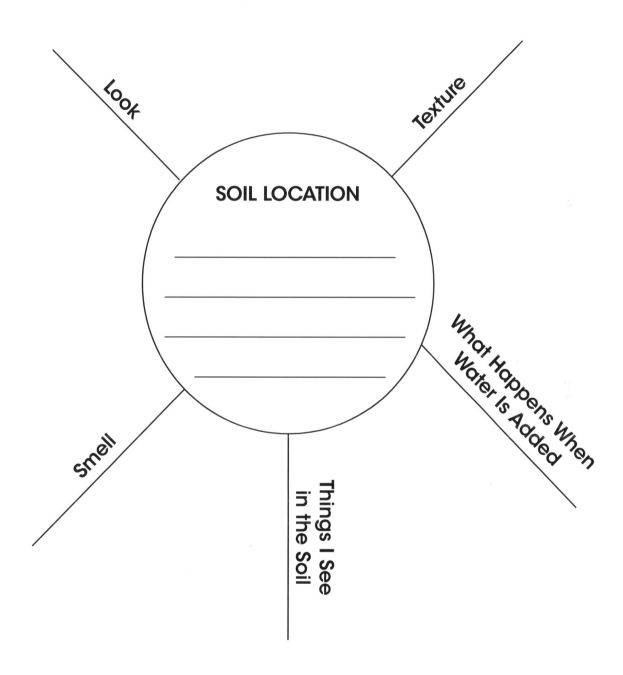

Look

Texture

SOIL LOCATION

_____

_____

_____

_____

Smell

What Happens When
Water Is Added

Things I See
in the Soil

Portage & Main Press, 2017 · Hands-On Science and Technology · Grade 3 · ISBN: 978-1-55379-709-8

# Creating a Model Soil Profile

Pretend you are a soil scientist.

1. Examine the diagrams of the soil profiles.

2. Conduct research to learn more about soil profiles.

3. Use the materials provided to create a model of a soil profile in a plastic cup.

4. Label each layer of your soil profile.

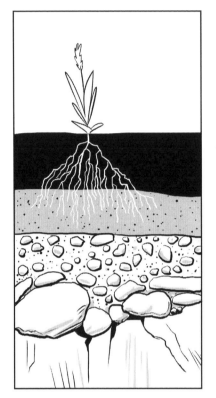

topsoil (humus, organic matter, dark brown or black)

subsoil (smaller particles, mostly clay, lighter brown in colour)

weathered parent material (broken-down rock)

parent rock (bedrock or glacial deposits)

topsoil

subsoil

parent rock

# 3 | How Can Soil Components Be Separated?

## Information for Teachers

Soil is a complex mixture of clay, loam, sand, pebbles, organic matter, and rocks. Each component is found in different layers of the ground. Soil relies on the interaction of its components to support life. In this lesson, students will explore to determine ways to separate soil components using sedimentation and sieving techniques.

## 21st Century Competencies

**Critical Thinking** and **Communication**: Students will use sedimentation to separate a soil sample into its different components, and then draw a picture of their results. Different samples of soil can be compared for similarities and differences.

## Materials

- soil samples from different locations and depths (Prepare one sample for each working group of students. Fill clear glass or plastic containers with lids about half full with soil, being sure to place an equal amount of soil into each container. Use masking tape to label the containers with the location of where the sample was collected.)
- water
- chart paper
- markers
- ruler with millimetre markings
- newspaper
- Activity Sheet: Separating Soil (4.3.1)
- Learning-Centre Task Card: Using a Sieve to Separate Soil (4.3.2)
- Learning-Centre Activity Sheet: Scientist's Recording Sheet: Separating Soil (4.3.3)
- several sieves of varying sizes (e.g., strainers, fine sieves, cheesecloth, mesh, nylon stockings, screening)
- large container of soil
- plate or plastic tub

- word splash (from lesson 1)
- Science and Technology Glossary (4.1.4)

## Activate

As a class, review lessons 1 and 2. Ask:

- What is soil?
- What are the different kinds of soil?
- Are different kinds of soil made up of the same things?
- What materials are found in soil?

Brainstorm a list of materials found in soil, and record these on chart paper (e.g., sand, leaves, rocks, clay) .

Introduce the guided inquiry question: **How can soil components be separated?**

## Action: Part One

Divide the class into small working groups, and have each group cover a work surface with newspaper. Give each group a magnifying glass, some water, a ruler, and a container half-filled with soil. Have students dump the soil onto the newspaper and observe the soil with a magnifying glass. Ask:

- Can you see different bits and pieces in your soil?
- What do you think the bits and pieces are?
- Can you separate out the various components—the bits and pieces—in the soil?

Have students share their ideas about soil separation techniques.

Next, ask students to put the soil back into the containers. Explain that you are going to have them add water to the containers and shake the containers. Ask:

- Why do you think you are going to do this?

▶

Portage & Main Press, 2017 · *Hands-On Science and Technology · Grade 3* · ISBN: 978-1-55379-709-8

Portage & Main Press, 2017 · Hands-On Science and Technology · Grade 3 · ISBN: 978-1-55379-709-8

Have students add water to their containers until there is only about five or six centimetres of space at the top. Have students put the lid on tightly, and shake the container 20 times. Tell students to set the container down on the desk and let it stand, without touching or moving it, until the soil settles (about three to five minutes). Ask:

- Can you see layers in the container?
- What is at the bottom of the container?
- What other layers do you see?
- Is anything floating?

Have students circulate the classroom and observe the samples of soil from other groups. Ask:

- How do the different soils compare?
- Do they have the same layers?
- Do they have the same kinds of particles in them?

Ask each student to formulate one new question about the soil or the separation technique. Record these on chart paper for further inquiry.

**NOTE:** The different layers in the containers are caused by different particles in the soil. Decaying materials—bits of wood, leaves, and roots—usually float on top of the water. The smallest particles dissolved in the water are clay. The fine grains are silt. The coarse grains are sand. The pieces of stone larger than the sand grains are pebbles. This technique of separating the components is called "sedimentation." Sedimentation is a natural process in which material (such as stones and sand) is carried to the bottom of a body of water and forms a solid layer with other less dense components layered above.

Distribute a copy of Activity Sheet: Separating Soil (4.3.1) to each student, and have students draw diagrams of their containers with the different layers inside. Ask students to make the diagram of the container as true to size as possible (students should use the ruler to

measure the size of the container, and then reproduce it in their diagram accordingly). Then, ask students to use the ruler to measure the height of each layer (in millimetres) found in the soil. Tell students to label the layers on their diagrams, using their own words to describe the layers and including the measurements, as well.

**Activity Sheet**

Directions to students:

Draw a true-to-size diagram of your container and the different layers inside it, then use a ruler to measure each layer found in your soil sample. Label the layers, including the measurements, and answer the question at the bottom of the page (4.3.1).

Have the groups present their diagrams to the class. Compare the different samples as reflected in the different diagrams. Also, compare the actual samples. Ask:

- How are these soil samples the same?
- How are they different?

## Action: Part Two

Learn about additives that might be in soil but that cannot always be seen (e.g., pesticides, fertilizers, salt). To safely investigate this topic, consider using videos and other sources of information. Videos on soil pollution include:

- **https://youtu.be/CcdXCVbeD4U**
  "Soil Pollution and Its Impact on Environment—Part 3." Iken Edu (13:35).

- **https://youtu.be/nGaONJ05UJc**
  "Soil Pollution." Flexiguru (00:28).

- **https://www.youtube.com/watch?v=UaVuLlwYEvA**
  "Soil pollution (Causes, effects and solutions)." Thanhh Nguyeen (3:53).

Other topics related to soil pollution the class could investigate include:

**3**

- the importance of bees for pollinating plant life, and the declining bee populations as a result of pesticides
- the impact of pesticides and fertilizers on local bodies of water

## Learning Centre

At the learning centre, provide a variety of different-sized sieves, including strainers, fine sieves, cheesecloth, mesh, nylon stockings, and screening; a large container of soil; and a plate or a large, plastic tub. Also, provide a copy of the Learning-Centre Task Card: Using a Sieve to Separate Soil (4.3.2), and copies of the Learning-Centre Activity Sheet: Scientist's Recording Sheet: Separating Soil (4.3.3).

Have students choose a sieve, pour some soil into it, and then shake the sieve over a plate or a large, plastic tub. Challenge students to identify the components as they are separated. Point out that different strainers can be used to separate out different components from the same sample of soil. Have students record their observations on the activity sheet.

### Assessment as Learning
Have students complete the Student Self-Assessment sheet, on page 31, to reflect on their learning during the lesson's activities and at the learning centre.

## Consolidate and Debrief

- Revisit the guided inquiry question: **How can soil components be separated?** Have students share their knowledge, provide examples, and ask further inquiry questions.
- Add to the class word splash as students learn new concepts, answer some of their own inquiry questions, and ask new inquiry questions.

- Add new terms, including *separation* and *sedimentation*, and illustrations to the class word wall. Include the words in other languages, as appropriate.
- Have students add new terms and definitions, as well as sentences that include the terms, to their Science and Technology Glossary (4.1.4). When possible, encourage students to use the words in other languages, including Indigenous languages, reflective of the class population.

## Enhance

- Remove the lids from the containers of soil samples (with water added) used during Action: Part One activity, and place the containers in a warm area. Have students predict what will happen to the soil samples over time. Leave the samples for several days so the water evaporates, then have students examine the layered soil samples again to see if their predictions were accurate.
- Access the interactive activity, Components of Soil, in the Grade 3, Unit 4 folder of the *Hands-On Interactive for Science and Technology, Grade 3* download. Find this download at: <www.portageandmainpress.com/product/hands-on-interactive-for-science-and-technology-grade-3/>.
- Have students continue their do-it-yourself projects at the Makerspace centre.

Portage & Main Press, 2017 · *Hands-On Science and Technology · Grade 3* · ISBN: 978-1-55379-709-8

Date: _____    Name: _____

# Separating Soil

1. Draw a diagram of the container.

2. Measure and draw the layers in the container.

3. Label the layers.

What do you think makes up each layer in the container?

_____

_____

_____

_____

Portage & Main Press, 2017 · Hands-On Science and Technology · Grade 3 · ISBN: 978-1-55379-709-8

# Using a Sieve to Separate Soil

1. Choose a sieve, strainer, or straining material (e.g., cheese cloth, screening) to separate soil.

2. Put some soil into the sieve, and shake it over the plate or the large, plastic tub. Watch what happens!

3. Use different sieves to separate the soil components, to see if some of them work better than others.

4. After the soil components have been separated, try to identify each component.

5. Record your observations on a copy of the Scientist's Recording Sheet: Separating Soil.

Portage & Main Press, 2017 · Hands-On Science and Technology · Grade 3 · ISBN: 978-1-55379-709-8

Date: _____   Name: _____

# Scientist's Recording Sheet: Separating Soil

1. List the soil components observed after separation.

   _____        _____

   _____        _____

   _____        _____

2. Which sieves did you use?

   _____        _____

   _____        _____

3. Which sieve separated the soil best?

   _____

4. Why do you think this sieve did the best job?

   _____

5. What else would you like to know about separating soil components?

   _____

   _____

   _____

Portage & Main Press, 2017 · Hands-On Science and Technology · Grade 3 · ISBN: 978-1-55379-709-8

# 4 How Much Water Can Different Soil Types Absorb?

## Information for Teachers

Soil's ability to absorb water is based on two factors:

1. permeability (how easily a soil is penetrated with water)
2. retention (how well the soil holds water)

Since sandy soils, for example, have very loose particles, they have a high water permeability. However, sandy soils do not retain water for very long. Clay soils, on the other hand, have low permeability and high water retention. Loam soils have medium permeability and rentention, and silt soils have low permeability and high retention.

## 21ˢᵗ Century Competencies

**Critical Thinking** and **Communication**: Students will experiment to test the water-holding capacity of different soil samples.

## Materials

- sets of four different soil samples in labelled containers (Label the type of soil [e.g., peat moss, potting soil, sand, clay soil] or the location from which the sample came. Samples from a preceding lesson can be used. You will need one set of four samples for each working group of students.)
- paper cups
- plastic cups
- pencils
- masking tape
- pens
- Popsicle sticks
- coffee filters or paper towels
- measuring cup or beaker (125 mL)
- water
- timers/stopwatches, or clocks/watches with a second hand
- plastic basin or container for water
- sponge
- brick
- Activity Sheet: Investigation: Absorption of Water (4.4.1)
- Learning-Centre Task Card: How Do You Like Playing With Mud? (4.4.2)
- *Mud Puddle* by Robert Munsch
- drawing paper
- colouring supplies (e.g., markers, pencil crayons, pastels)
- word splash (from lesson 1)
- Science and Technology Glossary (4.1.4)

## Activate

As a class, discuss how important it is for soil to be able to absorb water. Ask:

- Why is soil important?
- What is soil used for?
- What else do plants need to grow?
- How does a plant get water from the soil?
- What is meant by *absorption*?

To illustrate the meaning of absorption for students, take the sponge and dip it into water, allowing the sponge to soak up some of the water. Then, dip the brick into the water, and compare the sponge to the brick in terms of its ability to absorb water. Ask:

- What do you think would happen if soil could not absorb or hold water?
- Do you think all soil can absorb water equally well?

Introduce the guided inquiry question: **How much water can different soil types absorb?**

### Assessment for Learning

It is important for students to measure time accurately during the following investigation. Teachers are encouraged to conduct the first few tests as a class, so students know exactly how to calculate the amount of time needed for

▶

Portage & Main Press, 2017 · *Hands-On Science and Technology · Grade 3* · ISBN: 978-1-55379-709-8

Portage & Main Press, 2017 · Hands-On Science and Technology · Grade 3 · ISBN: 978-1-55379-709-8

the water to pass through a soil sample. During these tests, observe students' ability to measure time accurately. Use the Anecdotal Record sheet, on page 26, to record results.

Students will also be required to accurately measure water during the investigation; they will be adding 125 mL of water to each soil sample. Have students demonstrate their ability to measure this amount prior to beginning the following task, and also record these results on the Anecdotal Record sheet.

## Action

Divide the class into working groups of three to four students. Give each group a set of four different soil samples in labelled containers, and give each student a copy of Activity Sheet: Investigation: Absorption of Water (4.4.1).

Have students examine each sample and record their observations on their activity sheet. Ask:

- Which soil sample do you think will absorb water very well?
- Which soil sample do you think will not absorb water very well?

Encourage students to justify their predictions (orally).

Explain to students they will be testing the ability of water to pass through the various soil samples and then looking at the texture of the soil afterwards. Ask:

- Why might it be important to know how much water passes through a soil sample?
- If all the water does not pass through the soil, where does the water go?

Discuss the concept of variables with students, and the need to keep all variables the same in an experiment, except for what is being tested. Explain to students that they are going to test different samples of soil to see how much water they can hold.

Ask:

- What are some of the other things (variables) we should try to keep the same to make sure it is a fair test?

Discuss variables, including:

- amount of water
- amount of soil
- how quickly water is poured onto sample
- size of cup

Have the groups select one soil sample to test. Distribute paper cups, coffee filters or paper towels, and pencils. Have each group use a pencil to poke six holes in the bottom of the cup. Next, have them place a folded coffee filter or piece of paper towel in the bottom of the cup, to prevent granules of soil sample from falling out.

- Have the groups fill the paper cup half full with the soil sample they have selected. Distribute a piece of masking tape and a pen to each group, and tell the groups to label the paper cup with the name of the soil sample.

Now, distribute a plastic cup and two Popsicle sticks to each group. Have students set the plastic cup on a flat surface and place two Popsicle sticks across the top of the plastic cup. The Popsicle sticks will form a bridge for the paper cup (with the soil sample), which will allow water to seep from the paper cup into the plastic cup.

Have one student in each group act as a timer, and give that student a timer/stopwatch or a watch with a second hand (students can also use the classroom clock as a timer). Each group will also need a recorder. The timer should just focus on the time, and call out the times for the recorder to write down. Explain that the timer should tell the other group members to begin adding 125 mL of water to the paper cup when

**4**

the second hand reaches 12. Tell the timer to continue watching the time while the rest of the group watches the cup.

When the water begins to seep through the holes at the bottom of the paper cup and into the plastic cup, the other group members should let the timer know, and the timer will at that point note the time again. Students should also indicate when the water stops passing through the soil sample into the plastic cup, and the timer can also note that time. Students can then calculate how long it took for the water to pass through the soil. Tell students to record this result on the activity sheet. Have students measure how much water is now in the plastic cup and calculate the difference between the 125 mL poured into the soil and the amount of water now in the plastic cup. This will determine how much water was retained in the soil.

Afterward, have students remove the soil from the paper cup and try to form it into a ball. This task will encourage descriptive observations of the characteristics of different soils when they are wet.

Have the groups repeat the investigation for each of the different soil samples. Following the experiment, ask students:

- For which sample did the water seep through the bottom of the cup first?
- For which sample did the water seep through last?
- Did the same amount of water seep through each sample?
- How do you know?
- Did all of the water seep through the soil into the plastic cup?
- Where did the remainder of the water go?
- How would you describe the texture of the soil left behind?
- Which soil would be best for growing plants that need lots of water? Why?

### Activity Sheet

Directions to students:

For each soil sample, do the following: (1) Describe the soil. (2) Add 125 mL of water to the soil, and record how long it takes for water to begin to seep through into the plastic cup. (3) Measure the amount of water that seeps into the plastic cup. (4) Determine the amount of water absorbed by the soil (4.4.1).

### Learning Centre

At the learning centre, provide a copy of the book *Mud Puddle*, by Robert Munsch, a copy of the Learning-Centre Task Card: How Do You Like Playing With Mud? (4.4.2), and drawing paper, colouring supplies (e.g., markers, pencil crayons, pastels), and pens or pencils. Have small groups of students read the book and then discuss their experiences and ideas about playing with mud.

**NOTE:** For an interesting read about the value of having children playing in the mud, see the article "10 reasons why we should let children play in the mud" on the Let the Children Play website at <www.letthechildrenplay.net/2011/08/10-reasons-why-we-should-let-children.html>.

### Consolidate and Debrief

- Revisit the guided inquiry question: **How much water can different soil types absorb?** Have students share their knowledge, provide examples, and ask further inquiry questions.

**NOTE:** It is important for students to draw conclusions about the water-holding capacity of the different soil types (e.g., loamy soil holds more water than sandy soil). Encourage this type of discussion when sharing results of the investigation.

- Add to the class word splash as students learn new concepts, answer some of their own inquiry questions, and ask new inquiry questions.

▶

Soils in the Environment

Portage & Main Press, 2017 · *Hands-On Science and Technology · Grade 3* · ISBN: 978-1-55379-709-8

**4**

- Add new terms, including *absorb, absorption,* and *water-holding capacity,* and illustrations to the class word wall. Include the words in other languages, as appropriate.

- Have students add new terms and definitions, as well as sentences that include the terms, to their Science and Technology Glossary (4.1.4). When possible, encourage students to use the words in other languages, including Indigenous languages, reflective of the class population.

## Enhance

- Discuss the value of conducting multiple trials in a science investigation. Ask students how many trials might be necessary to draw conclusions. This encourages students to realize they are looking for consistency in data but not identical results. Outlier results may indicate a change in technique. Discussing such changes and differences is also important.

- Have students construct bar graphs of their results from the lesson's experiment, to compare how long it took before water began to seep through into the plastic cup for each of the different soil samples, or the difference in the amount of water collected in the plastic cup. Then, compare the class results by looking at the various bar graphs. Discuss the similarities, the differences, and what could cause such differences. In this way, you are looking at multiple trials with the class.

- Connect the learning in this lesson to gardening or taking care of house plants. Different soil compositions will require different amounts of watering. Explore how the water-holding capacity of soil used for house plants compares to the results found in this experiment.

- Have students identify ways water can affect soil (e.g., overwatering, under-watering, washing away nutrients, breaking up soil).

- Show students the video *The Mud Pony*, by Caron Lee Cohen (a reading of this book by Nicholas Kemper, along with the book's illustrations, is shown on YouTube at: <www.youtube.com/watch?v=hOSHIv__Vro>), or read the book to the class. Then, have students discuss how water affected the mud pony and why the boy covered the pony when it rained.

**NOTE:** Teachers are also encouraged to connect this discussion to the idea that rain is a strong force that can break and move soil.

- Access the interactive activity, Absorption of Water, in the Grade 3, Unit 4 folder of the ***Hands-On Interactive for Science and Technology, Grade 3*** download. Find this download at: <www.portageandmainpress.com/product/hands-on-interactive-for-science-and-technology-grade-3/>.

- Have students continue their do-it-yourself projects at the Makerspace centre.

Portage & Main Press, 2017 · Hands-On Science and Technology · Grade 3 · ISBN: 978-1-55379-709-8

**Date:** _____  **Name:** _____

# Investigation: Absorption of Water

Soil Sample #1: _____

Description:_____

_____

Length of time it took for water to seep through soil: _____

Amount of water in plastic cup:_____

How much water did the soil absorb? _____

---

Soil Sample #2: _____

Description:_____

_____

Length of time it took for water to seep through soil: _____

Amount of water in plastic cup:_____

How much water did the soil absorb? _____

---

Soil Sample #3: _____

Description:_____

_____

Length of time it took for water to seep through soil: _____

Amount of water in plastic cup:_____

How much water did the soil absorb? _____

---

Soil Sample #4: _____

Description:_____

_____

Length of time it took for water to seep through soil: _____

Amount of water in plastic cup:_____

How much water did the soil absorb? _____

Portage & Main Press, 2017 · Hands-On Science and Technology · Grade 3 · ISBN: 978-1-55379-709-8

# How Do You Like Playing With Mud?

Playing with mud might make you dirty, but it can also be a fun learning experience!

1. Read *Mud Puddle* by Robert Munsch.

2. After reading the book, think about the following questions:

   ▪ Have you ever played with mud?

   ▪ Have you jumped into a mud puddle?

   ▪ Have you squished mud through your fingers?

   ▪ Have you ever made things with mud?

3. Draw pictures of three different ways you could have fun with mud. Record a sentence with each drawing to describe your picture.

Portage & Main Press, 2017 · *Hands-On Science and Technology · Grade 3* · ISBN: 978-1-55379-709-8

# How Do Different Soils Affect the Growth of Plants?

**5**

## 21st Century Competencies

**Critical Thinking** and **Communication**:
Students will experiment to see how soil type affects plant growth.

## Materials

- Image Bank: Haudenosaunee Farming (see Appendix, page 442)
- three different types of soil (e.g., potting soil, soil heavy in clay, sandy soil)
- radish, pea, or bean seeds, or other relatively fast-growing seeds
- pots for planting seeds (one for each working group of students)
- small stones
- spoons
- measuring cups or labelled beakers
- masking tape
- chart paper
- markers
- centimetre rulers
- Activity Sheet A: Plant Journal (4.5.1)
- Activity Sheet B: Caring for the Soil (4.5.2)
- Learning-Centre Task Card: Graph Your Results (4.5.3)
- Centimetre Graph Paper (4.5.4)
- drawing and colouring supplies (e.g., pencils, crayons, pencil crayons, pastels)
- graph paper
- rulers
- sticky notes (several colours)
- word splash (from lesson 1)
- Science and Technology Glossary (4.1.4)

## Activate

Display the seeds for students to examine. Ask:

- How would you describe these seeds?
- How could you find out what kinds of plants these seeds will grow into?

Discuss the procedures for plant care. Ask:

- What do seeds need in order to sprout?
- What do plants need in order to grow?
- Do you think the type of soil will make a difference to the way the seeds grow?

Review plant location, and discuss other factors that affect growth, such as temperature and access to sunlight.

Have students examine the three different types of soil. Ask:

- How are these types of soil different from each other?
- How would you describe each soil type?
- How are they similar?
- In which soil do you think the seeds would grow best?
- In which soil do you think the seeds would not grow well?

Encourage students to justify their predictions. Also, discuss the importance of creating a fair test when conducting an experiment. For example, if students wanted to test their predictions, they would want to ensure that only the soil type varied in their samples. As a class, have students brainstorm which variables must be kept constant. This may include:

- amount of soil
- amount of water
- depth of seeds under surface of soil
- amount of light
- amount of heat

Introduce the guided inquiry question: **How do different soils affect the growth of plants?**

## Action: Part One

Organize the class into working groups, and distribute to each group a small pot, some stones, and some seeds. Instruct students to put a few stones at the bottom of their pots for drainage.

▶

Portage & Main Press, 2017 · *Hands-On Science and Technology · Grade 3* · ISBN: 978-1-55379-709-8

Portage & Main Press, 2017 · *Hands-On Science and Technology · Grade 3* · ISBN: 978-1-55379-709-8

Then, have students test their predictions by planting the seeds in their choice of soil. (Ensure all three soil types are used.) Predetermine with students the following:

- how much soil to measure and place into the pot
- how many seeds to plant in the pot
- at what depth to plant the seeds
- where the plants should remain (Help students choose a sunny location that is not next to or above a heater.)
- how much water to add when the soil is dry

**NOTE:** Students may be surprised to learn that seeds do not need sunlight to sprout, but they do need light once the plant emerges from the soil. Initially, the plant may look anemic but will turn green once it is exposed to sunlight.

Distribute a copy of Activity Sheet A: Plant Journal (4.5.1) to each student. While the plants are growing, observe them every few days. Have students use standard units of measure to determine the plants' growth. Also, have students note other changes, recording all observations on the charts. Discuss with students how to measure height (to what point on the plant) and the value of repeating measurements.

**NOTE**: A time-lapse app on a tablet, set to take photos every 30 minutes or so for three to four days, would be a valuable resource for observations and discussion.

For the duration of the experiment, have students use their activity sheets as observation journals. Discuss the growth of the plants in terms of the soil in which each is planted. Have students make comparisons, identifying the best soil in which to grow the plants and ordering the soil types from worst to best. They may discuss more than one criterion when ordering the soil types (e.g., plants that grow the tallest,

plants that have the most leaves). There will be a variety of effects students can observe. It is important to realize that not all plants will be identical, but each will provide valuable information leading to a conclusion about which type of soil is most suitable for plant growth. Ask students why more than one plant must be grown in order to get useful results from the experiment.

**NOTE:** While more than one type of soil will enable students to make comparisons, more than one seed in each pot will show multiple trials, which is scientifically appropriate practice.

### Activity Sheet A
Directions to students:

Record the name of the soil type at the top of the chart. Then, record observations about the growth of the plant(s), as well as the date you make each observation (4.5.1).

### Assessment for Learning
Observe students as they measure the growth of their plants to determine if they can measure accurately, using a centimetre ruler. Use the Anecdotal Record sheet, on page 26, to record results.

## Action: Part Two

As a class, learn about the Haudenosaunee techniques for preparing soil and keeping it healthy for plant growth. Display Image Bank: Haudenosaunee Farming. Have students examine each picture and describe their observations. Record these observations on chart paper.

Provide each student with a copy of Activity Sheet B: Caring for the Soil (4.5.2). Read the sheet as a class, taking time to discuss details and make connections to the pictures from the Image Bank. Have students illustrate the activity sheet, using the images for reference.

# 5

**Activity Sheet B**

Directions for Students:

Read about how the Haudenosaunee cared for the soil. Draw illustrations to match each paragraph (4.5.2).

## Learning Centre

At the learning centre, provide pencils, rulers, different-coloured sticky notes, scrap paper, a copy of the Learning-Centre Task Card: Graph Your Results (4.5.3), and copies of the Centimetre Graph Paper (4.5.4).

Have students create graphs to show the growth of their plants. Then, ask them to record, on sticky notes, three questions classmates can answer by reading their graph. Tell students to use all student graphs displayed at the centre to draw conclusions about the types of soil that are best and worst for growing indoor plants. Have students record these conclusions on the reverse side of their graphs. Also, ask them to answer questions posed by classmates (on their own graphs), recording the answers on sticky notes.

## Consolidate and Debrief

- Revisit the guided inquiry question: **How do different soils affect the growth of plants?** Have students share their knowledge, provide examples, and ask further inquiry questions.
- Add to the class word splash as students learn new concepts, answer some of their own inquiry questions, and ask new inquiry questions.
- Add new terms and illustrations to the class word wall. Include the words in other languages, as appropriate.
- Have students add new terms and definitions, as well as sentences that include the terms, to their Science and

Technology Glossary (4.1.4). When possible, encourage students to use the words in other languages, including Indigenous languages, reflective of the class population.

## Enhance

- Give students pure clay, sand, and humus. Have them develop their own recipe for ideal soil. Then, grow some plants and compare to the results found in the experiment above.
- Explore First Nations gardening techniques with the book, *Native American Gardening: Stories, Projects and Recipes for Families*, by Michael J. Caduto and Joseph Bruchac. The book includes cultural and historical information, as well as traditional stories, recipes, and activities about preparing soil, selecting seeds, planting, and harvesting. Invite a horticulturalist to present to the class about the components of a good soil mix.
- Have students investigate how specific plants have specific soil needs. To do this, have them select two different plants and research to determine the kinds of soil in which each grows best. Create a class chart identifying all plants researched according to their preferred soil type.
- Conduct experiments to investigate sprouting seeds without soil. Bean seeds, for example, will sprout on a dampened paper towel inside a plastic bag. Students can examine such seeds as they sprout, and determine what happens if the sprouting plant is not eventually placed in soil. Although the seedling will grow for some time, soil becomes an advantage in terms of providing nutrients, support, and a water source.
- Research hydroponics. Consider visiting a local retailer who sells these products.

▶

Portage & Main Press, 2017 · *Hands-On Science and Technology · Grade 3* · ISBN: 978-1-55379-709-8

**5**

- Take the class on a field trip to a local nursery, or invite someone who works at a local nursery to visit the class and discuss the composition of different types of soils used to grow different types of plants.

- As a class, dig up several weeds in the school yard or surrounding area. Note how easy or difficult it is to pull out or dig up the weeds, and relate this to the type of root system found on the plant. Examine the weeds in terms of their root systems, where they were found, and the type of soil in which they were growing.

- Have students visit local farms to see what types of crops are grown, and in which types of soil each one grows.

- Invite a local farmer into the classroom to talk about the importance of soil in the growing of crops.

- Access the interactive activity, How Different Soils Affect Plant Growth, in the Grade 3, Unit 4 folder of the *Hands-On Interactive for Science and Technology, Grade 3* download. Find this download at: <www.portageandmainpress.com/product/hands-on-interactive-for-science-and-technology-grade-3/>.

- Have students continue their do-it-yourself projects at the Makerspace centre.

**Date:** _____     **Name:** _____

# Plant Journal

Type of soil: _____

| Date | Observations |
|------|--------------|
|      |              |
|      |              |
|      |              |
|      |              |
|      |              |
|      |              |
|      |              |
|      |              |
|      |              |
|      |              |
|      |              |
|      |              |
|      |              |
|      |              |

Portage & Main Press, 2017 · Hands-On Science and Technology · Grade 3 · ISBN: 978-1-55379-709-8

Portage & Main Press, 2017 · Hands-On Science and Technology · Grade 3 · ISBN: 978-1-5379-709-8

Date: _____

Name: _____

# Caring for the Soil

1. The First Nations people who lived in what is now southern Ontario included the five nations of the Haudenosaunee (Iroquois). Traditionally, the Haudenosaunee were mainly farmers who grew corn, beans, and squash, which were grown together and called the Three Sisters.

2. The land was covered with trees, shrubs, and grass, so farmers had to clear it to plant crops. They cleared land by chopping down and then burning the trees. Ashes left on the land helped the soil by providing important nutrients. Farmers used hoes to mix the ash with the soil, which helped the corn, squash, and beans grow.

## Caring for the Soil (continued)

3. The farmers understood that after years of use, soil becomes worn out and crops are not as healthy. They understood that soil needs time to rest so it can build back its nutrients. This is called fallowing. To give fields time to regrow with grass, shrubs, and trees, farmers would move to another area and clear new fields. Years later, they would return to the first field, and give other fields time to regrow.

4. Farmers also kept their fields fertile by composting. They would throw unused plant parts from the beans, squash, and corn back onto the fields. As the plants decayed, they provided nutrients to the soil.

Portage & Main Press, 2017 · Hands-On Science and Technology · Grade 3 · ISBN: 978-1-55379-709-8

# Graph Your Results

1. Use the data from your experiment with plant growth in different soils to construct a bar graph.

2. On three different sticky notes, record three questions that can be answered by reading your graph. Attach the sticky notes to the front of your graph.

3. Use your graph, as well as the other graphs on display at the centre, to draw conclusions about the types of soil that are best and worst for growing plants indoors.

4. On the back of your graph, record three conclusions about the data from the class results and graphs.

5. Look at the graphs made by classmates, and try to answer some of the questions they have asked. You can record your answers on sticky notes.

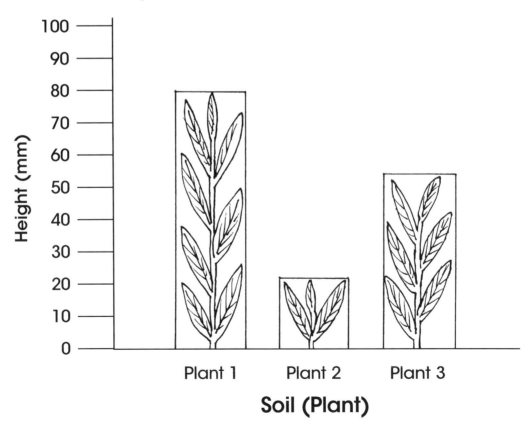

Portage & Main Press, 2017 · Hands-On Science and Technology · Grade 3 · ISBN: 978-1-55379-709-8

**Date:** _____     **Name:** _____

# Centimetre Graph Paper

Portage & Main Press, 2017 · *Hands-On Science and Technology* · *Grade 3* · ISBN: 978-1-55379-709-8

# 6 What Lives in Soil?

## Information for Teachers

Many living things make their home in soil. Some living things, such as earthworms, dig tunnels in the soil. This action allows air and water into the soil, helping plants grow. Worms eat dried-up leaves and dirt, as well. When they consume dirt, it passes through their bodies leaving rich, fertile nutrients behind. Other living things that live in soil include various insects, cutworms, and slugs. Soil also has massive amounts of bacteria, which is crucial for healthy soil. There can be up to one ton of bacteria per acre of soil.

## 21st Century Competencies

**Critical Thinking**, **Communication**, and **Creativity**: Students will examine soil samples to discover what living things can be observed. They will then communicate their learning in various ways, including designing and drawing a mural to show living things in the soil.

## Materials

- chart paper
- markers
- *Diary of a Worm* by Doreen Cronin
- newspaper
- computers/tablets with Internet access
- garden trowels
- trays or basins
- shovels
- large, paper bags
- containers of water (e.g., large, empty milk jugs)
- magnifying glasses
- digital cameras
- books and Internet resources about soil and its inhabitants (e.g., earthworms, snails, ants, centipedes)
- materials for constructing natural environments for living things (e.g., small aquariums, fishbowls, or other transparent containers; various soil samples; plants; soil animals [e.g., worms]; rocks)
- Activity Sheet: What Living Things Are Found in Soil? (4.6.1)
- Learning-Centre Task Card: Living in Soil (4.6.2)
- word splash (from lesson 1)
- Science and Technology Glossary (4.1.4)

## Activate

**NOTE:** Select a site for a field trip where students can investigate soil samples and organic things that live in the soil (e.g., local park, forest, green space).

Explain to students that they will be taking a field trip to investigate living things found in soil. Ask:

- What types of living things do you think you will see?

Record answers on chart paper. Ask:

- Will all these things be alive?
- Why will some of these things be dead, but still in the soil?

Before the field trip, read and discuss the book *Diary of a Worm* by Doreen Cronin.

Introduce the guided inquiry question: **What lives in soil?**

## Action

On the field trip, organize the class into small working groups, and provide each group with a garden trowel; a shovel; a tray or basin; a large, paper bag; a magnifying glass; and a digital camera. Have each group dig a deep hole in the ground, and spread out the extracted soil on a tray or in a basin, so organisms can be more easily spotted. As students dig, have them look for animals (e.g., worms, insects, spiders). Ask students to collect, if possible, some of the soil and animals and place them into their bags, or take a picture of what they find.

Portage & Main Press, 2017 · Hands-On Science and Technology · Grade 3 · ISBN: 978-1-55379-709-8

**6**

Once students have dug down about 30 centimetres, draw their attention to the sides of the holes they have dug. Ask:

■ What do you notice about the soil as you get deeper into the ground?
■ Does the colour of the soil change?
■ Does the texture of the soil change?
■ Is the soil wetter or drier the farther down you dig?
■ Is it harder or easier to dig?

Next, have students pour some water into the hole and observe. Ask:

■ Does any of the soil float?
■ Which parts?
■ Where do you think the water goes?

If possible, repeat the activity at another site so students can draw comparisons.

Back in the classroom, ask students to describe all the different living things they saw when they dug in the soil/dirt. Examine the photos taken during the field trip. Also, have students empty their samples onto newspaper and use magnifying glasses to examine the soil samples and look for any living things still in the soil. Have students identify the living things (if they know the names), or describe them. Give students the opportunity to photograph what they find in their soil samples. Ask:

■ What living things are in your soil sample?
■ How can you describe them?
■ How do they help soil?

Distribute a copy of Activity Sheet: What Living Things Are Found in Soil? (4.6.1) to each student. Tell students to use the activity sheet to describe and draw diagrams of the living things they have observed. Have them conduct additional research to identify animals, or other organic matter, by name if they would like, and to determine the organisms' roles in the soil or describe other interesting facts.

**Activity Sheet**

Directions to students:

Describe and draw diagrams of each living thing you found in the soil. If you want, research to identify the names or any other details of living things you have found. You can also print any photos you have taken, and attach them to Activity Sheet (4.6.1).

## Learning Centre

At the learning centre, provide a copy of the Learning-Centre Task Card: Living in Soil (4.6.2), access to books and Internet resources related to soil and its inhabitants (e.g., earthworms, snails, ants, centipedes), and materials for constructing natural environments for some of these living things (e.g., small aquariums, fishbowls, or other transparent containers; various soil samples; plants; soil animals such as worms; rocks). Have students do research to learn more about the habitats of these living things and then use the materials to recreate their natural environment.

**NOTE:** Ensure resources cover a variety of reading levels to engage all learners.

**Assessment of Learning**

Interview students to find out how they recreated natural environments for the living things found in soil, and why they used the materials they did. Use the Individual Student Observations sheet, on page 27, to record results.

## Consolidate and Debrief

■ Revisit the guided inquiry question: **What lives in soil?** Have students share their knowledge, provide examples, and ask further inquiry questions.

Portage & Main Press, 2017 · *Hands-On Science and Technology · Grade 3* · ISBN: 978-1-55379-709-8

**6**

- Add to the class word splash as students learn new concepts, answer some of their own inquiry questions, and ask new inquiry questions.

- Add new terms and illustrations to the class word wall. Include the words in other languages, as appropriate.

- Have students add new terms and definitions, as well as sentences that include the terms, to their Science and Technology Glossary (4.1.4). When possible, encourage students to use the words in other languages, including Indigenous languages, reflective of the class population.

## Enhance

- Have students use various references to identify the names of the living things found in their soil samples. Ask each student to select one living thing to research. Tell students to include a diagram and/or a photo, as well as written information in their reports. Encourage them to determine how the living thing affects the soil or the plants that live in the soil. Collect students' research reports, and bind them together in a class book called *Creepy Crawlies and Other Living Things Found in Soil*. Display the book in the classroom or school library.

- Have students investigate earthworms in greater detail (e.g., they can use a magnifying glass to look at the segments on a worm's body, observe how worms move through soil, design experiments to determine what worms eat).

- Using an aquarium or a wood box, raise a worm farm so students can study why earthworms are the "mixers and shredders" of soil.

- Explain, or have students research, why earthworm casts improve the nutrients in soil and indicate healthy soil.

- Have students design and draw a mural of life underground. Encourage them to incorporate all the different living things they found during their soil investigation.

- Access the interactive activity, Investigating Living Things Found in Soil, in the Grade 3, Unit 4 folder of the ***Hands-On Interactive for Science and Technology, Grade 3*** download. Find this download at: <www.portageandmainpress.com/product/ hands-on-interactive-for-science-and- technology-grade-3/>.

- Have students continue their do-it-yourself projects at the Makerspace centre.

# What Livings Things Are Found in Soil?

| Diagram | Description |
|---|---|
|  | _____ <br> _____ <br> _____ <br> _____ |
|  | _____ <br> _____ <br> _____ <br> _____ |
|  | _____ <br> _____ <br> _____ <br> _____ |
|  | _____ <br> _____ <br> _____ <br> _____ |

Portage & Main Press, 2017 · Hands-On Science and Technology · Grade 3 · ISBN: 978-1-55379-709-8

# Living in Soil

Create a home for some living things that are found in soil (e.g., earthworms, snails, ants, centipedes).

1. Think about what the animals that live in soil need to stay alive. Conduct research to learn more.

2. Use an aquarium or another clear container to recreate the natural environment of these animals.

3. Fill the container with soil, plants, rocks, and other things you think the living things need to survive.

4. Write a paragraph describing the environment you have created, and the living and nonliving things in it.

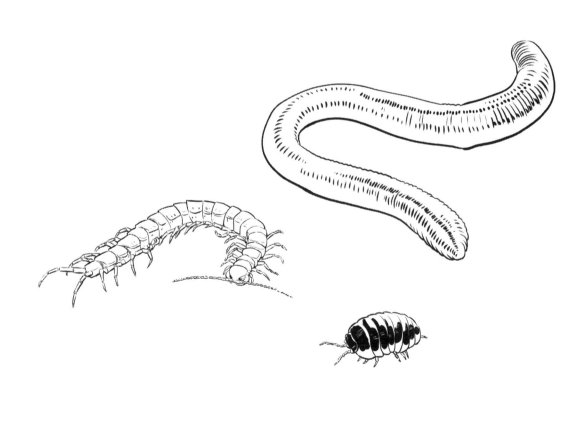

Portage & Main Press, 2017 · Hands-On Science and Technology · Grade 3 · ISBN: 978-1-55379-709-8

# 7 | How Does Rainfall Affect Soil?

## 21ˢᵗ Century Competencies

**Communication, Citizenship, Character**:
Students will explore soil erosion, and consider
ways to protect this resource.

## Materials

- patch of grass
- garden bed (on school grounds or local area
  where you have permission to conduct this
  activity)
- watering can
- spray bottle
- water
- *Peace Dancer* by Roy Henry Vickers and
  Robert Budd
- *Watakame's Journey: The Huichol Myth of
  the Great Flood and the New World* by Hallie
  N. Love
- *The Mud Family* by Betsy James
- *The Hopi: A True Book* by Andrew Santella
- Activity Sheet: Soil Erosion (4.7.1)
- word splash (from lesson 1)
- Science and Technology Glossary (4.1.4)

## Activate

Conduct a rainfall sound effects activity. Ask
students to imagine a rainstorm is coming, and
to follow your actions to "hear" the storm. Have
students sit in a semi-circle, with their hands
on their laps, and explain that when you walk
in front of them, they are to follow your action.
Begin at one end of the semi-circle, doing each
action, and having the students directly in front
of you begin that action, and continue it until you
are in front of them again.

Start by rubbing your hands together. Move
slowly from one end of the semi-circle to the
other, and have students join you in the action.
Once you are at the opposite end of the semi-
circle, move to the start again, and begin a
new action.

Encourage students to be silent, to watch you
carefully, and to listen to the sounds of
the rainstorm.

Do each of the following actions, and continue
doing it until it has propagated across the room:

- rub hands together
- snap fingers
- clap hands
- slap thighs
- stomp feet
- slap thighs
- clap hands
- snap fingers
- rub hands together
- hands on lap

The effect of these actions sound like a
rainstorm sweeping in and then passing by. After
completing the activity, have students share their
observations and experience with rainstorms.

Introduce the guided inquiry question: **How
does rainfall affect soil?**

## Action: Part One

Take students to a garden bed on school
property or in the local community. Ask students:

- What do you think will happen when I spray
  water from the spray bottle onto the soil?

Have students share their predictions.

Spray water from the spray bottle onto the soil.
Have students examine the soil closely and
discuss their observations.

Next, ask students:

- What do you think will happen when I pour
  water from the watering can onto the soil?

Have students share their predictions.

▶

Portage & Main Press, 2017 · *Hands-On Science and Technology · Grade 3* · ISBN: 978-1-55379-709-8

Pour water quickly from the watering can onto the soil. Have students take a close look at the soil and discuss their observations. Ask:

- Based on the results from our investigations, what do you think the effects of a light rain shower would be on soil?
- What do you think the results of a heavy rain downpour would be on soil?
- How would living things in the soil be affected by a light rain shower?
- How would living things in the soil be affected by a heavy rain downpour?
- What might happen to your garden or a farmer's field during a heavy rainstorm?

Have students share their ideas and background knowledge/experiences.

## Action: Part Two

Have students from a circle around a patch of grass in the school yard. Ensure students take a close look at the grass before you start the experiment. Ask:

- What do you think will happen when I spray the grass with the water from the spray bottle?

Have students share their predictions.

Spray water from the spray bottle onto the grass. Once students have looked at the grass closely, have them share their observations.

Next, ask students:

- What do you think will happen when I pour water from the watering can onto the grass?

Have students share their predictions.

Pour water quickly from the watering can onto the grass. Have students take a close look at the grass and then share their observations.

## Action: Part Three

Back in the classroom, compare the two investigations. Ask:

- Did the water have a greater effect on the grass or the bare soil?
- Why do you think this is?
- How can we use this new knowledge to protect soil?

As a class, discuss soil erosion and efforts to reduce soil erosion.

Divide the class into working groups and provide each group with Activity Sheet: Soil Erosion (4.7.1). Have the groups conduct research on soil erosion by watching online videos, and reviewing websites and print resources, then use this information to complete the activity sheet.

### Activity Sheet
Directions to students:

Use the sheet to record your research on soil erosion. Include labelled diagrams and writing, and record the names of the resources you used. (4.7.1)

## Action: Part Four

As a class, explore Indigenous stories of how rainfall affects soil and daily life. Have a local Elder or Métis Senator share stories and traditional knowledge on this topic.

Also, read related books, such as the following:

- *Peace Dancer* by Roy Henry Vickers and Robert Budd, tells the story of the Potlach, which came about after rainstorms flooded the Earth.
- *Watakame's Journey: The Huichol Myth of the Great Flood and the New World* by Hallie N. Love, a retelling of the traditional story of creation through colourful yarn paintings.

Portage & Main Press, 2017 · *Hands-On Science and Technology · Grade 3* · ISBN: 978-1-55379-709-8

- *The Mud Family* by Betsy James is set among the ancient Anasazi of the Southwest. In this fictional story, a young girl named Sosi and her family experience a difficult time when a summer drought dries up their cornfields.

- *The Hopi: A True Book* by Andrew Santella tells of the origin and geographic location of the Hopi who have resided in the desert lands of the American Southwest for generations. Their reservation is located in northeastern Arizona and the geographic region receives little rain. The book describes the unique cultural traditions of the Hopi including their foods and agriculture.

## Consolidate and Debrief

- Revisit the guided inquiry question: **How does rainfall affect soil?** Have students share their knowledge, provide examples, and ask further inquiry questions.

- Add to the class word splash as students learn new concepts, answer some of their own inquiry questions, and ask new inquiry questions.

- Add new terms and illustrations to the class word wall. Include the words in other languages, as appropriate.

- Have students add new terms and definitions, as well as sentences that include the terms, to their Science and Technology Glossary (4.1.4). When possible, encourage students to use the words in other languages, including Indigenous languages, reflective of the class population.

## Enhance

- Conduct investigations on other natural events (e.g., wind, ice storms) and their effects on soil.

- Have students investigate how different landforms (e.g., waterfalls, canyons, mountains) have been affected by natural events.

- Take students on a walk around the neighbourhood after a rainstorm. Have them observe the effects of the rainstorm on different surface areas (e.g., asphalt, grass, a creek, a garden bed).

- Conduct research on how soil erosion has affected farming communities in different regions of the world, and the techniques being used to save this important resource.

- Access the interactive activity, Effects of Rainfall on Surfaces, in the Grade 3, Unit 4 folder of the ***Hands-On Interactive for Science and Technology, Grade 3*** download. Find this download at: <www.portageandmainpress.com/product/hands-on-interactive-for-science-and-technology-grade-3/>.

- Have students continue their do-it-yourself projects at the Makerspace centre.

Portage & Main Press, 2017 · *Hands-On Science and Technology · Grade 3* · ISBN: 978-1-55379-709-8

# Soil Erosion

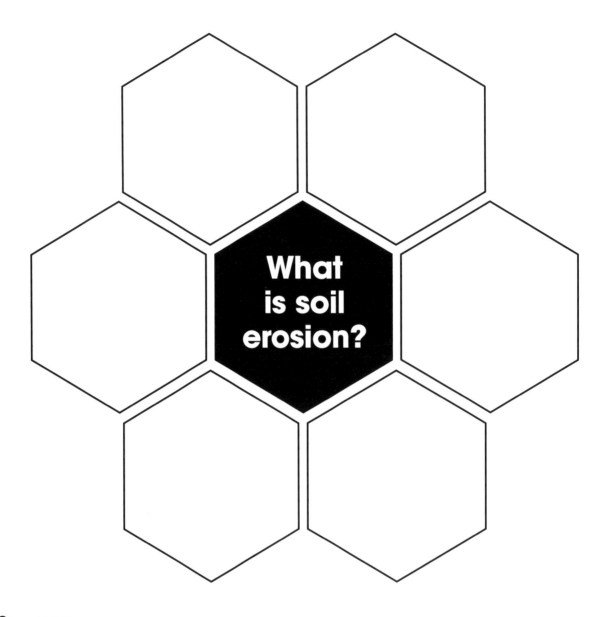

**What is soil erosion?**

Sources:

_____

_____

_____

_____

Portage & Main Press, 2017 · Hands-On Science and Technology · Grade 3 · ISBN: 978-1-55379-709-8

# 8 | How Can Organic Materials Be Recycled?

## 21st Century Competencies

**Critical Thinking**, **Communication**, and **Citizenship**: Students will research composting, and then design and construct their own composter. Students will learn the importance of composting organic material, instead of allowing it to enter other waste streams, such as a landfill.

## Materials

- reference materials about compost (e.g., Internet resources, books, brochures)
- shovel or trowel
- soil
- various containers for building compost bins (e.g., large plastic containers, large jars, large wooden boxes)
- other materials specified by students for building compost bins
- organic household or school garbage (e.g., fruit and vegetable remains, grass clippings, garden plants, eggshells, leaves, coffee grounds)
- chart paper
- markers
- paper
- computers/tablets with Internet access
- audio- or video-recording device
- completed Activity Sheet B: Caring for the Soil (4.5.2) (from lesson 5)
- Activity Sheet: Designing a Simple Composter (4.8.1)
- Learning-Centre Task Card: Compost Jingle (4.8.2)
- word splash (from lesson 1)
- Science and Technology Glossary (4.1.4)

## Activate

Review the various types of soil studied and investigated throughout the unit. Ask:

- What kinds of soil can you name?

- Which types of soil are good for a vegetable garden?
- What could you add to the soil to make it more fertile for growing plants?
- What is humus?
- What is humus made of?
- Can you think of a way you could make your own humus?
- What is compost?
- Have you ever seen a compost pile?
- What kinds of organic materials can be added to compost?
- What kinds of materials should not be added to compost?
- How did the Haudenosaunee farmers compost?

Review completed Activity Sheet B: Caring for the Soil (4.5.2) from lesson 5. Discuss how these Indigenous farmers enriched their soil by composting.

Introduce and discuss with students the term *organic*. Determine which plant and/or animal waste is suitable organic waste for a composter. For example, you would put cucumber skins in a composter but not chicken skins.

Introduce the guided inquiry question: **How can organic materials be recycled?**

## Action: Part One

Discuss the value of composting. Ask:

- Why do people compost?

Have students share their ideas. Explain that people often build their own compost heaps so they can produce fertile topsoil or humus for their gardens.

Have students explore various reference materials (e.g., Internet resources, books, brochures) to determine different ways of making a composter. As a class, identify common steps. Title a sheet of

▶

Portage & Main Press, 2017 · *Hands-On Science and Technology · Grade 3* · ISBN: 978-1-55379-709-8

Portage & Main Press, 2017 · Hands-On Science and Technology · Grade 3 · ISBN: 978-1-55379-709-8

chart paper "Directions for Making a Composter," and display these steps.

**Directions for Making a Composter**

1. Shovel a layer of soil into a container.
2. Add a layer of organic waste (e.g., grass clippings, leaves, vegetable peelings, fruit cores, pits and seeds, water).
3. Cover the organic waste with another layer of soil, and mix. This helps control bugs and smell.
4. Leave the composter outside where the rain will keep it moist.
5. Keep adding soil and organic waste. Mix every time you add to your compost.
6. In about two months, humus will be produced, which can be used to enrich soil.

## Action: Part Two

Discuss the various kinds of composters students researched in the previous activity. Explain they will now have an opportunity to design and construct their own composters. Co-construct criteria for an effective composter, with students. For example:

■ decomposes organic material reasonably quickly
■ produces minimal odour
■ does not attract nuisance animals
■ recycled materials used in its design

Organize students into pairs or groups of three, and have the groups use technological problem solving to design and construct their own simple composters. Provide students with materials as requested (e.g., containers [large jars, boxes, plastic containers], leaves, garden plants, food waste [fruit and vegetable peels, skins, tops; eggshells; coffee grounds], soil). Also, distribute a copy of Activity Sheet: Designing a Simple Composter (4.8.1) to each student, and have students record the project criteria on it, as well as their composter designs.

**Activity Sheet**

Directions to students:

Create a plan for a composter that meets the criteria established by the class. Draw and label your design. Once it is approved by the teacher, use the available materials to create your composter. Draw a labelled diagram of your completed design. Note the differences between your first design and the actual composter (4.8.1).

**NOTE:** This is a two-page activity sheet.

## Action: Part Three

Have students test and compare their composters to determine their effectiveness. Together with the class, agree on organic materials to decompose in the composters, and the amount of material to use, as well as a period of time, so the variables are consistent from composter to composter.

Over time, and based on students' observations, provide time for discussion related to the factors that speed up decomposition, by comparing and contrasting the various composters.

When the humus is ready to use, encourage students to mix it with soil for plants in the classroom, for a school garden, or for houseplants and gardens at home.

### Assessment as Learning
Have students complete the Cooperative Skills Self-Assessment sheet, on page 34, to reflect on their ability to work together to design and construct a composter.

### Assessment of Learning
Use the Cooperative Skills Teacher-Assessment sheet, on page 37, to assess each student as they work on the technological problem-solving project of building a simple composter.

**8**

## Learning Centre

At the learning centre, include an audio- or video- recording device, paper, and pencils, along with a copy of the Learning-Centre Task Card: Compost Jingle (4.8.2). Have students write jingles (or songs) about composting. Tell them to include in their jingles why composting is good for the environment.

## Consolidate and Debrief

- Revisit the guided inquiry question: **How can organic materials be recycled?** Have students share their knowledge, provide examples, and ask further inquiry questions.

- Add to the class word splash as students learn new concepts, answer some of their own inquiry questions, and ask new inquiry questions.

- Add new terms, including *organic*, and illustrations to the class word wall. Include the words in other languages, as appropriate.

- Have students add new terms and definitions, as well as sentences that include the terms, to their Science and Technology Glossary (4.1.4). When possible, encourage students to use the words in other languages, including Indigenous languages, reflective of the class population.

## Enhance

- Show students the video *What Is Backyard Composting?* ("Compost Kids." Hamilton County Recycling, 4:04), found at: <www.youtube.com/watch?v=Njbn34JrKnE>.

- Challenge students to share their knowledge about composting by creating posters or brochures to encourage members of the local community to compost.

- If you do not have a school compost program in effect, consider having students organize one. Place plastic buckets in classrooms (or lunchrooms) with the word "Compost" clearly marked. Once students are knowledgeable about the process and purpose of composting, have them visit classrooms to teach other students about the importance of composting, and to introduce the composting program. Encourage students to make posters to advertise the new program.

- Have students write letters to local government officials responsible for the environment, to request information about composting programs.

- Set up a vermicomposter (worm composter) to investigate how these living things affect decomposition. Usually vermicomposters use a small earthworm called a red wiggler, which create compost quickly. Worms can be purchased online at <www.gardeningknowhow.com/composting/vermicomposting/worms-for-vermicomposting.htm> or <www.cathyscomposters.com/>.

- Invite a local environmental group (e.g., conservation district) to work with students on vermiculture.

- Compare different types of soils to identify decomposers. Fill two containers with soil— one with sterilized potting soil and the other with soil from a local garden. Moisten both with water, and place lettuce leaves on top of each type of soil. The lettuce leaves in the container of garden soil should decompose faster because of the living things within the soil. The sterilized potting soil has no living things in it to speed up the decomposition process.

- Visit a local mushroom farm to learn about the importance of compost in the production of mushrooms.

▶

Portage & Main Press, 2017 · *Hands-On Science and Technology · Grade 3* · ISBN: 978-1-55379-709-8

**8**

- Have a class discussion about composting as it relates to Indigenous worldviews. Traditionally, Indigenous peoples have understood the importance of replenishing nutrients in the soil, such as spreading plants, fish bones, or other animal parts back on the land. Invite a local Elder or MétisSenator into the classroom to share stories and traditional knowledge.

- Access the interactive activity, Recycling Organic Materials, in the Grade 3, Unit 4 folder of the **Hands-On Interactive for Science and Technology, Grade 3** download. Find this download at: <www.portageandmainpress.com/product/ hands-on-interactive-for-science-and-technology-grade-3/>.

- Have students continue their do-it-yourself projects at the Makerspace centre.

Portage & Main Press, 2017 · Hands-On Science and Technology · Grade 3 · ISBN: 978-1-55379-709-8

# Designing a Composter

| Criteria | Met or Not Met |
|---|---|
| 1. | |
| 2. | |
| 3. | |
| 4. | |

**Design:**

**Materials Needed:**

Portage & Main Press, 2017 · Hands-On Science and Technology · Grade 3 · ISBN: 978-1-5537-709-8

**Date:** _____     **Name:** _____

## Designing a Composter (continued)

Final Product:

Did your final design change from the original?   YES   NO

Reasons why the final design changed:

What did you learn while using technological problem solving to make a composter?

What questions do you still have about composting?

Portage & Main Press, 2017 · Hands-On Science and Technology · Grade 3 · ISBN: 978-1-55379-709-8

# Compost Jingle

1. Pretend a local radio station is holding a jingle-writing contest, and any grade-three student can enter! Your task is to write a jingle (or song) about composting.

2. Include in your jingle (or song) why composting is good for the environment, and at least two other interesting composting facts.

3. Use the audio-record device or video-recording device to record your jingle (or song), and be prepared to share your masterpiece with the class!

Portage & Main Press, 2017 · Hands-On Science and Technology · Grade 3 · ISBN: 978-1-55379-709-8

# 9 | How Do Humans Use Earth Materials?

## 21ˢᵗ Century Competencies

**Critical Thinking**, **Communication**, and **Creativity**: Students will learn about items made from clay, and will design products of their own.

## Materials

- pictures (digital or printed) of local items made from earth materials (e.g., metal utensils for eating and cooking, pottery, bricks, jewellry)
- pictures (digital or printed) of items made from earth materials from various other countries and cultures (e.g., sod houses, utensils for eating and cooking, works of art, bricks, jewellry, dikes, sandbags, adobe bricks, soapstone carvings)
- interactive whiteboard or other projection device (optional)
- items made from earth materials (e.g., bricks, pottery, jewellry, metal, concrete)
- index cards
- clay
- rulers
- markers
- Activity Sheet: Clay Creations (4.9.1)
- word splash (from lesson 1)
- Science and Technology Glossary (4.1.4)

## Activate

Provide each student with a small piece of clay. Provide time for them to examine and manipulate the clay. Ask:

- What is this material?
- Where does it come from?
- What is clay used for?

Have the students create a small object from their clay. Ask:

- Why is clay good for moulding objects?
- What characteristics does it have that make it good for this purpose?

- When you are working with clay, what can you do if the clay starts to become dry and hard to work with? (add water)
- What happens to the clay when it hardens? (the water in it evaporates)
- What other ways do potters harden clay? (in an oven)
- What kinds of objects are made from clay?

Introduce the guided inquiry question: **How do humans use earth materials?**

## Action: Part One

As a class, investigate how Indigenous peoples made clay pots. The Haudenosaunee and the Wendat, for example, are well known for their clay pots. The shape and designs on these pots varied over time and by geographical location.

Take a virtual field trip to the Canadian Museum of History. The virtual tour, *Gather Around This Pot,* provides stunning visuals and descriptions of pottery made by Indigenous peoples from across Canada. Go to: <www.historymuseum.ca/cmc/exhibitions/archeo/ceramiq/cerart1e.shtml>.

The virtual exhibit tour can be projected an interactive whiteboard or other projection device, so that the pottery can be discussed and examined together as a class.

## Action: Part Two

Provide an opportunity for students to create more detailed objects from clay. Distribute copies of Activity Sheet: Clay Creations (4.9.1) to each student. Have students use it to record their ideas and process.

### Activity Sheet
Directions to students:

Use the sheet to record your ideas and process in making a clay creation. Use a ruler to measure your object (height, width, depth) and include

Portage & Main Press, 2017 · Hands-On Science and Technology · Grade 3 · ISBN: 978-1-55379-709-8

these measurements on a diagram of your object (4.9.1).

## Action: Part Three

Display the pictures and artifacts of various local items made from earth materials. Ask:

- What is the name of each of these items?
- What is each item used for?
- What do all these items have in common?

Have students share their background knowledge and ideas. Now, display the pictures and artifacts of items made from earth materials from various other countries and cultures. Ask:

Do you recognize any of these items?

- What are they?
- Where in the world would these items be used?
- Do we have items similar to these in Canada?
- Are they made of the same materials in Canada? Why or why not?

As a class, identify the objects made from earth materials (both locally and from other countries/cultures), and record the name of each item on a separate index card. Encourage students to suggest other items not displayed as pictures or artifacts, and record these on separate index cards, as well.

Have students sort the index cards according to two or more attributes. This will lead to discussion about different materials (e.g., rock, stone, clay, gems, metal), as well as other sorting rules such as use (e.g., tool, for building, jewellry) and cultural origin.

## Consolidate and Debrief

- Revisit the guided inquiry question: **How do humans use earth materials?** Have students share their knowledge,

provide examples, and ask further inquiry questions

- Add to the class word splash as students learn new concepts, answer some of their own inquiry questions, and ask new inquiry questions.
- Add new terms, and illustrations to the class word wall. Include the words in other languages, as appropriate.
- Have students add new terms and definitions, as well as sentences that include the terms, to their Science and Technology Glossary (4.1.4). When possible, encourage students to use the words in other languages, including Indigenous languages, reflective of the class population.

## Enhance

- Visit or invite into the classroom a local potter or artist so students can see how clay and pottery items are made.
- Have students cut out from magazines and newspapers pictures of items that are made of earth materials. They can also find pictures online to print and cut out. Then, have students use the pictures to make collages.
- Have students create their own works of art from clay.
- Have students research the environmental impact of extracting clay from raw soil and processing it into a material that can be used for pottery. Local potters can also share their techniques for gathering clay.
- Have students compare how houses were historically built from earth materials to how they are built from earth materials today (sod versus brick house). Ask students to present their ideas or designs to the rest of the class.
- Have students continue their do-it-yourself projects at the Makerspace centre.

Portage & Main Press, 2017 · Hands-On Science and Technology · Grade 3 · ISBN: 978-1-55379-709-8

# Clay Creations

What object did you create? _____

_____

Describe the steps you used to create this object.

_____

_____

_____

_____

_____

Draw a diagram of your object, and show its measurements:

```



```

Why is clay a good earth material for creating objects?

_____

_____

Portage & Main Press, 2017 · Hands-On Science and Technology · Grade 3 · ISBN: 978-1-55379-709-8

# Inquiry Project: What More Can We Learn About Products Made From Earth Materials?

**10**

## 21st Century Competencies

**Critical Thinking**, **Communication**, **Character**, **Citizenship**, and **Creativity**: Students will research how an item made from earth materials is manufactured. They may also explore the environmental costs of extracting the raw materials needed to make the product.

## Materials

- index cards from lesson 9 (with names of objects made from earth materials)
- pictures (digital or printed) of local items made from earth materials (e.g., metal utensils for eating and cooking, pottery, bricks, jewellry)
- pictures (digital or printed) of items made from earth materials from various countries and cultures (e.g., sod houses, utensils for eating and cooking, works of art, bricks, jewellry, dikes, sandbags, adobe bricks, soapstone carvings)
- items made from earth materials (e.g., bricks, pottery, jewellry, metal, concrete)
- research materials (e.g., nonfiction books, brochures, bookmarked Internet sites) about earth materials used to make products
- computers/tablets with Internet access
- chart paper
- markers
- scissors
- stapler and staples
- index cards
- audio- or video-recording device
- Activity Sheet: A: What Object in My Home Is Made of Materials From the Earth? (4.10.1)
- Activity Sheet: B: Inquiry Research Project Outline (4.10.2)
- Learning-Centre Task Card A: Reflecting on My Inquiry Project (4.10.3)
- Learning-Centre Task Card B: Unearth the Mystery! (4.10.4)
- Information Sheet: Earth Objects and Materials (4.10.5)
- word splash (from lesson 1)
- Science and Technology Glossary (4.1.4)

## Activate

Review the index cards from the previous lesson, and have students examine the items made from earth materials. Ask:

- From what materials are these items made?

List these materials on chart paper (e.g., soil, clay, metal, glass, rock, stone, gems). Point out that all of these materials come from the Earth. Ask students:

- Do you have items at home that are made of materials from the Earth?

Have students share ideas about items they have at home that are made from earth materials.

Distribute a copy of Activity Sheet A: What Object in My Home Is Made of Materials From the Earth? (4.10.1) to each student. Have students take the activity sheet home and complete it with family members.

**NOTE:** Along with the completed activity sheet, students can bring to school the actual object from home or a photograph of it (to attach to the sheet), or they can draw a picture or diagram of the object on the activity sheet.

Once students have completed and returned their activity sheets, have them share their items/pictures with the rest of the class.

Introduce the guided inquiry question: **What more can we learn about products made from earth materials?**

### Activity Sheet A

Directions to students:

Choose an item from home that is made from earth materials. Answer the questions, then bring the activity sheet back to school to share with the class (4.10.1).

▶

Portage & Main Press, 2017 · *Hands-On Science and Technology* · *Grade 3* · ISBN: 978-1-55379-709-8

**10**

## Action

Have students research one item made from (an) earth material(s). As a class, co-construct criteria for the research project. For example:

- identifies the earth material(s) used in the item
- describes how the item is made
- describes how the item is used
- includes answers to inquiry questions in written and picture form

Distribute a copy of Activity Sheet B: Inquiry Research Project Outline (4.10.2) to each student, and have students record the research project criteria on it.

Have students select one of the items made from earth materials to research. Tell students they may work individually or in pairs on this project. Begin by having students brainstorm a list of questions they have about their selected item and recording these on the activity sheet.

Review the research outline with students, provide research materials for students to use, and support them as they look for relevant information about their research topics.

Once students have finished their research, have them display their findings in a way that they choose (e.g., poster, song, puppet show, game, PowerPoint presentation). Display the completed research projects in the classroom or the school library. Later, have students present their projects to the rest of the class.

### Activity Sheet B
Directions to students:
Choose one object made from an earth material. Record the research project criteria, as well as questions you have about the object. Find the answers to at least two of the questions provided and two of your own questions (4.10.2).

**NOTE:** This is a two-page activity sheet.

## Assessment of Learning

Have students present their inquiry projects to the rest of the class. Use the Rubric, on page 36, to record the project criteria and the results as students present their projects.

## Learning Centre One

At the learning centre, display the co-constructed criteria for the inquiry project: How do humans use earth materials? Also, provide an audio- or video-recording device and a copy of the Learning-Centre Task Card A: Reflecting on My Inquiry Project (4.10.3). Have students record their thoughts on how they met the criteria for this project. Have them bring their projects with them to the centre when they are completing this self-reflection.

## Learning Centre Two

At the learning centre, provide a copy of the Learning-Centre Task Card B: Unearth the Mystery! (4.10.4). Tell students they are going to play a game show called "Unearth the Mystery!"

Before students visit the centre to play the game, have each create three questions to be used in the game: a 100-point question, a 200-point question, and a 500-point question. The answer to each question should be either an object made from an earth material (e.g., brick, sandbag) or a material found in the Earth (e.g., diamond, clay). For example: The wolf from "The Three Little Pigs" could not blow down this house. What did the pig use to build the house? (Answer: Bricks—100 points).

To each student, distribute three index cards and a copy of the Information Sheet: Earth Objects and Materials (4.10.5), which students can look at for ideas. Tell students to record each of their questions on one of the index cards and record the answer on the back.

Portage & Main Press, 2017 · *Hands-On Science and Technology · Grade 3* · ISBN: 978-1-55379-709-8

**Hands-On Science and Technology** · Grade 3

Once all students have created their questions, place all of the game cards they have created at the learning centre.

Have groups of four to five students play the game together at the centre. Ask students to choose one member of the group to be the host. The host will select one card and read the question on it to one of the other players. For the next round, have a new host ask a different player a question. (To help students keep track of turns, tell them to sit in a circle at the centre, and rotate the roles of host and contestant with the players—the contestant from the preceding round can be the host for the next round.) If the contestant gets the answer right, they keeps the question card until the end of the game. Once each student has had an opportunity to answer three questions, the game is over. Tell students to add up the points on the question cards they answered correctly; the player with the highest score wins.

### Assessment as Learning

Have students complete the 21st Century Competencies Student/Teacher Reflection sheet, on page 33, to reflect on their use of the 21st Century Competencies throughout the unit. Students record their reflections in the squares. The sheet also includes oval spaces for teachers to provide descriptive feedback to students.

## Consolidate and Debrief

- Revisit the guided inquiry question: **What more can we learn about products made from earth materials?**
- Have students share their knowledge, provide examples, and ask further inquiry questions.
- Review the class word splash and the class word wall created for the unit.

- Have students cut apart and alphabetize their Science and Technology Glossary (4.1.4) words, make title pages, and bind the pages together to create vocabulary booklets related to soils in the environment.

## Enhance

- Have students complete their do-it-yourself projects at the Makerspace centre.

Portage & Main Press, 2017 · *Hands-On Science and Technology · Grade 3* · ISBN: 978-1-55379-709-8

# What Object in My Home Is Made of Materials From the Earth?

Object: _____

Diagram or picture of the object:

[ ]

Which earth material is used to make the object? _____

_____

Why is this a good material for making this object? _____

_____

_____

What is the object used for? _____

_____

What else do you know about this object?_____

_____

_____

Portage & Main Press, 2017 · Hands-On Science and Technology · Grade 3 · ISBN: 978-1-55379-709-8

# Inquiry Research Project Outline

Project Criteria:

_____

_____

_____

_____

The object made from earth material I have chosen to research is:

_____ .

Questions I have about the object made from earth materials:

_____

_____

_____

Other possible questions to research (choose at least two):

1. Which country/culture does the earth material object come from?

2. Which earth material is used to make the object?

3. How is the raw material extracted from the Earth?

4. How is the environment affected by extracting the raw materials?

5. Why is this a good material for making this object?

6. How is the object made?

7. What is the object used for?

Portage & Main Press, 2017 · Hands-On Science and Technology · Grade 3 · ISBN: 978-1-55379-709-8

# Inquiry Research Project Outline (continued)

With your research project you may also include:

1. a model or diagram of the earth material object

2. a map of the country where the earth material object is found or made

3. a list of resources used in your research

Once the research is complete, choose a way to display your findings:

| | | | |
|---|---|---|---|
| ☐ song/rap | ☐ oral report | ☐ written report | ☐ journal |
| ☐ play/skit/ role play | ☐ poem | ☐ advertisement | ☐ bulletin board |
| | ☐ photo essay | ☐ picture book | ☐ pop-up book |
| ☐ diorama | ☐ dance | ☐ puppet show | ☐ interview |
| ☐ slide show | ☐ riddles | ☐ radio program | ☐ graphic chart |
| ☐ pamphlet/ brochure | ☐ video | ☐ news report | ☐ other: |

Portage & Main Press, 2017 · Hands-On Science and Technology · Grade 3 · ISBN: 978-1-55379-709-8

# Reflecting on My Inquiry Project

1. Review the criteria for the inquiry project.

2. Examine your own project.

   ■ How did you meet each of the criterion?

3. Record your reflections using the audio- or video-recording device.

Portage & Main Press, 2017 · *Hands-On Science and Technology* · Grade 3 · ISBN: 978-1-55379-709-8

# Unearth the Mystery!

Welcome to the game show *Unearth the Mystery!* Today, you are a contestant on the show!

1. Put all game cards into a pile.

2. Choose a game host and a contestant (take turns for each round).

   Host: Select a card from the pile, and read the question to the contestant (be sure to hide the answer on the back).

3. If the contestant answers the question correctly, they receive the point value for that question (and keeps the card until the end of the game, to keep track of points scored).

4. Rotate roles, having two different students act as host and contestant (or the host from the last round can move to contestant, and a new student is the host).

5. Repeat.

6. When every contestant has been asked and has tried to answer three questions of different values, the game is over. Add up all contestants' points to find out who wins the game.

Portage & Main Press, 2017 · Hands-On Science and Technology · Grade 3 · ISBN: 978-1-55379-709-8

# Earth Objects and Materials

| Objects | Materials |
|---|---|
| driveway | concrete or asphalt |
| brick | clay |
| stainless steel sink | nickel or chrome |
| plumbing pipe | copper |
| fertilizer | potash |
| countertop | granite |
| coins (quarters, dimes, nickels, pennies) | steel, nickel, and copper |
| Olympic medals | bronze, silver, gold plate |
| pottery | clay |
| jewellery | silver, gold |
| patio blocks | concrete |
| carvings | soapstone |
| arrowheads | stone |
| magnets | iron |
| nails and screws | steel |

Portage & Main Press, 2017 · Hands-On Science and Technology · Grade 3 · ISBN: 978-1-55379-709-8

# References

Ashbrook, Peggy. *Science Learning in the Early Years*. Arlington, VA: NSTA Press Book, 2016.

Bang, Molly, and Penny Chisholm. *Living Sunlight: How Plants Bring the Earth to Life*. New York: Blue Sky Press, 2009.

Bosak, Susan. *Science Is...* Richmond Hill, ON: Scholastic, 1991.

Bourgeois, Paulette. *The Amazing Dirt Book*. Toronto: Kids Can Press, 1990.

Brown, Harriet. *Food From the Sun: How Plants Live and Grow*. Life Science series. Vero Beach, FL: Rourke, 2008.

Burnie, David. *Plant*. Eyewitness series. New York: DK Publishing, 2011.

Butzow, Carol, and John Butzow. *Science Through Children's Literature*. Englewood: Teacher Ideas Press, 1989.

Conklin, Wendy. *Differentiation Strategies for Science*. Huntington Beach, CA: Shell Education, 2009.

Cross, Gary, and Elaine P. Simons. *Watch It Grow! Teacher's Guide*. Western edition. Pan-Canadian Science Place series. Markham, ON: Scholastic Canada, 2000.

Gallagher-Bolos, Joan and Dennis Smithenry. *Whole Class Inquiry: Creating Student-Centres Science Communities*. Arlington, VA: NSTA Press Book, 2016.

Georgopoulos, Demetra. *Growth & Changes in Plants*. London, ON: Geowat Innovative Teacher Publishing, 2002.

Hewitt, Sally. *Amazing Plants*. Amazing Science series. St. Catharines, ON: Crabtree Publishing, 2008.

Kalman, Bobbie. *The ABCs of Plants*. The ABCs of the Natural World series. St. Catharines, ON: Crabtree Publishing, 2008.

Konicek-Moran, Richard and Page Keeley. *Teaching for Conceptual Understanding in Science*. Arlington, VA: NSTA Press Book, 2009.

Kuhnlein, Harriet V., and Nancy J. Turner. *Traditional Plant Foods of Canadian Indigenous Peoples: Nutrition, Botany and Use*. Philadelphia: Gordon and Breach, 1991.

Lawson, Jennifer. *Hands On Science: An Inquiry Approach*. Winnipeg, MB: Portage & Main Press, 2015.

Manitoba Education and Training, and Joan Thomas. *Success for All Learners: A Handbook on Differentiating Instruction: A Resource for Kindergarten to Senior 4 Schools*. Winnipeg, MB: Government of Manitoba, 1996.

Martin, Tovah. *The New Terrarium: Creating Beautiful Displays for Plants and Nature*. New York: Clarkson Potter, 2009.

McGough, Julie V. and Lisa M Nyberg. *The Power of Questioning: Guiding Student Investigations*. Arlington, VA: NSTA Press Book, 2016.

Ontario Ministry of Education. *Aboriginal Perspectives: A Guide To The Teacher's Toolkit*. Toronto: Ontario Ministry of Education, 2009.

Ontario Ministry of Education. *Environmental Education*. Toronto: Ontario Ministry of Education, 2017.

Ontario Science Centre. Inquiry-Based Learning Video Series. <https://www.youtube.com/playlist?list=PLWJ3p5pi7LDEls45dP4MCQIT-xWM1t59q>.

Portage & Main Press, 2017 · Hands-On Science and Technology · Grade 3 · ISBN: 978-1-55379-709-8

# Appendix

Images in this appendix are for the Image Banks referenced in the lessons. Corresponding full-page, high-resolution images can be printed or projected for the related lessons, and are found on the Portage & Main Press website at: <www.portageandmainpress.com/product/HOSTBANKGR3/>. Use the password **MATERIALS** to access the download for free.

# Unit 1: Growth and Changes in Plants

## Lesson 1: What Do We Know About Plants and Their Needs?
### Local and Exotic Plants

1. Wild Rice in Lake

2. Wild Rice Plant

3. Corn Plant with Cobs

4. Corn Field

5. Squash Plant

6. Flowering Zucchini Squash Plant

7. Growing Bean Plant

8. Highbush Cranberries

9. Blueberry Plant

10. Sage Plant

11. Cedar Tree

12. Tobacco Plant

Portage & Main Press, 2017 · Hands-On Science and Technology · Grade 3 · ISBN: 978-1-55379-709-8

13. Sweetgrass

14. Birch Trees

15. Sugar Maple Tree

16. Chokecherry Tree

17. Swamp Milkweed with Monarch Butterfly

18. Poison Ivy

19. Black-Eyed Susans

20. White Trilliums

21. Black Walnut Tree

22. Pineapple Plant with Immature Fruit

23. Pineapple Plants

24. Flowering Cactus

Portage & Main Press, 2017 · Hands-On Science and Technology · Grade 3 · ISBN: 978-1-55379-709-8

25. Flowering Cactus 2

26. Banana Tree

27. Banana Tree 2

28. Orange Tree

29. Orange Tree 2

30. Venus Fly Trap

## Image Credits:

Portage & Main Press, 2017 · *Hands-On Science and Technology · Grade 3* · ISBN: 978-1-55379-709-8

# Lesson 4: How Do Plants Adapt in Order to Survive?
## Plant Adaptations

1. Venus Fly Trap

2. Flowering Cactus

3. Flowering Cactus 2

4. Poison Ivy

5. Black-Eyed Susans

6. Stinging Nettle

7. Stinging Nettle 2

8. Rosebush with Thorns

9. Rosebush with Thorns 2

10. Oak Tree with Acorns

### Image Credits:

1 – Venus fly traps by Anna Gardiner. Used under CC Public Domain Mark 1.0 licence.

2 – Cactus by Jonathan Kriz. Used under CC BY 2.0 licence.

3 – unidentified cactus flower by Michal Mañas. Used under CC BY 2.0 licence.

4 – CRW_0473_poison_ivy by David O'Connor. Used under CC BY 2.0 licence.

5 – Black-eyed_susans-kmf by Karen and Brad Emerson. Used under CC BY 2.0 licence.

6 – ladybug on nettle by F_A. Used under CC BY 2.0 licence.

7 – Stinging Nettle stinging bits by John Tann. Used under CC BY 2.0 licence.

8 – First rose of the season on backyard rose bush by Inga Munsinger Cotton. Used under CC BY 2.0 licence.

9 – flower of romance by mario. Used under CC BY 2.0 licence.

10 – Acorns by JB Kilpatrick. Used under CC BY 2.0 licence.

Portage & Main Press, 2017 · Hands-On Science and Technology · Grade 3 · ISBN: 978-1-55379-709-8

## Lesson 7: What Are the Different Ways in Which Plants Are Grown for Food?
### Three Sisters

1. Three Sisters Planting Method

2. Three Sisters Planting Method 2

### Wild Rice

1. Wild Rice in Lake

2. Harvested Wild Rice

3. Wild Rice Ready to Harvest

4. Wild Rice Harvesting Boat

5. Bagging Rice from the Harvester

6. Rice in the Bucket of the Harvester

7. Wild Rice Harvesting Boat 2

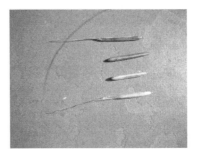

8. Unripened rice

9. Wild Rice Ready to Harvest 2

Portage & Main Press, 2017 · Hands-On Science and Technology · Grade 3 · ISBN: 978-1-55379-709-8

10. Wild Rice Harvesting Boat 3

# Unit 2: Strong and Stable Structures

## Lesson 1: What Is a Structure?

## Human-Made and Natural Structures

*General*

1. Playground structures

2. House

3. Alexandra Bridge, Ontario

4. Water Tower

5. Treehouse

6. Houseboat

Portage & Main Press, 2017 · *Hands-On Science and Technology* · *Grade 3* · ISBN: 978-1-55379-709-8

7. Wind turbines

8. Lighthouse

9. Hydroelectric dam

## Important Buildings in Ontario

10. Library of the Parliament of Canada

11. Parliament Buildings

12. CN Tower & Rogers Center

13. Rogers Centre

14. Air Canada Centre

15. Royal Ontario Museum

## Indigenous Structures

16. Igloo

17. Tipi

18. Longhouse

Portage & Main Press, 2017 · Hands-On Science and Technology · Grade 3 · ISBN: 978-1-55379-709-8

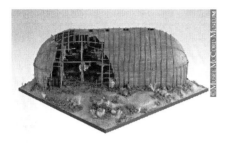

19. Model longhouse

20. Wigwam

21. Wigwam

22. Algonquin bark canoe

23. Dugout canoe

24. Western Greenland hunting kayak

25. Travois

26. Dogsled

27. Ilanaaq

## Natural Structures

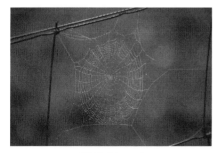

28. Spider web

29. Bird's nest

30. Beaver dam

Portage & Main Press, 2017 · *Hands-On Science and Technology · Grade 3* · ISBN: 978-1-55379-709-8

31. Anthill

31. Honeycomb with bees

33. Wasp Nest

34. Conch shell

35. Rabbit skeleton

Portage & Main Press, 2017 · Hands-On Science and Technology · Grade 3 · ISBN: 978-1-55379-709-8

# Lesson 2: Where Are Structures Found?
## Structures

1. APTN Newsroom and Studio

2. Wigwam

3. House

4. Playground structures

**Image credits:**

1 – APTN news room and studio by Lindsay Reid

2 – Ottawa Sept 17 2006 028 by Adam Kahtava. Used under CC BY 2.0 licence.

3 – Houses on Toronto Island by Jason Baker. Used under CC BY 2.0 licence

4 – Playground Primary Colors by Carl Wycoff. Used under CC BY 2.0 licence.

# Lesson 8: How Are Structures Around the World Similar and Different?
## Important Structures Around the World

1. Eiffel Tower in France

2. Great Wall of China

3. Taj Mahal in India

4. Canadian Museum for Human Rights in Canada

5. Canadian Museum for Human Rights in Canada

6. The Blue Mosque in Turkey

Portage & Main Press, 2017 · Hands-On Science and Technology · Grade 3 · ISBN: 978-1-55379-709-8

7. Golden Gate Bridge in the United States of America

8. Petronas Towers in Malaysia

9. Akashi-Kaikyo Bridge in Japan

10. Sydney Opera House in Australia

11. Burj Khalifa in the United Arab Emirates

12. Great Stupa at Sanchi in India

13. Eden Project in England

14. Eden Project in England

15. Shah Mosque in Iran

16. Great Sphinx of Giza in Egypt

17. Pyramids in Egypt

18. Temple of Kulkulcan in Mexico

Portage & Main Press, 2017 · Hands-On Science and Technology · Grade 3 · ISBN: 978-1-55379-709-8

## Image credits:

# Homes Around the World

1. Igloo in Canada

2. Igloo in Canada

3. Tipi in Canada

4. Longhouse in Canada

5. Longhouse in Canada

6. Wigwam in Canada

7. Wigwam in Canada

8. Apartment Building in the United States of America

9. Houseboat in the Netherlands

Portage & Main Press, 2017 · Hands-On Science and Technology · Grade 3 · ISBN: 978-1-55379-709-8

10. House on Stilts in Thailand

11. Mud architecture in rural India

12. A mud house in Rwanda

13. Yurts in Mongolia

14. Hill Houses in Brazil

15. Traditional House in Japan

16. More Modern House in Japan

**Image credits:**

1 – McCord Museum MP-1986.71.7.

2 – McCord Museum MP-1986.71.16.

3 – Tipi - Atlantic City by m01229. Used under CC BY 2.0 licence.

4 – Ottawa Sept 17 2006 024 by Adam Kahtava. Used under CC BY 2.0 licence.

5 – McCord Museum MR998.71.1.

6 – McCord Museum MP-0000.27.143.

7 – Ottawa Sept 17 2006 028 by Adam Kahtava. Used under CC BY 2.0 licence.

8 – Boston apartments 434 by Jeremy T. Hetzel. Used under CC BY 2.0 licence.

9 – Houseboat by Leandro Neumann Ciuffo. Used under CC BY 2.0 licence.

10 – Phra Mongkonbophit Thai house by Shankar S. Used under CC BY 2.0 licence.

12 – mud architecture - 360° panorama, bhirandiara kutch by nevil zaveri. Used under CC BY 2.0 licence.

13 – A mud house by John Cooke. Used under CC BY 2.0 licence.

14 – Ger Camp by Bernd Thaller. Used under CC BY 2.0 licence.

15 – Hill Houses by Francisco Anzola. Used under CC BY 2.0 licence.

16 – Shirakawa-go house by Esteban Chiner. Used under CC BY 2.0 licence.

17 – K's house by Beni Arnold. Used under CC BY 2.0 licence.

Portage & Main Press, 2017 · Hands-On Science and Technology · Grade 3 · ISBN: 978-1-55379-709-8

# Lesson 11: Inquiry Project: What More Can I Learn About Important Buildings and Structures?

## Indigenous Architecture

1. Mungo Martin House, Thunderbird Park - Victoria, BC

2. Église du Précieux Sang (Precious Blood Parish), Winnipeg, MB

3. Église du Précieux Sang (Precious Blood Parish), Winnipeg, MB

4. APTN Canopy, Winnipeg, MB

5. APTN Building Exterior, Winnipeg, MB

6. APTN Newsroom & Studio, Winnipeg, MB

7. APTN Newsroom and Studio, Winnipeg, MB

8. Waninitawingaang Memorial School, Kejick Bay, ON

9. Waninitawingaang Memorial School Exterior, Kejick Bay, ON

10. Waninitawingaang Memorial School Classroom, Kejick Bay, ON

11. Waninitawingaang Memorial School Hallway, Kejick Bay, ON

12. Makoonsag International Children's Centre Exterior, Winnipeg, MB

Portage & Main Press, 2017 · Hands-On Science and Technology · Grade 3 · ISBN: 978-1-55379-709-8

13. Makoonsag Spirit Room, Winnipeg, MB

14. Makoonsag Spirit Room Mozaic, Winnipeg, MB

15. Makoonsag Toddler Room, Winnipeg, MB

16. Waabanong Interpretive Centre (project rendering)

17. Waabanong Interpretive Centre (project rendering)

18. Urban Circle Training Centre, Winnipeg, MB

19. Urban Circle Centre, Winnipeg, MB

## Image credits:

1 – 4 Thunderbird Park Lodge House, Victoria by Lisa Andres

2 – Précieux Sang # 1 courtesy of Conseil de Développement économique des municipalités bilingues du Manitoba

3 – Précieux Sang 4 courtesy of Conseil de Développement économique des municipalités bilingues du Manitoba

4 – APTN Canopy by Lindsay Reid

5 – APTN Corporate Office & Studio by Lindsay Reid

6 – APTN news room and studio by Lindsay Reid

7 – APTN news room and studio by Lindsay Reid

8 – Kejick Bay School exterior & school yard courtesy of Prairie Architects Inc.

9 – Kejick Bay School exterior courtesy of Prairie Architects Inc.

10 – Kejick Bay School classroom courtesy of Prairie Architects Inc.

11 – Kejick Bay School hallway courtesy of Prairie Architects Inc.

12 – Makoonsag Intergenerational Children's Centre and Urban Circle by Derrick Finch

13 – Makoonsag Spirit Room by Derrick Finch

14 – Makoonsag Spirit Room mozaic by Derrick Finch

15 – Makoonsag Toddler Room by Derrick Finch

16 – Rendering of Waabanong Interpretive Centre 02 (not built) courtesy of Prairie Architects Inc.

17 – Rendering of Waabanong Interpretive Centre 03 (not built) courtesy of Prairie Architects Inc.

18 – Urban Circle Front courtesy of Prairie Architects Inc.

19 – Urban Circle Centre Space courtesy of Prairie Architects Inc.

Portage & Main Press, 2017 · Hands-On Science and Technology · Grade 3 · ISBN: 978-1-55379-709-8

# Unit 3: Forces Causing Movement

## Lesson 2: How is a Force a Push or a Pull?
### Forces in Traditional Indigenous Daily Life

1. Travois

2. Packing a Canoe

3. Assiniboine Bow

4. Eastern Cree or Innu Sling Shot

5. Eastern Cree or Innu Snare

6. Dogsled

7. Carved model of dogsled and team (Labrador Inuit)

8. Using bows and arrows

**Image credit:**

1 – McCord Museum MP-0000.2016.2
2 – McCord Museum M11443
3 – McCord Museum M10127.1
4 – McCord Museum M998.10.27
5 – McCord Museum M998.10.68
6 – Dogsledding in Greenland by Greenland Travel. Used under CC BY 2.0 licence.
7 – McCord Museum M924.1.1-3
8 – McCord Museum MP-0000.25.544

## Lesson 3: What is Friction?
### Traditional Indigenous Fire Starters

1. Inuit Bow Drill Set

2. Fire Drill

3. Bow Drill

Portage & Main Press, 2017 · Hands-On Science and Technology · Grade 3 · ISBN: 978-1-55379-709-8

4. Making Fire by Friction

# Unit 4: Soils in the Environment

## Lesson 5: How Do Different Soils Affect the Growth of Plants?
### Haudenosaunee Farming

1. Three Sisters Planting Method

2. Three Sisters Planting Method 2

3. Eastern Woodlands Village with Three Sisters Garden

# About the Contributors

**Jennifer Lawson**, PhD, is the originator and senior author of the Hands-On series in all subject areas. Jennifer is a former classroom teacher, resource/special education teacher, consultant, and principal. She continues to develop new Hands-On projects, and also serves as a School Trustee for the St. James-Assiniboia School Division in Winnipeg, Manitoba.

**Brad Parolin** is a junior division teacher at John A. Leslie Public School located in Scarborough, Ontario. Formerly, he was an Instructional Leader for Science and Technology with the Toronto District School Board.

**Kevin Reed** is the Indigenous Education Consultant for the Limestone District School Board in Kingston, Ontario. He is the the author of *Aboriginal Peoples: Building for the Future* and co-author of *Aboriginal Peoples in Canada*. He received a Prime Minister's Award for Teaching Excellence in 2008. He is a member of the Nacho Nyak Dun First Nation.

Portage & Main Press, 2017 · Hands-On Science and Technology · Grade 3 · ISBN: 978-1-55379-709-8